INDIVIDUALISM

INDIVIDUALISM

Theories and Methods

Edited by
Pierre Birnbaum and Jean Leca

Translated by
John Gaffney

CLARENDON PRESS · OXFORD
1990

Oxford University Press, Walton Street, Oxford OX2 6DP
Oxford New York Toronto
Delhi Bombay Calcutta Madras Karachi
Petaling Jaya Singapore Hong Kong Tokyo
Nairobi Dar es Salaam Cape Town
Melbourne Auckland
and associated companies in
Berlin Ibadan

Oxford is a trade mark of Oxford University Press

Published in the United States
by Oxford University Press, New York

First published in French as Sur l'individualisme:
Théories et méthodes © Presses de la Fondation
Nationale des Sciences Politiques, Paris, 1986
'The Gaffe-Avoiding Animal' by Ernest Gellner
© Cambridge University Press, 1985
Translation © Oxford University Press, 1990

British Library Cataloguing in Publication Data
Individualism: theories and methods.
1. Individualism
I. Birnbaum, Pierre   II. Leca, Jean   III. Sur l'individualisme: English
141.4
ISBN 0-19-827324-X

Library of Congress Cataloging in Publication Data
Sur l'individualisme. English.
Individualism: theories and methods / edited by Pierre Birnbaum
and Jean Leca; translated by John Gaffney
Translation of: Sur l'individualisme.
Includes bibliographical references.
1.   Individualism.   I. Birnbaum, Pierre.   II. Leca, Jean.
III. Title.
HM136.S8813 1990   302.5'4—dc20   90-7080
ISBN 0-19-827324-X

Typeset by Wyvern Typesetting Ltd, Bristol
Printed in Great Britain by Biddles Ltd.,
Guildford and King's Lynn

Contents

Part IV: Individualism and Democracy 267

Contributors

Bertrand Badie, *University of Clermont-Ferrand*
Pierre Birnbaum, *University of Paris I*
Raymond Boudon, *University of Paris IV*
François Chazel, *University of Bordeaux I*
Jon Elster, *University of Oslo and University of Chicago*
Ernest Gellner, *Oxford University*
Guy Hermet, *Fondation nationale des sciences politiques*
Georges Lavau, *Institut d'études politiques, Paris*
Jean Leca, *Institut d'études politiques, Paris*
Alessandro Pizzorno, *Harvard University*
Adam Przeworski, *University of Chicago*
Charles Tilly, *New School for Social Research, New York*

Publisher's note

The chapters by Ernest Gellner, Adam Przeworski, and Charles Tilly are published here in their original English form. The remaining chapters have been translated from the French by John Gaffney.

Introduction

PIERRE BIRNBAUM AND JEAN LECA

A spectre is haunting the West's intellectuals — the spectre of individualism. Individualism has, indeed, many spectral qualities: indeterminate shape, evocative power, and a myriad of other qualities attributed to it and which allow it to take many forms on a scale which ranges from benevolence to terror according to perceptions of it. Perhaps the most important quality ascribed to it when it appears (or reappears) is its power of annunciation: annunciation of historic changes which have taken place or are in the making, and which will shake the fragile foundations of our knowledge and our existence. Hence its incantatory use by visionaries, who are usually more concerned with invocation than with understanding. Conversely, it is the spectral quality ascribed to individualism which tempts many to refute it without due consideration or to reduce it to a 'pre-notion', or else to abandon it altogether to ideologues and (false) prophets.[1] The problem here is that spectres are not easily conjured away, especially if elements in their surrounding environment lend them a certain consistency, elements such as the wariness now expressed towards 'total' ideologies, the crisis of Marxism as a system of knowledge, the end of positivism, or the decline of group solidarity and collective identities. Perhaps, then, in the case of this particular spectre, we should go and take a closer look.

The present volume does not claim to be an exhaustive exploration of the subject. There are other excellent introductory works.[2] Nor is this volume a conceptual inventory of all the connotations and denotations of the term, of the contexts in which it appears, or of its meanings or uses in social practice. Still less are we attempting here a systematic breaking down of this enormous subject into simpler, less

---

[1] As did Lalande, with high seriousness, in his *Vocabulaire*: 'A bad and equivocal term whose use continually gives rise to sophisms' (*Vocabulaire technique et critique de la philosophie* (Paris: PUF, 6th edn. 1960), see 'Individualisme').

[2] Steven Lukes, *Individualism* (Oxford: Blackwell, 1974). A. Lindsay, 'Individualism', *Encyclopedia of the Social Science* (New York: Macmillan, 1930–5). On methodological individualism, see J. O'Neill (ed.), *Modes of Individualism and Collectivism* (London: Heinemann, 1973).

ambiguous component parts whose multiple combinations and sub-categories might then be analysed at leisure like some complex chemical process. We are not here following to the letter the advice of Weber or Lovejoy,[3] even though we would agree that to bring together the various types of individualism would make for an exciting confrontation: utilitarian individualism, and a society made up of equally weighted atoms, each driven by the pursuit of its own interests; romantic individualism, in which individuals are incommensurable and each one is irreplaceable; the market individualism of men and women liberated from their passions and constituting a new moral community formed by 'gentle commerce', and providing concomitantly a way of understanding their behaviour (economics); juridical individualism, and its echoes of the great controversies over the origins of law (can the individual be considered as the creative source of law(s)?) and its purpose (are there legal systems which strive for the autonomy of individuals to the exclusion of collective or community interests?). These latter two debates reappear with ethical individualism (should individual conscience be the ultimate court of appeal for the validity of ethical norms? Should the appraisal of a society be based exclusively upon the happiness and autonomy of individuals, or upon values which are not related to individual interests?); sociological individualism, with its multiplication and differentiation of social roles and the emancipation of the self from the social roles it performs (or the establishing of relational distance between these roles), and its tendency to depict the individual retreating into private life to the detriment of public obligation; epistemological individualism, and the individual as a knowing subject separated from its object (which it must construct), mistrusting what 'reality' presents to it, and searching to establish the conditions of true knowledge. We could cite many more 'great debates' involving Bentham and Simmel, Mandeville and Lamennais, Durkheim and de Tocqueville, Kant and Nietzsche, J. S. Mill and Schumpeter, and many others. What we propose, however, is to identify certain problems and establish the place of individualism (and the sense in which we mean it) in the

---

[3] Weber advocated systematic enquiry into a term which 'includes the most heterogeneous things imaginable'; M. Weber, *The Protestant Ethic and the Spirit of Capitalism* (London: Unwin, 1967), 222. Lovejoy points out that most works ending in 'ism' refer to combinations of distinct and often conflicting doctrines which writers and historians modify still further. It is appropriate, therefore, to isolate them and reduce them to their basic elements, in order to reconstitute the motives and historical influences which led

specific examination of these problems. We can illustrate these as a series of propositions:

1. Individualism can be an element in a process of *characterization* of institutions and social behaviour. It is in this sense that we speak of sociological individualism, economic individualism, or juridical individualism, even poetic individualism, or of whether, say, twelfth-century Europe or the Renaissance 'discovered the individual'.[4]

2. Individualism can also be part of the deliberate, more or less systematic ('doctrinal') process of *legitimation* of institutions and of norms and values, particularly political ones. It is in this sense that Macpherson discusses 'possessive individualism' and the difficulties this poses in resolving the problem of political obligation, which it has itself, in part, created.[5] Ethical individualism and, to a lesser extent, philosophical individualism are part of this debate, as is political individualism if one argues, for example, that 'contractualism' is the only logically conceivable, rational basis for the justification of political authority, or that the aggregating of individual preferences is the least costly way (rationally and ethically) of making collective decisions, or, more simply, that the play of individual strategies within a procedural framework which each individual observes is a more legitimate political process than the identification of holistic goals.

3. Finally, individualism can form the basis of a process of *explanation*. It can be a way of both posing problems and conceiving answers to questions of analysis. Methodological individualism, which aims to explain collective (macroscopic) phenomena on the basis of individual (microscopic) behaviour and strategies, is quite distinct from other individualisms because it is an attribute of the researcher, not of the object of study; it does not characterize the process studied, but the methodological approach itself. Furthermore, it is not a way of

to such combinations; Arthur O. Lovejoy, *The Great Chain of Being* (Cambridge, Mass.: Harvard University Press, 1936).

[4] We should note here the important works which followed the magisterial *Deutsches Genossenschaftrecht* of Otto von Gierke, and Jacob Burckhardt, *Die Kultur der Renaissance in Italien* (Basle: Schweighausers Verlagschandlung, 1860). The doubtful theme of the 'discovery of the individual' is examined by C. Morris, *The Discovery of the Individual, 1050–1200* (London: SPCK, 1972). Cf. Caroline Walker Bynum's notable analysis 'Did the Twelfth Century Discover the Individual?' in *Jesus as Mother: Studies in the Spirituality of the High Middle Ages* (Berkeley, Calif.: University of California Press, 1982), 82–109.

[5] C. B. Macpherson, *The Political Theory of Possessive Individualism: Hobbes to Locke* (Oxford, London: Oxford University Press, 1979).

legitimizing institutions or values, except for those values indissolubly linked to its function as a methodological approach.

We have, then, three types of problem, three series of individualisms with apparently no logical link between them. One could, like Durkheim, characterize the society where organic solidarity predominates as individualistic, and subscribe to this individualism normatively, without, nevertheless, making this the contractualist basis for the legitimation of power, and without accepting methodological individualism itself. Conversely, just as there are organicists of the right, there are also methodological individualists of the left. It would be interesting, however, to characterize the different 'schools' and constellations of meaning by examining the way in which these three problems are differentiated or combined, and how they relate to one another. On the surface, the climate of intellectual opinion in the West concerning the characterization of democratic capitalist societies as individualistic is perhaps less uniform today than it was only fifty years ago. Interestingly, this development comes at the same time as Zinoviev's highlighting of the contradictory aspects of Soviet society: holistic as the provider of an individual's identity; individualistic as the distributor of the values associated with the notion of 'every man for himself'.

On the other hand, the legitimation of individualism seems to have become much stronger: in Europe, Fascism, traditionalism, Christian democracy, personalism,[6] and Marxism are in decline, if not disappearing completely (none of these was ever very influential in the United States). But it is worth remembering that, for example, the impacting of capitalism and the crisis of the state upon Islamic society has produced rival legitimations with the result that the individualism of the 'liberal age' has been severely shaken. At the same time, the American 'new contractualists' have recently revived an individualist political theory, which had been somewhat in need of repair since John Stuart Mill, and which had been battered by Marxism and undermined — more discreetly, yet more profoundly — by Schumpeter's acid criticism. Finally, perhaps the newest addition to the many varieties of theoretical explanation is methodological individualism, which has emerged from economics, where it was dominant, and established solid bridgeheads in the fortresses of sociology and anthropology,

[6] See Emmanuel Mounier, *Communisme, anarchie et personnalisme* (Paris: Seuil, 1966).

where functionalism and structuralism had seemed immovable, propped up as they were by an impressive array of group, class, generational, ethnic, cultural, and other analyses. Individualist rereadings of Max Weber have not always been the same as the reading adopted by his most eminent American interpreter, Talcott Parsons.[7] But that Weber or Schumpeter, both of whom were sceptical about individualism as a principle of institutional legitimation, can be cited as masters of methodological individualism, and that Marx himself can be considered by Raymond Boudon as one of its founding fathers alongside Simmel and Popper, are in themselves indications of how attitudes have developed independently within the three areas we have identified.

But can these problems be classified so easily? Is there not an overall individualist apperception which incorporates both the social object and the researcher, and therefore governs characterization, legitimation, and explanation themselves (which is not, of course, to say that all those who are part of this *Zeitgeist* are necessarily in agreement on all the questions, still less on all the answers)? Louis Dumont's hypothesis is a useful reminder of the shared climate which includes sociological and doctrinal as well as methodological individualism.[8] Nevertheless, certain distinctions can still be made. Methodological individualism would never posit the individual as 'non-social', nor would it subscribe to an 'atomistic' view of society. Similarly, methodological individualism does not necessarily involve adherence to economic liberalism or ethical individualism. To use an individualist methodology does not mean that one considers all societies as being governed by individualist values. It is equally the case that to hold the view that modern society (ourselves included) is imbued with the ideology of individualism does not preclude the use of a 'holistic' methodology. Relationships and situations which are perceived and understood (particularly by protagonists) as communitarian can be explained on the basis of individual strategies. There is, therefore, no reason to link methodology and object as if, at each stage of its — sometimes imaginary — development, a social fact should be analysed by means of a specific method.

There is, undoubtedly, a strong inclination to include several

---

[7] It is true that François Bourricaud has called Parsons an 'institutional individualist'. The debate is too technical to go into here. See, however, *L'Individualisme institutionnel: Essai sur la sociologie de Talcott Parsons* (Paris: PUF, 1971).

[8] L. Dumont, *Homo aequalis* (Paris: Gallimard, 1977) and *Essais sur l'individualisme* (Paris: Seuil, 1983).

individualisms in the same category and to examine simultaneously problems specific to the object of study and those specific to the researcher. A good illustration of this is provided by monetarist theories and the development of the neo-liberal credo associated with James Buchanan and the Virginia school, which combines political individualism, classic economic liberalism, and methodological individualism.[9] The latter is all too often reduced to (monetarist, rational-choice) economic theory, which is itself elevated to the status of an explanatory and prescriptive theory of the ensemble of social mechanisms. We can ask, however, whether these elegant hypotheses follow on from the premisses which give rise to them. Monetarist theory, viewed from a particular perspective, is more holist than individualist. Take the case of governments which create inflation by increasing the money supply beyond what is 'necessary' to the economy because they are unable to resist formidable interest groups (in particular, the bureaucracy), and then court the electorate by lulling it with false hopes. What is implied here is a view of society where all-powerful historical subjects work to strip the unhappy individual of the rational choice which he[10] is in fact supposed to be

---

[9] J. M. Buchanan and G. Tullock, *The Calculus of Consent: Logical Foundations of Constitutional Democracy* (Ann Arbor, Mich.: University of Michigan Press, 1962); J. M. Buchanan, *The Limits of Liberty: Between Anarchy and Leviathan* (Chicago, Ill.: University of Chicago Press, 1975); J. M. Buchanan and R. E. Wagner, *Democracy in Deficit: The Political Legacy of Lord Keynes* (New York: Academic Press, 1977). Cf. the criticisms of Brian Barry: 'Review', *Theory and Decision*, 12 (Mar. 1980), 95–106; 'Methodology versus Ideology: The "Economic" Approach Revisited', in E. Ostrom (ed.), *Strategies of Political Inquiry* (London: Sage, 1982), 123–47; 'Does Democracy cause Inflation? Political Ideas of Some Economists', in Leon N. Lindberg and Charles S. Maier (eds.), *The Politics of Inflation and Economic Stagnation* (Washington, DC: Brookings Institution, 1985), 280–317.

[10] The pronominal denomination of 'the individual' in this book raises the question of gender. In the French, the use of 'il' is uncontentious because *l'individu* is a masculine noun. We have translated this as 'he' for several reasons. First, it is explicit or else implied that the authors are generally referring to an imagined 'he', either because they consider this conventional and uncontentious (Przeworski is an exception), or because the historical subjects they are referring to are invariably men (peasant heads of household, capitalists, warriors, priests, and so on). In some instances (Lavau's chapter, for example) this is not the case, though here I have retained 'he' in order not to throw the use of 'he or she' into direct contrast with the use of 'he' elsewhere. Another point worth making here is that *l'individu* is, in part (though only in part and this adds to the difficulty), a concept or theoretical category rather than simply the signifier of a given historical or social person. Having said this, however, it does not follow that 'it' would properly express such a concept. On this question too, therefore, the use of the term 'he' remains the best, as is the case in the discourse of psychoanalysis where 'he' refers to the patient even though the patient might be female and, indeed, where the discipline itself

exercising according to the theory itself. Suddenly, the so-called rational individual is afflicted by schizophrenia: rational as an economic actor, he is incompetent as a citizen. The problem here is not that, according to this type of theory, the market individual is privileged in relation to the individual who acts within a political organization (such a view, though not very original, is plausible). Nor does the problem lie in the fact that economic and political behaviour are treated as obeying different rules (this also is plausible, even uncontentious, though, we might add, unexpected, coming as it does from those who generally believe in the unifying rationality of all behaviour). The problem is that, at a certain point, the explanation of the overall process abandons methodological individualism and moves towards the notion of the irrational (in the case of the electorate), or towards that of the collective subject (in the case of the bureaucracies—an unexpected variation on the theme of the '200 families' or of 'capital').[11] The incautious mixing of characterization, legitimation, and explanation clearly has its drawbacks.

We can, therefore, take as a methodological rule the logical separation of descriptive, justificatory, and explanatory individualisms. This should not, however, preclude a closely integrated examination of the problems we have identified. Thus, for example, Ernest Gellner examines the characterization of modernity in terms of a *Zweckrationalität* which takes sociological individualism as its cultural framework and methodological individualism as its epistemology. He questions, however, whether this offers a means of locating oneself in the world, or a basis for political legitimation. Alessandro Pizzorno criticizes methodological individualism as a means both of understanding and of legitimating democracy. Georges Lavau questions individualism as a means of characterizing electoral behaviour and as a methodology underlying such characterization. Pierre Birnbaum adopts the same approach with regard to working-class strategies: are these informed by individualism? How? And are they better explained by methodological individualism? Birnbaum highlights the weaknesses of holistic

is concerned with the analysis of identity not only in terms of gender but also in terms of individualism itself (translator's note).

[11] Cf. Leon N. Lindberg, 'Models of the Inflation–Disinflation Process', in Lindberg and Maier, *The Politics of Inflation*, pp. 37–44, and Leon N. Lindberg and Charles S. Maier, 'Alternatives for Future Crises', *The Politics of Inflation*, pp. 569–71. Not all individualist-based economic theories are so contradictory, even though they all tend, more or less, to see political mechanisms (real or desired) as procedures whose sole aim is to allow the rational individual to treat politics as a market-place. This view means that models which do not conform are seen as conspiracies or aberrations.

approaches which see collective actors as unified groups possessing consciousness and will. Bertrand Badie analyses individualist and communitarian representations and takes issue with the view which considers concepts of 'community' and 'individual' as indicators of worlds sealed off from one another and of methodologies adequate to apprehend them. Charles Tilly and François Chazel focus their analyses on the value of individualist methodologies (game theory, Olson's paradigm) in explaining the phenomenon of collective mobilization, while Jon Elster and Adam Przeworski concentrate upon the challenge to Marxism of methodological individualism. Jean Leca analyses the relationships between sociological individualism and citizenship, and the problems these relationships pose for the legitimation of political obligation. Individualism–citizenship relations are also examined by Guy Hermet, who flushes out both the implicit and the explicit legitimations at work within the theory, wrongly termed Weberian, which considers the Protestantism–individualism relation as the touchstone and model for the process of the individualization of Western societies.

In spite of their diversity, the contributions to this volume come together on a series of points. They agree upon the individualist character of democratic capitalist societies; they express doubts concerning individualist legitimations put forward by authors such as Robert Nozick; they accept (with varying reservations) the growing importance of explanations based upon methodological individualism. Differences of nuance, and even oppositions, remain, however, concerning (1) the nature of sociological individualism, and (2) methodological individualism as a system of explanation.

1. Every contributor is in agreement in refusing to view societies as totally 'individualist' or 'holist'. It is not to deny notions of sequentiality or change to stress, as do Ernest Gellner (the most sensitive to the notion of massive historical change), Bertrand Badie, Pierre Birnbaum, and Georges Lavau, the dual presence of holistic and individualistic traits in a given concrete historical society (in Gellner's terms, the combination of fixed and variable cognitive capital). We must first, however, join the heady debate concerning the isolation and identification of univocal individualist qualities attributed to behaviour and to institutions. Should, for example, all behaviour induced by the rules of the game of a particular strategic site, such as that involving the supporters of Lian Po, the illustrious general of the kingdom of Zhao, be termed 'individualist'?:

At the time of his disgrace, his supporters had abandoned him. When he was reinstated to his post they came back to him. 'Go away', he shouted at them. And one of them replied: 'Come now, sir, be realistic. Didn't you know that it is market forces which govern human relations? You are disgraced and we leave you; you find the king's favour once again and we serve you once again. It is as simple as that. There is no need to make such a fuss about it.'[12]

This is a good illustration of the 'exaltation of the self', wherein the uninformed reader would (perhaps rightly) see the opposite of the Confucian moral code extolling respect for old people and tradition, compliance with codes and rites, restraint, and obedience. In the above example there is only rational calculation, a cold and cynical utilitarianism, a strategy related to circumstance, the notion of flexible attitudes, and the rejection of prescribed behaviour (loyalty for the sake of honour alone). Is this, then, an illustration of individualism? Viewed in this way, one might well find individualism almost anywhere, or at least anywhere where people, confronted with problematic relationships involving distinctions between the 'self', 'other', and 'world', bring their own thoughts to bear, even those of the most practical and cynical kind.[13] However, is it not just as plausible to put forward, in opposition to the notion of the utilitarian conduct of the supporter, another form of behaviour which is just as, if not more, 'individualistic', though grounded not in self-interest but in 'free' choice made within a range of motivations: the play of the aesthetic, for example, or the cult of prowess, or the passion for honour?[14] Or perhaps individualism is that of the pre-Islamic Arab warrior who breaks ranks in order to hurl his own defiance at the enemy.[15] This

[12] The story is derived from the *Mémoires historiques* of Sima Qian written two thousand or so years ago and cited by Simon Leys, *La Forêt en feu: Essais sur la culture et la politique chinoises* (Paris: Hermann, 1983), 191–2.

[13] What certain authors would call 'primary individuality'. Cf. Uwe Schottmann, *Primäre und sekundäre Individualität* (Stuttgart: Enke, 1968).

[14] In the West, many authors have linked individualization to Nordic military heroes, and seen in the military community an 'individualizing' effect (R. Nisbet, *The Social Philosophers: Community and Conflict in Western Thought* (New York: Cromwell, 1973), 11–90). To call such individualization 'individualist' would doubtless have horrified the defenders of the French army, when it was threatened by 'individualism' during the Dreyfus Affair. On this kind of reasoning see Vytaulas Kavolis, 'Logic of Selfhood and Modes of Order: Civilisational Structures for Individual Identities', in Roland Robertson and Burkart Holzner (eds.), *Identity and Authority* (Oxford: Blackwell, 1980), 40–60.

[15] Shelomo Dev Goitein, 'Individualism and Conformity in Classical Islam', in Amin Banani and Speros Vryonis (eds.), *Individualism and Conformity in Classical Islam* (Wiesbaden: Otto Harrassowitz, 1977), 3–18. Goitein qualifies this type as 'model individualist' (p. 12).

view in turn is opposed by those who interpret the heroism of the Christian knight or Arab warrior not as individualism but as conformity, and the songs glorifying heroes as a means of socializing those who listen to them, and of communicating a particular view of warfare.[16]

We could develop the argument further to include, for example, poetic aesthetics, scientific enquiry, the laws of inheritance (is the abolition of the law of primogeniture individualist?), or decision-making processes (the secret ballot or the drawing of lots, for example). We would do well to remind ourselves here of two methodological rules. The first is to distinguish the codes within which the different 'selves' operate — utilitarian in the market-place, heroic on the battle-field, altruistic in collective action — in order to identify what distinguishes them one from another, and, with the help of a properly defined concept, to call one form 'individualist'. The second is to combine selected empirical characteristics with their wider contexts. Just as it would be misguided to identify individualism on the basis of attributes isolated from their context, it would be equally wrong to reconstruct totalities ('individualist' or 'holist') within which empirical observations would be univocally interpreted, as if the ensemble comprising the totality and its attributes had one meaning and one alone. To do this would give exaggerated importance to the overall reconstructions effected by contemporary (and subsequent) theoreticians, and would mean that we took as valid empirical information which was being put forward only as interpretation (in itself valid). We should, therefore, be sensitive to context where it throws light upon the meaning of institutions and practices, and should draw comparisons between attributes which have been properly extracted from their context. In this way we can counter the double danger of unrestricted characterizations and overall descriptions. There is individualism (but which?) in the city of antiquity, in medieval Europe, and in classical Islam, and there is not only individualism in 'modern' societies. Apposite confirmation of this last point is provided by Mary Douglas and Aron Wildavsky who, borrowing directly from Louis Dumont the concept of 'hierarchy', oppose it to 'individualism', and apply it to organizations (regulating agencies) and to very contemporary small groups (certain sects).[17] These kinds of observation

[16]   John F. Benton, 'Individualism and Conformity in Medieval Western Europe', in Banani and Vryonis, *Individualism and Conformity*, pp. 145–58, and particularly p. 152.

[17]   Mary Douglas and Aron Wildavsky, *Risk and Culture: An Essay on the Selection of Technical and Environmental Dangers* (Berkeley, Calif.: University of California Press, 1982), 90–113.

are useful in that they enable us to bear in mind the complexity of the issues involved, and to maintain a healthy mistrust of generalizations.

2. One of the essential lessons of methodological individualism is that a society is not a system.[18] In parenthesis, this lesson makes such a paradigm unsatisfactory, not only for those who wish to understand the 'whole', but also for those who would like to ground their beliefs on 'solid' foundations (that is to say, present their beliefs as explicitly rational on the one hand yet sheltered from examination, suspicion, and the risk of refutation on the other). There are rules which enable us to analyse human behaviour, offer explanations of interaction, and thus analyse social phenomena as an effect of the aggregation of such behaviour. As explanation, however, social 'laws' do not go much further than this, those of 'social change' being even less satisfactory. In other words, the difficulties of interpretation only begin afterwards. A close reading of Adam Przeworski's tightly argued (almost despairing) analysis, and of his opposition to Jon Elster and Alessandro Pizzorno (whose analysis he criticizes directly), is instructive here: Przeworski sees no theoretical alternative to methodological individualism; even the 'undeniable' fact that individual identities 'are continually moulded by society' does not invalidate the notion that people act rationally in response to their preferences (a view held for a number of years by William Riker, among others). Even so, Przeworski himself is not happy with the theory. At one with Elster in his rejection of the collective historical subject, the 'meaning' of History, and the cunning of Reason, and of the revivification of these ideas in the form of the teleonomic functionalism of G. A. Cohen, he is, nevertheless, more pessimistic than Elster about the fruitfulness of both Marxism and methodological individualism.

The ballet of these two prima ballerinas (Marxism and methodological individualism) is not without a certain baroque charm. Elster believes they are capable of a *pas de deux* which would assure them both continuing fame. Elster's is a three-act ballet (I. Productive forces and relations of production; II. Class and class-consciousness; III. Ideologies) which sees the curtain fall on the triumph of the celebrated dancers who have thrown off their more absurdly idiosyncratic mannerisms (and, God knows, they have quite a repertory), and embraced the subtle interplay of game theory and the typology of false

[18] Boudon is not, for all that, alone in this view. Ernest Gellner agrees, even though he is sceptical about methodological individualism, especially given his suspicion that the ends–means model turns real society into *one* system.

consciousnesses. Przeworski's scenario has four acts (I. The theory of action; II. Collective actors; III. Class conflict; IV. Equilibrium analysis). For him, none of Marxism's counter-arguments to methodological individualism is convincing. He considers Marxian theory of class action and of the structure of class conflict in democratic capitalism to be out of date and inadequate, logically invalid, and empirically false. Nor is a theory of collective action founded on individualism pertinent, at least at the present time: its ontology is defective, given its notion of society as a collection of undifferentiated and unrelated individuals; its disdain of historicity draws it into formal analyses which are not founded upon 'historically descriptive concepts of equilibrium'; and it cannot explain how individual actions in given conditions will produce new conditions. A comment here which bears on the psychology of knowledge: it is the view which expects the most of Marxism as a general method of elucidation of social movements and of History which finds Marxism the most lacking (Przeworski); it is the views which see in Marxism only an analytical methodology bearing on specific processes, and decoupled from any 'grand theory' of History, which are the most sympathetic to it (Boudon and Elster).

From the perspectives expounded in this volume, we can draw several conclusions: a common rejection of the 'despotism of structures' and of an 'oversocialized' view of mankind; the importance (subscribed to by most of the contributors, including Charles Tilly) of game theory and the recognition of the challenge presented by the 'free-ticket' or 'free-rider' notion of Mancur Olson; the (perhaps temporary) inadequacy of methodological individualism when faced with certain problems where (for the moment?) it is impossible to explain the macroscopic in individualist terms, that is, to elevate a statistical correlation to the status of a conclusion concerning a set of individual behaviours which obeys a definite logic. Charles Tilly widens the critique made by both Ernest Gellner and François Chazel: many relations which constitute and frame social life manifest so little mutual strategic action that they call for other modes of analysis; networks of communication, daily interaction between employers and workers, financial and fiscal movements, the itineraries of sickness, and the chain reactions of migrations, for example, occasionally contain within them elements of mutual strategic action. However, their crystallization or transformation also necessitates, according to Tilly, a structural analysis. How are social networks, the orientations of action, and the structural stimuli which act upon the potential responses of actors constituted? And what is the place of these in explanation? With these questions posed by Tilly and Chazel (and which Elster endeavours to answer, without convincing Przeworski) there remains uncertainty as to whether methodological individualism is able to offer a satisfactory answer.

In the view of some of the contributors, this inadequacy is possibly only a temporary one. Others are clearly more sceptical. Perhaps Alessandro Pizzorno takes this latter view the furthest: there are problems (and, in the first instance, that of the processes of individual and collective identification) which methodological individualism cannot address. Self-identification cannot be reduced to utility.[19] The world in which individuals exercise their individual strategic abilities is not the result of these abilities. The world both precedes and constitutes rational choices. It is not that the world is unchanging, but its macroscopic change is not (or is not solely) the product of microscopic changes. Belonging and its corollary self-identification are the sites where individual and collective rationality articulate with one another (though in relation to which models remains uncertain). The relations between these are perhaps easier to analyse in so-called 'holistic' societies where identities, being strongly prescribed, can be taken as given. This allows for the easier examination of how real individuals, already identified a priori by their respective positions and material and cognitive resources, manœuvre strategically by means of their rationality. Of course, the 'holistic' individual can find himself 'different' at the end of the game but, at the start, identities are clear. Here the identities of players in the game are taken as unproblematic (this explains why the processes of the constitution of prescribed identities—language, ethnic identity, etc.—have been relatively under-researched);[20] only their mobilization and strategic games can be examined legitimately, and methodological individualism can contribute here, at least in part.

The situation is clearly quite different in more strongly individualistic bourgeois societies. Here 'class' mobilization is the *pons asinorum* for many analyses, and understandably so: it is grounded—as is

---

[19] Arthur Stinchcombe has, however, put forward a sophisticated version of this view. See Jean Leca's discussion of this in this volume.

[20] Except, and this too is very recent, when these processes occur in 'modern' or at least nation-state societies. Cf. Nelson Kasfir, 'Explaining Ethnic Political Participation', *World Politics*, 1 (1979), 345–64; Crawford Young, 'Patterns of Social Conflict: State, Class and Ethnicity', *Daedalus*, 3 (1982).

'national' mobilization[21] — in collective identities which are not a priori constructs. Pizzorno even makes the freedom to participate in processes of collective identification, and not freedom of political choice, the central value in individualist modern democracy (in other words, the individual is powerless to influence the outcome of the game but can select the teams). If this proposition is correct, it explains both the attraction and the inadequacy of methodological individualism. Its attraction resides in the fact that if groups are not assumed as given, it is more valuable to interpret macro-processes on the basis of the aggregation of individual preferences rather than on the basis of hypothetical conflicts of structurally oriented groups. Its inadequacy lies in its offering an explanation of neither the constitution of collective identities nor the conflict of rationalities.[22] Thus, ironically, if these propositions were correct, it would be in societies where sociological individualism ruled that methodological individualism would dash the high hopes it had raised. One might argue that the question has been wrongly put: that it is not the function of methodological individualism to resolve the historical problems posed by sociological individualism. The difficulties raised by such a question, however, do not disappear just because of possible inadequacies in the formulation of the question itself.

[21]   There has been more work done on the construction of 'national' identities (which are not constitued a priori but are created to produce a prescribed effect, or illusion). Cf. E. Gellner, *Nations and Nationalism* (London: Blackwell, 1983); P. Birnbaum, 'Nation, État et culture: L'Exemple du Sionisme', *Communication* (June 1986).

[22]   For the observations of a recent (though not fanatical) convert to cultural anthropology, see Aron Wildavsky, *From Political Economy to Political Culture, or, Rational People Defend their Way of Life* (Paris: World Congress of the International Political Science Association, July 1985).

PART I

WHAT IS METHODOLOGICAL
INDIVIDUALISM?

The Gaffe-Avoiding Animal or A Bundle of Hypotheses

ERNEST GELLNER

There are a number of notions of rational behaviour. The most important, and also most readily intelligible, is *Zweckrationalität*. Conduct is rational if it is optimally effective in attaining a given specified aim. (Alternative reading: if, in the light of the evidence available to an agent, there is good reason to believe it to be so.) Instrumental rationality contains, as an important part or corollary, the requirement for the efficient use of relevant information. He who wills the end must will the means; information relevant to the choice of most effective means is itself a means, perhaps the most important one. Thus *Zweckrationalität* required not merely that one should choose the optimal means, but also that one's beliefs, in the light of which the means are chosen, should themselves be in some sense optimal, given the data at one's disposal. The second most important sense of rationality is rule-observance, consistency, like treatment of like cases. Unless an authority, an organization, or for that matter a segment of nature is rational in this sense, we feel rather helpless in the face of its unpredictability, its caprice. This sense can be extended to a third one, namely the rationality of a coherent system of rules. *Wertrationalität* does not strictly seem to me a form of rationality at all: the idea behind it seems to be the implementation of a value, as contrasted with the attainment of an end. But this only differs from, say, the fulfilment of any whim whatever in so far as a 'value' is solemnly adhered to, consistently respected in its diverse manifestations, and 'deep', i.e. coherently related to other aspects of one's identity. In other words, when we look at what it is that makes a *Wert* into a *Wert* we find *Wertrationalität* dissolving into one or more of the other types of rationality.

This chapter was first published in Gellner, *Relativism and the Social Sciences* (1987). It is reprinted here by permission of Cambridge University Press.

The Consistency and Instrumentality senses of rationality overlap: inasmuch as optimal effectiveness is uniquely determined, in any given situation or assessment thereof, efficient instrumental behaviour will also be consistent. The same aim in similar circumstances will call for the same action. There is another and more debatable overlap: consistent, rule-abiding behaviour on the part of an organization or individual may be held to be the most efficient from the viewpoint of a wide range of possible ends.

The easy intelligibility of the notion of instrumental rationality is liable to give the impression that the thing itself is fairly unproblematical; or that the problems which it engenders are mainly technical rather than fundamental. (The most important instrumentalist theory of ethics, Utilitarianism, generates a host of technical-seeming issues in connection with its own implementation, such as the problems of interpersonal comparisons and discounts for risk or future.)

The notion of instrumental rationality, or efficiency for short, seems to me problematical in a way far more profound than that; and the reasons and factors that make it so appear to me to have become particularly prominent of late. This is not an artificial, academic problem: in real life, the sheer identification of what is to count as rational conduct has become much harder.

There are two elements which enter into the definition of *zweckrational*, instrumentally rational, conduct: means and end. The notion presupposes that we can isolate, identify, ends, aims, criteria of that which will satisfy us, which will warrant our treating the endeavour as having been crowned with success. It also assumes an objective world of causally interconnected things, some of which are under our direct control. A 'means' is in the first instance something that is under our control and also in turn has an effect on our ends, and, by an extension which can be repeated, anything which is under our control indirectly and/or indirectly affects our end.

These assumptions underlying the idea of efficiency seem relatively uncontentious, or alternatively, problematical only in such a very general philosophical way that the problems raised ought not to create any specific difficulties for efficiency as such. There may be problems about the existence or accessibility of an objective world, or about causality, but need we worry about them specifically in connection with efficiency? Those problems would seem to touch virtually everything in the world; like the rain which falls on the just and unjust alike, they do not discriminate, so why should they bother us?

This is an illusion.

The notion of efficiency does not merely presuppose an external world, it presupposes a *single* world. I think that most theoreticians of knowledge, philosophers of science, and so on have indeed assumed something of the kind in their very formulation of the problem. The model with which they more or less tacitly operated was something like this: the individual, using the tools and materials supplied to him (the mix of external material and self-supplied tools varying with the epistemological theory in question), constructed one world. Of course, on occasion his world was fractured, but that constituted an anomaly, a problem, and it was up to him to set it right by reordering his ideas.

David Hume considered man to be *a* bundle of sensations, but note that the famous phrase was in the singular. It was assumed that the sensations would coagulate into one single bundle, as a lot of small snowballs may congeal into one large one in the process of making a snowman. It is not at all clear why this should be so, nor why the bundles should be as relatively neat and discrete as in fact they mostly are. For Immanuel Kant, the process of gluing the bits together so as to make a single bundle plays an important part in the construction of the world-picture, and is given a name—the synthetic unity of apperception. In fact, for Kant, the central job for the epistemic ego is precisely this, to be a kind of link man or anchor man, as they say in television: when the ego is attached to each single one of the sensations, it causes them to become indirectly fused to each other and make up a World. For Hume, the bundle arose mysteriously by some kind of spontaneous generation or accretion. So Kant at any rate has the merit of seeing the problem, or half-seeing it: for he used the unity of the perceived and conceived world as a step in solving the problem of causation, rather than being imbued with the problematical and dubious status of that unity itself. (His left-handed 'proof' of causality amounted to the following: if we have or assume a single world, with each thing assigned a definite place within it, then causality is already presupposed, for without it, things could not be given unambiguous locations in the world; so causality must be taken or left in a single package deal with an unambiguous single world; none would forgo that single world (so Kant assumed), and hence causality is established.)

One bundle, one world. During the period when the epistemological question was reformulated in terms of language, this assumption was nevertheless retained. The question about the relationship of language to the world was formulated on the basis of the tacit assumption that one language faced one world.

I think I can say, without fear of immediate and virulent contestation, that I am not widely known as an uncritical and enthusiastic admirer of Ludwig Wittgenstein's later work. Nevertheless, if I were asked to single out some idea in his work which seems to me both valid and important, I should pick out the denial of the Single-Bundle thesis which, *nur mit ein bißchen anderen Worten*, thoroughly pervades his approach to language. One does not need to sympathize with the philosophical uses to which he put the idea of the plurality, disparateness, and incommensurateness of diverse 'language games' to recognize that this plurality and disparity have profound implications. The matter is really simple: Wittgenstein supposed that this plurality and disparity, or rather its recognition, somehow solved something, and absolved us from the unnecessary and self-imposed burden of seeking general validations. In fact it does nothing of the kind. Used in that way, his discovery seems to me to have little merit. But if treated as a problem, not as a solution, the idea becomes significant.

Language games, i.e., presumably, clusters of tokens and the rules governing their use, do not add up to one single overarching language with one set of rules and casting a single categorical shadow on the world, as Kant supposed. I take this to be the central philosophical point associated with the notion of 'language games'. Games are many and not one. Moreover, they do not all interact with extra-linguistic reality, whatever it is, in the same kind of way, and some of them perhaps do not interact with it at all. In so far as they do interact with it, they do so in diverse ways for diverse purposes in diverse contexts; thus the 'bits' of reality which they capture, record, or report are not all of the same kind. The diversity of the games is reflected in the diversity of the material they dredge up. The incommensurateness of the various games is reflected in the incommensurateness of the material which they pull into their respective nets. And just as you cannot meaningfully reply to a move in chess by a move from dominoes, replying then with a move from Scrabble, so equally you cannot expect the diverse 'worlds' to add up to one perspective, one vision, one system. A plurality of interrelated but incommensurate worlds replaces that unitarian world tacitly assumed by classical epistemology, a world rather like one of those reconstructed panoramas of battles one sometimes finds in museums which offer a single picture as it may have appeared from one definite viewpoint, with all objects obeying the requirements of perspective from that viewpoint. Traditional epistemology saw the cognizing individual as located within his single prospective cocoon, assembling one mosaic from the items supplied to him.

Within such a world, he could then, if he chose, be instrumentally rational. To be rational in this way might have required exceptional clarity of mind, firmness of purpose and character, and great ability or luck in extrapolation towards the as yet uncompleted parts of the mosaic. But allowing for these practical difficulties, which were not insurmountable for someone with character and ability, *Zweckrationalität* was an available option.

Is it, in fact? A man can be a good, *zweckrational* chess player, bridge player, poker player, and so on. The criteria of success and the connections between available means and desirable ends are adequately defined within each of these universes of discourse, and efficiency is consequently identifiable within them without undue difficulty — and is indeed on occasion contrasted with other considerations which influence players, such as elegance, truculence, or sociability. But what conceivable *Zweckrationalität* can be credited to a life as a whole, where that life encompasses a multiplicity of diverse games?

The question is not rhetorical and is not intended, or not yet, to provoke an immediate reply — any reply. It may be that the multiple games add up to one world after all, and it may be that some more abstract aim can be identified in terms of which scores from disparate games can be added and subtracted. Possibly: but it is obviously no easy matter, and there is no immediately evident answer.

It is interesting and relevant, though perhaps not conclusive, that I instinctively find the model of plural and incommensurate overlapping games much closer to life as I know it than the single-bundle observer, assembling one homogeneous world with one perspectival structure based on a single vantage-point. Each mood, each milieu, each relationship, has its own idiom. Communication between them does exist, but it is partial, incomplete, awkward, sometimes merely embarrassing. They commit treason against each other. That which is sacred in one context may be trite and easy to treat ironically in another. You have to know your way about if you are not to make a fool of yourself. What is known as *savoir-faire* is largely the ability to switch from one key to another and to recognize the clues which make such switches appropriate. But too much *savoir-faire* is morally suspect. It suggests pliable, adjustable principles. Yet moral consistency, the unwillingness to switch from the conventions of one game to another, the insistence on staying within the bounds of one of them, is a kind of madness — admirable madness, perhaps.

A great part of our life is spent not so much (as those social sciences which are inspired by the ends–means model would suggest) in the pursuit of aims, but in the avoidance of gaffes. We try to learn our part as we go along and to get by without too much unfavourable comment. Of course you could say that 'avoiding gaffes' either is, or constitutes part of, an overall aim, but that is twisting the facts a bit into the mould of the ends–means model. It is of course notoriously a feature of the ends–means model of human conduct that it can, if necessary, be imposed on all human behaviour. When this is done, we are then rational whether we like it or not. By inventing appropriate ends, any conduct becomes *zweckrational*. Whether it is useful so to impose that vision is another matter.

But if we are, as seems to me to be the case, gaffe-avoiding rather than rational animals, treading our way gingerly through a variety of games to which we are only in part habituated, then our condition is very different from what the theory of instrumental rationality suggests. Thus far, at any rate, I agree with those romantic thinkers who, in opposition to the means–ends rationalists, see social life as the mastering of a language, the use of a code, the participation in a conversation. They are right to this extent — for much of their life, men are not maximizing anything or striving for some concretely isolable end, but are simply eager to be included in, or to remain within, a continuing play. The role is its own reward, not a means towards some further end-state. The point at which these romantics go wrong is this: the role can indeed be understood only through the concepts internal to the play. The role is a fulfilment and not an instrument, they say. So far so good. But from this there is only a small, but disastrously wrong, step to an idealist view which ignores material, non-conceptual, non-conventional constraints. Man may indeed be a convention-seeking, gaffe-avoiding animal; but even the perfect mastery of an idiom will not save you from violence or starvation if objective conditions impose them on you, and conversely, if you are powerful enough, you may commit any gaffe you choose, you may violate the local code or idiom, you may write your own ticket, impose your own code with impunity.

But these (quite fashionable and pervasive) errors of sociological idealism, current under various names, are a side issue to the present argument, which is concerned with the plurality of idioms in life, the plurality of 'worlds' which are their shadows or correlates, and the consequent plurality of overlapping worlds, within which, according to my argument, a general, pervasive *Zweckrationalität* simply makes no sense. Such rationality is possible within delimited areas; if the argument sketched out is correct, it simply makes no sense as an overall life-style. If this argument is correct, what is at issue is not whether a life-style of this kind is attractive — romantics find it repellent — but whether it is logically possible. On this view, when John Stuart Mill was plunged into a depression and concluded that it was not possible to live life in the direct pursuit of a single aim, namely happiness, as utilitarianism commended, what he was facing was not a psychological but a logical impossibility.

The point is this: not only is it questionable whether there is, in the required sense, a single world; it is equally questionable whether there can be a single aim. On this point, let me first of all specify my conclusion before indicating the argument which supports it. There is a kind of Inverse Law: the Specificity and the Plausibility of aims vary inversely. By Specificity of an aim I mean its usability as a criterion for efficiency, for the success or failure of an enterprise — in other words, the testability of assertions concerning its attainment. For the purpose of measuring efficiency, an aim can be of a simple yes–no variety, or can allow of measurable degrees. For instance, if my aim is to ascend a certain mountain, I either succeed or fail, and it is normally easy to tell which. A miss is as good as a mile. If my aim is to amass wealth as measured in a given currency, the precise amount of it can also normally be measured. Climbing mountain peaks or making money are *specific* aims, and in consequence the *Zweckrationalität* of strategies for attaining these ends is open to fairly reliable assessment.

By contrast, each of these aims has very low plausibility as an overall end of the life of a human individual or community. If we perform the *Gedankenexperiment* once recommended by G. E. Moore for the evaluation of the intrinsic goodness or desirability of things, and think of the states of affairs satisfying these ends in complete isolation, as if there were nothing else in the world, we end up with something which is absurd in itself, let alone as an object of desire. Standing on a peak in a universe containing naught else, or possessing gold ingots in an otherwise empty world: each has a somewhat surrealist quality. (G. E. Moore, if I remember rightly, also used this method to discredit pleasure as an end, with the further aid of the somewhat odd argument that pleasure alone meant pleasure without the consciousness that you had it, and there you were …)

But something quite serious and important does underlie Moore's rather Dali-esque method. It is this: the kind of aim which can plausibly be ascribed to a human life or a human community is a highly complex, holistic state of affairs, which contains the specific objects of isolated endeavours only as components or internal options; these insulated sub-aims, however, are worthless or meaningless in isolation. The moral philosophy which tried to articulate itself in the idiom of Means and Ends, utilitarianism, only attained plausibility through the use of an ambiguous, stretch-and-contract notion, namely happiness, the meaning of which fluctuated between being the attribute of an approved total way of life, and (when defined as 'pleasure and absence of pain') being the alleged name of a more or less measurable and isolable specific experience.

Social sciences which operate with means–ends models require, so as to be able to reach testable consequences from the premises of their models, that men should maximize or aim at *something*, never mind what. The trouble is that they are caught in a fork: either they choose realistic aims, which, however, are complex and diffuse and thereby frustrate all calculations of instrumental efficiency, or they choose aims which allow of such calculations, but whose resemblance to actual human aims is generally minimal.

Thus it is doubtful whether *Zweckrationalität* often has, in important contexts, any plausible aims on which to work. It does of course have application in limited fields. If Weber is to be believed, the paradigmatically *zweckrational* conduct of capitalist enterprises came as the consequence of the compulsive enactment of a role. The role was compulsively enacted in an illogical, double-think-permeated effort to demonstrate to the agent himself something which was at the same time outside the power of the person attempting to provide the demonstration through his own conduct, and something which was already decided and thus not the possible object of *zweckrational* behaviour. (By a further irony, if Weber is right, the instrumentally rational world, in which human activities and roles become volatile under the impact of the requirements of efficiency, was brought about by a rigid attachment to the notion of a *calling*, an attachment which, through that rigidity, was itself impervious to instrumental considerations of efficiency.)

This unavailability of plausible aims is important for the ideal of instrumental rationality, but the unavailability of a single world, within which efficiency could be judged by a single measure, so to speak — if the aim were there — is even more important. I believe that this plurality of worlds has always been part of the human condition, and thus constitutes nothing new — but that we have recently become more aware of it.

There are interesting reasons for this development. It is precisely because recent times have witnessed a more persistent and determined effort to unify our world that we have become sensitive to the failure of these unification attempts. In the past, precisely because the world as a whole was seen as some kind of coherent cosmos, qualitatively distinct incommensurate sub-realms within it, each with its own style of being and evidence, were perfectly tolerable. But something quite different has happened to the modern, post-Cartesian vision. (Note, incidentally, that the latest exegesis of Descartes, that of Bernard Williams, sees him primarily — though this is not the terminology used — as a kind of hero, clown, or martyr of *Zweckrationalität*; as a man who adopts the method of doubt in consequence of abandoning temporarily the normal plurality of human aims, and serving instead one end exclusively and ruthlessly, that end being the augmentation of truth in his possession, with a manic disregard — while in this temporary condition — of other considerations; a truly paradigmatic case of *zweckrational* lunacy.)

What is it that has happened?

The basic plot of post-Cartesian philosophy is the perfectly sensible attempt to find a general criterion, or legitimator, of our ideas about the world, as a reaction to the erosion, fragmentation, and destabilization of previous world-visions.[1] This endeavour leads in due course to the empiricist theory of one-kind-of-evidence-only, namely sensory grains. The homogenization of evidence leads automatically to the unification of the world (which, as I insisted early in the chapter, this tradition anyway assumed to hold, and on the whole uncritically). Man, as Hume put it, becomes a bundle of sensations; and of course other subjects in the world are likewise bundles, and made up of similar raw materials. On this account, the world really does become a remarkably homogeneous place.

There is, however, a sense in which (within this picture) the world at large is a bit different from things within it, including people. 'The world' is not just an accumulation of things (or facts, according to Wittgenstein's *Tractatus*, in many ways a fine specimen of that

---

[1] I have argued this in detail in *Legitimation of Belief* (Cambridge, CUP 1975).

tradition), it is also the system of connections between them, of 'laws' and so on. The vision of approach which turns man into a bundle of sensations turns the world itself into a *Bundle of Hypotheses*. The question now is — and this leads us straight back to our general problem of Rationality — can one, and if so how, live in or with a Bundle of Hypotheses? *Ein Zollverein ist keine Heimat*: and is a Bundle of Hypotheses a livable world?

Note the route along which the world was made into a Bundle of Hypotheses. It was a consequence of the attempt to rationalize evidence and conviction, which in turn is a pre-condition or part of the *Zweckrationalität* ideal. *Zweckrationalität* called for standardization of evidence, so as to evaluate it systematically and by a common yardstick. Unless you assess evidence rationally, you cannot assess efficiency, for efficiency is conduciveness to some aim. Choice of means on the basis of sloppily selected evidence is worthless. But if various beliefs are to be compared, they must be in a similar idiom. Thus world-levelling, unificatory epistemologies were elaborated in the service of instrumental rationality. If you are to choose the most efficient Means, you must *know* (and not take on trust, uncritically) the world within which means are links in those causal chains which you manipulate in getting, in the most economical way possible, to your desired Ends. This means suspending faith in objects, realities, unbased on evidence. The end-point of this story is that the world becomes a Bundle of Hypotheses, selected either for optimal corroboration, or for maximum daring and anticipated future fertility (to take two relatively recent rival philosophies of science).

At this point I wish to become dogmatic and make some unsubstantiated assertions (not because I wish to avoid discussion of them, which on the contrary I would find interesting, but because there is no space for it, and intelligibility of exposition requires that the point be asserted long before it is defended): mankind has never in the past tried to live within a Bundle of Hypotheses. It is extremely difficult and probably impossible to do this. Instead, mankind has generally lived by means of the joint employment of Fixed and Variable Cognitive Capital, to borrow phrases from another context and to give them a new sense.

Anthropologists and philosophers of anthropology sometimes raise the question of whether or to what extent peoples who held or hold very strange, and to us eccentric, views were also capable of recognizing and using ordinary sound empirical evidence in the way which is so highly prized amongst us and which has made us the men we are. Field observation suggests that they are perfectly capable of it. That then raises the puzzled question—if so, how can they also believe that other nonsense? For instance, how can those fishermen be so intelligently sensitive to all the sound empirical pre-conditions (as we would say) of a successful fishing expedition, and yet also say and evidently believe that their success is conditional on various ritual performances and omens which, to our minds, have not the slightest connection with it ...?

I suspect that part of the answer is to be sought in the distinction between what I have called Fixed and Variable Cognitive Capital. At any given time and in any given society, a large, probably an overwhelmingly large, part of the view of the world is frozen into the Fixed Cognitive Capital. To treat this part of the society's beliefs as a set of hypotheses is misleading and somewhat offensive. It is not just that they are held with a rigidity which makes them quite insensitive to contrary evidence, should it turn up. There is more to it than that. The identities, roles, personal relationships, power and hierarchy structure, allocation of resources of the society, are all articulated and legitimated in terms of the concepts and ideas of this Fixed Cognitive Capital. This means that, on the one hand, a tangled and weighty network of vested interests and habits helps ensure that the Fixed Capital cannot be changed: anyone inclined to tamper with any single part of it soon finds that he is trying to dislodge a vast and intertwined mass of other things, and he rapidly desists from so enormous, and perhaps dangerous and bewildering, an effort. It also means, on the other hand, of course, that if for some reason that interconnected mass were dislodged, the movement of the resulting avalanche would be hard to arrest, and unpredictable and destructive in its course. This happens rarely, but plainly it did and does happen when the fundamental changes associated with slogans such as 'industrialization' or 'modernization' dislodge either social/institutional or intellectual elements in the mass.

But in the relatively stable traditional situation there is no avalanche, and the big bulk is in a stable, frozen condition. Variability of opinion, sensitivity to evidence, permitting the rapid inversion of the truthvalue attributed to individual and isolable bits in the world-picture mosaic ('propositions'), are restricted to a fairly small and reasonably well-insulated area. The superstitious fishermen do not revise either their cosmology or their social organization, and would not understand what was being suggested if someone were to propose it to them; but within the limited field of connections between various weather signs and tomorrow's state of the sea, they make perfectly rational inferences from the former to the latter, and are quite capable of *Zweckrationalität* and of the construction of an evidence-sensitive sub-world, within which instrumental efficiency can be practised and assessed.

And it is this which brings us to the greatest problem for the notion of *Zweckrationalität*: rational, evidence-sensitive cognitive behaviour is perfectly feasible within such delimited spheres. If the framework is fixed, then a subset of details, of specific ideas, can be variable, and can be tied to 'evidence' (or, no doubt, to other things, for not all flexible ideas are also rational, in the sense of meeting the recommendations of scientific method). But it is by no means obvious that any sense can be attached to evidence-sensitivity, to cognitive rationality, to a system as a whole. Alternatively, even if some sense can be attached to it, it is doubtful whether the practice of such rationality is psychologically tolerable.

When I say that it is doubtful whether any sense can be attached to evidence-sensitive, rational assessment of total visions, I do not have in mind the familiar point about the infinite regress of justification, which leads people to say that 'in the end' there is a blind leap of faith in any vision whatever (and therefore, to the delight of believers, all faiths are in the end equal in the eyes of Reason, and so never have any need to feel inferior *vis-à-vis* agnostics and rationalists). The point is rather that there is not much sense in attaching probability weightings to *sui generis* hypotheses, which are not parts of any kind of series or wider class, and whose probability consequently cannot be derived from a background hypothesis, because either there is no such hypothesis, or, if there is, it is simply the idea-to-be-assessed restated. Pascal attempted to assess the rationality of belief in God in precisely this manner, in a remarkable essay in cost–benefit analysis of *Zweckrationalität*. But his famous Wager is a bit of a joke, it does not feel serious, it is not to be taken seriously; more than half its point is, precisely, to bring out the uniqueness of the question posed, through the ineptness of a procedure which in other and more limited spheres would be perfectly rational and sensitive. Fixed Cognitive Capital simply cannot be dealt with in the same way as Variable Capital.

In ordinary life, we bang our heads against the wall of the Fixed Cognitive Capital not merely, like Pascal, when we encounter theological issues, but also in much more mundane matters. To hazard a sociological generalization: the presence of *ritual* is a good sign of the limits of the variable world, of impinging on the fixed. The essence of ritual is, precisely, its rigidity, its evidence-*in*sensitivity, which makes it the very antithesis of *Zweckrationalität*. (No wonder the Puritans, who were the instruments by which the cunning of Reason introduced instrumental rationality into the world, also minimized ritual in their religious life.) Now what is the point of that rigidity?

A man can be instrumentally rational in choosing, let us say, a business partner, a tennis partner, or a holiday companion. There are moderately precise and formulable criteria for the successful occupancy of such a role. But does it make sense to speak of a rational choice of a spouse? No doubt the mystique of romantic love, the requirement of a *coup de foudre*, arises in part in a society which has abandoned prescriptive or preferential marriage, and where the requirement of this allegedly quite unpredictable, free-floating element of 'love' provides an ever-ready excuse for those who do not propose to otherwise suitable and eligible partners; without the presence of such an in-built excuse, the matter could often be embarrassing. But the other reason is that for such a weighty and many-stranded relationship, rational calculation breaks down, and is bound to do so. Calculation is of course present, but it is overruled by some kind of global consideration or summation, in which so many imponderables, incommensurables, and unpredictables are weighted in a mysterious half-conscious and private algorithm that to pretend to fit it into *Zweckrationalität* is a bit of a fraud. The change of status and identity which is involved in a *rite de passage* such as marriage involves far too much to be eligible for rational calculation. Yet the participants have to go through with it. The ritual and its rigidity are a kind of hand-rail which guides them through a passage in which reason is no longer available, and where they might otherwise waver.[2]

Likewise, and notoriously, no rational attitude is possible in the face of death, whether one's own or that of others. The enormity of the thing makes it impossible to weigh it against other things, and it is offensive and repugnant to try. Judges and insurance companies are of course often obliged to assess death in calculable, monetary terms, but

---

[2] In complicated modern conditions, it can also work in reverse, by a kind of double-take. I knew a young woman who came from a country in which, traditionally, the preferred form of marriage was with the parallel patrilateral cousin. In fact, she was educated in Britain, and lived the life of an emancipated Western woman. She did, however, *marry* in her own background; a young man who was in fact her parallel

that is viewed apologetically and with embarrassment, and the judges themselves are protected by a certain ritualization of their own procedure. Armies are perhaps the most ritualized institutions in society, more so even than churches (whose special business is the global and incalculable), and the reason for this is not only that ritualization helps enforce discipline by creating so many secondary transgressions which can be invoked against the defiant. It is said that during the last war, the German army had a set drill for the capture of machine-gun nests, doing it by numbers, and that it worked. One would think that a highly specific concrete task, like the capture of a fortified point, would be eminently suitable for pliable, evidence-sensitive *Zweckrationalität*; but when the actions involved also imply, for the participants, the facing of an incalculably weighty risk — their own death — then ritualization, by freeing the mind from the need to ponder, is probably effective.

Unique and weighty political decisions are similarly incalculable and thus evade *Zweckrationalität*. For a Jew in the 1930s or early 1940s, in a country occupied or about to be occupied by Hitler, was it rational to flee, whatever the dangers involved? With hindsight, we know of course that it was. But genocide and coldly organized mass murder were so discontinuous with, at least, European history for some centuries, that assigning some precise probability to them in advance of the event would have been absurd. The *sui generis* nature of the possibility made it virtually impossible to evaluate evidence about the contingency.

Or take the much-debated and emotive issue of nuclear disarmament. It is said that, as part of an intelligence exercise, military experts advising the US government have on occasion ascribed a definite figure to the probability of nuclear war breaking out within a defined period. These figures have an air of silliness about them similar to that which attaches to Pascal's calculation of the rationality of the belief in God. It is, of course, easy to construct an argument which shows that nuclear war is, in the long run, overwhelmingly probable. But once again, we have reached the limit of our Variable Cognitive Capital, we are tinkering with something like the total stock, we are trying to deal

patrilateral cousin, and whom she knew only for a brief period before their wedding. No doubt she was embarrassed at the thought that she might seem to her 'Western' friends to be a slave of tradition and of social constraints. So she made a point of telling people that she and her cousin did in fact experience a *coup de foudre*, and that had they met in the West, they would of course simply have lived with each other as is right and proper, but that they promptly married simply as a concession, on a superficial matter, to the

with the Fixed Capital as if it were variable, and calculations acquire an air of unreality.

Or to take something not so ultimate, consider the dilemma which recently faced West European liberal socialists—whether to take liberal Eurocommunism at face value and co-operate with communist parties. There is no record of a communist regime in power remaining liberal, which of course does not entail that the thing is impossible. The issue is exactly like that of immortality and the existence of God, in that by the time we know the answer, it will be too late to revise the wager if we have made the wrong one.

A competent stockbroker, whose job and essence is to practise *Zweckrationalität* on behalf of his clients, can more or less advise them about the instrumental rationality of alternative forms of investment, within the assumption of an overall economic/political stability. His views on the probability of the maintenance of that framework are about as worthless as those of anyone else. The boundary between areas where instrumental efficiency can be a guide (owing to the easy insulation of Variable Cognitive Capital, and the availability of fairly clear aims and criteria) is, I suspect, also closely linked to the delimitation of economics and politics. (This, amongst other reasons, makes the recent revival of social-contract theories in politics, in a form which tries to incorporate them within instrumental rationality, so weird.)

To sum up my contentions (and I have no illusion that they are adequately substantiated):

Instrumental rationality is feasible only within limited sub-spheres of our world, where rational evidence-sensitivity, which it presupposes, is also possible, and where fairly precise aims are too. In other words, it is possible within sub-realms within which hypotheses can be evaluated within a wider given framework.

The modern industrial/scientific world is simultaneously impelling us in two incompatible directions. By eroding the old frameworks and requiring neutral, homogeneous legitimations of beliefs, it pushes the world into becoming a Bundle of Hypotheses, and thus a home fit for instrumental rationality, if not perhaps for much else. It has diminished Fixed Capital, it has extended Variable Capital. This after

feelings of their archaic relatives. I am not suggesting that her story was untrue. But it is interesting to see an upside-down situation, in which the idea of an irresistible, sudden, and spontaneous passion is invoked not as an excuse for avoiding, but as an explanation of conforming to, traditional requirements.

all was the essence of the Scientific Revolution. It has led rapidly to cumulative knowledge and an unprecedented control over the environment. At the same time, this extension of the Bundle of Hypotheses and the corresponding reduction of the rigid framework also eventually make rational calculation harder in many areas where it is now expected and which were previously exempt from it. The more general or fundamental features of the world, though now demoted to the status of mere hypotheses, often elude rational assessment because they are unique or *sui generis* or very fundamental. They have become relativized, optional, and deprived of their privileged, entrenched status—but without becoming, for all that, eligible for rational, instrumental evaluation.

By secularization and 'disenchantment', our world reduces or eliminates the ritually protected, entrenched areas, thereby propelling us towards an ever more general 'rationality'. By increasing human power over nature and society, it also greatly increases the number of occasions on which fundamental, unique, imponderable choices need be made. But by including, by these two processes, a far bigger dose of issues not easily amenable to *Zweckrationalität* within our collective agenda, so to speak, it also makes it that much harder for us to live by the principles of instrumental efficiency. (In the days in which the area in which those principles were to be applied was restricted, it would at least have been possible, within that restricted area, to implement it.)

Thus we need *Zweckrationalität* most when we can least use it. I'm not clear where this leaves us.

2

Individualism and Holism in the Social Sciences

RAYMOND BOUDON

In a much quoted letter Max Weber once wrote: 'Sociology itself can only proceed from the actions of one or more separate individuals and must therefore adopt strictly "individualistic" methods'.[1] Interestingly, Weber put the term 'individualistic' in inverted commas, doubtless to indicate that he did not mean it in its traditional ethical or sociological sense. In its ethical sense, individualism is a doctrine which makes of the person—the individual—a point of reference which cannot be transcended. In this sense, 'individualism' is opposed particularly to 'collectivism'. In its sociological sense, a society is taken as individualist when the autonomy conferred upon individuals by law, custom, and social constraints is very wide. Durkheim identified such societies with the related, although not quite synonymous, term of 'egoism'. Similarly, de Tocqueville noted the development of 'individualism' in mid-nineteenth-century American society, and used the term to denote the fact that the American citizen seemed especially preoccupied with private life and little concerned with public life.

Methodologically, the notion of individualism has a quite different meaning. And it is in order to indicate that he is referring to what we shall identify below as 'methodological' that Weber puts the term in inverted commas. In its methodological sense, 'individualism' can be contrasted with 'holism' or, in Piaget's terms, with 'totalitarian realism'. In short, the two senses of individualism, on the one hand, its methodological sense and, on the other, its ethical or sociological sense, have the same relation as 'bad' in Persian and 'bad' in English.

[1] W. Mommsen, 'Max Weber's Political Sociology and his Philosophy of World History', *International Social Science Journal*, 17 (1965), 44; J. E. T. Elridge, *Max Weber: The Interpretation of Social Reality* (London: M. Joseph, 1970, 1971); P. Birnbaum, *Dimensions du pouvoir* (Paris: PUF, 1984), 192.

According to A. Martinet, the two words are pronounced in exactly the same way, but because they belong to two different languages, their meaning is different. Similarly, the notion of individualism has a quite different meaning according to whether it appears in the context of sociology or ethics, or in that of the theory of knowledge.

The principle underlying 'methodological individualism' is that in order to explain a social phenomenon, whether of demography, political science, sociology, or any other social science, the reconstruction of the motivations of the individuals concerned is indispensable to an understanding of the phenomenon as an aggregate of the individual forms of behaviour prompted by such motivations. And this proposition is valid whatever the form of the phenomenon to be explained, whether a singular instance, a statistical regularity, the expression of a set of quantitative or qualitative data, and so on. Take, for example, a simple relation between two economic phenomena: under certain conditions, if the price of a product goes up, the demand for the product goes down. One could, of course, simply record this macroscopic relation. It is, however, considerably more interesting to pose the much more easily identifiable question of causes. We need only imagine the likely reasoning of a consumer who notes that the price of a particular product has risen: except in the case of the product's being both an unavoidable necessity and in a monopolistic market, or else in competition with other products the price of which has risen in the same way, the consumer, obeying a perfectly understandable motivation, would endeavour to maintain his purchasing power by buying a different product. And because many, if not all, consumers would probably react in the same way, all having the same reason so to react, the aggregation of their conducts would have a collective effect, that is to say, the reduction of the overall demand for the product in question.

Let us call the phenomenon we wish to examine M, in this case the macroscopic relation between price and demand. The explanation proceeds from the observation that M results from the aggregation of microscopic, that is to say individual, behaviours. We can represent it thus: $M + M(m)$, where $M()$ means 'function of' and m indicates the behaviour of a particular individual. The behaviour itself is a function of a set of data, which are not themselves microscopic but macroscopic, that is to say, defined at the level of the system. We can represent these macroscopic data as P: $m = m(P)$. In our example, P indicates that the price of the product in the market has gone up, but also that this product is not a vital necessity or in a monopoly position. The explanation can be represented thus: $M = M [m (P)]$. In other words, the overall phenomenon M is derived from a set of individual behaviours *m* which are the result of motivations which are themselves affected by the macroscopic data P.

When Weber writes that 'sociology *itself* can only proceed from the actions of one or more separate individuals', he means (because the letter from which this quotation is taken was to an economist) that sociology should use what we today call 'methodological individualism', a notion traditional to the discipline of economics. Such a conviction is certainly not a pious hope. If, for reasons we shall examine, the principle of methodological individualism is often criticized in the social sciences that lie outside economics, it is, nevertheless, widely used by them. In classical sociology, as I have tried to show elsewhere,[2] many of Marx, de Tocqueville, Max Weber, Sombart, and Simmel's analyses adhere strictly both to the principle itself and to the form of explanation it denotes. When we turn to modern sociology it is clear that, even though it is far from dominant, the individualist paradigm is present in much, and often the most interesting, research. In order to support this view I shall give a few brief examples.

The first concerns the analysis of social movements, mobilization, and collective action. In this area there are, of course, many examples of the holistic approach. Le Bon's contention that social movements are only comprehensible from the postulate that the individual is as if dissolved in the group is sometimes still taken seriously,[3] although I doubt whether there has been one example of a collective movement successfully explained using this type of perspective. It is probable, moreover, that Le Bon's theory explains, at best, very marginal phenomena. Conversely, certain sociologists still analyse social movements, as did Hegel, as the bearers of the meaning of history, and as the focus of historicity, using a perspective which is both holist and teleological.[4] In contrast, a considerable number of studies concerning social movements use the paradigm of methodological individualism. We can mention here just one example, A. Oberschall's analysis of

[2] R. Boudon, *The Logic of Social Action* (London, Boston, Mass.: Routledge & Kegan Paul, 1981).

[3] F. Le Bon, *Psychologie des foules* (Paris: Alcan, 1895; Paris: Retz, 1975). See also S. Moscovici, *L'Âge des foules* (Paris: Fayard, 1981).

[4] A. Touraine, *Production de la société* (Paris: Seuil, 1973); *Le Retour de l'acteur* (Paris: Fayard, 1984).

the Black movement in America in the 1960s.[5] His analysis conceptualizes the movement and interprets its different forms as being the effect of the strategies deployed by the protagonists in response to the context they found themselves in. A brief illustration of this is the section of Oberschall's book where he explains why the Black movement was violent in the North and non-violent in the South. The non-violence of the movement in the South had often been ascribed to the more oppressive nature of White domination in the Deep South. Oberschall has shown that this holist explanation is quite inadequate, and that it is necessary to conceptualize the non-violence employed by the Southern Black leaders as a strategy which was well adapted to the Southern context. It is true that violence brought with it the risk of greater reprisals than in the North. But it is also necessary to note that, in 1960, the Black movement in the South enjoyed the sympathy of Northern White élites who viewed segregation in the South as an unacceptable archaism. Moreover, the movement was able to draw upon the support of government agencies endeavouring at this time to promote equality between Whites and Blacks. In the South, the Black movement also enjoyed the support of the Protestant clergy, the Black Protestant churches being the only organizations not dominated by Whites. The churches played a significant role in that they performed, outside their religious context, all kinds of social, cultural, and political functions. In the particular conjuncture of the 1960s, Black leaders were in a strategically favourable situation where they could count on the support of enlightened Northern opinion, government agencies, and the Protestant Southern clergy. It is clear that by adopting a strategy of non-violence they could minimize Southern White reprisals and maintain their other support. By resorting to violence they would have risked alienating the Protestant clergy, placed the government agencies in a difficult situation, strengthened the position of conservative Southern politicians, and reduced their audience on the Northern university campuses.

In the North, the situation was completely different. To begin with, the Black community was segregated, with a middle class separated from its old attachments, and an atomized proletariat participating in no form of group activity, and crowded into the ghettos. The Black middle class was not committed to the Black issue, and the atomization of the Blacks in the ghettos made for little mobilization. Nor did

[5]   A. Oberschall, *Social Conflict and Social Movements* (Englewood Cliffs, NJ: Prentice-Hall, 1973).

the Church play the support role which it did in the South. This is why the Black movement in the North, often sparked off by police heavy-handedness, took on an explosive character. And later, as the attention of the Northern élites turned from the Black problem to the problem of Vietnam, the Black movement in the North took a radical and sectarian form, in an attempt once again to attract the attention of the political and intellectual élites, either by laying claim to spontaneous violence, or by stimulating violence itself.

It is clear that an individualist methodology is being used here: the Northern context (P) is different from that of the South (P'). Moreover, the conjuncture, in the case of the Southern strategy of non-violence, was different from that in the North where radical forms of the Black movement appeared. We can express this conjuncturable variable as N/N'. The analysis takes the form of demonstrating that the system (P, N) induced, on the part of Black leaders and the Black community, attitudes *m* and strategies different from those attitudes *m'* which developed later in the North as a result of the context P' and the conjuncture N'.

This example, incidentally, illustrates an important point: that methodological individualism in no way implies an atomistic view of societies, indeed, it requires that individuals be seen as inscribed in a social context. Moreover, it allows us to treat in a similar way individuals in the same situation, and thus facilitates analysis of collective phenomena. It differs, however, from holistic methodology in that it requires that the individual reasons for these collective phenomena be demonstrated, thus denying in principle the possibility of treating a group as an actor endowed, like individuals, with self-identity, consciousness, and will. And when it does treat a group as an individual it has sound reasons for doing so. This individualist economic sociology has no difficulty in treating the family group as a decision-making unit. Finally, and I shall come back to this point, methodological individualism treats the individual as fundamentally 'rational'. In order to show that the individualist paradigm occupies an important place in the most divergent branches of modern sociology, let us turn to a very different area, that of the sociology of development.

In the sociology of development also we can identify a holistic mode of thought. Authors as different as Margaret Mead and Hoselitz[6] have

---

[6] B. F. Hoselitz, *The Progress of Underdeveloped Areas* (Chicago, Ill.: University of Chicago Press, 1952); M. Mead, *Cultural Patterns and Technological Change* (Paris: UNESCO, 1953).

argued that it was extremely difficult to draw traditional societies out of under-development because, essentially, in societies of this type, tradition is so constraining and family, religious, economic, and other institutions so interdependent that economic progress means ultimately the complete overturning of their social structures. In a similar way, authors such as Lerner[7] put forward the view that the introduction of technical change or of an educational or communications system are, given the close interdependence of institutions in traditional societies, bound to cause a generalized upheaval in their social structures.

Other authors, such as Dumont,[8] argue that societies are dominated by an ideology — often referred to more recently as a culture — in which the social totality is immersed. According to such a view, India is a society organized around the principle of *homo hierarchicus*, whereas Western societies are those of *homo aequalis*. Dumont's work is a good illustration of the classical *Gemeinschaft–Gesellschaft* distinction. Underlying Tönnies' and Dumont's classical distinction is the holistic postulate that societies are coherent wholes, that the underlying principles of this coherence can be identified, and that discontinuous forms of society also exist.

This holistic view has been widely criticized and qualified by sociological studies which have adopted an individualist methodology. In order to illustrate this point, let us look at one of the many studies of the effects of technical change within traditional societies. Epstein's study on the effects of irrigation in India demonstrates that holistic theories of development, along with those which believe in the existence of coherent and discontinuous social systems, are often, to use Feyerabend's expression, 'fairy tales'. In Epstein's study,[9] we find neither Mead's 'timeless and changeless Indian village' nor Lerner's mechanical processes of chain reaction. And one is left with the impression that although Indian society is dominated by *homo hierarchicus*, it contains within it processes of considerable social significance which are barely distinguishable from those identified in the

[7] D. Lerner, *The Passing of Traditional Society: Modernising the Middle East* (London: Collier-Macmillan, 1964).

[8] L. Dumont, *Homo hierarchicus: Essai sur le système des castes* (Paris: Gallimard, 1966); *Homo aequalis: Gènese et épanouissement de l'idéologie économique* (Paris: Gallimard, 1977); *Essais sur l'individualisme: Une perspective anthropologique sur l'idéologie moderne* (Paris: Seuil, 1983).

[9] T. S. Epstein, *Economic Development and Social Change in South India* (Manchester: Manchester University Press, 1962).

study of societies dominated by *homo aequalis*. A good illustration of this is Mendras's work on the modernization of French agriculture.[10]

Irrigation enabled the peasants of southern India to replace traditional subsistence crops such as ragee with sugar cane. Generally speaking, we can say that the villages of southern India moved from subsistence to an exchange economy. More importantly, however, irrigation had contrary effects, some of which contributed to the reinforcement, others to the breakdown, of traditional structures. In this way, irrigation indirectly undermined the paternalist structure of the family: the peasant could not process the cane himself so he sold it to state-owned factories. The state bureaucracy itself was subject to two functional constraints: it had to avoid the overproduction of cane, and deal with the peasants on an equal basis. Thus quotas were established, the state committed to buying an established quantity of cane from each household. This, however, encouraged a strategic response on the part of the peasants. They soon understood that in order to overcome the limitations imposed upon them by the quota system, they needed only to bequeath plots of land to their offspring. The result was that whereas before irrigation actual transfer preceded juridical transfer, after irrigation there was a tendency towards the opposite. Of course, this process encouraged both the economic and legal independence of sons *vis-à-vis* their fathers. Irrigation also led to a similar tendency towards independence in husband–wife relations. The creation of surpluses caused by the cane crop meant that the peasant's wife was able to develop an autonomous function. It was her role to redeploy a part of the surplus in, for example, the rearing of poultry for sale. Whereas before irrigation she was just a part of the overall division of labour, afterwards she became an autonomous economic actor. These two tendencies contributed to the undermining of traditional structures.

Other factors, however, had a contrary effect. For example, clientelist relations between peasants and Untouchables were reinforced indirectly by the introduction of irrigation. Before irrigation, under-employment was very high: Untouchables could work for peasants for only a short period of the time they were available. After irrigation, under-employment decreased, the Untouchables profiting from the economic boom created by the cane crop. At the same time, however, they were more directly involved with the peasants and, therefore, more dependent upon them. It is worth noting, in this respect, that

[10] H. Mendras, *La Fin des paysans* (Paris: SEDEIS, 1967).

there was an opposite tendency in non-irrigated neighbouring villages. The peasants there, although they could not grow cane, nevertheless profited from the economic boom created by the irrigated villages, becoming, for example, horse traders or repairers of agricultural machinery. Generally speaking, the peasants complemented their traditional agricultural work with service or artisanal activities. Here, however, these new activities loosened the traditional ties between peasants and Untouchables because the peasants began to recruit their workers from beyond their traditional clientele networks.

The above study is only one example among many. Many similar examples could be given where development processes are analysed as being an aggregate result of the reaction of social actors to circumstances which have changed as the result of, say, innovation. Taken together, these studies indicate the over-simplistic nature of general theories of development which try to analyse directly the results of structural or cultural factors, while avoiding the analysis of motivation and individual behaviour.

Let us look finally at a recent addition to classical sociology, that of social stratification and social mobility, an area I have myself researched.[11] It is an interesting example because the form of holistic thought which informs it has been dominant for a long time and, to a large extent, remains so.

Generally speaking, sociologists in this area limit themselves to the study of, for example, certain independent variables such as the effect of the extension of education on social mobility, without seeking to analyse the individual behaviour which creates the structure of mobility flux. We know that it has generally been assumed to be the case that the extension of education leads automatically to social mobility. Moreover, many holistic analyses undertaken in the area of social mobility assume that, through 'subtle' mechanisms, individuals adopt behaviour which allows social structures to reproduce themselves[12] or else to move in the direction prescribed by the direction of history itself.

In this type of analysis, it is the structures of society that are taken as the active elements, individuals being characterized as behaving in a passive manner, and having only the freedom to enact a pre-ordained destiny. It is worth noting here a very particular form of holist

---

[11] R. Boudon, *Education, Opportunity and Social Inequality* (New York: Wiley, 1973; Paris: Hachette, 1985).

[12] P. Bourdieu and J.-C. Passeron, *La Reproduction* (Paris: Minuit, 1970).

methodology which we can call here minimal individualism or dis-simulated individualism, in which the individual is characterized as merely the site or point at which collective forces or ideas cross. An individual's expectations and plans are determined entirely by his social environment. The beliefs of other individuals, and the character-istics of the social actor's general environment, are not considered as data which the actor takes into account, but as quasi-mechanical forces which determine both the goals he sets for himself and the means he uses in order to attain them.

It is this kind of methodology which explains, for example, econ-omic stagnation as the product of the traditionalism of social actors. Here, the macroscopic phenomenon that is to be explained is analysed as the product of microscopic conduct. But as the actor is conceptu-alized as being deprived of autonomy, the microscopic stage of analysis is, in fact, valueless: the actor is described as obeying invisible mechanisms whose existence can only be demonstrated on the basis of conduct which these mechanisms are supposed to produce and indeed explain.

Our critique here does not mean that an idea like traditionalism has no reality or use, only that it can easily be — and often is — used tautolo-gically. It is clearly acceptable to refer to attitudes, to the Aristotelian ῞εξις or the Thomist *habitus*, when explaining the behaviour of social actors. If, however, one refers to *habitus* to explain behaviour which is itself the only evidence of the *habitus* itself, then one is clearly in a vicious circle.

In my work on social mobility, I tried to demonstrate that if the extension of education did not seem to have had the anticipated effects upon mobility, then this could be explained as the aggregate result of a multiplicity of individual rational behaviours made in response to first the education system and, consequently, the job market. Just as it is not necessary to have recourse to the tautological hypothesis of traditionalism or resistance to change to explain why an innovation which is individually or collectively advantageous is only accepted after a significant time lapse, neither is it necessary to assume that individuals subconsciously obey a desire to reproduce social structures in order to explain that the structure of mobility flux takes longer to change than would have been predicted, even after the education system had become 'democratized'. This relative stability can be explained as an aggregate effect of individual strategies, individual strategies which are not irrational but, on the contrary, understandable if viewed from the perspective of the situation in which the actors find themselves. It seems to me, therefore, undeniable that the individualist paradigm when properly applied is more theoretically sound than the holist one. If this view is correct we still need to explain why the holist approach remains dominant in the social sciences. There are, I think, several reasons for this.

First, it must be said that the paradigm of methodological individualism is somewhat difficult to apply. In an observation full of insight George Simmel writes:

For perfect understanding, it has to be admitted that only individuals exist. For an understanding that goes to the heart of things, any phenomenon which seems to constitute a new and independent unity above the level of individuals will express itself in the reciprocal actions exchanged by individuals. Unfortunately, this perfect understanding is not available to us.[13]

It is important to grasp the significance of this quotation. Simmel stresses first that no social phenomenon can be conceptualized other than as an aggregate effect, that is, as the result of actions, attitudes, and individual behaviour. And when he points out that this is a chimera, he means that it would simply be impossible to try to analyse in a controlled and objective way the behaviour of each individual. Instead, the actors should be classified into types and the behaviour of these ideal-typical actors described (a description which can only, however, be a very simplified representation of them). This representation will always involve, as Simmel points out, an 'abstract psychology' or 'a psychology of convention'.[14] In short, individual explanations always involve the construction of models. In the same way as the economist assumes the right to describe the conduct of the consumer or the producer in given circumstances, so must the sociologist create ideal-types of actors to whom he or she ascribes a behavioural 'logic' which has been infinitely simplified in relation to reality. Simmel adds, however:

Having said this, just as the biologist has already replaced the vital force, which seemed to control the different organs, with the reciprocal action of the latter, so too the sociologist, in his turn, must aim more and more to identify the specific processes which actually produce social phenomena, even though this means a certain denial of the sociologist's ideal.

This passage indicates that research should construct individual

[13] G. Simmel, *Sociologie et epistémologie* (Paris: PUF, 1981).
[14] Ibid. 174.

models, and that the advancement of knowledge in the social sciences goes by way of moving from holist to individual explanations. At the same time, however, the passage (and the context in which the text itself was written) indicates that this change is often difficult and that, in any case, it does not apply equally to all objects of study.[15] The problems raised by the application of the individualist paradigm is the first reason for the dominance of the rival paradigm.

It is true that the logic informing economic behaviour can usually be easily reconstructed. As a result, macroscopic economic phenomena, such as those referred to above, can be analysed convincingly by models of the individualist type. It is the same, for example, for stratification or mobility: these can be relatively easily characterized as aggregate effects of behaviour which is itself subject to a relatively simple logic.[16] Such an analysis, however, is much more difficult in the case of suicide rates, for example. Suicide rates are the result of behaviour which is subject to complex and infinitely variable logics which differ from individual to individual. This is why, in this case, it is much more difficult to analyse the macroscopic by reference to its constituent microscopic elements.

The example of suicide is, of course, not unique. Public opinion surveys also resist individualist analysis. This is why the researcher has no alternative but to assert that the frequency of a given opinion varies in relation to a particular socio-demographic characteristic without being able to explain why this is so, that is to say, without being able to explain the correlation as the result of a set of behaviours obeying a clear logic. Similarly, it is generally known that demographers cannot always explain the results they observe at the aggregate level in terms of individual behaviour. Why, for instance, was the First World War followed in France by a decrease in births, and the Second by an increase?

These trivial observations have important and often unappreciated consequences. They explain, for example, in part at least, why individualist methodology is more frequently used in economics than in sociology. Yet on the other hand we should bear in mind another of Simmel's points, and one to which I subscribe whole-heartedly: that advances in knowledge usually involve the movement from the holist to the individualist paradigm. And there are many instances of changes of this kind, some of which I have given above.

[15] G. Simmel, *Les Problèmes de la philosophie de l'histoire* (Paris: PUF, 1984).
[16] Boudon, *Education, Opportunity and Social Inequality*.

These remarks, however, still do not explain the lack of popularity of the individualist paradigm in sociology. Resistance to it is also the result of a frequent occurrence in the social sciences and what Wrong calls an 'oversocialised conception of man':[17] the social actor is often conceptualized as a clay on to which are inscribed environmental influences which subsequently dictate his behaviour in a given situation. Thus sociologists of development often admit that social actors obey strictly the rules imposed upon them by tradition and culture. It is in this way that certain writers have explained, for example, why Indian peasants continue, against their own and the collective interest, to have numerous children. In such a view this is the result of mechanical allegiance to secular traditions. Apart from the fact that such an 'explanation' explains nothing, it overestimates the passivity of the social actor in his relation to tradition.

In a case such as this, the individualist approach should be that of examining the situation of the actor and attempting to show that if tradition is followed it is not simply because it generates unconditional and mechanical respect, but because it does not conflict with the situation; in short, that it is 'rational' for the actor who follows that tradition, that it makes sense to him. We have shown that, in India, the economic context is often such that it is in the interests of families to have numerous children for *reasons* of social and economic security.

This 'oversocialized' view of man—of the social actor, to be more exact—is not at all uncommon, and can be found in the most diverse sociological writings. In my view, it proceeds, in the first instance, from the fact that it is difficult to avoid what Piaget calls 'socio-centrism'. It is easier to interpret as unconditionally irrational a given behaviour which the observer does not understand than to seek to show that it is irrational only in terms of its relation to the observer, and not in terms of its relation to the actor. One of the advantages of the individualist paradigm, and of the assumption of rationality contained within it (that is to say the Weberian[18] view according to which all behaviour is in principle capable of being comprehended by the observer on condition that the observer is sufficiently well informed of the context in which the actor moves) is that it enables the sociologist to avoid falling into the trap of sociocentrism.

The 'oversocialized conception of man', moreover, has quite clear

[17] D. Wrong, 'The Oversocialised Conception of Man in Modern Sociology', *American Sociological Review*, 26/2 (1961), 183–93.
[18] M. Weber, *Economy and Society* (New York: Bedminster Press, 1968).

ideological roots. It is derived from a widely held and easily under-standable belief in the despotism of social structures. Although this belief may be a legitimate one, it does not mean that the ideological position derived from it, which perceives the social actor as a puppet whose strings are pulled by social structures, is also well founded. We should add that the belief is not, of itself, sufficient to establish the holist ideology, especially when the observer holds the further belief that the structures are themselves nefarious, and that those who sub-mit to them must consequently be viewed as irrational or else alienated.

These two reasons, the despotism of structures and the tendency towards sociocentrism, explain the widespread nature of the holistic approach; when the actor is perceived as the puppet of the structures, he can be dismissed, in which case the individualist perspective loses all meaning and can be easily viewed as irrelevant. Thus societies can be conceptualized as simple systems which can be described with the help of a few oppositional concepts: *Gemeinschaft–Gesellschaft*, modern–traditional society, or industrial–post-industrial society, for example. As for social processes themselves, these can, in a similar way, be reduced to elementary notions such as class struggle, domina-tion, and dependence.

3

Marxism and Methodological Individualism*

JON ELSTER

'God is the productive forces.' This joke of Paul Lafargue's[1] expresses well enough a particular Marxist approach that I shall take issue with in the present chapter. Such an approach involves seeking out the motor forces of history, as well as the stabilizing forces of societies. It uses abstractions such as 'productive forces', 'relations of production', 'classes', 'state', or 'ideologies' without indicating how these are anchored in individual actions, motivations, and beliefs. According to this view, history is the self-realization of Humanity, of Man rather than of men.[2] Capitalist exploitation and domination are the fact of Capital, which takes precedence in the order of explanation over individual capitals. The appeal to these supra-individual entities usually goes hand in hand with two other equally dubious procedures. On the one hand, methodological collectivism is linked to a functionalism which accounts for social phenomena by invoking consequences rather than causes. On the other hand, it adopts a form of dialectical reasoning which uses a kind of conceptual deduction to understand historical change. Although one can put forward a reasoned defence of functionalism, and—even more so—of a particular version of the dialectic,[3] these salvage operations are only possible through recourse

* This chapter is adapted from J. Elster, *Making Sense of Marx* (Cambridge: Cambridge University Press, 1985). For reasons of convenience I have omitted here textual references to Marx's work. I should like to thank G. A. Cohen and John Roemer for their many discussions which helped to clarify the ideas expressed here.

[1] Quoted in K. Papaioanou, *De Marx et du marxisme* (Paris: Gallimard, 1983), 59.
[2] See G. A. Cohen, 'Karl Marx's Dialectic of Labour', *Philosophy and Public Affairs*, 3 (1974).
[3] On the relationship between Marxism and functionalist explanation, see G. A. Cohen, *Karl Marx's Theory of History* (Oxford: Oxford University Press; Princeton, NJ: Princeton University Press, 1978), and J. Elster, 'Un marxisme anglais', *Annales économies, civilisations, sociétés*, 36 (1981). On the construction of a non-mystifying

to individualist based arguments.

This critique of Marxist methodology presupposes a substantial interest in Marxist theory; otherwise such a critique would be a waste of time. It is precisely because historical materialism and the critique of capitalism remain living and vital theories—which does not mean that they are without failings, far from it—that it is worth extricating them from their peculiar strait-jacket. Some sample sketches of this process will be offered below. Let us begin with the principles of methodological individualism.

Methodological Individualism: What it is and what it is not

Methodological individualism is a form of reductionism. It offers to the social sciences the explanatory ideal of the other sciences, namely, the analysis of complex phenomena in terms of the most simple phenomena. More precisely, it claims that all social phenomena— whether process, structure, institution, or *habitus*—can be explained by the actions and properties of the participating individuals.

There are essentially two reasons why the explanation of the macro by the micro is preferable to that of macro by the macro. On the one hand, there is an aesthetic reason: even if the macro–macro explanation is robust and reliable, it is always more satisfying to open the black box and see the workings of the mechanism. On the other hand, there is a more scientific reason: by descending from the macro to the micro, one goes simultaneously from the long to the short term, thus reducing the risk of confusing explanation and correlation, or of assuming that a law necessitating a certain event also explains it.[4]

It is worth noting several limitations of this reductionist principle, and clearing up several quite common misunderstandings. First, reduction can only take place in transparent contexts. To explain this idea, an example is more valuable than a definition. In the sentence 'France fears Germany', the first reference to a supra-individual entity (France) can, in principle, be replaced by a reference to the fears of individual French people. Conversely, the second reference (Germany) cannot be because—and in as much as—what individual

theory of the dialectic, see J. Elster, *Logic and Society* (Chichester, London: Wiley, 1978), chs. 4–5, and 'Négation active et négation passive', *Archives européennes de sociologie*, 21/2 (1980), 329–49.

[4] See also J. Elster, *Explaining Technical Change* (Cambridge: Cambridge University Press, 1983), ch. 1.

French people fear is precisely a supra-individual, perhaps mythical, nebulous entity (which does not mean that it has no psychological reality). Marx was doubtless wrong to see in capital such a supra-individual entity, although in the sentence itself 'Marx saw in capital a supra-individual entity', one could not, without entering the realms of the absurd, eliminate the reference to capital, *salva veritate*.

There is a second constraint at the level of the application of doctrine; it is the risk of premature reductionism. We shall see below that in certain aspects of Marxism, the reductionist approach exposes itself to this danger. Nevertheless, we cannot overemphasize the difference between the idea that we must sometimes accept methodological collectivism for want of something better, and the idea that there is nothing better, between a non-reductionism which makes a virtue of necessity, and one which insists on its intrinsic virtues.

Among the misunderstandings to be cleared up, let us begin with the idea of methodological individualism as a theory of individual motives. There are no assumptions in the doctrine about rational motives, nor about selfish behaviour. Without doubt there are good reasons for giving a methodological primacy to the rational over the irrational, as well as to selfish motives over non-selfish motives.[5] These reasons, however, do not proceed from the individualist principle itself. Moreover, this methodological primacy in no way excludes the possibility, as we shall see below, that in a particular case the behaviour of actors must be explained in terms of irrational or non-selfish motives.

Methodological individualism is not an atomistic doctrine confined to the extrinsic or causal relations between social agents, like billiard balls hitting each other. It is, in fact, perfectly compatible with the idea that there are intrinsic or intentional connections. On the one hand, there is the *interdependence of utilities*, in altruism, envy, and other such sentiments. On the other hand, there is the *interdependence of decisions*, such as is studied by game theory. However, in order that there be interdependence, it is necessary, first of all, that the entities thus interlinked are distinct; this is what is claimed by methodological individualism.

Schumpeter, the inventor of the term 'methodological individual-

---

[5] On the primacy of the rational over the irrational see D. Davidson, *Essays on Actions and Events* (Oxford: Oxford University Press, 1980). On the methodological primacy of selfish motives over non-selfish ones, see J. Elster, 'Rationality, Morality and Collective Action', *Ethics*, 95 (1985).

ism', himself insisted that there was no necessary link with liberalism or with political individualism. The idea should have been obvious: there remains, however, a strong prejudice which places methodological individualism naturally 'on the right'. Durkheim—its most famous adversary—was undoubtedly a man of the left; the Austrian economists—its staunchest defenders—placed themselves clearly on the right. Today, the same opposition can be found between Pierre Bourdieu and Raymond Boudon, to name only two. It is necessary, however, to remember that there is also an organicism of the right. Why should there not be an individualism of the left?

Finally, there is the confusion between methodological individualism and ethical individualism. The latter is the doctrine according to which only happiness, rights, and the freedom, or autonomy, of individuals count in the ethical evaluation of societies; excluded are values such as the protection of nature, or the growth of scientific knowledge, in as much as these are not the object of man's desire; excluded also are supra-individual categories such as class or nation. It would be necessary to reject, for example, a redistribution of wealth which, while creating a more equal average income of nations, would increase inequality between individuals. In this sense, Marx was an ethical individualist. Class societies have seen man's fulfilment in the creation of works of art and scientific theories. Only communism would allow the true fulfilment of each individual person. Having said this, Marx's ethical individualism stopped him from leaning quite so closely towards explanatory individualism.[6] Although one can offer strong arguments for each one of these doctrines, they are essentially independent of one another.

Productive Forces and Relations of Production

History, according to the 1859 Preface, is the history of the productive forces and the relations of production. The advent and decline of successive relations of production can be explained by their tendency to promote or obstruct the productive forces. In order better to understand this doctrine and its fatal lack of 'microfoundations', we must first of all eliminate certain ambiguities.

[6] These two forms of individualism do not seem sufficiently distinguished from one another in Dumont's (otherwise very enlightening) analysis. See L. Dumont, *Homo aequalis* (Paris: Gallimard, 1977). For a thorough analysis see S.-C. Kolm, *Le Bonheur— liberté* (Paris: PUF, 1982), ch. 5.

In an initial phase, the relations of production are in 'correspondence' with the productive forces, and later enter into 'contradiction' with them. The idea of contradiction can be interpreted in many ways, according to whether one perceives it in a static or a dynamic, actual or counterfactual way. As a static-counterfactual notion, contradiction means that inefficient use is made of the productive forces. Thus, in capitalism, the anarchy of the market creates crises, unemployment, overproduction, etc., which require, for their elimination, a planned economy. As a dynamic-actual notion, contradiction means the stagnation of technology: the rate of development of productive forces is lower than it was in the initial phase. There are texts which allow us to impute to Marx both of these ideas, but the most plausible reading, nevertheless, is to understand contradiction as a dynamic-counterfactual phenomenon: the rate of development of the productive forces is lower than it would have been in other relations of production.

We can therefore summarize the theory in two propositions. At all *levels* of development of the productive forces there is an ensemble of relations of production which maximizes their *rate* of development; there is a tendency for relations of production, which maximize the rate of development, to be created. As G. A. Cohen has shown, this is a functionalist explanation.[7] The relations of production can be explained by their beneficial and, in fact, optimal consequences for the productive forces. However, this explanation immediately comes up against the central problem of all explanations of this type: what is the mechanism by which the productive forces create the relations of production which maximize their development? More precisely, who are the individuals who, acting in their own interest, tend to realize the aim of history? Who are the men of flesh and blood who incarnate this god, the productive forces?

Marx offers no answer to this question, but we can attempt to give one for him. A priori, there seem to be two principal possibilities. Either the individual producer finds that it is in his interest to transform the relations of production at the level of the unit of production; or else there is a group of individuals with the power and the motivation to transform the relations of production at the level of the economy.

The first idea comes up against the social nature of the relations of

---

[7] See, in particular, Cohen, *Karl Marx's Theory of History*, ch. 6.

production. Take the transition from feudalism to capitalism,[8] the latter being characterized by the conjunction of wage labour and production for the market. It is clear why the creation of the market is a social process outside the control of the individual producer. Conversely, the transition from serfdom to wage labour could, in principle, have taken place at the level of the unit of production, but it is difficult to see how it could be explained by the development of the productive forces; at most, wage labour would allow a more efficient utilization of existing productive forces. It is the same with the transition to communism: even if workers' self-management can emerge spontaneously at the level of the workplace, central planning—that is to say, the abolition of the market—would require the conquering of political power. Moreover, there is no reason why the introduction of workers' self-management should be explained by the more rapid development of the productive forces.

The other aspect of the dilemma is scarcely more attractive. Let us take the case of the transition to communism. Marx wanted us to believe that the communist revolution would take place when and because communist relations of production would allow a higher rate of development of the productive forces. However, the idea that the promise of faster technological innovation would encourage the working class to revolution is doubly implausible. First, there is the general problem of the prisoner's dilemma: we shall come back to this below. Also we must remember that according to Marx the rate of innovation in capitalism is very high and is even growing. He did not reckon on the stagnation of capitalism but on the superiority of communism. It is, however, to display a staggering naïvety to think that the workers would abandon a system in full economic expansion for a purely hypothetically superior alternative, given the costs of transition and the uncertainty which would inevitably hover over the outcome. Doubtless one could reply that the revolution will take place following capitalist crises: this, however, would be to repudiate the idea of its occurrence when *and because* communism will allow faster technological development.

For Marx, therefore, it was a question of explaining the relations of production by the rate of development of the productive forces. It is instructive to compare the Marxist explanation with two other theories which, though still functionalist, substitute other explanations.

[8] See, in particular, R. Brenner 'The Social Basis of Economic Development', in J. Roemer (ed.), *Analytical Marxism* (Cambridge: Cambridge University Press, 1986).

On the one hand, the neo-classical theory of property rights claims that these are justified and explained by their tendency to maximize the net social product.[9] Here, too, one must ask what is the mechanism which assures this result. It is not sufficient to show that laws are such that the net product effectively attains its maximum; it would also be necessary to prove that laws are what they are because they tend to have this effect. The theory addresses neither of these propositions. On the other hand, the 'neo-Marxist' theory of Douglas North explains the relations of production by their tendency to maximize the *surplus* received by governments.[10] This 'predatory theory of the state'[11] has the methodological advantage of being able to name an agent with the power and the motivation to realize maximization. Of course, methodological individualism reminds us that the state should not be conceptualized as a monolithic agent, and that we must take account of the conflict of interests not only between the state and social classes, but also between the head of state and his agents.[12]

The 1859 Preface claims that history is the history of the relations of production and the productive forces. The *Communist Manifesto* stresses just as clearly that the history of humanity until the present is that of class struggle. The central problem for the Marxist theory of history is the absence of mediation between these two propositions. Marx never explained how social classes are led to act in a way which serves not only their own interests, but also those of humanity. Moreover, he did not really resolve the following problem: how does a social class manage to promote its collective interest when this differs from the individual interests of the members of the class?

Class and Class-Consciousness

A class, as such, is unable to act. The notion of collective action is, in fact, just a way of speaking; in reality, only individuals are capable of acting. Yet can we not speak of the interest of a class as such? Moreover, is it not only too clear that such interest often animates social movements? We shall outline here how we can give affirmative

[9] See R. Posner, *The Economic Analysis of Law* (Boston: Little Brown, 1977).

[10] D. North, *Structure and Change in Economic History* (New York: Norton, 1981).

[11] M. Levi, 'The Predatory Theory of the State', in M. Hechter (ed.), *The Micro-foundations of Macrosociology* (Philadelphia: Temple University Press, 1983).

[12] For a recent analysis, see G. M. Macdonald, 'New Directions in the Economic Theory of Agency', Discussion Paper 84/7 (Economics Research Center/NORC, University of Chicago).

responses to these questions without, however, violating the doctrine of methodological individualism.

It is not necessary here to explain what a class is according to Marx; it is sufficient to say that the question, although complicated, is not insoluble.[13] In any case, the problems posed by the notion of class-consciousness are largely independent of the notion of class itself. It seems that the most useful approach for empirical applications is to define class consciousness as the ability to overcome the problem of the 'free rider' in collective action. Let us indicate briefly what this means for the capitalist class and for the working class.

The interest of the capitalist is to maximize his profit; that of the capitalist class to maximize total profit. A certain restriction on production is the necessary means of realizing this last aim. To simplify, let us suppose that each capitalist has the choice between two strategies; to limit production (L) and to maintain it at a competitive level (C). We have here a structure similar to the prisoner's dilemma. For each capitalist, profit is higher if all choose L than if all choose C, but it is always more profitable for the individual to choose C, whatever the others do. The interest of 'capital', that is to say, of the capitalist class, often differs from the interest of the individual capitalist. Marx, moreover, knew this very well, as his analyses of the Factory Acts show in volume i of *Capital*.

In the same way, the actions of the working class — whether reformist or revolutionary in nature — involve the temptation for each individual to profit from the solidarity of others. Why strike when one can reap the benefits without the costs, and leave to others the risk of the effort of confrontation? And if others, authors and victims of the same reasoning, decide to abstain as well, this only reinforces such a view. The fact that the strike is better for the working *class* does not of itself encourage the individual worker.

Such at least is 'the logic of collective action' as it has been studied for the last twenty years.[14] It is a strong case — too strong even, given that it makes cartels and trade unions impossible, although neither the existence nor the importance of these can be denied. Before, the difficulty was to explain why collective action, indispensable for the survival of the group in question, often faltered; today, political

[13] See, in particular, J. Roemer, *A General Theory of Exploitation and Class* (Cambridge: Harvard University Press, 1982).

[14] The classic analysis is that of M. Olson, *The Logic of Collective Action* (Cambridge, Mass.: Harvard University Press, 1965).

observers are confounded when it succeeds. Even if their earlier reaction was somewhat excessive, it was nevertheless fundamentally healthy. The enduring legacy of the 'logic of collective action' is that one can no longer explain collective action simply through the public goods it produces, because the principal characteristic of these is to be accessible to everyone, whether or not they have contributed.

How then can we explain collective action? We can dismiss immediately explanations which appeal to differential and selective benefits and punishments.[15] Once established, a trade union can maintain itself by offering pensions to the workers or by threatening them with social ostracism or worse, but these private goods and evils cannot explain its initial creation. We can also dismiss explanations which see participation in collective action as a benefit rather than a cost.[16] Even for trade-union action, this suggestion is not very plausible; applied to the formation of cartels, it becomes absurd. The co-operative strategy can only be explained by the extrinsic benefit produced by co-operation rather than by secondary or intrinsic benefits.

Let us begin with explanations which only involve rational and selfish individuals. Game theory — both formal and experimental — has allowed us to clarify these explanations, as well as define their validity.[17] Co-operation which takes place between rational individuals and which does nothing other than serve their particular utility requires prudence from each one among them, that is to say, the ability to take into account long-term benefits, as well as sufficient information on the motivation and information of others. In other words, voluntary co-operation between rational egoists is hindered by avarice and suspicion.

This kind of explanation seems plausible in the case of capitalist cartels; it seems less so for the creation of trade unions. Even though one cannot exclude, a priori, the idea that working-class solidarity is just an ultra-sophisticated form of prudence, it is not easily compatible with our knowledge of the great social movements of the modern period. Hence the temptation for Sartre, in his analysis of the group in fusion, to explain collective action as a phenomenon that is irreducible

[15] This is Olson's explanation, ibid.

[16] See A. Hirschman, *Shifting Involvements: Private Interests and Public Action* (Princeton, NJ: Princeton University Press, 1982).

[17] The essential works are A. Rapoport and A. Chammah, *Prisoner's Dilemma* (Ann Arbor, Mich.: University of Michigan Press, 1956); M. Taylor, *Anarchy and Cooperation* (Chichester, New York: Wiley, 1976); R. Axelrod, *The Evolution of Cooperation* (New York: Basic Books, 1984).

to the individuals who constitute it.[18] However, there is an alternative approach, and one which conforms with methodological individualism: the rejection of the egoism hypothesis, but the retention of the idea of rationality. There is a whole range of altruistic and moral motives capable of inducing individuals to co-operate.[19] In a heterogeneous group, one often finds several individuals, strongly motivated towards co-operation, whose presence creates a snowball effect, picking up others who, by themselves, would have remained passive. It is possible to identify quite precisely the conditions in which this effect will be produced.[20]

The rationality hypothesis, although more profoundly embedded than that of egoism, is not, however, sacrosanct. Among the attempts to interpret participation in collective action as fundamentally irrational, let us mention a study of experimental psychology concerning voting behaviour.[21] The 'voter's paradox' is, in fact, a famous example of the prisoner's dilemma: on the one hand, it is better for our candidate and us that he receive all our votes rather than none; on the other hand, however, each one of us has only an infinitesimally small influence on the result of an election, to the extent that it does not seem worth going to the polls.[22]

The subjects of the experiment in question expressed voting intentions which seem to correspond to the following sophism:

I am quite a representative member of the political grouping to which I belong. If I vote, it is quite probable that the other members will vote as well; because they are like me, they will behave like me. I am, therefore, going to vote, in order to ensure that they will vote too.

The last sentence expresses the 'Calvinist' slide[23] from a diagnostic

[18] J.-P. Sartre, *Critique de la raison dialectique* (Paris: Gallimard, 1960), 220 ff.
[19] See Elster, 'Rationality, Morality and Collective Action'.
[20] See O. Oliver, G. Marwell, and R. Teixeira, 'Interdependence, Group Heterogeneity, and the Production of Collective Action', *American Journal of Sociology*, 9 (1985).
[21] G. Quattrone and A. Tversky, 'Self-Deception and the Voter's Illusion', in J. Elster (ed.), *The Multiple Self* (Cambridge: Cambridge University Press, 1986). For another attempt to explain co-operative behaviour in terms of irrational motives, see Rapoport and Chammah, *Prisoner's Dilemma*, p. 29.
[22] See, in particular, B. Barry, *Sociologists, Economists and Democracy* (Chicago, Ill.: University of Chicago Press, 1979).
[23] A notable example of this mode of reasoning is the following extract from a Baptist pamphlet of the 18th century: 'Every soul that comes to Christ to be saved ... is to be encouraged ... The Coming soul need not fear that he is not elected, *for none but such would be willing to come*', quoted in E. P. Thompson, *The Making of the English Working Class* (Harmondsworth, Penguin, 1969), 38 (our emphasis). There is a large

reasoning which is seen as perfectly acceptable to a causal reasoning which is itself manifestly false. It goes without saying that the subjects are not explicitly conscious of the slide; it is a piece of bad faith rather than a logical deduction.

A sociological theory of collective action could not accept these abstract and rather simplistic models. Account would have to be taken of the historical background, as well as of the economic, social, cultural, and political context.[24] In any specific case, there would be a unique mixture of motivations which makes collective action possible. These motives do not fall out of the sky, but have a precise social causality which must be demonstrated. However, even if the social structure (at the macro level) comes into the explanation of (equally macro) collective action, it does so through the intermediary of actions, motivations, and individual beliefs. We need only remember the virtues of reductionism pointed out above; the discovery of micro-foundations assures an explanation which is both more satisfying and more solid.

Having said that, it should be added that, in practice, the social sciences cannot yet accommodate the above findings of game theory and experimental psychology. Even if the historian or the sociologist can draw inspiration from game theory or the sciences of decision-making, macro-sociological correlations often offer more solid evidence. We know, for example, that collective action is facilitated by the stability of the group, whereas a higher rate of renewal hinders it.[25] Moreover, it is generally more difficult to determine whether the causal effect of this macro-variable is mediated by influence on individual motivations, by the impact of beliefs, or by both. Given the difficulty of sounding the hearts of a large number of individuals, especially when it is a question of the past, it is often better to remain at the macro-sociological level than to expose oneself to the risk of premature reductionism. Progress in this area will take the form of the interrelated development of more refined theoretical models, more macro-sociological correlations, and more precise techniques of observation.

body of literature on the philosophical aspects of the problem, beginning with R. Nozick, 'Newcomb's Problem and Two Principles of Choice', in N. Rescher (ed.), *Essays in Honour of Carl Hempel* (Dordrecht: Reidel, 1969).

[24] For a good example of this, see S. Popkin, *The Rational Peasant* (Berkeley, Los Angeles, Calif.: University of California Press, 1979).

[25] On the importance of the rate of renewal in the analysis of collective action see Elster, *Logic and Society*, ch. 5.

Ideologies

Both cognitive and moral belief systems seem to offer the best counter-example to the principles of methodological individualism. It is absurd, in fact, to hope to explain a language, a religion, a social norm, or a tradition as a 'logical construction' on the basis of dispositions or individual beliefs. Is it not much more plausible to see them as supra-individual entities which are presupposed by all acts or by all individual states of mind, themselves the conditions of possibility of all such phenomena?[26]

We cannot here answer this question in all of its generality.[27] Let us simply note that traditions, beliefs, and norms are far from being immutable and monolithic. It is impossible, even at a given moment, to define what *the* French language is, given the infinite variation of its uses. Doubtless there is an authorized version—but it is certainly not the Dictionary of the French Academy which is the condition of possibility of daily French. Moreover, linguistic and cultural practices are in permanent, although slow and imperceptible, flux. If the individual feels norms as objective constraints, independent of his will, it is because at any given moment, their range of variation among the individuals he frequents is severely limited, just as the price of milk is more or less the same in all the shops in one locality.

Marxist theory of ideologies offers a good example of this problem. It deserves, in fact, a pre-eminent place in the chamber of horrors of scientific thought, through its arbitrary and often absurd explanations. Reading, for example, Franz Borkenau or Lucien Goldman, one has the impression that between a social and economic system and its corresponding ideology, there is a relation of emanation which seems to ignore completely mediation by individuals. We need only remember Borkenau's claim that Cartesian physics is socially determined 'in every line'.[28] These phantasmagorical excesses are based either on functionalist explanations of the *Cui bono?* type, or on so-called 'structural homologies'. The arbitrary nature of both modes of analysis is shown by their ease of application, which meets no resistance or friction whatever from what is being explained. Everything resembles

[26] For a clear formulation of such objections to methodological individualism see C. Taylor, 'Interpretation and the Sciences of Man', *Review of Metaphysics*, 25 (1971).
[27] For more detailed attempts at refutation, see J. Elster, 'Reply to Comments', *Inquiry*, 23 (1980), and 'Reply to Comments', *Theory and Society*, 12 (1983).
[28] For references and discussion see J. Elster, *Leibniz et la formation de l'esprit capitaliste* (Paris: Aubier, 1975), ch. 1.

everything else; everything serves everything else's interests, as long as one chooses the right temporal horizon and angle of approach.

Marx himself began this sorry tradition. In his observations on the Christian religion, he sometimes explained it in terms of the service it renders to the dominant classes, sometimes by its 'correspondence' with economic fetishism. One could multiply these examples. However, there are also in Marx far more interesting elements which justify an effort of reconstruction. The attempt to do so must be guided by the principle that all social determination of thought operates at the level of the individual, and through psychological mechanisms which must be identified and not simply postulated.

To this end we can offer a typology of forms of false consciousness. We should distinguish, on the one hand, between the cognitive and affective consciousness, that is to say, between factual beliefs and beliefs of value, and, on the other hand, between the mechanisms of 'cold' or cognitive distortions[29] and 'hot' or affective mechanisms.[30] The combination of these distinctions produces the following:

	Cognitive content	Affective content
Cognitive distortion	1	2
Affective distortion	3	4

1. This is an important category in Marx's thought because it includes his sociology of daily economic consciousness. He did not believe that the erroneous beliefs held by the economic agents of the capitalist system were hot, that is to say, motivated errors. They are illusions which are created spontaneously because each agent perceives the system from a particular point of view, which falsifies his perspective. The clearest case is that of monetary fetishism. An individual capitalist always has the choice between investing his capital in a productive enterprise in order to get profit, and putting it into a bank in order to get interest. Apparently—that is to say, from his particular point of

---

[29] On theoretical discussion and numerous applications of these see, in particular, the research brought together in D. Kahneman, P. Slovic, and A. Tversky (eds.), *Judgement under Uncertainty* (Cambridge: Cambridge University Press, 1982), and R. Nisbet and L. Ross, *Human Inference: Strategies and Shortcomings of Social Judgement* (Englewood Cliffs, NJ: Prentice-Hall, 1980).

[30] See, in particular, the work of L. Festinger, beginning with his *A Theory of Cognitive Dissonance* (Stanford, Calif.: Stanford University Press, 1957). For comparisons between 'cold' and 'hot' mechanisms see Nisbet and Ross, *Human Inference*, and D. Pears, *Motivated Irrationality* (Oxford: Oxford University Press, 1984).

view—the capital is productive in both cases. Monetary fetishism confuses appearance and essence, partial and general equilibrium.[31] He claims that gold or money—and not only men, land, and tools— are part of the real wealth of a country, as if all capitalists could put their money into the bank and receive interest from it. This *fallacy of composition*[32] is an important mechanism of ideological thought.

2. The idea that norms and values are susceptible to purely cognitive distortions does not exist in Marx's thought, though it does have a place in the more general theories of ideological thought. The 'framing' phenomenon[33] is of particular importance here. It is noticeable that the choice between two elements of an alternative depends not only on their 'objective' properties but also on the way they are presented. A banal example is the description of the glass that is either half empty or half full. Another is the description of a surcharge on credit cards as a discount on cash purchases. In the domain of collective action a good illustration is the ambiguity of the notion of co-operation which is dependent upon the chosen reference group. The motivation of a striker can disappear if he begins to see himself as a consumer rather than as a worker. The cause for such a change in perspective might be the self-interest of the agent, if he is looking, for example, for an excuse to withdraw from the efforts and risks of the strike. It is also possible, however, that the change is the result of a kind of optical illusion.

3. The central phenomenon is that of bad faith, in the sense it is used by Freud, Sartre and analytical philosophy.[34] For Marx, the most important example is the tendency for each class to represent its particular interests as the general interest. Rather than refer here to the well-known analyses of *The German Ideology* and *The Eighteenth Brumaire*, let us quote from a text by the young de Tocqueville who expressed, better than Marx ever did, the psychological need which underpins and supports bad faith:

What I call the big political parties, those which refer to principles and not to their consequences, to generalities and not to particular cases, to ideas and not to men, these parties have, in general, the noblest traits, the most generous

---

[31] This interpretation of the Hegelian doctrine of essence and appearance is drawn from a course given by J. Hyppolite at the Collège de France in 1966.

[32] For an analysis of the logical structure of this sophism see Elster, *Logic and Society*, ch. 5.

[33] See A. Tversky and D. Kahneman, 'The Framing of Decisions and the Psychology of Choice', *Science*, 211 (1981).

[34] See Pears, *Motivated Irrationality*, for a recent analysis.

passions, the most real convictions, a more frank and audacious bearing than the others. Particular interest, which always plays a major role in political passions, can hide itself in big political parties more easily, under the veil of the public interest. It even manages often to hide itself from those it stimulates and causes to act. Small parties, on the other hand, are generally without political faith; their character is complete and marked by an egoism which is ostensibly produced by each one of their acts. They remain cold, however heated they become.[35]

4. Religion as 'the opium of the people' falls into the category of ideological beliefs. In a more general way the phenomenon of *adaptive preferences*[36] — the adapting of desires and aspirations to what seems possible and accessible — is affected both by the mechanism and by the result. According to Paul Veyne, on Léon Festinger's work on the reducing of cognitive dissonance, this was the dominant form of political ideology in the classical world.[37] There are also numerous more recent examples.[38] We should stress here that it is not a question of an ideology imposed by the dominant class. It is precisely because it is an endogenous and spontaneous process that the dominant class needs only minimal recourse to indoctrination and manipulation, and these latter, when attempted, rarely have the desired effect.

This sketch of the principles of methodological individualism and the illustrative applications of Marxism is intended to convince the partisans of both doctrines that they are not incompatible. For several years now, especially in the Anglo-Saxon world, and, to a lesser degree, in continental Europe, there has been a certain schizophrenia among academics and intellectuals who want to be both analytically rigorous and on the left. In its most benign form this has led philosophers, economists, and others to dismiss Marxism from their professional life, while picking it up again in their atheoretical activist lives outside work. Too lucid not to see the pathetic state which theoretical Marxism had got itself into, they instead espouse resolutely one of the numerous variants of practical Marxism. There is a more unhealthy version of this duality of mind among many researchers (and not the least significant either), who have felt it necessary publicly to defend

[35] A. de Tocqueville, *Voyages en Sicile et aux États-Unis*, in *Œuvres complètes* (Paris: Gallimard, 1957), 260.

[36] On this phenomenon, see J. Elster, *Sour Grapes* (Cambridge: Cambridge University Press, 1983), ch. 3.

[37] P. Veyne, *Le Pain et le cirque* (Paris: Seuil, 1976).

[38] See e.g. J. Levenson, *Confucian China and its Modern Fate* (Berkeley, Calif.: University of California Press, 1968).

doctrines whose intellectual tenor they would never tolerate in their own research.

The first step towards getting rid of such a state of affairs is the introduction of a Marxist methodology which conforms to generally accepted and practised canons. It is possible that the originality and specificity of Marxism will suffer as a result—so much the better. The aim of theoretical Marxism does not lie in securing its own indefinite perpetuation, but in its self-transcendence as a separate doctrine or sect.

4

Marxism and Rational Choice

ADAM PRZEWORSKI

Social sciences are beleaguered today by an offensive not seen since the 1890s: a deliberate thrust to impose the monopoly of the economic method over all study of society. According to neo-classical economists, everything that happens falls into two categories: economic phenomena and seemingly non-economic phenomena. The challenge of methodological individualism is not directed specifically to Marxism; it defies equally all that used to be called political science, sociology, anthropology, or social psychology. Karl Marx's concept 'relations of production' is exposed to the same challenge as Georg Simmel's 'shared social a priori', Émile Durkheim's 'collective consciousness', and Talcott Parsons's 'value orientations': the challenge to provide microfoundations for social phenomena, specifically, to ground all theory of society in goal-orientated, rational actions of individuals.[1]

This offensive has been quite successful. The intellectual influence of social psychology — the queen of social sciences twenty years ago —

Versions of this chapter have been published in *Politics and Society*, 14/4 (1985), 379–409, and in *Prokla* (Berlin, 1986). I benefited from comments by and discussions with Pierre Birnbaum, G. A. Cohen, Jon Elster, Barry Hindess, Juan Lopez, Alessandro Pizzorno, George Tsebelis, Robert van der Veen, Michael Wallerstein, and the editors of *Politics and Society*.

[1] One difficulty in labelling this challenge is that it is based on two positions that need not necessarily go together: (1) the requirement of 'methodological individualism' — that all social phenomena must be comprehensible as an outcome of actions of individuals; and (2) the substantive assumption of 'rational choice' — that individual behaviour is rational in the instrumental sense of this term. We could have methodological individualism based on a theory of action different from rational choice. We also could have, and do have within the formal choice perspective as it stands, actors other than individuals: firms, unions, committees, bureaus, and so forth. In fact, the challenge presented during the last few years to collectivistic sociologies combines a methodological individualism that admits strategic actors other than individuals with various, stronger and weaker, versions of the rational-choice perspective. 'The strategic action perspective' would be my preferred label for this amalgam but to observe standard usage I will speak of 'methodological individualism' and 'rational-choice approach' almost interchangeably.

has vanished almost completely. The functionalist school, both its psychological and structural aspects, has lost its dominance over sociology. The 'public choice' approach reigns over political science. Even Marxism, which during the 1950s and 1960s used to hide in the American academia under the label of 'political sociology', has now rediscovered its roots as a political *economy*. Several writers have recently addressed traditional Marxist problems within the framework of rational choice or even of standard general equilibrium theory. Many more launch counter-attacks demonstrating the weakness of the individualistic perspective. But references to 'ahistorical individualism of the bourgeois economic theory' seem no longer sufficient. Apparently, Marxism is no longer impervious to the challenge presented by methodological individualism.

Not so long ago one could draw a clear and sharp contrast between Marxism and 'bourgeois social science'. Individual behaviour was viewed by Marxists as an execution of class positions; it was viewed by bourgeois economists as self-interested, rational action. The actors that moved Marxist history were classes, collectivities-in-struggle; the actors of bourgeois history were individuals-citizens-consumers, who at most sometimes banded together into ephemeral 'interest groups'. For Marxists, the central relation organizing the capitalist society was the irreconcilable conflict of interests of the two antagonist classes; for bourgeois social scientists, it was the basic harmony of interests, which permits individuals to exchange until they arrive at the best possible solution. Finally, Marxists saw the capitalist society as economically and politically dominated by capital, while bourgeois thinkers saw it as a competitive market with the government as neutral and universalistic institutions.

None of these contrasts can be drawn clearly today: both the rational-choice framework and Marxism are highly heterogeneous and rapidly evolving. In what follows I do not pay any attention to differences within the rational-choice framework unless they are directly relevant for the discussion. I consider this framework in the most standard, and brutal, form of well-informed, self-interested utility maximizing with an instantaneous adjustment to equilibrium. Thus I use the terms 'methodological individualism', 'rational-choice framework', and 'neo-classical economics' interchangeably.[2]

---

[2] The best treatment of distinctions among them is J. Elster, *Ulysses and the Sirens* (Cambridge: Cambridge University Press, rev. edn. 1984).

To make the discussion intelligible a shared conception of 'Marxism' is also necessary. Marxism for me is an analysis of the consequences of forms of property for historical processes.[3] Any Marxism, as far as I am concerned, is a theory of history, perhaps not necessarily of humanity, *à la* G. A. Cohen, perhaps not even of modes of production, *à la* Louis Althusser, but of the lawful reproduction and transformation of social relations.[4] Theories of history provide explanations of connected successions of events. They explain not only how particular institutions arise but also how they continue to function, not only how particular conflicts are terminated but how their termination affects future conflicts. Static comparisons of equilibria do not constitute theories of history unless they specify why and how transitions between such equilibria occur. This turns out not to be such a minimalist requirement: Raymond Boudon argues that no such theory is possible in principle; Jon Elster is satisfied with game-theoretic analyses of isolated, punctual events; and even John Roemer's treatise relies exclusively on comparisons of static equilibria.[5] A Marxist explanation of history, in any case, originates from assumptions concerning the structure of property of alienable productive resources: the 'means of production'. I will say more about such assumptions below.

The discussion that follows is organized around four topics: the theory of individual action; the ontology of collective actors; the structure of class conflict; and game theory as a technical apparatus. A brief conclusion, orientated toward the future, follows. With regard to each topic, I identify the specific challenge presented to Marxism by the rational-choice framework; if there are any, I summarize Marxist counter-arguments; and, finally, I try to see who can learn what from whom. Much of the discussion is inconclusive, but a general point does emerge: the critique of Marxism offered by methodological individualism is irrefutable and salutary, but the ontological assump-

---

[3] It has been pointed out to me that this definition includes Robert North's *Structure and Change in Economic History* (New York: Norton, 1981); and Svetozar Pejovich's 'The Relevance of Marx and the Irrelevance of Marxian Revivals', *Modern Age* (1977), 30–8. I see no reason why it should not.

[4] G. A. Cohen, *Karl Marx's Theory of History: A Defense* (Oxford: Oxford University Press; Princeton, NJ: Princeton University Press, 1978); and Louis Althusser and Étienne Balibar, *Reading Capital* (New York: Pantheon Books, 1970).

[5] R. Boudon, *La Place du désordre* (Paris: PUF, 1984); J. Elster, 'Marxism, Functionalism, and Game Theory: The Case for Methodological Individualism', *Theory and Society*, 11 (1982), 453–83; and J. E. Roemer, *A General Theory of Exploitation and Class* (Cambridge, Mass.: Harvard University Press, 1982).

tions of the rational-choice framework — in particular, the assumption of undifferentiated, unchanging, and unrelated 'individuals' — are untenable. Thus, while any theory of history must have microfoundations, the theory of individual action must contain more contextual information than the present paradigm of rational choice admits. The task of understanding history as an outcome of individual actions is still ahead of us.

Theory of Action

The challenge

The specific challenge presented to Marxism with regard to the theory of action is to provide an explanation of individual acts under particular conditions, that is, to provide microfoundations for the theory of history. Historically, we thought of individual actions as either preordained, biologically driven, norm ruled, or goal orientated. The current debate is between the psychosociological views of behaviour as execution of internalized norms and the view of behaviour as intentional, strategic action.[6]

This is not a new challenge: Jean-Paul Sartre posed it in 1946, when he observed that Marxism can explain that Paul Valery is a *petit bourgeois* intellectual but not *why* he is a *petit bourgeois* intellectual.[7] This challenge is directed not only to Marxism but to any theory that takes as its point of departure the level of collective organization or consciousness. Marxism, however, has always been in a peculiar predicament, and the present challenge is much more exacting than the traditional dissatisfaction with the absence of 'humanism'.

The peculiar predicament is that Marxists were never completely prepared to embrace any alternatives to methodological individualism,

---

[6] The most extensive polemic along these lines concerns the moral versus the rational peasant. See: James Scott, *The Moral Economy of the Peasant* (New Haven, Conn.: Yale University Press, 1976); S. L. Popkin, *The Rational Peasant* (Berkeley, Los Angeles, Calif.: University of California Press, 1979); and a review by Bruce Cummings, 'Interest and Ideology in the Study of Agrarian Politics', *Politics and Society*, 10 (1981), 467–95. Similar issues have appeared in studies concerning unions' decisions to strike (for a review, see Michael Shalev, 'Trade Unionism and Economic Analysis: The Case of Industrial Conflict', *Journal of Labour Research*, 1 (1980), 133–73) and to organize (A. Przeworski, 'Union Growth: A Literature Review' (unpublished paper, 1984)) as well as concerning the micro-economics of production (Michael Reich and Paul Devine, 'The Microeconomics of Conflict and Hierarchy in Capitalist Production', *Review of Radical Political Economics*, 12 (1981) and the discussion that follows).

[7] J.-P. Sartre, *L'Existentialisme est un humanisme* (Paris: Nagel, 1946).

whether the psychosociological explanation adopted by functionalist sociology or explanations based on Freudian theories of personality. Functionalists explained that people behave in accordance with shared values because individuals are taught norms and values, which they first 'internalize' and eventually act out. Functionalists viewed all individual behaviour as an act of execution of the internalized society, with the implication that all persons exposed to the same norms and values should behave in the same manner.[8] Marxists, I think, adopted this mode of explanation in practice, explaining individual behaviour by the class position but, perhaps because of the lingering utilitarian aspects of Marx's legacy, they have never accepted the psychological principles on which this particular view of individual behaviour is based.[9] Althusser tried to purify this mechanism of mentalistic connotations, but the result was a behaviouristic black box of *appelation*.[10] Herbert Marcuse and Gilles Deleuze relied on Freudian psychodynamics to establish the formative effects of the social organization of repression on individual behaviour, but neither went beyond the assertion that capitalism generates standard personality patterns.[11] By and large, Marxists were satisfied with the intuitive belief that people act out their class positions: Marx's phrases about

[8] For critiques of the theory of action underlying functionalist explanation, see George Homans, 'Bringing Men Back In', in Alan Ryan (ed.), *The Philosophy of Social Explanation* (London: Oxford University Press, 1973); and P. Bourdieu, 'Marriage Strategies as Strategies of Social Reproduction', in Robert Forster and Orest Ranum (eds.), *Family and Society* (Baltimore, Md.: Johns Hopkins University Press, 1976).

[9] The most thorough treatment of the Marxist theory of action to date is David Lockwood's 'The Weakest Chain? Some Comments on the Marxist Theory of Action', *Research in the Sociology of Work*, 1 (1981), 435–81. Lockwood argues: that the traditional Marxist theory of action was basically utilitarian; that the concepts of ideological domination and false consciousness played the role of explaining why the proletariat acted irrationally (specifically, not in a revolutionary manner); and that the role of norms, values, and traditions—the non-rational as distinct from irrational aspects of action—was underestimated. As the result, the Marxist theory of action is highly unstable, as 'manifested by the tendency to shuttle back and forth between positivistic and idealistic explanations of working-class radicalism and acquiescence' (456–7). Lockwood attributes the source of this weakness to the reliance on utilitarianism and advocates an emphasis on normative components of action: just the contrary of my own views. I think that treating the actions of workers as rational is sufficient to explain why under most circumstances they would not be revolutionary and thus no reference to norms, traditions, or values is necessary. See below and A. Przeworski, *Capitalism and Social Democracy* (Cambridge: Cambridge University Press, 1985).

[10] Louis Althusser, 'Ideology and Ideological State Apparatuses', in his *Lenin and Philosophy* (New York: Monthly Review Press, 1971).

[11] Herbert Marcuse, *Eros and Civilization* (London: Sphere Books, 1959); and Gilles Deleuze, *Anti-Œdipe: Capitalisme et schizophrénie* (Paris: Maspero, 1973).

studying capitalists as 'personifications', 'carriers', or 'representatives' of capital seemed sufficient, and that Marx referred to profit as sometimes 'the motor', sometimes 'the aim', sometimes 'the motive', and still at other times 'the need' of capitalists, capital, or capitalism somehow did not seem confusing. What was important about history happened at the level of forces, structures, collectivities, and constraints, not individuals. Hence, microfoundations were at most a luxury it would have been nice to have, to explain other minor variations. Marxism was a theory of history without any theory about the actions of people who made this history.[12]

This position is no longer tenable, because criticisms derived from the postulates of methodological individualism go to the centre of Marxist theory of collective action and thus of history. The actions of individuals can no longer be taken as given by their class positions; they must be explained under each set of conditions. Statements about individuals and collectivities must be carefully distinguished: attributions of the status of collective actor to 'capital', 'the working class', or 'the state' must be subjected each time to critical scrutiny to see whether the collective action is consistent with individual rationalities. The challenge originating from the rational-choice framework is specific: a satisfactory theory is one that can explain history in terms of the actions of individuals who are goal orientated and rational. All theory of society must be based on such foundations: this is the challenge.

Marxist objections to methodological individualism

The assumptions of methodological individualism, however, have been met with several objections, some of which are deeply grounded in Marxist traditions. These objections fall into three main categories: preferences are not universal or stable but are contingent upon conditions and thus change historically; self-interest is a poor description of preferences for at least some people; and under some conditions 'rational' action is not possible even if individuals are 'rational'. I discuss these in turn.

---

[12] The extreme position on this issue was the Althusserian school. Balibar, in a brilliant argument that 'individual' is not a theoretical concept, maintained that people act only as 'carriers' of particular social relations (classified, as this school tended to, into economic, political, and ideological), never as integral subjects. Étienne Balibar, 'Fundamental Concepts of Historical Materialism', in *Reading Capital*. A scorching critique of this position was made by Fernando H. Cardoso, 'Althusserianismo o Marxismo?' in B. N. Zenteno (ed.), *Las classes sociales in América Latina* (Mexico: Siglo XXI, 1973).

Historical character of preferences   The most traditional objection to methodological individualism, namely, that individual preferences change historically, is not specific to Marxism. But Marxist theory provides the analytical framework to explain historical changes of individual rationality. I would like to distinguish two separate arguments about social formation of individual rationality. One concerns comparisons of different economic systems, the second concerns the process of collective identity formation under capitalism.

Marx claimed that individual goals and the courses of action available to individuals depend on how a system of production and exchange was organized: a peasant who pays rent in cash and who can, therefore, use information provided by the market to choose crops is a different person from a peasant who pays rent in kind, can choose at most techniques of production, and does not participate in market relations.[13] Witold Kula's theory of feudalism is built on the assumption that landowners try to satisfy a constant level of needs under very restricted information about the value of alternative resources.[14] Examples are countless, and the point is not that peasants, landlords, or anyone else do not behave rationally, but that we must know what they want, what they know, and what they can choose from before we can explain their behaviour. The assumption that owners of resources maximize profit in a market full of information will be of no use under historical conditions other than developed capitalism. As Jon Cohen and Martin Weitzman have argued, in the medieval world, 'the preconditions that would have made profit maximization even a feasible objective were not evident'.[15] To put it differently, methodological individualism is not enough; one needs substantive assumptions to explain behaviour of individuals under specific historical conditions.

To some extent this issue is an empirical one. When Roemer assumes that economic agents under all historical conditions seek to maximize income (or leisure) or when Margaret Levi assumes that 'rulers' under all historical circumstances seek to maximize revenue, they formulate theories that imply that all variations in behaviour are attributable to changes in constraints.[16] In principle, such theories can

---

[13] Karl Marx, *Capital*, vol. iii (New York: International Publishers, 1967).

[14] Witold Kula, *Teoria ekonomiczna ustroju feudalnego* (Warsaw: Panstwowe Wydawnictwo Naukowe, 1963).

[15] Jon S. Cohen and Martin L. Weitzman, 'A Marxian Model of Enclosures', *Journal of Development Economics*, 1 (1975), 293.

[16] Roemer, *General Theory*; and Margaret Levi, 'The Predatory Theory of Rule', *Politics and Society*, 10 (1981), 431–65.

be evaluated empirically, and Levi, in a series of papers, undertook exactly such a project. All I am saying is that the traditional Marxist presupposition seems to be that medieval lords wanted something different from what capitalists wanted, not just that they faced different constraints (or that they wanted something different because they faced different constraints).

The second Marxist argument against the assumption of fixed stable preferences originates mainly from Antonio Gramsci's theory of formation of personal identities under capitalism — the specifically Marxist view of a general sociological emphasis on the social origin of identity formation.[17] In this view, politics is not just about who gets what but first about who is who, not only an arena but first an *agora*. Collective identity is continually being transformed — shaped, destroyed, and moulded anew — as a result of conflicts in the course of which political parties, schools, unions, churches, newspapers, armies, and corporations strive to impose a particular form of organization upon the life of society. The relation between places occupied by individuals in society and their identity is thus a contingent historical outcome of conflicts: conflicts over whether something is a source of satisfaction, whether a particular goal appears within reach, whether a particular course of action is admissible. Voting behaviour provides clear examples: people vote sometimes out of class loyalty, sometimes as Catholics, southerners, or women, and at other times as individuals calculating freely which party is more likely to do things to their advantage.[18] Thus even within a relatively short period the assumption of exogenous stable preferences does not seem promising.

This traditional Marxist emphasis on the historical formation of identity is most damaging to the rational-choice perspective. Individual identities and thus preferences are continually moulded by society: this seems unquestionable. Yet I believe that the proponents of this view are too eager to celebrate their triumph.

Almost all writers who emphasize the social character of preference

[17] See Lockwood, 'The Weakest Chain?' for an interesting comparison of the rules of Gramsci and Durkheim.

[18] A. Przeworski and J. Sprague, *Paper Stones: A History of Electoral Socialism* (Chicago, Ill.: University of Chicago Press, 1986). Note that invocations of Schumpeter as the intellectual father of the economic theory of democracy are misleading: Schumpeter saw the political process as one of persuasion. 'What we are confronted with in the analysis of political processes', he insisted, 'is largely not a genuine but a manufactured will.... the will of the people is the product and not the motive power of the political process.' Joseph A. Schumpeter, *Capitalism, Socialism, and Democracy* (New York: Harper & Row, 1975), 263.

formation mistakenly jump to the conclusion that the view of behaviour as rational action is invalidated by this assertion. This is true of Roemer in his 1978 article, of Johannes Berger and Claus Offe, Alessandro Pizzorno, and Barry Hindess.[19] Roemer has argued that 'the individual formulation of the economic problem in its very conception prevents a fruitful inquiry into the most important aspects of change and history, namely, how social reality produces social beings who then act to change reality'.[20] The same point has been made by Pizzorno and by Hindess. Berger and Offe observed that 'logically, the game starts only after the actors have been constituted, and their order of preferences has been formed as a result of processes that cannot themselves be considered as part of the game'.[21]

Once, however, preferences have been formed, people do have them and act upon them at a particular instant of time: the power of the neo-classical economics lies in being able to separate the analysis of action at a particular moment from everything that created the conditions under which this action occurs.[22] In addition, the rational-choice approach certainly does not prevent an enquiry into preference formation, even if within neo-classical economics preferences are taken as given (and within classical utilitarianism as random). Hence, the belief that preferences are formed historically and the belief that people act rationally upon the preferences they have are not contradictory. Moreover, there is no reason to think that the processes that result in preference formation could not involve rational actions, a 'game' even if not 'the same' game. Indeed, I believe that John Sprague and I have demonstrated that the reason some individuals under some historical circumstances identify as workers is a consequence of strategies pursued by leaders of left-wing electoral parties.[23] I am far from certain

[19] J. E. Roemer, 'Neo-classicism, Marxism, and Collective Action', *Journal of Economic Issues*, 12 (1978), 147–61; Johannes Berger and Claus Offe, 'Functionalism vs. Rational Choice? Some Questions concerning the Rationality of Choosing One or the Other', *Theory and Society*, 11 (1982), 521–7; A. Pizzorno, 'Sulla razionalità della scelta democràtica', *Stato e mercato*, 7 (1984), 3–47; and Barry Hindess, 'Rational Choice Theory and the Analysis of Political Action', *Economy and Society*, 13 (1984), 255–77.

[20] Roemer, 'Neo-classicism', p. 149.

[21] Berger and Offe, 'Functionalism vs. Rational Choice?', p. 525.

[22] This point has been made by Schumpeter: 'Historically, the consumer's desire for shoes may, at least in part, have been shaped by the action of producers offering attractive footgear and campaigning for it; yet at any given time it is a genuine want, the definiteness of which extends beyond "shoes in general" and which prolonged experimenting clears of much of the irrationalities that may originally have surrounded it.' *Capitalism, Socialism, and Democracy*, p. 258.

[23] Przeworski and Sprague, *Paper Stones*.

how feasible are theories of history that consider preferences as formed endogenously, but I see no methodological grounds on which the possibility of such theories could be rejected.[24]

Altruism The second counter-argument to the offensive of methodological individualism is that self-interest is a poor description of preferences of at least some people under some historical circumstances. Some individuals may care about others, whether these are members of their family, class, nation, or other human beings in general. About this there seems to be little disagreement and, indeed, several recently developed economic models are based on non-egoistic assumptions.[25] In principle, models that involve states of other people as arguments of everyone's utility functions present at most mathematical difficulties.[26]

A debated question is whether altruistic preferences, meaning any

[24] The feasible grounds would be to argue for some true individual determinacy, as Boudon does in some parts of his *La Place du désordre*, or for multiple and numerous equilibria. Since I would be satisfied, however, with theories of possible histories, I do not find the latter argument damaging.

[25] David Collard, *Altruism and the Economy: A Study in Non-selfish Economics* (Oxford: Oxford University Press, 1978); Howard Margolis, *Selfishness, Altruism, and Rationality* (Chicago, Ill.: University of Chicago Press, 1982); Gerald Marwell, 'Altruism and the Problem of Collective Action', in *Cooperation and Helping Behavior* (New York: Academic Press, 1982); and S.-C. Kolm, *La Bonne Économie: La Réciprocité générale* (Paris: PUF, 1984).

[26] This is not to say that we now have an adequate language for describing utility functions. A number of distinctions need to be clarified; unfortunately, their discussion exceeds the limit of this article. First, the definition of 'altruism' in the text is too broad, since one can care about the states of others out of purely selfish motivations, when there exist externalities in consumption. For example, the usefulness of a telephone to me depends upon the number of others who have one. For a general equilibrium model that incorporates such externalities, see Michael L. Katz and Carl Shapiro, 'Network Externalities, Competition, and Compatibility', *American Economic Review*, 75 (1985), 424–41. A narrower definition of altruism would be one in which the satisfaction of others would enter as argument(s) in ego's utility function. Such a definition would pose, however, more serious mathematical problems and would create a need for additional distinctions. For example, I may weigh someone's pleasure more than my own but not if this pleasure is derived from consumption of heroin. Second, we can think of preferences as contingent, either upon actions of others or upon circumstances. A. K. Sen, 'Rational Fools: A Critique of the Behavioral Foundations of Economics', *Philosophy and Public Affairs*, 6 (1977), 317–44, argued that people have several preference orderings that they activate contingently according to some meta-ordering. Altruism conditional upon co-operative behaviour by others constitutes one way out of the prisoner's dilemma. Third, to be 'altruistic' may not be the same as being 'ideological' in the sense of A. Pizzorno, 'Introduzióne allo studio della partecipazióne politica', *Quaderni di sociologià*, 15/3–4 (1966), 235–86, for whom to be ideological is to include in one's utility function states of a collectivity, rather than of other individuals.

utility function that takes among its arguments states of other individuals, should and can be always derived from selfish motivations. Particularly interesting is the notion of change of preferences through a dialogue, which Offe and Helmuth Wiesenthal see as essential for the organization of workers as a class, and Serge-Christophe Kolm's notion of 'general reciprocity'. This and related issues are discussed by Jon Elster as well as Scott Lash and John Urry, and I have nothing to add other than perhaps a dose of scepticism.[27]

Whether we should abandon, however, the assumption of self-interest is not apparent, for three reasons.

First, if we abandon the hypothesis that individuals are invariably selfish, what should we assume instead? Certainly, the assumption that people are invariably altruistic would be equally ahistorical and equally arbitrary. What we need to know is the relation between conditions and preferences, perhaps even between actions of some and preferences of others. Yet, somehow, in spite of widespread attention of sociologists to collective identity formation, we do not know when to expect which people to be selfish, when to expect them to be altruistic, and when ideological. Among more individualistically orientated writers, A. K. Sen suggested we should think in terms of 'sympathy' and 'commitment' as two distinct mechanisms of preference activation; Howard Margolis proposed a rule according to which individuals derive utility from self-interested versus group-interested ends; Albert Hirschman proposed that we distinguish between 'values' (about which we reason and argue) and 'tastes' (which are 'wanton') and argued that individuals deliberately allocate time and energy to instrumental or to non-instrumental activities.[28] But these are conceptual distinctions, not substantive propositions. Thus, the assumption of self-interest is easier to reject than to replace.

Second, one should not suppose that strategic problems would vanish in an altruistic or even ideologically motivated society — something critics of economic theory like to believe. Just think of a situation in which my satisfaction would be more important for you than your

---

[27] Claus Offe and Helmuth Wiesenthal, 'Two Logics of Collective Action: Theoretical Notes on Social Class and Organizational Forms', in Maurice Zeitlin (ed.), *Political Power and Social Theory* (Greenwich: JAI Press, 1980); Kolm, *La Bonne Économie*; Elster, *Ulysses*; and Scott Lash and John Urry, 'The New Marxism of Collective Action: A Critical Analysis', *Sociology*, 18 (1984), 33–50.

[28] Sen, 'Rational Fools'; Margolis, 'Selfishness, Altruism, and Rationality'; and A. Hirschman, 'Against Parsimony: Three Ways of Complicating some Categories of Economic Discourse', *Economics and Philosophy*, 1 (1985), 7–21.

own, your satisfaction would be more important for me than mine, and we would meet in front of a door through which we could not pass simultaneously. This 'after you' paradox just gives a taste of strategic problems to be encountered in an altruistic society.[29]

Finally, a realistic description of society, in which selfish, altruistic, and ideological individuals coexist at any time, may make any deductive analysis next to impossible. The strength of methodological individualism is methodological: it lies in the willingness of neo-classical economists to ignore all complications that would impede getting answers to central questions. To introduce descriptive realism is to cut Samson's hair. This is why Elster's carefully measured assessment of human rationality in *Ulysses and the Sirens*, welcomed by Scott Lash and John Urry as 'an ontology of social process and ... not merely a heuristic or instrumental device for generating predictions about the social world', may be subversive of the project of methodological individualism.[30]

Irrational society   Finally, the third criticism of the rational-choice framework is probably due to Sartre. The point is generally understood and admitted among game theorists: some games have no solutions. One's actions do have consequences, but when one acts these consequences cannot be predicted (often because they depend completely on actions of others who are in the same situation). Sartre's point (in *Le Mur*) was that consequences of one's action were unpredictable and at times perverse. In an irrational world there is no possibility for rational action. Thus irrational action is a reflection not upon individuals but upon conditions. Suppose, for example, that the

[29] Such problems are discussed by Collard, *Altruism and the Economy*. See also the argument by Alan Buchanan, 'Revolutionary Motivation and Rationality', *Philosophy and Public Affairs*, 9 (1979), 59–82, that the 'paradox of revolution' would exist even if workers were ideological. Robert Van der Veen shows, however, that certain non-selfish preference orderings would make socially desirable outcomes more likely to obtain, in 'Meta-rankings and Collective Optimality', *Social Science Information*, 20 (1981), 345–74. Note that the outcomes of the political process in a perfectly altruistic democratic (one-person one-vote) society would be the same as the outcomes in a perfectly selfish society: the interests of every individual would receive an equal weight in both societies. See e.g. Koichi Hamada, 'A Simple Majority Rule on the Distribution of Income', *Journal of Economic Theory*, 6 (1973), 243–64.

[30] Lash and Urry, 'The New Marxism', p. 39. This point may be too strong, given that there already exist reasonable analyses of situations in which only some people behave strategically while others follow a habit. See John Haltiwanger and Michael Waldman, 'Rational Expectations and the Limits of Rationality: An Analysis of Heterogeneity', *American Economic Review*, 75 (1985), 326–41 and the bibliography therein.

conditional probability that a government would follow the policies that it advocated during an election campaign is zero: if this is all voters have to go on, no rational voting would be possible.

If I understand it correctly, Pizzorno's version of this argument goes as follows: since sources of individual satisfaction are determined socially, individuals cannot rationally commit themselves to the pursuit of any longer-term goals because by the time they would reach these goals they might no longer receive satisfaction from them.[31] This is thus a social version of Friedrich Wilhelm Nietzsche's observation that satisfaction of desires is never as intense as the pain caused by deprivation—a phenomenon economists call 'regret' and rule out. Pizzorno seems to believe that this situation represents a general social condition and renders goal-orientated behaviour futile.

To evaluate this argument we must be careful to distinguish games without (unique) solutions, such as 'chicken' or the 'battle of the sexes', from the general class of games in which individually rational strategies lead to a solution that is collectively suboptimal, epitomized by the 'prisoner's dilemma'.[32] In no-solution games, no individual rational action is possible; in games with solutions, each individual has a unique rational strategy. If games without (unique) solutions are frequent enough, rational-choice framework is moot as an instrument of analysis. The ubiquity of prisoner's dilemma, however, makes this framework most useful.

I am not certain how to assess the frequency of such irrational situations in the real world, and thus I suspect that differences of views are not based on empirical assessments. The choice of factor bias in technical change provides one extensively studied example of a game without solution.[33] Kenneth Arrow's theorem and the subsequent developments demonstrate that, given fixed individual preferences, no voting procedure will in general produce a unique ordering of collective preferences.[34] Bargaining situations also seem indeterminate,

[31] Pizzorno, 'Sulla razionalità della scelta democràtica' and 'Some Other Kind of Otherness (A Critique of "Rational Choice" Theories)' (manuscript, 1985).

[32] For general discussions of counterfinal effects, see R. Boudon, *Effets pervers et ordre social* (Paris: PUF, 1977); and J. Elster, *Logic and Society* (Chichester, London: Wiley, 1978).

[33] J. Elster, *Explaining Technical Change* (Cambridge: Cambridge University Press and Universitetsforlaget, 1983).

[34] Kenneth J. Arrow, *Social Choice and Individual Values* (New York: Wiley, rev. edn. 1963); Richard D. McKelvey, 'Intransitivities in Multidimensional Voting Models and Some Implications for Agenda Control', *British Journal of Sociology*, 30 (1979), 472–82; and Norman Schofield, 'Instability and Development in the Political Economy',

although this may be a reflection on the bargaining theory rather than on reality. These illustrations are sufficient to demonstrate that the concept of irrational conditions—conditions that do not allow individuals to act rationally—constitutes a useful, perhaps even under-used, instrument of analysis. Yet I continue to doubt that the world is as irrational as existentialists have portrayed it. In turn, situations in which the individually rational course of action results in states of the world that are collectively suboptimal are ubiquitous under capitalism and, as Karl Korsch noted in 1928, would be present under social-ism.[35] The existence of such situations may also be interpreted as indicating that the society is organized irrationally—a traditional component of Marxist critique of capitalism—but it does not imply that individually rational actions are impossible.

Collective Actors

The challenge

The most damaging implication of methodological individualism is that people who share life conditions and interests would not, in general, act collectively to promote these interests. Even if the results of collective action were beneficial to all workers, each worker would not participate if he or she would benefit from the results regardless of participation. If Mancur Olson and his followers are correct, then we cannot expect that the working class would ever become a collective historical subject, a class-for-itself, with all the consequences that would follow.[36] Understandably, most Marxist reactions to methodological individualism have concentrated on this issue.

Grounds for rejecting workers' collective-action dilemma

The validity of the 'free-rider' problem with regard to the working class has been rejected for a long list of reasons. (1) The problem is irrelevant on the grounds of methodological collectivism.[37] (2) People,

in P. A. Ordeshook and K. A. Shepsle (ed.), *Political Equilibrium* (Boston, Mass.: Kluwer-Nijhoff, 1982).

[35] Karl Korsch, 'What is Socialization?', *New German Critique*, 6 (1975), 60–82.

[36] M. Olson, *The Logic of Collective Action* (Cambridge, Mass.: Harvard University Press, 1965).

[37] Nancy Holmstrom, 'Rationality and Revolution', *Canadian Journal of Philosophy*, 13 (1983), 305–25; and Pizzorno, 'Sulla razionalità della scelta democràtica'.

at least workers, are not selfish.[38] (3) Workers are so narrowly constrained by their conditions that they have no choice; concerning workers the rational-choice framework poses a false problem.[39] (4) Workers are particularly prone to alter each other's preferences through communication.[40] (5) Workers satisfy the conditions for co-operation in an iterative prisoner's dilemma:[41] they are in the same situation repeatedly; they do not know how long they will remain in this situation; and they have a low rate of time discount.[42] (6) Workers satisfy the conditions for an endogenous change of probabilities of success: when some of them initiate the collective action, the probability of sucess of collective action increases, which means that the expected benefit also increases, and it outweighs the expected cost for additional workers, whose participation in turn further increases the probability of success, and so on.[43]

The first three positions reject the free-rider problem out of hand; the latter three admit that the assumptions of the neo-classical theory of collective action may be valid in some contexts but find reasons why the implications of this theory would not hold for workers. None among the last three arguments has even been shown to be empirically or even formally true of workers: they constitute at best wishful conjectures. And note the peculiar way in which the problem tends to be formulated: all these arguments assume that something is wrong with a theory that predicts that workers in general would not organize as a class and would not undertake collective action, including, most importantly, that of a socialist revolution. There is something surrealistic about the question, 'What would induce the proletariat to make

[38] D. E. Booth, 'Collective Action, Marx's Class Theory, and the Union Movement', *Journal of Economic Issues*, 12 (1978), 263–85.

[39] Roemer, 'Neo-classicism'.

[40] Elster, *Ulysses*, esp. p. 146; Offe and Wiesenthal, 'Two Logics of Collective Action'.

[41] Martin Shubik, 'Game Theory, Behavior and the Paradox of the Prisoner's Dilemma', *Journal of Conflict Resolution*, 14 (1970), 181–202; and Michael Taylor, *Anarchy and Cooperation* (Chichester, New York: Wiley, 1976).

[42] Matthew Edel, 'A Note on Collective Action, Marxism, and the Prisoner's Dilemma', *Journal of Economic Issues*, 13 (1979), 751–61; and William H. Shaw, 'Marxism, Revolution, Rationality', in Terence Ball and James Farr (eds.), *After Marx* (Cambridge: Cambridge University Press, 1984).

[43] For the general model, see Mark Granovetter, 'Threshold Models of Collective Behavior', *American Journal of Sociology*, 83 (1978), 1420–43. Used with regard to workers by Gregory S. Kavka, 'Two Solutions to the Paradox of Revolution', in P. A. Finch, T. E. Uehling, jun., and H. K. Wettstein (eds.), *Midwest Studies in Philosophy*, vol. vii (Minneapolis, Minn.: University of Minnesota Press, 1982).

the socialist revolution?'[44] The proletariat has never made a socialist revolution. Workers are typically not even organized as a class: although in a few countries most workers are members of one centralized union federation, in general, many do not belong to or even vote for left-wing parties, and many abstain from participating in other collective endeavours. Furthermore, particular unions, parties, and other organizations often adopt strategies that are adverse to the collective interests of the working class. Certainly, unions and working-class parties do exist and enjoy sizeable participation, but empirically the neo-classical theory of collective action is no less valid than collectivist theories.

The central question posed by methodological individualism is the following: under what conditions, from always to never, is solidarity (class co-operation) rational for individual workers or particular groups of them? Michael Wallerstein has recently shown that particular unions will try to organize all and only those workers who compete with each other within the same labour market and that particular unions will co-operate with each other in small economies forced to depend on foreign trade but will seek to co-operate with employers if they can benefit from any form of monopoly rents (in particular, protection).[45] Wallerstein's theory provides the microfoundations of the phenomenon of 'neo-corporatism' and goes far in explaining the different patterns of union structure in different capitalist societies.

Note that all the above discussion concerned workers. The notion that capitalists may be unable or unwilling to organize and act collectively as a class was traditionally present in Marxism. In Marx's own analysis, competition among capitalists results in a falling rate of profit, but they can do nothing about it since their situation is one of a prisoner's dilemma. The observation that peculiar capitalists have conflicting interests that impede their collective action was important in the work of Nicos Poulantzas.[46] The question of the unity of the bourgeoisie has always loomed large in the Latin American literature,[47] while in the United States much interesting empirical

[44] Shaw, 'Marxism, Revolution, Rationality', p. 12.

[45] M. Wallerstein, 'The Micro-foundations of Corporatism: Formal Theory and Comparative Analysis' (paper presented at the Annual Meeting of the American Political Science Association, Washington, DC, 1984), and 'Working Class Solidarity and Rational Behavior' (Ph.D. diss., University of Chicago, 1985).

[46] Nicos Poulantzas, *Political Power and Social Classes* (London: New Left Books, 1973).

[47] Fernando H. Cardoso, *Ideologías de la burguesía industrial en sociedades dependientes (Argentina y Brasil)* (Mexico: Siglo XXI, 1971); Peter Evans, 'Reinventing

work was done on the separation of ownership and control, overlapping directorates, and other forms of capitalist class organization.[48] Finally, the problem of capitalist class organization has been recently formulated systematically within the rational-choice framework by John Bowman.[49]

Altogether the perspective of methodological individualism forces a complete re-evaluation of Marxist theory of class action. As formulated by Olson, the free-rider problem most likely constitutes a poor description of collective action among workers, but the effect of the neo-classical attack on the Marxist theory of class action has been exceedingly salutary. One symptom is that things written just a few years ago, in which 'the working class' marched throughout history in the interest of workers, now seem uncomfortably naïve. Whether anything in the end will be left from Marxist theory of class action, I am far from certain. Since the formal theory of collective behaviour is itself developing rapidly, I am persuaded that we have only begun to consider the question of class action.

Weaknesses of the neo-classical theory of collective action

At the same time, the traditional Marxist perspective highlights two weaknesses of the neo-classical theory of collective action: the strategic problem facing individual workers does not consist of free riding in the provision of public goods but of competing with each other to obtain employment, and the problem of organizing each class (and

the Bourgeoisie: State Entrepreneurship and Class Formation in the Context of Dependent Capitalist Development', in Michael Burawoy and Theda Skocpol (eds.), *Marxist Inquiries*, the supplement to the *American Journal of Sociology*, 88 (1982), 210–48; Guillermo O'Donnell, 'Notas para el estudio de la burguesía local, con especial referencia a sus vinculaciones con el capital transnacional y el aparato estatal', *Estudios sociales*, 12 (Buenos Aires: CEDES, 1978); and Maurice Zeitlin and Richard Ratcliff, 'Research Methods for the Analysis of the Internal Structure of Dominant Classes: The Case of Landlords and Capitalists in Chile', *Latin American Research Review*, 10 (1975), 5–61.

[48] Maurice Zeitlin, 'Corporate Ownership and Control: The Large Corporation and the Capitalist Class', *American Journal of Sociology*, 79 (1974), 1073–119 provided a seminal formulation. This literature has been recently reviewed by Davida S. Glasberg and Michael Schwartz, 'Ownership and Control of Corporations', *Annual Review of Sociology*, 9 (1983), 527–40. See also J. A. Witt, 'Can Capitalists Organize Themselves?' *Insurgent Sociologist*, 9 (1979), 51–9, for a fascinating example in which capitalists did organize in spite of conflicts of interests among them.

[49] John Bowman, 'The Logic of Capitalist Collective Action', *Social Science Information*, 21 (1982), 571–604; and 'The Politics of the Market: Economic Competition and the Organization of Capitalists', in Maurice Zeitlin (ed.), *Political Power and Social Theory*, vol. v (Greenwich: JAI Press, 1984).

other collectivities) cannot be considered in isolation from the relation of the individual members of one class to the other class.

Workers' strategic situation Somewhat surprisingly, all Marxist writers responding to the free-rider paradox accept Olson's description of the problem facing individual workers. But Olson's description is inaccurate.

Imagine a crossroads with four petrol stations, one on each corner. According to Olson and his followers, the owners of these petrol stations encounter the free-rider problem when they try to install at the intersection a street light that would bring more customers during night hours. They would all benefit from the increased traffic, but since each would benefit anyway once the street light was there, none would want to pay for the cost of installing it. Until the problem of the street light appears, the petrol stations do not face strategic problems; as Olson puts it, they are in a 'pre-strategic context'. But is this true? The petrol stations compete with each other: each lowers the price (or increases the service) to attract customers from the others. The result is a price war: the price goes down, and the station owners all lose. Clearly, one solution to this problem is some kind of price collusion (or service differentiation), and we could say that this collusion constitutes a public good. But I think that this terminological manœuvre obscures a fundamental difference: the petrol stations are in a prisoner's dilemma, because of the interdependence of their private and rival consumption, before and independently of any action that would result in providing goods that are non-rival in consumption (so-called 'public goods').

Workers (and in some aspects capitalists)[50] are in a situation analogous to the price war. Individual workers compete with each other, bidding down their wages in search for employment. The result is a general lowering of wages. Thus workers are in a prisoner's dilemma over their private consumption. It is true that when workers form a union or engage in other forms of collective action they may run into the free-rider problem, that is, the prisoner's dilemma associated with actions designed to provide goods non-rival in consumption. But they need to organize not to provide public goods but to avoid competition with one another as they pursue private goods.[51]

[50] See Bowman, 'The Politics of the Market'.
[51] Note the confusion, as exemplified by Peter H. Aranson and Peter C. Ordeshook, 'Public Interest, Private Interest, and the Democratic Polity', in Roger Benjamin and

Note that it is impossible to represent particularistic interests of individuals who are embedded in a prisoner's dilemma situation: impossible because the particularistic interests are those that pit individuals against one another. If individuals are in a situation in which the particular state of the world that is best for them is simultaneously the best for all, then indeed their 'common' interests can be represented simultaneously: in Sartre's terminology, their 'group' interest is identical with their 'serial' interests.[52] But if individuals compete with each other, then their 'common', group interests are no longer the same as their serial, particularistic interests: their group interest is to avoid the collective suboptimality associated with competition, while the realization of this group interest is not the best outcome for each individual. But the only interest that can be 'represented' is precisely the one associated with co-operation among potential competitors. Thus 'representation' must necessarily involve coercion, sanctions that would dissuade the individual members from non-co-operation. Unless unions or parties are capable of disciplining workers away from competing with one another, no class organization is possible. At the same time, one should expect that the discontent of individual members would be a perennial condition of class organizations: their particularistic interests are not being represented, and each might improve his or her situation by defecting from co-operation.

Social relations and collective action   A major weakness of the neo-classical formulation of the problem of collective action is that the organization of each group is considered in isolation from the rest of the society (because there is no 'pre-strategic' nor any other context of social relations in this theory). Workers organize 'unions', capitalists organize 'lobbies'; they encounter their own problems in the process; and only if they succeed may they perhaps encounter each other. But workers and capitalists (and others) are related to each other without and before any organizing, and they always organize with regard to the other class. Workers compete with each other in bidding down wages

Stephen L. Elkin (eds.), *The Democratic State* (Lawrence, Kan.: Kansas University Press, 1985), 93. They write: 'Free riding occurs in several contexts. The term's traditional usage refers to those who enjoy the putatively higher wage rates and improved working conditions derived from union striking and bargaining efforts, without themselves paying union dues or the costs of striking.' Workers' strategic dilemma is not whether to pay union dues but whether to abstain from accepting employment when this acceptance would lower the general level of wages.

[52] J.-P. Sartre, *Critique de la raison dialectique* (Paris: Gallimard, 1960).

as they offer their labour power for sale to firms. The intensity of their competition is affected by the decision of firms concerning the rate of investment, factor intensity of technological change, capacity utilization, and by what those firms expect of other firms and of consumers. Moreover, as Philippe Schmitter and Donald Brand have shown, the organizational problem of workers is affected by the association among capitalists.[53]

Indeed, there is evidence that this may have been the way in which Marx himself conceptualized class relations. In *German Ideology*, Marx and Frederick Engels noted that 'the separate individuals form a class only insofar as they have to carry a battle against another class; otherwise, they are on hostile terms with each other as competitors'. In *Poverty of Philosophy*, Marx wrote, 'Combination always has a double aim, that of stopping competition among the workers, so that they can carry on general competition with the capitalist.' Similar phrases can be found in the *Communist Manifesto* and several other writings.[54] The view of society entailed here is one of individual workers who are simultaneously in a relation of competition to other workers and in a relation of collective conflict with capitalists. Each worker is best off competing against other workers, but all workers can improve their situation by organizing against capitalists.[55] What is thus wrong with methodological individualism, I believe, is not the idea that collective actions must be explained by referring to individual rationality but the idea that society is a collection of undifferentiated and unrelated individuals. The appropriate view is neither one of two ready-to-act classes nor of abstract individuals, but of individuals who are embedded in different types of relations with other individuals within a multidimensionally described social structure.

Class Conflict

The structure of class conflict under democratic capitalism

The traditional Marxist theory of the structure of class conflict has been exceedingly crude and, I believe, both logically invalid and

[53] Philippe C. Schmitter and Donald Brand, 'Organizing Capitalists in the United States: The Advantages and Disadvantages of Exceptionalism', paper presented at the Annual Meeting of the American Political Science Association (Chicago, 1979).

[54] Karl Marx and Frederick Engels, *German Ideology* (Moscow: Progress Publishers, 1964); and Karl Marx, *Poverty of Philosophy* (Moscow: Progress Publishers, n.d.).

[55] Interesting formal ideas for analysing this kind of game have been offered by George Tsebelis, 'When Will the Prisoners Cooperate?' (unpublished manuscript, (Washington University, St Louis, 1985).

empirically false. I am referring here to Marx's own theory, specified most explicitly in *Wage Labour and Capital*, in which he claimed that interests of workers and capitalists constitute a zero-sum game, both statically and dynamically.[56] This model has been mechanically used in most subsequent Marxist theory, particularly in the theory of the state, in which interests of workers are not even specified since they are always treated as the zero-sum complement to the interests of capitalists.

The static claim is trivially true: since at any instant of time the social product is by definition constant, one person's gain is another person's loss. But if we allow for the existence of a future, the picture becomes much more complex. Gramsci was the first to analyse the dependence of the entire society upon capital, the dependence that makes possible the hegemony of the bourgeoisie. His central thesis—which I think should be treated as an empirical hypothesis, the validity of which is not certain—is that because of the private property of wealth, that is, because decisions to allocate productive resources are made privately and in pursuit of private interests, the advancement of material interests of everyone in a society is contingent upon the compatibility of their interests with those of the owners of wealth. I will refer to this hypothesis as the 'structural dependence upon capital'.[57]

Specifically, the hypothesis of structural dependence upon capital is based on the following assumptions: investment is a necessary condition for improving the future material conditions of anyone within a society; investment decisions are a private prerogative, attached to property, and are made in pursuit of profit; any demands that threaten the profitability of investment cause the rate of investment to fall; therefore, whether any particular interests can be satisfied depends upon their compatibility with the privately appropriated profit of the owners of wealth.[58] What must be emphasized is that this mechanism applies to everyone, not just the working class. To the extent to which material means are required to satisfy their interests, this hypothesis applies to minorities seeking economic equality, women seeking to

---

[56] Karl Marx, *Wage Labour and Capital* (Moscow: Progress Publishers, 1952).

[57] Antonio Gramsci, *Prison Notebooks*, ed. Quintin Hoare and Geoffrey Nowell Smith (New York: International Publishers, 1971). For an interpretation of Gramsci along these lines, see Przeworski, *Capitalism and Social Democracy*, ch. 4.

[58] For a more extensive discussion and critique of this model, see A. Przeworski and M. Wallerstein, 'Popular Sovereignty, State Autonomy, and Private Property', *Archives européennes de sociologie*, 27/2 (1986), 215–59.

transform the division of labour within the household, old people seeking material security, workers seeking better working conditions, politicians seeking re-election, and the military seeking more bombs. It is in this sense that capitalism is a class society: not in the sense that there are always two, ready-made classes, but in the sense that the structure of property characteristic of capitalism makes everyone's material conditions contingent upon the privately made decisions of owners of wealth.[59]

The structural dependence upon capital opens the possibility of compromises between organized workers and capitalists. In such compromises workers consent to the institution of profit (and thus private property of wealth), while capitalists invest and consent to political arrangements, democracy, that permit workers to process their claims to a part of the societal product. Since Michael Wallerstein and I have analysed such compromises elsewhere,[60] I will emphasize here only the game-theoretic structure of the relation between interests of workers and capitalists.

Examine Fig. 4.1. The straight line with a slope of -1, $W = Y - P$, represents all possible allocations of the national product between wages and profits at any particular instant of time, when the product Y is fixed (the distance of this line from the origin measures the size of the product). Along this line there is a zero-sum relation between wages and profits: whenever wages increase, profits fall, and vice versa. This is the traditional Marxist model of the conflict of class interests. Now examine the second straight line, in which wages are measured as the sum of present wages and what the wages workers expect to receive in some discounted future, W^*. If this line still slopes monotonically downward, then Marx's extension of the static to dynamic conditions is valid and the conflict of material interests irrevocably pits classes against each other: workers would want to confiscate the capital stock even if the product grows, since the present value of future wages is smaller if the present profit is larger. But if workers' future wages depend upon present investment and if this investment depends upon present profits, then it is possible that the function that relates present and future wages to present profits,

---

[59] John Manley, 'Neopluralism: A Class Analysis of Pluralism I and Pluralism II', *American Political Science Review*, 77 (1983), 368–84, recently revived the view that Marxist theory maintains that in every capitalist society there are always two and only two classes. All that could be said about such a theory is that it is false.

[60] A. Przeworski and M. Wallerstein, 'The Structure of Class Conflict in Democratic Capitalist Societies', *American Political Science Review*, 76 (1981), 215–36.

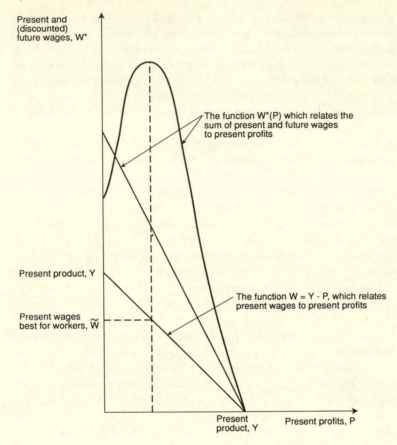

Present and (discounted) future wages, W*

The function W*(P) which relates the sum of present and future wages to present profits

Present product, Y

The function W = Y - P, which relates present wages to present profits

Present wages best for workers, W̃

Present product, Y

Present profits, P

FIG. 4.1

W*(P), looks like the uppermost line: a maximum of wages at some positive value of present profits. The level of present wages that corresponds to the level of present profits that maximizes the sum of present and future wages, W̃, is lower than the present product: hence workers concerned about the future will in this case offer wage restraint and will consent to capitalists appropriating profits. Whether this is the situation workers face, that is, whether the function W*(P) has an internal maximum, depends on the function that relates the rate of investment to profits and on political institutions and conditions that determine whether workers can reasonably expect to benefit in the future from present investment. It has been shown that conditions under which both classes would opt for a compromise do exist.[61]

This is just one model of the conflict of interests under capitalism formulated within the assumptions of rational choice. Several other analyses conceptualize somewhat different aspects of this conflict. Kevin Lancaster provided the seminal formulation of the intertemporal trade-off, and his work was extended by Michael Hoel.[62] Sam Bowles and Herbert Gintiss focused on the Keynesian aspects of class compromise, which they call 'the accord'.[63] Yvo Dirickx and Murat Sertel analysed the impact of taxation on class conflict, while Ephraim Kleiman studied the impact of the revolutionary (and counter-revolutionary) threats on taxation.[64] Frans van Winden, V. K. Borooah and Frederick van der Ploeg, and Kerry Schott provided analyses of conflicts involving unions, firms, and the state.[65]

Comparative welfare of economic systems and transition to socialism

Suppose that among all strategies available to workers under capitalism, they are best off by offering a high degree of wage restraint. Does this imply that capitalism is better for workers than socialism? Or conversely suppose that under capitalism workers are best off by being highly militant economically: is it now true that workers would be better under socialism? The question of the comparative welfare associated with different modes of production turns out to be exceedingly complex, and I believe that we do not yet know how to answer the above questions. Wallerstein and I were able to formulate the question but were not able to find an answer.[66] Elsewhere, I have focused on

[61] Ibid.

[62] Kevin Lancaster, 'The Dynamic Inefficiency of Capitalism', *Journal of Political Economy*, 81 (1973), 1092–109; and Michael Hoel, 'Distribution and Growth as a Differential Game between Workers and Capitalists', *International Economic Review*, 19 (1978), 335–50.

[63] Sam Bowles and Herbert Gintiss, 'The Crisis of Liberal Capitalism: The Case of the United States', *Politics and Society*, 11 (1982), 51–93.

[64] Yvo M. I. Dirickx and Murat Sertel, 'Class Conflict and Fairness in "Democratic Capitalism"', *Public Choice*, 34 (1979), 99–116; and Ephraim Kleiman, 'Fear of Confiscation and Redistribution: Notes towards a Theory of Revolution and Repression', Seminal Paper no. 247 (Stockholm: Institute for International Studies, 1983).

[65] V. K. Borooah and Frederick van der Ploeg, *Political Aspects of the Economy* (Cambridge: Cambridge University Press, 1983); Kerry Schott, *Policy, Power, and Order: The Persistence of Economic Problems in Capitalist States* (New Haven, Conn.: Yale University Press, 1984); and Frans van Winden, *On the Interaction between State and Private Sector: A Study in Political Economics* (The Hague: Drukkerij J. H. Pasmans BV, 1983).

[66] Przeworski and Wallerstein, 'The Structure of Class Conflict'. See also Tsebelis, 'Comment on Przeworski and Wallerstein', and our response in the *American Political Science Review*, 78 (1984), 785–90.

the transitional aspects and have come to the conclusion that the costs of transition might lead workers to cling to capitalism even if socialism were a superior system for satisfaction of their material needs.[67]

From the point of view of methodological individualism, the general question of the theory of revolution is: under what conditions would people, characterized by their specific endowments of alienable and inalienable resources under one economic system, prefer a specific alternative economic system, that is, different property rights and/or allocation mechanisms. Roemer's fundamental work set a framework for the analysis of such questions.[68] He has shown under what conditions a particular class of economic agents in one economic system would be better off in a given alternative economic system. Roemer's recent papers relate this analysis to the distributional theory of justice, with some startling results concerning the institution of private property of wealth.[69] Unfortunately, the conceptual apparatus of instantaneous adjustment to a general equilibrium does not allow for studying transitions between economic systems, only for comparing their static equilibria.[70]

Note that, from the viewpoint of methodological individualism, the question about transition to socialism is whether socialism is preferred by the concrete individuals living under capitalism, individuals as they are, with their endowments and their preferences.[71] Clearly, this formulation is too rudimentary to provide unambivalent answers: are the concrete individuals living under capitalism autonomous and therefore responsible for their preferences, and what methods are there for aggregating individual preferences? But the methodological perspective suggests a certain democratic scepticism: the question to be asked

---

[67] A. Przeworski, 'Material Interests, Class Compromise, and the Transition to Socialism', *Politics and Society*, 10 (1980–1), 125–53.

[68] Roemer, *General Theory*.

[69] J. E. Roemer, 'Public Ownership and the Private Property Externalities', Working Paper no. 252 (Davis: Department of Economics, University of California, 1985).

[70] Przeworski, *Capitalism and Social Democracy*, ch. 7.

[71] It might be tempting to rely instead on one of two alternative formulations. (1) under socialism, people would have different preferences and once they had the new preferences they would prefer them to those they had under capitalism: hence their preferences under capitalism need not be considered, even if these 'capitalist' preferences would lead people to oppose socialism. Or (2) preferences change endogenously in the course of struggle for socialism. I find the first position unacceptable on the grounds that it permits dictatorship over current preferences, and I find the second, Rosa Luxemburg's, position unpersuasive because we do not know whether and how preferences change.

about any blueprint of the future is first whether the concrete individuals living under their given historical conditions would express and continue to express a preference for this blueprint through some reasonable voting mechanism.

To summarize, even those writers who are sceptical about the individualistic point of departure agree that it is in analysing class conflict that the strength of the rational-choice perspective becomes most evident. Some students of class alliances disavow the use of formal strategic calculus,[72] but in fact they are forced to use such a calculus throughout their analysis. After all, game theory is but a formal theory of conflict and, for better or worse, the only theory there is.

'The Economy', Politics, and Equilibrium Analysis

While most discussions concern the general posture of methodological individualism, to close this review I would like to point out a crippling technical weakness of the formal apparatus of game theory. But first let us step back.

Marxist economic theory shares with neo-classical economics the reliance on equilibrium analysis as the main methodological device. The equilibrium is a state of the world in which actors, individual or collective, do not alter their courses of action because no one can be better off given the expected response of others.[73] Even if situations other than equilibrium are admitted by Marxist theory, underconsumption, overproduction, or wage pressure are always identified and analysed with reference to equilibrium.

Now, there is no consensus that equilibrium is a useful concept, in economics and beyond. Views range over the entire spectrum: from the insistence of neo-classical theory that the economy is always in equilibrium, through the standard neo-classical position that the economy tends to the equilibrium every time it is displaced by exogenous actions and events, through the standard Keynesian position, that while the economy may never be in equilibrium, this concept

---

[72] Notably Fernando H. Cardoso and Enzo Faletto, *Dependencia y desarrollo en América Latina* (Mexico: Siglo XXI, 1969).

[73] Economists tend to confuse the meaning of this term: for them an equilibrium is a situation that will not be departed from without an external displacement and one in which the relevant markets clear. What economists call 'disequilibrium' is, then, equilibrium in which some market does not clear. As used here, the concept of equilibrium has no market-clearing connotations one way or another.

is nevertheless useful as an analytical device, to the view that this concept is misleading descriptively and useless methodologically.[74] In this last view, social systems are complex and the flow of information takes time: when one actor learns about the results of actions of other actors (say, prices), some of these other actors will have already changed their behaviour because of the information they have received in the mean time. In such a world, expectations are never fulfilled; there is no equilibrium nor any tendency toward one.[75]

I am not certain again to what extent these theoretical and methodological differences can be resolved empirically. There may be times when things are so much in flux that strategic calculations are impossible: take the recent inflation in Brazil, where prices seem to change faster than anyone can learn about them and thus vary widely from seller to seller.[76] There are most likely periods when everything is stable and predictable: I suspect that electoral phenomena tend to be quite orderly in general. I do not think that the difference is one between markets versus other social institutions. I am persuaded, however, that most of the time strategic calculations are possible and that some of the time they are fulfilled. Thus, I am not ready to reject the apparatus of the game theory in general and the concept of equilibrium in particular.

The question, however, is 'which equilibrium?' Note that the models of the economy used in Marxist and neo-classical theory are the same. The traditional object of analysis for both is the model of competitive economy. There is a large number of agents, households or firms, who are capable of moving their alienable resources or their bodies from sector to sector and of exchanging commodities and services. For each of the agents, the rest of the system is given as a parameter that this agent takes into account in the maximization problem.[77] On the other extreme of perfect competition, both theories

---

[74] Good discussions of the concept of equilibrium are: Eugene Silberberg, *The Structure of Economics: A Mathematical Analysis* (New York: McGraw-Hill, 1978), ch. 16; and, at the other end of the spectrum, Harvey Gram and Vivian Walsh, 'Joan Robinson's Economics in Retrospect', *Journal of Economic Literature*, 21 (1983), 518–50.

[75] This is the view of the economy held by some interpreters of Keynes, and the view of politics held by Pizzorno.

[76] I owe this observation to Sergio Abranches.

[77] In the 'new classical economics', private actors anticipate decisions made by the government as they compete with each other, but here again each individual faces a parametrically given environment. See Thomas J. Sargent, 'Beyond Demand and Supply Curves in Macroeconomics', *American Economic Review*, 72 (1982), 382.

employ models of monopoly and duopoly, as well as models in which the only actor is the government, which anticipates the behaviour of economic actors.[78] Between the two—the competitive market with many actors or systems with at most two strategic actors—there are no analyses, neo-classical or Marxist.

This state of affairs may appear surprising given that most descriptions of contemporary capitalist societies emphasize that the relevant actors are a limited number and that their actions comprise non-market strategies. If we wanted to list the domestic actors whose strategies shape a typical capitalist economy, we would include: the government, the Parliament, perhaps some specialized regulatory agencies, and in some countries the central bank; employers' associations, some large corporations, and perhaps private banks; unions and often some other organizations; and then households and firms in general. If we were to list the actions available to these actors, we would certainly not stop at moving resources and bodies across sectors but would include all forms of collective organization, collusion, negotiation, pressure, and so on. To make the point bluntly, most descriptions claim that we live in corporatist societies while theoretical analyses vacillate between studying competitive equilibria and duopolies.[79]

This may not be an accident. The technical apparatus of game theory is almost unusable for all situations that involve fewer than many but more than two actors. As the number of actors becomes large, the Nash non-co-operative solution converges to the competitive equilibrium, and the solution is technically immediate. With two actors it is not always clear which is the appropriate solution: the Nash equilibrium in which the two actors decide independently, a Stackelberg equilibrium in which one actor anticipates the reactions of the

---

[78] The government anticipates the behaviour of producers and consumers in the model developed by Sam Peltzman, 'Towards a More General Theory of Regulation', *Journal of Law and Economics*, 19 (1976), 211–40. It anticipates the actions of several interest groups in the model of Gary S. Becker, 'A Theory of Competition among Pressure Groups for Political Influence', *Quarterly Journal of Economics*, 68 (1985), 371–400. In the innumerable models of electoral business cycles, it anticipates the behaviour of voters. Yet the only actor that anticipates the behaviour of others in all these models is the government; everyone else predictably responds in their best interest.

[79] See Philippe C. Schmitter, 'Still the Century of Corporatism', in Frederick Pike and Thomas Stritch (eds.), *The New Corporatism* (Notre Dame, Ind.: University of Notre Dame Press, 1974). The enormous literature on corporatism has been collected by Alan Cawson and John Ballard, 'A Bibliography of Corporatism', Working Paper no. 84/115 (Florence: European University Institute, 1984).

other, or some more complicated solution involving binding commitments. But all these are standard solutions in the two-person case, and while the solution concepts remain the same for any number of players, technical difficulties become formidable when the number of strategic actors exceeds two. I am thus not particularly optimistic about the future of formal applications of game theory to the study of intergroup conflicts and, in particular, to the study of class alliances.

What is apparent is that the formal game-theoretic analyses will remain unpersuasive unless the concepts of equilibria they employ are descriptive of particular historical conditions. I suspect, therefore, that methodological individualism will force us to be more cautious and more explicit in analysing strategic situations, especially class alliances and the relations among social groups and state apparatuses, but I do not see much future for formal deductive analyses of this kind, at least not before game theory crawls out of its mathematical infancy. Be that as it may, non-technical analyses of political and economic dynamics caused by shifting class alliances have resulted in some remarkable studies, foremost among them Guillermo O'Donnell's analysis of Argentina.[80]

Summary and Perspectives

I hope that it is apparent from these pages that if one accepts the methodological validity of individualistic postulates, most if not all traditional concerns of Marxist theory must be radically reformulated. Whether the eventual results will confirm any of the substantive propositions of Marxist theory of history and whether the ensuing theory will be in any distinct sense 'Marxist', I do not know.

I believe that the challenge of methodological individualism must be accepted. The only alternative would be to agree with G. A. Cohen that '... Marxism is *fundamentally* concerned not with behavior, but with the forces and relations constraining and directing it. When we turn from the immediacy of class conflict to its long-term outcome game theory provides no assistance, because that outcome, for historical materialism, is governed by a dialectic of forces and relations of production that is background to class behavior, and not explicable in terms of it.'[81] This seems to me more like a screenplay for *Star Wars*

[80] Guillermo O'Donnell, 'State and Alliances in Argentina, 1956–1976', *Journal of Development Studies*, 15 (1978), 3–33.

[81] G. A. Cohen, 'Reply to Elster on Marxism, Functionalism, and Game Theory', *Theory and Society*, 11 (1982), 489.

than for social theory. Somehow I would think that for historical materialism the motor of history is class struggle, not The Force.[82]

At the same time, I find Elster's programmatic statement barren: 'By methodological individualism, I mean the doctrine that all social phenomena (their structure and their change) are in principle explicable in terms of individuals—their properties, goals, and beliefs.'[83] Elster is in good company: he could have cited Marx's phrase (from *Holy Family*) according to which 'history is nothing but the activity of men in pursuit of their ends'.[84] These are nice-sounding phrases but, as Marx himself noted in the letter to Annenkov, their explanatory power is minimal.[85] They may be true, but only if we admit that results of individual actions are often indirect, unanticipated, and sometimes unwanted by anyone.[86] The conditions we face today constitute consequences of actions undertaken yesterday, but yesterday we acted in pursuit of other goals than producing conditions for tomorrow. As François Furet observed, 'men make history but they do not know which one'.[87] Thus the central difficulty of individualistic views of history is to explain how actions of individuals under given conditions produce new conditions. Most people would agree about this postulate in principle, but I think that Berger and Offe as well as Anthony Giddens are correct to return the challenge to Elster.[88] For the problem is that, as it stands now, the technical apparatus of methodological individualism, game theory, is woefully inadequate for this task. Today, the apparatus of game theory can at best elucidate isolated, singular events that occur under given conditions. It has nothing to say about history.

The critique implied by methodological individualism is thus more impressive than the alternative explanations based on rational-choice postulates. Sen observed a few years ago that economic theory 'has *too little* structure'.[89] This is true not only about individual rationality but

[82] See J. E. Roemer, 'Methodological Individualism and Deductive Marxism', *Theory and Society*, 11 (1982), 513–21, for a more measured response.

[83] Elster, 'Marxism, Functionalism, and Game Theory', p. 453.

[84] Karl Marx, *The Holy Family* (Moscow: Progress Publishers, 1956).

[85] The letter to Annenkov (from 1846) is reprinted in *Karl Marx: Selected Writings*, ed. David McLellan (Oxford: Oxford University Press, 1977).

[86] How lawful social outcomes result from individual actions was a source of unending confusion for Frederick Engels. See his letter to Joseph Bloch of 21 Sept. 1890, in *Marx and Engels*, ed. L. S. Feuer (New York: Doubleday, 1959).

[87] François Furet, *Penser la Révolution française* (Paris: Gallimard, 1978), 44.

[88] Berger and Offe, 'Functionalism or Rational Choice?'; Anthony Giddens, 'Commentary on the Debate', *Theory and Society*, 11 (1982), 527–40.

[89] Sen, 'Rational Fools', p. 335.

also about social relations, which endow individuals with objectives and possibilities of action. I am persuaded, however, that the objections and preoccupations of social theorists will lead to, and in fact are already leading to, a rapid development of the game-theoretic apparatus. I thus see a long perspective of constructive interaction between formal theorists and students of society. If successful, this interaction will lead to: treating preference formation as an endogenous, continuous outcome of social processes; distinguishing categories of actors by their strategic situations; using historically specific concepts of equilibrium; while explaining history, including the origins of conditions, in terms of the goal-orientated actions of individuals.

PART II

THE HISTORICAL CONDITIONS OF SOCIOLOGICAL INDIVIDUALISM

5

Community, Individualism, and Culture

BERTRAND BADIE

One of the classic distinctions in sociology is that between community and association, between community feeling and individual rationality. It can be found in various forms in analyses of social change which identify community with tradition, and association with modernity.[1] The distinction also informs comparative analyses such as those which compare individualist Western societies with African or Middle Eastern societies that are presented as archetypes of the community model.[2] As with most clichés, there is some truth in this view, and the classifications on which it is based deserve, no doubt, a place in socio-historical and comparative analyses, now in a process of reappraisal.

There are several difficulties related to Ferdinand Tönnies' initial theoretical construct. In comparative sociology, his theoretical framework poses certain problems of method. The key concept of a natural, instinctive 'organic will', which, for Tönnies, is the basis of community, is difficult to use comparatively in the classification or comparison of the various social structures identified in historical or anthropological studies.

For Tönnies, *Gemeinschaft* signifies the relation which links 'those who care for one another' and who 'understand' one another, and live together, organizing their shared experience, and constructing between them a natural and spontaneous solidarity. It is based upon 'understanding' and 'agreement' and is expressed through the family, neighbourhood relations, and friendship. Association (*Gesellschaft*),

---

[1] This opposition is an essential postulate of 'neo-evolutionist' sociology; cf. on this subject, A. Smith, *The Concept of Social Change* (London: Routledge & Kegan Paul, 1973), 14ff.
[2] Cf. e.g. K. Deutsch, 'On Nationalism, World Regions and the Nature of the West', in P. Torsvik (ed.), *Mobilization, Center Periphery Structures and Nation-Building* (Bergen: Universitetsforlaget, 1981), 51–93.

on the other hand, involves 'an aggregate of human beings which superficially resembles the *Gemeinschaft* insofar as the individuals peacefully live and dwell together. However, in the *Gemeinschaft* they remain essentially united in spite of all separating factors, whereas in the *Gesellschaft* they are essentially separated in spite of all uniting factors.' *Gesellschaft* applies to 'a multitude of natural and artificial individuals, the wills and spheres of whom are in many relations with and to one another, and remain nevertheless independent of one another and devoid of mutual familiar relationships'.[3] These criteria are far too unclear especially in the present climate in which methodological individualism tellingly reminds us to be wary of any characterization of the social involving the organic as a primary and irreducible reality.[4]

Tönnies' typology has been much criticized in modern sociology. For the most part, critiques involve the clash of paradigms within sociological theory. Naegele makes the specific point that Tönnies' characterization takes place within a framework whose unit of analysis is social relation rather than social action.[5] The notion of social ties is thus treated as a privileged variable and is, therefore, more likely to be accorded a recurring quality. These factors encourage the creation of marked distinctions between types of society. Such a tendency is less likely within a sociology which accords privilege to social action. Moreover, the taking into account of social action, which is, by definition, more volatile and less amenable to social typologies, may well overturn or at least qualify all classifications of social forms derived from Tönnies' categories.

The privileged position enjoyed by the sociology of social relations also poses the more serious problem of the relationship between the micro-sociological and macro-sociological. On this question, Gurvitch stresses that community relations are inadequate to describe the structure of a whole society, and are barely more adequate than the concepts of mass or communion in his own typology of social relations. Stressing that, depending upon circumstances, community can assert itself at any time within any social ensemble, Gurvitch downgrades this form of social relations which he likens to 'social electrons' of

[3] F. Tönnies, *Community and Association* (London: Routledge & Kegan Paul, 1955), 74, 87.
[4] R. Boudon, *La Place du désordre* (Paris: PUF, 1984), esp. pp. 64 and 231.
[5] K. D. Naegele, 'The Institutionalisation of Action', in T. Parsons *et al.*, *Theories of Society* (New York: Free Press, 1965), 185.

different kinds, none of which exclusively characterizes the societies from which history is itself made.[6]

Gurvitch's work also demonstrates the problematic nature of a binary typology, which endows community with a unity that hinders 'the diversity of mental states and acts',[7] and so leads either to an over-restricted use of the concept, or to the creation of a category which is too heterogeneous. In order to cope with this problem, Gurvitch distinguishes between community and 'communion', the latter referring to a higher level of fusion and membership participation. In the same way Schmalenbach distinguishes between community and the league (*bund*), assigning to the former ties of blood and proximity and, to the latter, the intensity of commonly held feelings and collective emotions which constitute integration and common will.[8] The creation of this third category, especially in Schmalenbach's work, shows the dangers inherent in Tönnies' approach, that is to say, an approach which conceptualizes the community relation as singular and homogeneous and which, above all, postulates a necessary continuity between, for example, societal relation and individualist act or between community relations and community feeling.

Parsons was well aware of the difficulty of establishing a firm criterion for distinguishing community and association.[9] Rejecting Tönnies' idea of will — organic will being unable to explain the genesis of a friendship or marital relationship — Parsons proposes a series of supplementary criteria. That of the goal which contrasts the restrictive nature of the aims which govern society with the impossibility of conceiving community by means of a precise teleology. That of the nature of obligation or sanction, defined strictly in the *Gesellschaft*, tendentially unlimited in the *Gemeinschaft*, and linked to rule in the former, to social control in the latter. Above all, Parsons points out that the totality of these criteria demonstrates the discriminatory character conferred by Tönnies upon social relations. In the case of

[6] G. Gurvitch, *La Vocation actuelle de la sociologie* (Paris: PUF, 1963), i. 167.

[7] Ibid. 163.

[8] H. Schmalenbach, 'Communauté et ligue', in P. Birnbaum and F. Chazel, *Théorie sociologique* (Paris: PUF, 1975), 157–60.

[9] T. Parsons, *The Structure of Social Action* (New York: Free Press, 1968), ii. 689–90. The difficulty involved in constructing a criterion also explains the polysemic nature of the concept of community, and the widening of meaning apparent in notions such as 'local community' which signifies both an intense sociability and all forms of local groupings. This ambiguity appears particularly in American sociology. Cf. R. M. MacIver, *Community* (London: Macmillan, 1917); it was vigorously denounced by P. Sorokin in *Society, Culture and Personality* (New York: Harper & Row, 1947), 243.

society, the relation is specific, and is strictly related to immediate action. In the case of community, the relation is diffuse, 'organic', independent of immediate action, and inscribed in a wider, more enduring context.[10] In the meaning conveyed by the actor, action loses its significance as an individual act to the benefit of social relations.

Two lessons can be drawn from this reconstruction of the concept of community. First, against Tönnies' theory, community can no longer be identified a priori as 'a historical phase in the development of global society';[11] nor can it be made synonymous with the idea of traditional society. Second, the notion cannot be used to characterize or describe types of apparently homogeneous social formations; it can be used to understand structures of significations, and to show how certain practices or social institutions have been constituted in history on the basis of a privilege accorded to them by actors in terms of their insertion into a diffuse social relation rather than the specific orientation of their action. As a cultural rather than a structural phenomenon, community thus becomes a less rigid, less exclusive, less uniform category than when it is seen as the objective model for the structuration of human relations. Historical sociology can thus use the term in relation to the networks of significations which form the principal categories of social life, such as the conceptualizing of the political, the economic, and the religious.

Moreover, this distinction becomes even more significant when one addresses the question of social processes, the mechanisms of change, of resistance, or of crisis, as opposed to the static interpretation of social reality. It is worthy of note that Tönnies' work has been far more convincing in the analysis of social dynamics, whether in the construction of the state or in political mobilization, than in the straightforward comparison of social formations. This second point is linked to the first and suggests that the processes of social transformation depend directly upon their relation to the 'signification' which underpins interactions within a given social space.

Community and Socio-history: Towards a Cultural Construct

The use of the concept of community in historical sociology reflects therefore certain of the inadequacies of the term in sociological theory: the heterogeneity of the category of analysis; the inclusive nature of

[10] Parsons, *The Structure of Social Action*, p. 691.
[11] Gurvitch, *La Vocation actuelle*, p. 163.

community relations, and the absence of transitivity which characterizes them. This negative balance-sheet suggests the necessity for a return to the cultural perspective derived unequivocally from the Weberian tradition.

The dangers of a concept

The principal ambiguity of the concept results from the extreme variety of historical structures it refers to: to speak of the community model in the singular, as is often the case, is a misuse which reflects the imprecision of the concept. From a socio-historical perspective, community structures refer to very varied and differing social formations. Community structures can refer to blood relations of a tribal, clan, or family nature, as well as to political communities such as village communities, economic communities such as corporations, religious communities such as the parish, monastic orders, or even brotherhoods. Community structures can, moreover, be restricted to the ownership and use of goods (patrimonial communities), or else be the organizing principle of people's lives (neighbourhood communities) or labour (work communities).

These several distinctions are all the more self-defining given that, far from being complementary or historically interdependent, they are sometimes mutually exclusive and correspond to quite different settings. The family community, for example, was little developed in the Middle Ages where village communities dominated.[12] It was the decline of these, coupled with economic crisis, which saw the rise, during the fourteenth century, of family communities.[13]

Both of these communities seem, however, to correspond to the criteria elaborated by Tönnies. The village community found all over medieval Europe was based upon neighbourhood relations, themselves based upon a shared life and a truly 'natural' solidarity. J. Blum has remarked that there were frequent collective meetings, worship, and profane celebrations all organized communally. Residence was controlled, all newcomers having to undergo a probationary period before being integrated into the community, as in Alsace, Switzerland, or Austria where one had to pay a fee in order to be admitted into the village community. Community organization gave rise to common

[12] Cf. J. Gaudemet, *Les Communautés familiales* (Paris: Rivière, 1963), 89, 97, 179.

[13] Family community holdings, for example, comprised between 10 and 15% of the holdings in Auvergne from the 14th century onwards. Decline was marked from the 14th century; cf. P. Charbonnier, 'Les Communautés familiales en Auvergne d'après les terriers', *Revue d'Auvergne*, 95/4 (1978), 257–81.

distribution of payment to the local lord, to a defining of the modes of the exploitation of land, and to the political organization of the communal territory.[14]

There is, however, a significant and decisive distinction between Western feudalism, where community organization was most often limited to the socio-political domain, and Eastern 'feudalism', where it extended to land ownership and to the defining of family roles. J. Gaudemet has noted the counterweight power of individualism in the West as early as the medieval period, which includes the Germanic world wherein the importance of blood relations (*Sippe*) was amplified by a historical tradition which grew out of German romanticism.[15] On the other hand, village and family communities seem to have combined in certain Slavic regions, for example, in the southern areas dominated by the *zadruga*, which E. Sicard depicts as an organization of rural society whose members are united by family ties and who share the exploitation of land not subject to any individual rights of succession. The family community, expressed by the individual household which grouped the members of the extended family, organized religious feasts, the management of commonly owned goods, and the distribution of roles in the productive process.[16] This structuration was of a much more patriarchal character than that of the Russian *mir*, which was related to a quite different socio-historical reality in which the community principle was derived not from consanguinity, but from the shared administering of land which was periodically redistributed among several families.[17] The distinction between these different underlying forms can be clearly seen in the institutions which structured them and which, in each case, referred to a concept of power or clearly specified law. Each case, moreover, throws into sharp relief the inadequacy of the view which posits the community phenomenon as a single category.

It is worth mentioning here the elective view of power which predominated in the Western village community, the *mir*, and the Serbian *zadruga* (the designation of the chief is related to age in the

[14] J. Blum, 'Village et famille', in *Histoire des paysans* (Paris: Berger-Levrault, 1982), 11–12.

[15] Gaudemet, *Les Communautés familiales*, pp. 84–8.

[16] E. Sicard, *La Zadruga sud-slave dans l'évolution du groupe domestique* (Paris: Ophrys, 1943), chs. 3–5 (part i).

[17] R. Portal, *Les Slaves, peuples et nations* (Paris: Colin, 1965), 15–16; cf. also Blum, 'Village et famille', p. 10, and *Lord and Peasant in Russia* (Princeton, NJ: Princeton University Press, 1961), 504 ff.

Montenegran *zadruga*). We can also mention the predominance in the West of individualist rights of inheritance which encouraged the progressive institutionalization of private property, and which is distinct from the whole of the Slav world with its normative system which forbade distribution, based as it was on the principle of collective ownership.[18]

These observations seem to suggest a major distinction between an essentially political community model incarnated in Western feudalism, and the family community model of Eastern Europe, the existence of which is confirmed by J. Blum, who notes the importance of 'multiple families' in the Balkans, Bohemia, Moravia, Southern Poland, and as far as Russia, in contrast to the rapid rise of the individual farms in England and Scandinavia.[19] Medieval historians show us, however, that such a distinction is, in its turn, too summary, and inadequate to the description of the complexity of feudal society. Even though the Western village community became the model for the political organization of the community, ties of vassalage appear, on the contrary, to have been an essentially individualist political relation. Even though the existence of rights of inheritance protecting individual ownership is evidence of the reality of the independent organization of the family, the sporadic occurrence of family communities and, on another level, the control of private wars and the limiting of the division of fiefs, seem to suggest the opposite. The analysis could be developed in even more detail. But we have here sufficient indication that the concept of community remains far too general in the discriminatory conceptualization and classification of the social formations we wish to compare. The problem becomes even more complex if we take into account North African society where the nature of the community is derived not from neighbourhood relations nor from the extended family, but from membership of the same tribe, that is to say, from a model which transcends the distinction between the village community and the family community.[20]

Communities, therefore, are not all the same, nor do they exclude social relations of an individualist nature. Herein lies another weakness in a concept of community which reconstructs the social reality it

[18] Blum, *Lord and Peasant*, and Sicard, *La Zadruga sud-slave*, p. 113 ff.

[19] Blum, 'Village et famille', p. 22.

[20] This raises further questions concerning the notion of community. Cf. E. E. Evans-Pritchard, *Nuer* (Oxford: Oxford University Press, 1987), see in particular ch. 4; regarding North African societies, see E. Gellner, *Muslim Society* (London, Cambridge: Cambridge University Press, 1979).

describes on the basis of a common and natural will, when in fact it can be easily shown that it derives from individual strategies. Village communities were organized, at the dawn of feudalism, as much upon the initiative of the villagers who grouped themselves together as a rational means of resisting the lords, as upon the initiative of the latter who saw in such groupings an expedient means of delegating part of their political role, notably that involving the distribution among the peasants of seigneurial dues.[21] The taking into account of the individual strategies of actors thus suggests a cluster of explanations concerning the origin of communities which are not reducible to the hypothesis of a natural will which generates sociability.

The same observation also applies to family communities. We know, for example, that the family communities which appeared in the West at the end of the Middle Ages were derived from individual marriages designed to cope with the economic difficulties which followed the crisis of the fourteenth century. Even the brotherhood ties which occurred at this time in Provence and the Auvergne (as well as in Italy, Spain, and the Germanic world) were, primarily, individual contracts entered into freely between brothers in order to bring together their production. The artificial nature of the intent informing these actions is clear from the fact that the fraternity involved was derived as much from association as from blood ties.[22]

C. Geertz makes the same observation concerning Bali society and the organic *dadia* groups. He shows in particular that the constructing of the *dadia* was derived from a choice related to the will to domination of one family group. When one among them had accumulated sufficient power resources, notably riches and prestige, it endeavoured to express its power within the hamlet by grouping the households around an elected chief and under the protection of an ancestral temple. In this way *dadia* became collective groups which governed political, economic, and social relations.[23]

On the one hand, therefore, it is power strategies which, by and large, constitute community groups, natural will being at the most an effect, and certainly not an origin, of the phenomenon. On the other hand, it is too simplistic to claim that relations of the community type

[21] Blum, 'Village et famille', p. 11.

[22] Cf. R. Aubenas, 'Réflexion sur les fraternités artificielles au Moyen Âge', in *Études d'histoire à la mémoire de Noël Didier* (Paris: Montchrestien, 1960) and Sicard, *La Zadruga sud-slave*, p. 491.

[23] C. Geertz, 'Form and Variation in Balinese Village Structure', *American Anthropologist*, 61/6 (Dec. 1959), 991–1012.

can displace individual rationality or the 'free-rider' strategy. P. Birnbaum has shown that individualism as a method facilitates the identification of modes of individual strategies in any social formation.[24] In the same way S. Popkin has demonstrated, from his research into the Tonkin peasantry, that even within relations of a community type, action will still be elaborated in relation to individual calculation.[25] These observations are pertinent to institutions as well as to action. The identification of models of community organization does not mean that individual forms of social organization do not exist within them.

To take issue with certain approaches — which we regard as highly suspect from a methodological point of view — it is not sufficient to identify the parameters of family communities in order to refute the existence, or social relevance, of the nuclear family. J. Goody has aptly demonstrated that although the reality of the family community can be attested, using co-residence, for example, it is not possible, in any definitive sense, to show the non-universality of the nuclear family. The same can be said of the family community. Social forms are irreducibly intermingled, and are only distinguishable by establishing the cultural models and institutional types they give rise to.

In historical sociology the use of the concept of community is also limited by its non-transitive nature. The highlighting of a community characteristic only implies the characteristic which theoretical reflection ascribes logically to it. Wider ascription is, however, common, especially in recent historical sociology. It is, for example, at the centre of the current of moral economics attacked by Popkin. E. Wolf, one of the main exponents of this view, has attempted to demonstrate how peasant revolutions can be explained as the contestatory behaviour of the small independent, conservative-minded peasantry reacting against the advance of the market economy, adopting as a result a protectionist community attitude.[26] Popkin has empirically undermined this thesis by his work on the Vietnamese revolution, the community foundation of which he contests.[27] Paige, from a systematic comparative analysis, has offered a more complex interpretative model which demonstrates the equivocal nature of explanations of the

[24] P. Birnbaum, *Dimensions du pouvoir* (Paris: PUF, 1984), ch. 10.
[25] S. Popkin, *The Rational Peasant* (Berkeley, Los Angeles, Calif.: University of California Press, 1979), see, in particular, pp. 251 ff.
[26] E. Wolf, *Peasant Wars of the Twentieth Century* (New York: Harper & Row, 1969), esp. conclusion.
[27] Popkin, *The Rational Peasant*, pp. 245 ff.

revolutionary phenomenon which use the notion of the peasantry's community identity: small family property and the link with the land, which together create competitive behaviour between peasants and encourage the rejection of radical political actions. Conversely, such actions are encouraged by those tenant farmers who do not perceive their relations with their peers in a competitive manner.[28] In both cases, therefore, it is a calculation of an Olsonian kind which separates the social formation from political behaviour, and which precludes transitivity between them. Tilly and de Bois's work on the revolution and counter-revolution in the Vendée and in the Sarthe region can be interpreted in the same way. Here one could define the conduct of the peasantry *vis-à-vis* the new regime not as a function of the community character of the social formation, but as a perceived opportunity by individuals to align themselves with the political choices of the bourgeoisie who controlled the neighbouring towns.[29]

To sum up, the notion of community has a plurality of meanings. It is contradictory when analysed in terms of concrete expressions, is never exclusive of processes exterior to it, and governs directly no known model of political behaviour. All in all, the concept of community is an ambiguous category of socio-historical analysis. We can, therefore, question the relevance of a concept which purports to describe such diverse realities, and to explain, within a given social practice, elements which have been isolated without real justification or which have been arbitrarily privileged, and which therefore only allow for the most fragile of hypotheses concerning the behaviour of actors.

Towards a Cultural Perspective

Our assessment becomes less negative if we take into account research which has drawn upon the duality elaborated by Tönnies but which uses this duality more rigorously by adopting the notion of the ideal-type. K. Dyson has analysed Western political development with reference to two axes in order to describe the movement from, on the one hand, a form of stateless political organization to that of state organization and, on the other, from a social formation of the community type to that of an associational type. The author's main hypothesis is that the processes of transition are constitutive of crises, and

[28] J. Paige, *Agrarian Revolution* (New York: Free Press, 1975), 29ff.
[29] C. Tilly, *The Vendée* (Cambridge, Mass.: Harvard University Press, 1964); P. Bois, *Paysans de l'Ouest* (Paris: Flammarion, 1971).

that these are more serious in cases where the social formation is confronted with a double transition affecting its political organization and its form of social relations, in which case it will undergo a 'crisis of modernity'.[30]

This kind of analysis is helpful in that it transcends the static, binary character normally associated with the community–association distinction. It also questions the double dualism generally posited by evolutionist sociology which systematically links state and society, on the one hand, and 'non-state' and community on the other. On the first point, Dyson demonstrates clearly that the concept of community does not draw its significance from its ability to describe a social structure, but from its ability to account for political tensions which are encouraged by the coexistence of community and individualist drives. He shows in particular how these tensions can undermine the feudal, patrimonial, and clientelist forms of the political organization of communitarian social formations operative within a weak, a developing, or an already institutionalized state.

This ideal-typical construction highlights the two conditions which will permit the 'salvaging' of the communitarian hypothesis. The first is the inscription of the communitarian hypothesis into the notion of crisis, itself based upon the notion of decisive breaks which have effects upon equilibria between different social forms. The second is its analysis not simply in its own terms but in terms of its relation to and lines of compatibility with other imagined constructs of political life. In both cases, we come up against the cultural significance of the problem, that is to say, that the sociologist is concerned with relations of the communitarian and associational type inasmuch as these affect the understanding social actors have of social change and of the political order associated with it.

Such an approach allows for the cautious identification of different types of historical situation and the development of a comparative analysis. In this vein, MacFarlane has noted the individualist orientation which characterized social relations in England from the thirteenth century, distinguishing them from continental models, as well as from societies in Eastern Europe and Asia.[31] For MacFarlane, three comparative elements which bring out the mediating function of

[30] K. Dyson, *The State Tradition in Western Europe* (Oxford: Martin Robertson, 1980); 'State and Society in Western Europe: A Model for Comparative Analysis', *West European Politics* (May 1980), 166–87.

[31] A. MacFarlane, *The Origins of English Individualism* (Cambridge: Cambridge University Press, 1975), 5.

so many cultural models and political strategies deserve examination. The first is the role of Christianity and its place in the advance of individualism as distinct from, for example, the community orientation of Islamic or Chinese culture. Second is the question of the political will of actors whose aim was to destroy the peasantry and establish a commercial agriculture. Thirdly, and above all, is the question of the establishment of an individualist view of law which was more quickly developed than anywhere else, and which saw, in particular, the strong individualization of the land market as early as the thirteenth century (non-existent at this time in the rest of Western Europe), and a clear freedom of legacy (the freedom to disinherit existed neither in France nor in the Germanic world).[32] This individualist culture and strategy thus preceded and encouraged the commercial and capitalist revolution. They were not, therefore, simply superstructural phenomena. Nor, however, did they derive from a trans-historical permanence of social structure, given that historians have shown the strong community character of pre-Norman English society.[33]

The cultural and mutable nature of community has been accepted for a long time. Weber formulated the concept of 'communalization' in order to point out the relevance of 'a subjective feeling of the parties, whether affectual or traditional, that they belong together'.[34] Further on he notes that 'it is only when this feeling leads to a mutual orientation of their behaviour to each other that a social relation arises between them'.[35] Weber thus demonstrated that the concept of community was dependent not upon objective elements constitutive of the social structure, such as neighbourhood relationships, co-residence, familial organization, or a village grouping, but upon the significance this distribution model had for the actor.

Two points can be made here. First, it is essential that the sociologist understands the origin of these community or individualist representations and the subjective sentiment upon which such views of social relations is grounded. Comparative sociology illustrates, at this level, the function of the sacred and the religious, and the role of Christianity in the rise of individualism[36] (and which can be dis-

[32] Ibid. 50, 121ff., 130ff.

[33] R. Bendix, *Kings or People* (Berkeley, Calif.: University of California Press, 1978), 178.

[34] M. Weber, *Economy and Society* (New York: Bedminster Press, 1968), 40.

[35] Ibid. 42.

[36] Cf., in particular, L. Dumont, *Essais sur l'individualisme* (Paris: Seuil, 1983), 33 ff.

tinguished from the roles of Chinese religion and of Islam).[37] On this latter point, Gellner notes, for example, the complexity of relationships which link Islam to the communitarian model, whereas J. Chelhod shows its strict relation to the tribal form of social organization.[38] Second, the structuring role of representations of law should, at this level of analysis, be stressed, that is to say, the juridical culture which gave meaning in particular to relations between men and material goods, and land in particular.

Furthermore, the Weberian perspective demonstrates the pertinence of the community constructs of different categories of social action and offers the means of distinguishing them, through an ideal-type methodology, from associational constructions. In this way, the major axes of a communitarian political culture can be established: the political refers to the group rather than to territory; the political identity of the actor is defined more in terms of other actors than in terms of a fixed centre; power corresponds to a given idea, that is to say, one that relates to the community, and is thus devolved either to law or to an actor to whom each individual is personally subject, rather than to an abstract delegatory system.

This reading of the political should not, however, be taken as a homogeneous one. It varies according to the nature and extent of the community, and to its claim to the direct exercise of political power (as in tribal societies), and to its incorporaiton into a model of a confederal type (such as tribal states and, in particular, the Islamic state such as is described by Ibn Khaldun), or to its claim to be only the basic unit which underpins, through cohesion, a much larger political form (such as the imperial Chinese model). The differences between these different community constructs are therefore very real, even though they converge in the way they perceive essential political categories.

One last point remains, that of how to reconcile the privilege given to this form of cultural explanation with the overall hypothesis which rejects the idea of the irreversible nature of models of social organization, while giving greater credit in its explanation of social phenomena to 'total history' than to changes in ideas and representations. It is probably here that the limits of such an analysis lie. On the one hand,

[37] On the comparative aspect of this, see B. Badie, *Culture et politique* (Paris: Economica, 1983), part ii.

[38] E. Gellner, 'The Distinctiveness of the Muslim State', in E. Gellner and J.-C. Vatin, *Islam et politique au Maghreb* (Paris: CNRS, 1981), 163–75, and J. Chelhod, *Introduction à la sociologie de l'Islam* (Paris: Berson-Chantemerle, 1958).

the socio-historical hypothesis can only interpret known historical sequences. Not only is it not predictive, it can only offer an understanding of social dynamics which have already taken place, rather than pretend to a deductive approach involving the illusion that a change was programmed or that a cultural code 'had to' control social changes indefinitely, along the lines of communitarian or associational relations. On the other hand, by admitting that systems of representation and signification are not primary factors, and that they come into being through the play of social practices, cultural analysis renounces its claim to reconstitute the totality of the process of origins, thus avoiding the danger of falling into the illusions and implications of a macro-historical approach. Its role thus becomes, in a more modest way, that of demonstrating the community or individualist significance which individual or collective actors give to their social action at a given moment.

The Political Crisis of Community Constructs

In an analysis of the social dynamics and of the crises which affect the community model, two aspects of historical sociology are significant: on the one hand, the move away from the community model, that is, the processes by which certain associational forms substitute themselves for community forms; and on the other, community resistances, that is to say, the tensions created by the coexistence of developing processes of individualization and continuing community models.

Departure from community models

The move away from the community model can result either from the establishing of relations of substitution which are seen, in a functionalist way, as an internal solution to the community crisis, or from the spread of individualist cultural models which coexist with community cultural models.

The first process involves primarily the genesis of the state. History shows that the institutionalization of the state is in inverse proportion to the rise of community models. The rise of village communities follows the disappearance of the Carolingian Empire which, by creating the notion of expectation *vis-à-vis* state power, began the individualization of social relations.[39] At the end of the Middle Ages, village communities in their turn disappeared with the construction of

[39] Gaudemet, *Les Communautés familiales*, p. 175.

the modern state. In this sense, the construction of the state is related to the monopolization process (described by Weber) which imposes, simultaneously, a spatial political construct and an individual-related notion of citizenship, both of which undermine community models of political organization.

Several studies have shown, however, that this type of solution was intrinsic to feudal society, the dual individualist and community nature of which we have demonstrated. The conditions necessary for the formation of an autonomous political space in fact relate to the incapacity of the lord to manage the community structures he controlled, and to the competition between individual lords which led gradually to a process of political monopolization.

Such a move away from the community model did not, however, take place either in the weakly feudalized societies of Northern Europe, or in the patrimonial societies of Eastern Europe. In the first case, the absence of tension between lords and peasants, on the one hand, and between lords themselves on the other, withdrew from politics its mediating function in the construction of an individualist social space.[40] The move away was a direct result of the processes of social mobilization unconstrained by the state. There took place, in the case of Eastern European societies, the reactivation of community models, the 'centre' of which is found in Russia and in Prussia as a result of the strength of rural communities and the reinforcement of the coercive power of the lord over the peasants. The resulting type of development thus superimposed a hierarchical and centralized statist rationality upon a dispersed communitarian social formation. This tension explains the patrimonial, personal, and, in the final analysis, a-statist nature of the prevailing models of domination.

However, these different forms of movement away from the community model are only intelligible in the context of the culture in which they occur. The role of Christianity is, from this perspective, crucial, and helps explain the processes of individualization which have informed European societies. At this level of analysis, the distinction between different types of development remains. The first is that of the Roman Christian societies whose individualization process was reinforced by the activity of the Church. As an institution, the Church played a decisive role in the destruction of communities and the

---

[40] We agree here with P. Anderson's hypotheses, see *Lineages of the Absolutist State* (London: New Left Books, 1974).

introduction of individual rights which allowed the Church to profit
from the alienation of goods.[41] As a differentiated hierocratic domain,
the Church encouraged the creation of an area specific to political
issues and, therefore, the rise of the individual-related roles of the
citizen. It is clear that the Calvinist Reformation, in terms both of its
genesis and of the action of its forerunners, involved the exaltation of
an individualist and extra-institutional view of all forms of practice.

The case of Eastern Christianity is noteworthy in two respects.
Formed within the context of an empire which was not in decline, it
brought together institutional legitimation and the negation of the
autonomy of the political *vis-à-vis* the religious. In this way, it contributed to the conceptualization of the role of the emperor as being
that of a supreme legislator designated by and representing God, thus
encouraging the construction of a patrimonial type of domination
model. However, as R. Bendix has noted, its extension beyond its
Byzantine framework, and notably deep into Russia, was like a graft
which led to a break with former cultural traditions and coincided
with the destabilization of community models through the flux and
interplay of exogenous cultural factors.[42]

Bendix notes that this flux was related to the Byzantine Empire's
hegemony and to the strategy of the Kiev princes, who profited from it
to lay the foundations of their autocratic power and contain tribal and,
therefore, community organization, which was the aristocracy's power
base, particularly the *duma boyar* and the institutions at local level
which undermined imperial rationality. It was upon this basis that
rural communities and a patrimonial state were, for many centuries,
able to coexist.

Community resistances

The move away from the community model occurred within the wider
context of social mobilization, especially the growth of towns, communication systems, and all the factors which contributed to the formation of a mass public, and questioned models of community
allegiance.[43] This process created varying degrees of resistance on the
part of community structures, a resistance perceptible to varying
degrees in the history of Western development. The circumstances of

[41] Gaudemet, *Les Communautés familiales*, p. 121.
[42] Bendix, *Kings or People*, p. 92.
[43] On social mobilization and the break with community allegiances see, in particular, D. Lerner, *The Passing of Traditional Society* (London: Macmillan, 1958, 1964).

such resistance varied according to macro-sociological factors and the
nature of the states involved. MacFarlane shows that it was weak in
England,[44] and we can note that the state itself remained weak because
of this,[45] that it was uneven in the case of French feudalism, thus
contributing to the growth of a strongly institutionalized state, and
strong in Mediterranean societies, thus explaining, as in the Italian
case, for example, the formation of a clientelist state.[46]

Several studies of Fascism and Nazism support this hypothesis by
identifying the relationship between movements of this type and the
phenomenon of community resistance. Using electoral material,
Heberlé has already shown how Nazism mobilized, above all, not the
urban population or an atomized public, but a clientele which was
essentially rural and traditional. In terms of Tönnies' hypothesis, this
can be seen as a formation of the community type, seeking protection
from change.[47] More recent studies reinforce these conclusions, showing, on the one hand, that mobilization was more extensive among
Protestants than among Catholics, that is to say, within groups Oberschall would call more segmented, less organized, and less represented
as such on the political scene.[48] On the other hand, they indicate that
the response to Nazism was greater among the lower middle classes
than in any other social stratum, that is to say, in a milieu where the
value system was the most clearly orientated towards the community
tradition and its protection.[49] This interpretation of Nazism cannot, of
course, be taken as exclusive of other interpretations. It shows,
however, the conditions in which Tönnies' distinction can be fruitful
in an analysis of social phenomena. In this way, its importance is
twofold. In the first place it suggests that the concept of community is
only fully operative if one adds the concept of segmentation which

[44] MacFarlane, *The Origins of English Individualism*, p. 163.

[45] Cf. B. Badie and P. Birnbaum, *Sociologie de l'État* (Paris: Grasset, 1979), 217 ff.
English translation, *The Sociology of the State* (Chicago: Chicago University, 1983),
121 ff.

[46] See, in particular, L. Graziano, 'Patron–Client Relationship in Southern Italy',
European Journal of Political Research, 1 (1973), 3–34, and 'La Crise d'un régime libéral
démocratique: L'Italie', *Revue française de science politique* (Apr. 1988), 259–89.

[47] R. Heberlé, *From Democracy to Nazism* (Baton Rouge, La.: Louisiana State University Press, 1945).

[48] B. Hagtvet, 'The Theory of Mass Society and the Collapse of the Weimar
Republic', in S. U. Larsen, B. Hagtvet, and J. P. Myklebust (eds.), *Who were the
Fascists?* (Bergen: Universitetsforlaget, 1980); Birnbaum, *Dimensions du pouvoir*, p. 160.

[49] To argue in this context, as does Birnbaum, in class terms (*Dimensions du pouvoir*,
p. 162) is not appropriate to the communitarian hypothesis, and implies a quite different
level of analysis.

indicates the relations between the group and the exterior environment, and if the value system is taken into account. It is also helpful in that it facilitates analysis of the socio-historical development of relations between the political and the social and identifies forms of community resistance which explain social movements.

The phenomenon of community resistance becomes especially significant in historical situations where the dominant cultural model, far from encouraging the individualization of social relations, reinforces their community character and denies legitimacy to the process of state-building. The orientation of the kind found in Islamic societies is an example of this. Gellner has noted the inversion which characterizes Islam *vis-à-vis* Western Christian culture. Whereas the latter, in its mainstream tradition, imposes a ritualized and hierarchical model of action, Islam is characterized by a mainstream tradition which is egalitarian, weakly structured, and deprived of leadership, and which leaves to its periphery its most ritual and hierarchical organizational forms.[50] This type of model encourages the maintenance of peripheral community forms while undermining the dynamics of centralization necessary to state-building.

All erratic forms of social mobilization, therefore, run the risk of increasing critical community resistances which can be depicted as natural forms of social protest against any social change perceived as pernicious. Movements such as those of the Islamic type are most typical here. The determining role played by rapid urbanization processes in Middle Eastern and North African societies is clear. The effect of these processes is increased when they are not accompanied by the raising of standards of education or other indicators of social mobilization. Community protest occurs, therefore, in the Islamic world, not as a non-modern or residual expression of discontent, as was the case in the West, but, on the contrary, as a form of protest stimulated by the dominant cultural mode.[51]

The essential question here is that of establishing the extent to which central political structures could, in the Islamic world, overcome these community resistances, as was the case in the West. Two approaches are worthy of note here. The first is that of modernizing

---

[50] E. Gellner, *Muslim Society* (London, Cambridge: Cambridge University Press, 1979), 54ff.

[51] See B. Badie and R. Santucci, 'Essai d'analyse de la contestation fondamentaliste et marxiste dans plusieurs pays islamiques', in *Contestation en pays islamique* (Paris: CHEAM, 1984), 11–29.

political systems of the secular or revolutionary type which, from the Turkish to the Baathist political systems, endow the state with a new charismatic or rational-legal legitimacy, and attempt to supplant claims to community legitimacy. The second is that of more conservative — more precisely 'endogenous' — political systems which attempt, by re-utilizing traditional forms of legitimacy, to coexist with community allegiances.

The most persuasive example of this approach is that of the traditional Moroccan political system in which the sultan draws his legitimacy both from the *baraka* and from his role as conciliator between rival tribes. The central role of the prince does not, therefore, establish itself to the detriment of the segmentary and community organization of social relations but, on the contrary, is a functional element within this.[52] The Qajar monarchy in Persia is another variant of this model, notwithstanding its affinity to the Khaldunian type, given that here we have an example of a tribe which itself constructs the state, drawing support from its own community resources in order to impose its domination on the totality of Persian territory. These two examples can be considered as two archetypes of community political system, more than say, the 'clientelist state' which Dyson places in this category, using as illustrative examples the French Third Republic, Spain, and Italy. In these cases, the state seeks to impose individual relations of citizenship which are designed to supplant community allegiances, clientelist practices only having as their aim to reconcile or make compatible community and individualist rationales. In the Moroccan and traditional Persian cases, on the other hand, the centre draws its support from one source of legitimacy which is ultimately a community one.

The essential problem is to evaluate the potential for compatibility between the logic of the modern state, that is to say, one which occurs in the context of the social division of labour, and implies the rise of the functions of the centre, and the maintenance of the community aspect. We should note that the modernization models applied to date indicate the failure to achieve this reconciliation, the progressive development of clientelism being merely a palliative. The limits of this latter development are clear in that it establishes social relations of a vertical type, thus arresting the segmentation of the social space and

[52] See R. Jamous, 'Interdit, violence et baraka: Le Problème de la souveraineté dans le Maroc traditionnel', in E. Gellner, *Islam: Société et communauté* (Paris: CNRS, 1981), 34–54.

impeding the rise of the social division of labour.[53] Neither statist nor communitarian, this type of political system indicates in a telling manner the irreconcilability of the two forms in the context of modernity.

As a differentiated institution, we can say, with Dyson, that the state's ideal-type form is 'diametrically opposed' to that of *Gemeinschaft*: the standardization of behaviour rather than the particularist construction of social relations; a system of clearly defined expectations rather than one of mutual obligations of an ill-defined nature; privilege accorded to performance rather than status, and so on.[54] This observation throws into relief the depth of the political crisis—notably the legitimation crisis—which affects societies in which social mobilization is confronted by community resistances. It also throws into relief the patent failure of intellectual and political élites to define a political centre which is compatible with the orientations of community culture.

Several developments can thus be identified which demonstrate both the pertinence and the limits of Tönnies' distinction in historical sociology. The confrontation between the concept of community and history reveals, in the first instance, the former's ambiguity and, above all, its inappropriateness in the description of social reality, and the impossibility of inscribing it into a binary typology of a trans-historical kind. The value of the concept is essentially analytical. Its value resides not so much in its ability to create models of social solidarity, or to conflate certain of these, but in its providing a way to interpret social processes, in particular the diversity of their consequences depending upon which form of social solidarity they affect. Ultimately, this conferring of privilege on the analyses of crises, rather than on that of the social order, confirms our view that solidarities are not a property which is known a priori to the sociologist, but are rather models of interaction which can then give rise to community resistances.

This privilege accorded to community resistances should in its turn be qualified by a series of safeguards, and above all by the necessity of introducing a distinction between situations which are all too often subsumed under the same heading. It is in this way that, in the context of contemporary Western individualism, many examples of community practices can be provided in the sociology of political mobiliza-

[53] See E. Banfield, *The Moral Basis of a Backward Society* (New York: Free Press, 1958).
[54] See Dyson, 'State and Society in Western Europe', p. 174.

tion, electoral sociology, or the sociology of political personnel.[55] The totality of these phenomena, which cannot be considered merely as residual, would constitute by themselves an axis of research over and above those we have suggested. They inform, moreover, the cultural hypothesis which we have put forward: that their compatibility with state processes draws its significance, it seems, from the meaning ascribed to them by the actors involved, who themselves do not consider them, contrary to what we can observe in other contexts, as excluding or being incompatible with the exigencies of citizenship, but, on the contrary, as being one of its essential channels.

The cultural approach has, therefore, a triple function in an understanding of the phenomenon of community. It gives it, as Weber demonstrated, a true identity which a study of social morphology could not identify. Community solidarity can only be apprehended via the meaning conferred by actors upon their interactions. Second, it allows us to identify the concrete and tangible manifestations of the community phenomenon: political, legal, and power constructs and institutional models related to them. Thirdly, it facilitates differentiation between community models, and the identification of the plurality of types subsumed by it, and in particular the different forms of compatibility between community models and types of social change.

[55] We refer here to Oberschall's work on mobilization, *Social Conflict and Social Movements* (Englewood Cliffs, NJ: Prentice-Hall, 1973), and to the criticism of the individualist postulate in the analysis of voting decision, particularly by the Chicago school, and to the clientelist and community bases of the nobility.

6

The Citizen-Individual in Western Christianity

GUY HERMET

Any discussion of the relationship between politics and religion within Western Christianity must begin with the work of Max Weber. However, although *The Protestant Ethic*[1] illuminates a specific aspect of individualism in Northern Europe, it is not the only key to an understanding of the values underlying the emergence of modern citizenship.

Although its importance cannot be overstated, the Weberian interpretation is neither exhaustive nor universally applicable in the European context. Given its emphasis upon a particular phase of one particular expression of Calvinism, it ignores significant areas relevant to the dynamics of individualization in our societies. This is due, in the first instance, to the narrow cultural context defined by Weber and, in the second, to his almost exclusive preoccupation with the economic rather than the political aspect of one of the forms of 'Protestant' individualism. Over and above this, the 'comprehensive' scope wrongly and misleadingly attributed to Weberianism and its application in the political domain, which was not Weber's explicit pre-occupation, encourages our caution. Such a reading of Weber, itself biased and value-judgemental, has conferred privilege on one of the organizing elements of Western citizenship, and created a situation whereby the claim to its Protestant origin has become the accepted yardstick and agreed model of democratic development. In this way, other forms of political development appear not as aspects or facets of a composite process but as deviations or exceptions, particularly those of a cultural or religious kind. Moreover, they are perceived as being in

[1] M. Weber, *The Protestant Ethic and the Spirit of Capitalism* (London: Unwin, 1967).

opposition to an individualism which has been given normative status rather than as encouraging the creation of 'civic' attitudes and an individualism that is counterbalanced by conformism and deference. This view is encouraged by their apparent relation to traditional forms of community solidarity, and to the development of conflicts considered contrary to the consolidation and equilibrium of the orthodox, right-thinking Protestant democracies of Europe and America.

To attack Weber is not a solution to this problem, and Weber himself is not responsible for it. His critics, moreover, sometimes display a committed obstinacy which serves only to obscure three important questions which are fundamental to an understanding of the religious context of the creation of the Western citizen-individual. The first concerns not a misplaced criticism of Weber's having failed to address the political impact of Calvinism, but the development of the political aspects of his analysis which could only have been of a limited nature, given that his preoccupation was with the economic origins of the rise of capitalism. The second question is related to the first. Beyond the processes he identified, there are others he did not elucidate, concerning other contradictory aspects of Protestant development in which authoritarian and even totalitarian drives coexist with the more edifying drives of citizenship and democracy. The third question, often ignored in spite of its major importance, concerns the Catholic dimension in the genesis of modern citizenship. On the one hand, the political developments influenced by Protestantism always involved reaction to or evolution in terms of the political development of Catholicism. On the other hand, the importance and relative specificity of the Catholic contribution to the new tradition of citizenship are such that it cannot be reduced to the notion of resistance to change, or to that of a perverse interpretation of a political orthodoxy shaped by the spirit of the Reformation.

Political Consequences of the Weberian Thesis

The Weberian thesis is based upon two observations. The first refers to the original and privileged development of capitalism in the Calvinist areas of Holland, England, and the German-speaking countries. The second proceeds from the fact that this coincidence cannot be attributed to the economic creativity of religious minorities. The Protestants soon ceased to be a minority in these areas and came to dominate the Papists. For their part, the Catholics, who had themselves become the minority, exhibited no particular economic *savoir-faire*, and the Jewish minorities, in spite of their trading and financial expertise, were not the source of the rise of capitalism.

As we know, on the basis of these observations Weber posits a relation—rather than a causal link—between the Calvinist Puritan ethic of certain of the pioneers of modern capitalism and their economic behaviour. More precisely, Weber believed that the Protestant concept of *Beruf*—a profession as a vocation—proclaimed for the first time the equal legitimacy and moral dignity of all forms of reputedly virtuous activity: religious, of course, and political activity, but also family, professional, and particularly commercial and financial activity. Moreover, this legitimation was not simply that of the spirit of profit or of greed, these being, as Claude Polin notes, immemorial. Nor was it the sacralization of a rationality 'intrinsic to all economic action'.[2] Conversely, the ethical value of *Beruf* proceeds from its disinterested nature, from its notion of the fundamental nature of efficient individual achievement and of each person's professional duty. This duty, which hitherto appeared only as the means—a transcendent goal—and was pernicious for those who worked beyond the simple satisfaction of their needs and obligations, was itself transformed into a morally worthy goal.

Moreover, as Polin points out, the mysterious process by which economic activity ceases to be servile, or else justifiable in terms of a drive towards self-sufficiency, and becomes one of the sacred imperatives of indefinite material accumulation constituted the core of a new individualist religious feeling. It is true that individualist religious feeling was not born with Protestantism; the idea of personal salvation goes back at least as far as the origins of Hinduism and Buddhism. But the idea of salvation, now familiar to the West, remained until the Reformation one of, in Louis Dumont's expression,[3] 'renunciation' and the flight from the corruption of the things of this world in order to save oneself. Conversely, the Calvinist notion of individual salvation is not confined to simply rehabilitating commitment in worldly matters, but makes of it an imperative. Moreover, the Calvinist doctrine of predestination makes personal success in such commitment a sign of God's recognition of rank, and eternal salvation.

In this, Calvinism breaks not only with Indian religions and Catholi-

---

[2] C. Polin, *L'Esprit totalitaire* (Paris: Sirey, 1977), 59.
[3] L. Dumont, *Homo hierarchicus* (Paris: Gallimard, 1966), 299.

cism, in which acquired wealth is disdained, but also with the medieval heresies brought from eleventh-century Italy[4] and from Bohemia and Holland in the fifteenth and sixteenth centuries.[5] Professing scorn for the flesh and the equality of a rediscovered paradise in this world, the medieval sects condemned in a general way speculation on the labour of others, recognizing legitimacy only in the manual labour of each person in relation to his needs or those of his restricted community. On the contrary, Calvinist sensibility creates a horizontal realignment of values, putting, in principle, all men, and especially all levels of social life, at the same level of dignity, whether religious, political, economic, or familial.

The economic consequences of this upheaval were immediately evident. Calvinism had an ambiguous secularizing effect, inasmuch as it depicts religious life as operating horizontally and not vertically or hierarchically as is the case in Catholicism. Reduced in this way, the sacred becomes compatible with the discharging of interest loans, commercial and manufacturing activities, and, more generally, with wealth creation hitherto hindered by Catholic restrictions. Moreover, this sacralization of economic initiative established not just its moral legitimacy. Individual success in the carrying out of *Beruf* is an indication of what the beneficiary is promised in salvation, in short, that the hand of God is upon him. In this way, the prosperity of individuals ceases to appear as the cause of the poverty of others, while charity becomes a personal option and not a collective duty. In this perspective, Calvinism not only provides the ethical basis for rising capitalism, but justifies inequality through its opposition to a certain evangelical egalitarianism to which the Church of Rome had remained loyal. For the Roman Church, the powerful — in practice, princes and nobles — could only attain grace through its explicit or implicit unction. For Calvinists, those who attained wealth demonstrated by so doing that they were anointed by God, and that for this transcendent reason were entitled to power.

This unequal material power draws additional legitimacy from the use to which it is put. Calvinist asceticism is opposed to the conspicuous and immediate consumption of acquired wealth. As the concrete symbol of divine will, wealth is but a usufruct whose holder must cultivate its indefinite growth in order to confirm his effective virtue.

---

[4] On these heresies, see G. Duby, *Les Trois Ordres ou l'imaginaire du féodalisme* (Paris: Gallimard, 1978), 163 ff.

[5] With the Hussites and the Anabaptists.

In this moral context, capitalist accumulation illustrates the grand design of the All-Powerful.

Without doubt, the political consequences of this upheaval of values formed one of the contributions of Protestantism to the development of representative systems and Western citizenship. For the Calvinists, the political undergoes, even more than does the religious, a revolutionary levelling through its rejection of essentially monarchical or seigneurial hierarchies. The political is no longer inscribed at the summit of the profane world but on the same—horizontal—level as other aspects of human existence. It is exercised in an instrumental way in the cleavages of society, without any longer having the pretension to dominate or govern them. The political no longer has a vocation of authority; it is but the technical exercise of the minimum of ever-necessary government. The American Declaration of Independence of 1776 illustrates this view when it proclaims that the 'Creator' has endowed men 'with certain unalienable Rights, that among these are Life, Liberty and the pursuit of Happiness', and goes on to affirm that 'to secure these rights, Governments are instituted among Men'. Unlike the state which dominated in countries with a Catholic or Lutheran tradition, the government apparatus in areas influenced by Calvinism saw its ethical claims challenged—claims which otherwise would have allowed it to maintain its supremacy over society. For a time, in fact long gone, the central political apparatus of Anglo-Saxon countries influenced by Calvinism was reduced to the role of providing shared services for the benefit of free citizens. The state was thus subordinated to the will of its users. In this framework, elective parliamentarianism became the expression of this revocable consensus and the means of controlling this residual and limited power. Basically, society governs itself, having recourse where necessary to governmental agencies which are themselves devoid of exclusive sovereignty.

These are the positive aspects of the political consequences of Weber's analysis. Although politically innovative, ideologically Calvinism was socially conservative, even reactionary. By claiming that the profits of some people are not the cause of the misery of others, it sidesteps concern for social justice and even withdraws ethical justification from it. Recurrent until the eighteenth century and again threatening—in another form—in the nineteenth, popular revolt against inequality became morally reprehensible because it was orientated against a wealth which is legitimate, being the result of a divine plan. If the disinherited experience some discomfort in their situation, they have only to endeavour to orientate the plan in their favour by trying in their turn to enrich themselves as recommended to them by the Protestant Guizot.[6] Or else they can go off in search of a new promised land — America — given the biblical precedent. Whatever the case, Calvinism is only egalitarian at its starting-point. Unequal at its point of conclusion, it marks a retrograde step even in terms of the representative forms of the *ancien régime*, where peasants and townspeople were able to elect representatives to the village assemblies and the House of Commons.

In this élitist version, the Calvinist view contained within it the exclusive claims of the tax-paying voter which over a long period challenged the notion of the active citizenship of ordinary people. This in turn led on to a more disguised idea of the tax-paying voter which for a long time restricted to an enlightened caste the task of representing the English electors, and expelled from the pale of American citizenship all those suspected of being un-American, and which today salves the conscience of the Afrikaners in the Messianic South African Republic. The Calvinist sensibility analysed by Weber led tax-paying parliamentarianism astray, and later engendered the political credos which made of consensus a prescription pushed to intolerable limits.

Protestantism and Forced Consensus

It is true that this interpretation of citizenship is based upon only one version of Calvinism which itself was only one of the movements which grew out of the Reformation. On the question of the Calvinist sphere of influence, Weber only addresses its Anglo-Saxon and Germanic expressions. He neglects, in particular, the fact that the movement launched by Calvin was of French or Romance origin, and that although it very rapidly eclipsed Dutch Lutheranism, it was introduced there via the Walloon provinces by the young nobles who had studied in Geneva, and by French workers involved in the growing Dutch and Antwerp textile industry. Until 1566, Valenciennes remained the main fortress of Calvinism in the northern countries, and the division from France took place only after the Saint-Barthélemy massacre in 1572. From then on, the Dutch reformed Church could no longer count upon the support, until then essential, of the

---

[6] François Guizot, French statesman (1787–1874), author of the expression 'Enrichissez-vous!'.

Huguenots, and it is only from this period that Holland became the sanctuary of Calvinism. This retreat cut it off from the more aristocratic French Calvinist tradition which virtually incarnated a form of aristocratic dissidence, given that it was supported by almost half of the nobility during the wars of religion (against between only 10 and 20 per cent of the overall population). In total, the Dutch reformed community in fact represented a bourgeois manifestation of Calvinism in a country in a state of siege, and in which the Catholic provinces were themselves treated like subordinate territories.

It was here that the English Puritans found refuge at the beginning of the seventeenth century, and where they developed ideas and practices which, although derived from Calvinism, have little to do with the élitism of the capitalist ethic. These ideas and practices were derived from two factors on which Weber placed little emphasis, even though they were extremely influential. The first is also related to the exalting of individual responsibility inherent in Protestantism, but in this case only applied to the affirmation of the free will of the individual in his reading of the Bible. Religious in its initial form, free will came to hold sway for the Puritans in all domains, including the political. Rejecting all orthodoxies, Puritanism turned the political into an open, egalitarian, and pluralist debate within the parameters of a given community (an important qualification). Concomitantly, Puritanism pushed the second principle, concerning the rejection of pre-established hierarchies, to its logical conclusion by advocating the revocable election of the leader of the religious community (the *presbyter*[7]) who thereby became the leader of the whole community in all domains, given the position of isolation of the English Puritans in Holland. The result, at both levels, foreshadowed what became the new legitimating base of all Western democratic systems, a legitimacy based upon the sovereignty of individual free will expressed via the electoral procedure and within the context of a plurality of choice.

This is the organizing principle which runs counter to tax-paying parliamentarianism and which, even though it was countered by the devotion felt by the Puritans for community consensus, contributed to the English revolution and to Cromwell's Commonwealth. However, it runs up against the other current of the English Reformation, the Anglican, which remained faithful to an episcopal view of the ecclesiastical hierarchy and, above all, to a doctrinal orthodoxy

---

[7] See R. Bendix, *Kings or People* (Berkeley, Calif.: University of California Press, 1978), 292.

elaborated from above. The English élites were perhaps Calvinists in economic matters but were not Puritan in political ones. The monarchist preferences of the Church of England which became the brake that established religion put upon popular movements suited them better. The Church's view was also perfectly compatible with the parliamentary power of the merchants and of the new bourgeois and aristocratic agricultural entrepreneurs. Moreover, the monarchical façade of a weakened state did not undermine the self-government of society whose sole representatives they claimed to be.

According to Samuel P. Huntington 'England had a Puritan revolution without creating a Puritan society', which élitist Calvinism and Anglicanism attempted to marginalize from citizenship. It is true, however, that Huntingdon contrasts the British case with that of America, which 'created a Puritan society without enduring a Puritan revolution'.[8] In reality, the difference is only a relative one. It is true that the architects of the independence of the thirteen British colonies of North America were patricians—and in some cases pro-slavery—who were little inclined to offer themselves to the popular vote and to scrutiny by the majority of the colonials. Their intellectual guide could have been Godwin, for whom universal consensus does not change falsehood into truth, who believed that even partial popular sovereignty would lead society to its ruin, and who advocated giving power to an enlightened élite liberated from the constraints of a representative regime. It is also true that Washington and the 'Virginians' did not succeed in imposing this aristocratic view and had, in part, to bow to the expectations of participation on the part of a people which perceived itself as an elect, and who, strongly influenced by this Puritan belief, achieved within half a century the practice of an active and sustained citizenship for the whole of the population of European origin (more or less from Jackson's presidency, the first non-patrician president, elected in 1832). However, even though this widened consensus saw the suppression of the patrician caste outside its central political sphere, it nevertheless reinforced rather than undermined the immutability of the system. The religious exalting of the community sentiment of an elect led in time to ideological conformism. The condemnation of heterodoxies which were considered anti-American resulted in a latent totalitarianism of which the hostility to communism and socialism is an expression. The Manichaean deism

[8] S. P. Huntington, *American Politics: The Promise of Disharmony* (Cambridge: The Belknap Press, 1981), 153.

resulting from earlier attitudes legitimated the self-perception which enables Americans to see themselves as the role-model for the liberation of other peoples. Such a view allows them to avoid questioning their own situation and the inequality from which they profit or suffer.

An agnostic, like other founding fathers of American democracy, Thomas Jefferson sensed that his own lack of faith in the divinity of Christ, to whom he attributes only 'every *human* excellence',[9] should not hinder him from asserting that God had led this people to establish a new social order which would be revealed to all nations. He must surely have thought that for the masses of Puritan persuasion the politico-religious credo of independence might become 'the substitute for an aristocracy which, although it had itself disappeared, left behind it its ideology'.[10] The terms of the *Confiteor* of American citizenship, still in use in primary schools at the beginning of the twentieth century, symbolized with astonishing clarity the value of order acquired according to this logic by the consensual political postulates of the Puritan tradition:

I believe in the United States of America as a Government of the people, by the people, for the people; whose just powers are derived from the consent of the governed; a democracy in a republic; a sovereign Nation of many sovereign states; a perfect union, one and inseparable; established upon those principles of freedom, equality, justice and humanity for which American patriots sacrificed their lives and fortunes. I therefore believe it is my duty to my country to love it; to support its Constitution; to obey its laws; to respect its flag and, to defend it against all enemies.[11]

Even though it reinforces American democracy, this form of democratic indoctrination nevertheless carries within it the serious problem of encouraging a passive citizenship and the alienation of those who become aware of this phenomenon. The propensity of Americans for electoral abstention is the clearest expression of this passivity, a passivity which right-thinking people see as tacit acquiescence, whereas it could equally be evidence of frustration. Electoral abstention was widespread in the nineteenth century, becoming less so in the politically innovative period between 1930 and 1950. It grew again, however, after this, attaining 37.2 per cent of the

[9] Quoted in W. Berns, 'Religion and the Founding Principle', in R. H. Horwitz (ed.), *The Moral Foundations of the American Republic* (Charlottesville, Va.: University of Virginia Press, 1979), 174.

[10] H. Gourdon, 'Dieu aux États-Unis à propos de Watergate', *Revue française de science politique*, 26/2 (Apr. 1976), 236.

[11] Quoted in Huntington, *American Politics*, p. 159.

electorate in the presidential election of 1960, 45.6 per cent in 1976, and 62 per cent of eligible voters in the elections to the legislature of 1982. Moreover, abstentionism affects the Protestant community more than the Catholic.[12] In fact, the classic idea of, on the one hand, a European Catholic citizenship which is sceptical and conflictual and, on the other, an ordered and civic-minded American-Calvinist citizenship is reversed. 'Americans', writes Michel Crozier, 'seemed in an earlier period, much more capable of generosity than Europeans. However, less inoculated against adversity, the Americans who, in an earlier period, were more naïve drift more easily into cynicism and alienation.'[13]

It is possible that this erosion of the Puritan-inspired tradition of citizenship is related to the discreetly veiled Calvinist political temperament, a temperament imbued with totalitarianism; the integrative aspects of the American credo being its benign illustration. In certain respects, Calvinism was derived from the German-Dutch Anabaptist movement which, in the sixteenth century, awaited the coming of the 'Kingdom of the Millenium', and which fought for civil and political equality, and the abolition of private property. Guided by the prophet Jean de Beukelz, the Anabaptist New Jerusalem, born in Munster, foreshadowed Calvin's Geneva. Although a republic, it instituted, beneath an egalitarian façade, a sacralized totalitarian system which, though based upon majority Calvinist consent, adopted values which were the opposite of the productionist and liberal values identified by Max Weber. Popular rather than centralized, Genevan totalitarianism[14] did not simply survive in the sects which grew out of Anabaptism, such as the Mennonites, it contributed to the Manichaean and generally intolerant state of mind of sectarian movements, including those which derived from Calvinism. Still endemic in the US, the 'witch hunt' is the illustration of a millenarianism which, acceptable as 'an impatient version of the eschatological Christian tradition',[15] is less so when it becomes the oppressor in the name of a monist vision of society, and still less again when the totalitarian seed of Calvinism seems to have encouraged, as in Switzerland in the 1930s, the growth of the Nazi *Neue Front* in the predominantly Protestant

[12] This is also true of Switzerland, where Protestant abstentionism is particularly high in a general context of weak electoral participation.

[13] M. Crozier, *Le Mal américain* (Paris: Fayard, 1980), 205–6.

[14] See B. J. Moore, *Political Power and Modern Society* (New York: Harper & Row, 1969), 30–88.

[15] C. Rangel, *L'Occident et le Tiers Monde* (Paris: Laffont, 1982), 206.

German areas. For Richard Morse, Protestant civilizations have a peculiar ability to bloom in out-of-the-way places.[16] This ability is perhaps related to a para-totalitarian tendency towards a citizenship based upon ostracism, and which is enhanced by a scorn for other forms of political expression.

Whether in its patrician, Puritan, or para-totalitarian form, Calvinism does not account for all the influences which Protestantism has had on Western forms of citizenship. Chronologically, the Lutheran contribution in its original form pre-dates it, and is diametrically opposed to the Calvinist view of the role of the state. As we know, Calvinism is at one here with pure liberalism, in that it anticipates Adam Smith's notion of the 'invisible hand' and society's self-regulation by sole virtue of the forces within it, and without the intervention of a parasitic central political apparatus. This view prevails in both the patrician idea of Parliament as the transparent site of this autonomous self-regulation of interests, and in the Puritan, para-totalitarian idea of society governing itself from within homogeneous, delimited communities where permissiveness is severely constrained. In a completely opposite way to this, Lutheranism leads to a perverse legitimation of the primacy of the state in some of its most oppressive and arbitrary forms.

Nevertheless, Luther's preaching was received as a liberating message by the Saxon peasants who rose against their rulers in the 1520s. Their mistake, however, was soon apparent. Too dangerous to be handed over to the masses, the libertarian content of the Wittenberg theses was to be reserved for the powerful. And with the crushing of the peasants' revolt in 1525, Lutheranism was transformed henceforward into an aristocratic movement which would uphold the quintessentially despotic principle of *cujus regio, ejus religio*, a principle which asserted the right of rulers to impose upon their subjects their own religion, and reinforced their authority by giving them control of this exclusive ideological resource. This claim had been denied them for a time by the extra-territorial, would-be hegemonic power of the Catholic Church. Henceforward the princes could adapt it as they wished: Lutheran in Prussia, Saxony, and Scandinavia, or simply 'established' in the para-Catholic case of the Church of England after its separation from Rome.

This gift to the absolutism of the rulers of 'national ideology-reli-

---

[16] R. M. Morse, 'L'Héritage de l'Amérique latine', in L. Hartz (ed.), *Les Enfants de l'Europe* (Paris: Seuil, 1968), 186.

gions' was not the most influential of Lutheranism's contribution to the omnipotence of the state. Not satisfied with ignoring the hitherto accepted principle of 'Render unto Caesar that which is Caesar's, and to God that which is God's' the Lutheran doctrine effectively freed the holders of power from the need to observe a common religious morality.[17] Already Catholicism perceived power as 'an instrument for the punishment of man'[18] desired by God. Luther went further. For him, power is not simply a form of expiation which people cannot evade, but a morally necessary evil which, because of this, escapes ethical obligation. As the exercise of brute force, it acquires a legitimacy which, though perverse, places it beyond the teachings of the Gospels and Christian natural law.

Doubtless, this free rein conferred, in the name of a supernatural plan, upon shrewd, all-powerful rulers was only an implicit principle and did not everywhere create unlimited tyrannies. We need only contrast the political developments of the Scandinavian countries and Germany. All of these were influenced by the Lutheran culture, but the effect of this influence was not identical. In the case of Germany we can speculate on the interaction of the very pronounced status accorded to power by the Lutheran culture with the long subordination of the German concept of citizenship to authoritarian or totalitarian values. The barrack-state of Frederick-William I, and the strong Bismarckian state, found perhaps their ideal ground in an environment prepared for obedience. Later, the National Socialist paroxysm coincided with the moral pre-conditioning of a part of German society. If a majority of the Germans were not racist in 1930, they nevertheless abstained later from rebelling against the abject anti-Semitism of Nazi rule. This is partly explained by fear but also perhaps by a religious tradition of submission to the sins of their rulers. Whatever was the case, between 1930 and 1933 the Nazi vote was particularly strong in the eastern Lutheran regions of the country, in Pomerania, in Prussia and in Eastern Prussia, in Saxony and in Schleswig,[19] while remaining weak in the Catholic Rhenish–Bavarian areas.

There was, moreover, no contradiction between the Lutheran idea

---

[17] See B. Badie, *Culture et politique* (Paris: Economica, 1983), 123–4.
[18] Polin, *L'Esprit totalitaire*, p. 27.
[19] N. Passchier, 'The Electoral Geography of the Nazi Landslide', in S. U. Larsen, B. Hagtvet, and J. P. Myklebust (eds.), *Who were the Fascists?* (Bergen, Universitetsforlaget, 1980), 283–300.

of expiation through politics and the acceptance of the total state imposed by Hitler. In 1933, the Minister of the Interior, Frick, claimed that, for National Socialists, law was that which served the German people, injustice that which harmed them.[20] Given that the German people had no say in the matter, it might be more accurate to say that a certain politico-religious tradition prepared them to bow to the ignominy that their masters committed in their name.

The widespread conviction that Protestant forms of citizenship were less favourable to the extension of the state is therefore in need of qualification, especially as it is not only Lutheranism which demonstrates this. Without here exhausting the theme of the impact of the Reformation on Western political development, we can say that Protestant societies with a non-Lutheran tradition have revealed themselves to be equally statist. On the one hand, the British Welfare State has offered for decades a strong example of the tutelary status of its citizens *vis-à-vis* state institutions. On the other hand, among the Commonwealth countries of European extraction, it has been shown that state development or lack of it is a function of circumstances rather than of value systems. Faced with the threat of American assimilation, the strongly centralized power in Ottawa responded vigorously, for almost a century, to the expectation of English-speaking Canadians for whom the authority of 'the Crown' was more than folklore. And faced with the threat, very few opposed the unifying diktat represented by the British North America Act of 1867, which nevertheless imposed on the weakest provinces the defensive, protectionist, and statist regime desired by Ontario and (English-speaking) Quebec. In the same way, the Australian state never abandoned the tutelary power, and has turned to it to resolve its problems right up to the present day:

When the American settlers crossed the Appalachians they moved, for a time, beyond the reach of the centres of government back on the coastal plain. They set up their own forms of independent local government ... When the Australians crossed the Great Dividing Range it did not occur to them to provide their own government.[21]

---

[20]   Quoted in the foreword to the 1983 French edition of Hitler's *Mein Kampf* (Paris: Nouvelles éditions latines), 11.

[21]   'Australians under the Skin', *The Economist*, 288 (7301) (6 Aug. 1983), 14. Moreover, state pre-eminence in initiative was also the case in Australia; from 1850 to 1914, 90% of railway tracks were created and run by the state, J. Bogarty, E. Callo, and H. Dieguez, *Argentina y Australia* (Buenos Aires: Instituto T. di Tella, 1979), 57.

Catholicism and Citizenship

Notwithstanding the ambivalence of the effect of Protestantism on the Western concept of citizenship, sociology has, in the religious sphere, by and large held Catholicism responsible for the vast majority of obstacles to the development of democracy. There is no doubt that Catholicism's reactionary character and the political and ideological strategy of the Church as an institution were highly significant. These aspects, however, are sufficiently well known for them to be simply noted here. Thus we can note the struggle waged by the Church against an emerging liberalism at the end of the eighteenth century,[22] and those in southern Europe and Latin America at the beginning of this century.

At first reticent towards absolutism, the Church was later converted to traditionalist legitimism in order better to protect its land owner-ship and other privileges threatened by the secularizing measures of bourgeois liberalism. To this end it drew natural support from its peasant base, which it had recently gained effective control of within the framework of the vigorous Counter-Reformation.[23] The Church was alone in having a personnel which was in a symbiotic relationship with the rural masses and which spoke their language. And given their ill-treatment by the bourgeois architects of centralization and agri-cultural reform, the clergy found themselves even able to guide the peasants, overwhelmed as they were by the commercial and capitalist upheaval in agriculture. The Church thus provided the shepherds and the guerrilla-priests of the *chouannerie*, Spanish Carlism, Portuguese Miguelism, the traditional revolt of the ancient Kingdom of the Two Sicilies annexed by northern Italy, Brazilian Sebastianism, Mexican Christiade, and other anti-bourgeois 'agricultural counter-revolu-tions'. It was only later, however, that the Church was transformed into — to use Gramsci's expression — an 'organic intellectual' of reac-tion for the declining aristocracy and that fraction of the upper bourgeoisie fearful in its turn of the political consequences of liberalism.

This transformation implies that the Church was unable to identify

---

[22] The royalist fraction of the Anglican clergy also resisted the liberals between 1710 and about 1760.

[23] Weber rightly reminds us that for a long time the connotation *paganus* existed within the term 'peasant'. Christianity was, first of all, an urban phenomenon, and the peasant revolts of the Middle Ages were against the established Church. The religious socialization occurred only afterwards, in response to the Lutheran threat in particular, M. Weber, *Economy and Society* (New York: Bedminster Press, 1968), 472.

itself with an established liberalism. Conservative clericalism and anti-clericalism, which in general is no less conservative, were in a recip-rocal relationship in that they were the extreme expressions of the rivalry between Church and state for the control of the rural popula-tion in a decisive phase of the construction of modern national identi-ties. Committed to the land and transnational by virtue of its doctrine and its organizing principle, the Church could only be, initially, the enemy of centralizing states in political as well as linguistic, educa-tional, and ideological matters. In these conditions it was unable to align itself completely with the new dominant élites at the moment when the liberal order and the proletariat clashed. And, as Emile Poulat has noted,[24] this clash involved not two but three parties of which the Church was one.

The Church was for a long time closer to the rich and affluent than to proletarians. It was not, however, the 'organic' intellectual of extreme conservatism, nor the 'ideological apparatus' of the bourgeois state as defined by Gramsci. In Italy the *non expedit*[25] through which the Holy See enjoined Catholics, from 1868 onwards, not to become involved in the political life of the new unified state illustrated the paroxysm of this three-way relationship. And the reserved neutrality of the Spanish episcopate *vis-à-vis* the parliamentary regime between 1875 and 1923, employer-dominated Catholic trade unionism, and the confessional political parties which emerged in Belgium, Germany, Austria, and later in France were less antagonistic expressions of this same relationship. We should remember, however, that none of these was faced with the problem the Italians faced, the annexation of the papal state. This specific situation helps us understand the subsequent establishing of relatively privileged relations between the Church and Fascism which resolved the conflict in the Vatican's favour, and the pro-Fascist leanings of a fraction of the Catholic élite, not only in Italy, but also in France and Belgium during the 1930s.

The notion of a Catholicism beatifying liberal conservatism, though not completely misplaced, is as simplistic as that of the Inquisition and the *autos da fé*. Even though Catholicism often took the side of resistance to certain types of social change and certain more open

[24] E. Poulat, *Église contre bourgeoisie* (Paris: Castermann, 1977), 9, 37.

[25] The *non expedit* not only applied to the occupation of the pontifical states, and then the city of Rome, by Piedmontese troops. It also sanctioned the boycott of elections by the Catholics of Piedmont-Sardinia, after the form of the elections had been changed by the liberals after 1857. The *non expedit* was lifted in 1905 by the bull *Il fermo proposito*, which allowed bishops to authorize voting by Catholics in their dioceses.

expressions of citizenship, it did so always in relation to its own development and via structures and institutions rich with contradictions. Doubtless non-permissive over the longer term, given that it had based its power over a long period upon the community solidarities which served its own spiritual and social power, Catholicism was, and for this very reason, pulled in a multiplicity of directions; towards authoritarianism borne of its suspicion of a new atomized and critical citizenship; towards a certain libertarianism which reflected, sometimes in an unpremeditated way, its long struggle with emerging national states; and towards a political socialization which, focusing on the past and a sense of ideal community, contributed subsequently not only to its resistance to dictators but also to the emergence of certain forms of modern democracy.

In this way, Catholicism's long influence on the orientation and differentiation of types of citizenship and types of Western governments was the result of a strategy elaborated by the Church as early as the twelfth century. The strategy itself, as Otto Hintze points out,[26] was designed to slow down the developing strength of territorial rulers by undermining their claim to religious power, and by controlling their claims to divine blessing. The Church also resurrected to this purpose the millenarian principle of 'render unto God', 'render unto Caesar', which it had itself abused in the Caesaro-papist period. The re-emergence of this principle allowed the ecclesiastical apparatus to recuperate its monopoly of the sacred. However, in the medieval context, the reconquest of the religious domain amounted in practice to complete ideological domination, and to an enormous political influence, given that the essential quality of politics is its legitimation of the sacred status—conferred with good grace by the Church—of rulers.

Conversely, the rulers themselves gained the monopoly of temporal authority. It remained the case, however, that the Church's right of coronation and its overall ideological hegemony meant that this concession was limited. The Church retained the key to legitimacy, and remained the pre-eminent sovereign, first supra-territorial and later supra-national, a situation which, while reaffirming the separation between the religious and the temporal, impeded the re-emergence of a vast unified state in Europe. The primary preoccupation of the papacy was to undermine the hegemonic ambitions of Germanic Holy Roman Emperors who saw themselves as the new Caesars of medieval

[26] O. Hintze, *Historical Essays* (Oxford: Oxford University Press, 1975), 169.

Europe. These emperors wanted the sovereign pontiff as their chaplain, whereas the Roman pontiff's intention was that under no circumstances would a continental political area be created whose ruler would certainly diminish the Pope's power. In the face of such claims, the distinction between the two powers benefited the papacy. Until the end of the eighteenth century, the papacy was able to maintain an invincible barrier not only to the resurgence of any kind of new European empire, but also to the unification of the central area of Christianity of the time, Germany and northern Italy. A corollary to this divide and rule tactic adopted by the Church meant a certain accommodation towards the strengthening of the smaller kingdoms peripheral to the Holy Roman Empire such as France, England, and several other less powerful and less successful kingdoms.

Herein lies the weakness of Catholic policy. Although only of secondary importance at first, this tactic eventually countered the hegemonic designs of the Church. In spite of its success *vis-à-vis* the Empire, such an approach had long-term consequences for the Church which undermined its domination by encouraging the emergence of the first secular states. The benevolence which the papacy displayed towards France or England did not only lead, in these countries, to the early development of a quasi-national identity which the kings supported because of the religious powers' tolerance of it. In a more decisive way, this particular approach to Europe's peripheral kingdoms involved the Church in establishing the legitimacy and the dynamics of the modern state. As Bertrand Badie and Pierre Birnbaum have noted, 'The secular, legal, bureaucratic state is the product of the fundamental dissociation within Catholic culture between the temporal and the spiritual'.[27]

These rulers, at first of little threat to the Church, were to reinterpret the doctrine of the two powers to their advantage by inverting its meaning. In fact, the monopoly of the temporal, conceded to the rulers of emerging states, increased their overall legitimacy. In England and France in particular, the Pope lost the contest each time he attempted to subject the kings to his authority. Via the religious apparatus, these rulers cut themselves off from Rome, and acquired in practice an autonomous authority which soon became pre-eminent. More generally, this authority and pre-eminence became that of the state itself in both its material and abstract sense. Henry VIII of England was able very rapidly to send the Church off to its prayers

[27] B. Badie and P. Birnbaum, *Sociologie de l'État* (Paris: Grasset, 1979), 164.

when it attempted to treat the king once again as a vassal. Similarly, even though the strengthening of royal power remained compatible in France with the proffering of ritual respect to the illustrious Pope and to Catholic doctrine, the result was an even greater consolidation than in England of a powerful state governing the nation. This situation prevailed until 1789 when the pontifical cord was cut completely as it had been, though in a different way, in England two centuries earlier.

French kings used this two-century period to achieve the consolidation of the absolutist state, a development England was unable to achieve because of the parliamentary revolution of 1688. Moreover, this achievement was concomitant with an uneven separation between political power and the subordinated interests of private individuals. It is not enough to say, with Otto Hintze, that by absorbing 'the magical and the sacral' the Church freed Western societies from the constraints which 'stood in the way of the rationalisation and intensification of economic and social activity'.[28] What should also be noted is the way this phenomenon — associated with the rise of capitalism in Protestant countries — enabled the state to 'impose itself in Catholic societies not as the extreme example of a universal logic of differentiation, but as a specific form of this, which, while attempting to disconnect in a radical way the temporal from the spiritual, the civil from the political, overvalued the latter, conferring upon it an autonomous and sovereign legitimacy'.[29]

In England, the Reformation and the political revolution of the seventeenth century ended this uneven distinction between the public and the private. In an opposite way, the French Revolution enhanced the distinction further by conferring democratic integrity upon it and creating a model for the rationalism of the modern state whose origin was based upon the religious distinction between the sacred and the profane. This inversion legitimated, first in France and then in most of continental Europe, the recognition of the autonomous authority of the state *vis-à-vis* society. Moreover, this autonomy in fact masked the subordination of the private to the public, inscribing it in law according to an opposite hierarchy to that of Calvinism.

Thus we return to the Weberian point of departure: the vertical and hierarchical organization both of the political sphere and of citizenship in Catholic countries as opposed to their horizontal and less authoritarian, if not more democratic, characteristics in the countries

[28] Hintze, *Historical Essays*, p. 431.
[29] Badie and Birnbaum, *Sociologie de l'État*, p. 164.

influenced by Calvinism. In this way, the distant origins of Jacobin centralism lie in the confounded political strategy of the twelfth-century Church. Also in this way, Prussian respect for the state is itself derived from an extreme Lutheran form of this strategy.

Even though Catholicism was the initial channel of the authoritarian principle of statist centralization and an obstacle to the emergence of democratic citizenship in southern and central Europe and in Latin America, it nevertheless played a part in the development and extension of representative government. In the first place, an understanding of the link between the 'Catholic factor' and the complex process of the development of the Western state should not obscure its democratic effects in terms of the secularization of attitudes. The impetus given by the Church to the legitimacy of the state cannot be understood only as an assertion of the state's supremacy. The strength of the modern state is drawn above all from its secularized nature, which offered a legitimacy other than those of divine blessing or Protestant reference to divine will. Conversely, it had to establish itself as the directing agency of society by means of an intellectual claim separated from religious faith, involving explicit consent obtained from its citizens at one time or another. Such consent can be measured initially in a very restricted sense, in terms of an exclusive constituency as well as by its plebiscitary dimension, even though the end result is almost necessarily universal suffrage, to which Catholic societies are more exposed than societies with a Calvinist tradition whose elect are of divine nomination. Moreover, the rationalism which grew out of Catholicism created a political domain which tended to become more profoundly secularized and diversified than its Protestant counterpart which was underpinned by the idea of a consensus on certain fundamental values. In order to establish its legitimacy, the Protestant political domain had to function in a way which was acceptable to the totality of the community. Catholicism is not subject to this exigency, tolerating, encouraging even, the development of a political domain which is almost totally secularized and fragmented into a multiplicity of ideological areas free from cohesive constraints.

For Lipset,[30] the narrowness of political and partisan choices in Protestant societies is modified to a certain extent by the proliferation of religious sects. Schematizing this argument, we can say that societies with a Catholic tradition had the opposite experience. Until relatively recently, the religious divide was only apparent in the two inter-

[30] S. M. Lipset, *Political Man* (Garden City, NY: Doubleday, 1963), 97–9.

dependent areas of clericalism and anti-clericalism, whereas political cleavages multiplied with no limits other than those of the spirit of the age and the state of social relations. They superimposed themselves upon one another without eradicating each other, creating a kind of disordered proliferation which in fact represented the inexhaustible reserves of a certain form of free-will citizenship. In Stein Rokkan's view,[31] this 'Catholic' form of antagonistic citizenship is a variation on the community identity shaped at an early stage by reformed national religions in Protestant areas. According to Rokkan, it is one of the co-determinants of the conflictual mode of the political game in the countries in which it dominates, notably via the exalting of the class struggle and the creation of strong communist parties which take on the role of a counter-state. Perhaps it would be more exact to argue that the sacralization of the community spirit, a feature of the Protestant milieu, inhibits freedom up to a certain point by repressing the critical expression of citizenship, whereas the majesty of the state in the Catholic milieu is not sufficient to make it sacred or untouchable. In the latter case, if the autonomous object which the state has become maintains its pre-eminence, this does not constitute an inherent underlying superiority which would protect it from becoming itself one of the stakes in political debate and struggle. Whereas the 'American Way' or 'English-style politics' represent value systems which are presented as intangible, in Catholic countries, the state is a site to be conquered, that is to say, it is the objective of the political game itself.

The democratic result of such developments is ambivalent. On the one hand, the 'Catholic' demythification of the principle of supreme authority makes citizenship both freer and more rational. On the other hand, the fact that political action becomes centred upon the conquest of the state means that parties and ideologies are defined by this single aim. Struggle for control of the state shapes the whole political system, including the working-class movement which—in the Catholic Latin countries—develops in relation to it. This is so even when it is a question of negating the state (as in the case of the anarcho-syndicalist movement) as well as when it is a question of appropriating it (as in the case of Marxist trade unions).[32] In this way, citizenship is trapped in one single perspective: that of the exercise, by a majority will, of an

---

[31] See, in particular, S. Rokkan, 'Dimensions of State-Formation and Nation Building', in C. Tilly (ed.), *The Formation of National States in Europe* (Princeton, NJ: Princeton University Press, 1975), 562–600.

[32] See P. Birnbaum, *La Logique de l'État* (Paris: Fayard, 1981), 13–17.

uncompromising authority, which can only be fulfilled through the monopolizing of state power.

However, the influence of Catholicism on Western forms of citizenship cannot be reduced to the question of its relations with the state. First of all, the unintentional support which the Church gave to the emergence of the modern state did not destroy its older and manifest anti-statist prejudice. It was in order to oppose strong central power that it renewed, in the Middle Ages, elective and representative procedures forgotten since antiquity. As early as the sixth century, religious orders elected their leaders, inventing, as Léo Moulin has shown, several of the antecedents of many present-day voting systems. Moreover, the election of the Pope by the cardinals became the model for the election by the aristocracy of certain rulers until the eighteenth century. The tradition of the assemblies of the *ancien régime*, which was even more widely used, also came from Catholicism, and was transmitted to the Protestant world. It is true that assemblies such as the Estates General, the Cortes, the Diet, and the House of Lords or Commons have part of their origin in ancient Germanic practice. However, the Church reactivated these at the same time as it was emphasizing the distinction between the temporal and spiritual spheres. And this with the sole aim of limiting the power of emerging states. Widespread in Western Christianity, this embryonic representative form remained unknown in Russia and in the regions of Orthodox Christianity, and *a fortiori* in Islamic and Asiatic countries. Even though the absolutist reaction of the sixteenth and seventeenth centuries brought an end to this advance almost everywhere, it was the direct source of British parliamentarianism, whose two Houses were renewed after 1688, thanks to the adoption of the tax-paying restriction.

Catholicism contributed at least in two other ways, the second being of particular significance to the emergence of modern citizenship. The first, whose consequences are difficult to appraise, probably derives from the different orientations of the Protestant and Catholic forms of preaching in the course of the two centuries following the Reformation and Counter-Reformation. It is worth noting in this respect the relative obscurantism ascribed to a Protestantism considered too tied to a literal and somewhat totalitarian reading of the Bible. Jean Delumeau[33] suggests that its opposite was the, equally relative, rationalism of Catholic Counter-Reformation preaching. On the one hand,

[33] J. Delumeau, *La Peur en Occident* (Paris: Fayard, 1978).

the Catholic sermon — and its Jesuitic prototype in particular — tended to confine religious discourse to the abstract domain of a formalist representation of the Beyond, or else to the concrete and itemized domain of the temporal administration of the sacred and the moral. In this way, it lent support to the elimination of former connections of the religious to the political, and participated in the secularization process by confining the sacred in impressive but inaccessible clouds; contributed, in a word, to the secularization of the political. On the other hand, Protestant sectarian preaching mixed the spiritual and temporal registers in the millenarian vision of the reign of God in a sublimated terrestrial society. This mixing of registers later encouraged an intolerance which echoed the holocaust of the witches of Salem; the execution, for example, of Sacco and Vanzetti.

More convincing still are the arguments related to the Catholic contribution to the processes of political socialization of certain milieux. It is true that the multiplicity of explicit and implicit forms of the *non expedit* had effects and contributed to a fraction of the Catholic community refusing for a time any involvement in the circuits of democratic participation. The *non expedit* did not, however, apply in all circumstances and only lasted several decades. It coexisted, moreover, with other formative factors within Catholicism influencing citizenship, the most disparaged example being that of clientelist mobilization. In the peasant societies of southern Europe and Latin America, the caciques and other political patrons held, in some cases until the very recent period, a legitimacy often adorned with the seal of religious sacredness. 'You know very well that each person leans upon his master', wrote St Augustine in order to assimilate the ascendancy of the nobility of his time with that of Christ, the master of mankind. Clientelism, the cement of social relations in the Roman world, and transferred subsequently to the feudal system, continued to enjoy in the nineteenth and twentieth centuries a legitimacy derived from religious faith. In other words, clientelism possessed a cultural base which went beyond the illiteracy and isolation of the peasants, transcending this context by virtue, in particular, of the personal relations which sublimated it in the name of Christian values. Patronage, in particular, meant that the master became, in both the Christian and superstitious sense of the term, the honoured guardian of the children of those of his clients he became especially attached to. In Spanish-speaking countries, this widespread custom is known by the term *compadrazzo*. But it existed also in Sicily, Sardinia, in southern Italy, and in Malta, where the word—*qaddis*—means both saint and master. In this way, the master is not only the strongest person, but can be, in the biblical sense of the metaphor, the respected guardian of the clientelist flock, he through whom the gregarious vote is drained of the sins of fraud and complicity, and this all the more in that such legitimate authority was supported by the clergy itself.

Of course this mode of deferent and servile political socialization has generally been evaluated in a negative way. However, this view is only valid in reality if clientelist servitude exists to the point where the electoral act is itself discredited in the eyes of those constrained to exercise it for too long under tutelage. On the other hand, we should remember that it was networks of patronage which facilitated the masses' apprenticeship of universal suffrage (on the condition that these networks did not continue to exist to the point of impeding the development of voting behaviour of an individualist and apparently more autonomous type). At the dawn of universal suffrage, a self-conscious citizenship was almost entirely absent within peasant populations. Clientelism represented, therefore, the most 'propitious' initial framework for the mobilizing of electors who otherwise would have remained, possibly permanently, abstentionist. In this context, the religious legitimacy of agrarian clientelism had a positive side which Bossism in Anglo-Saxon countries replaced with corruption pure and simple.

In certain countries, moreover, through the intermediary of confessional political parties, Catholicism has participated in an even more positive way in the democratic involvement of its believers. In the multi-confessional societies such as those of Holland or Germany, political parties of Catholic origin allowed marginal citizens to acquire their own political identity·and call for the creation of a more egalitarian democracy. The German *Zentrum* even converted itself into the organizational expression not only of Catholic minorities but of ethnic minorities too, thereby facilitating their entry into political life.[34] For its part, the Dutch Catholic party became, in alliance with conservative Calvinists, the architect of the first real alternation of power in the country, in 1901, after the universalization of the suffrage. Moreover, the confessional parties lent respectability to the electoral and parliamentary game in Catholic countries, particularly in Austria, Belgium, Italy, and Switzerland, but also, to a lesser degree, in France where the Popular Republicans (MRP) achieved, after 1945,

---

[34] In particular, Polish, Hanoverian, Alsatian, and Lorraine minorities.

the political liberation of the Catholic areas of the west, east, and north which had been until this point subject to a kind of mental block *vis-à-vis* the republican principle. As late as 1960, moreover, the confessional parties channelled the political expression of approximately one-third of the electorate in the countries of continental Europe.

TABLE 6.1. *Percentage of the vote for 'Catholic' parties around 1960*

Country	% Sunday church attendance around 1960	% of votes for 'Catholic parties'
Austria	36	44 (1959)
Belgium	48	41 (1961)
France	23	12 (1958)
Holland	32	32 (1959)
Italy	43	42 (1958)
Switzerland	21	23 (1959)
West Germany	23	45 (1961)

Source: J.-H. Whyte, *Catholics in Western Democracies* (New York: Saint Martin's Press, 1981), 93.

Without the confessional parties, electoral mobilization would probably have been slower in several countries, especially in terms of the female vote and women's access to citizenship. Without them also, hundreds of thousands of activists trained in secular associations would have been unable, after 1945, to renew the personnel and style of the political parties and the trade unions. Finally, without them, a number of the democracies formed after the War would not have been able to regain their equilibrium as quickly as they did, as in, for example, Italy and Germany but also in Venezuela and Ecuador. Moreover, these new political cadres had already shown themselves, along with the communists, as the best equipped to resist Fascist or military dictatorships. And this because the solid structure of the Catholic Church offered them both a refuge and a framework for their action which did not exist in regimes which excluded all forms of independent partisan organization.

In conclusion to this brief and provisional inventory of the influence of religion upon the development of the Western citizen-individual, one must confess that the profusion of routes of enquiry and the wealth of potential hypotheses also reveal their fragility. Too many questions remain unaddressed, in particular, an exhaustive study of the religious dimension of authoritarianism in Europe and Latin

America.[35] Equally important is the role played by local religious apparatuses, Catholic in particular, in the preservation of regional and subregional identities, which is one of the keys to an understanding of contemporary national identities. Or, again, there is the question of how properly to structure analysis of the rather flippantly addressed issue of Catholicism and the great communist concentrations, and which is contradicted by many neglected cases: first that of eastern Germany before 1933 or after the War; later that of Protestant Finland and Iceland; or the extreme Calvinist canton of Geneva which became, in 1945, the bastion of Swiss communism. We should also remember the enigma of the religious connection to modern revolutionary currents which, according to Jean Jaurès—in the case of Lutheranism—, nourished German socialism and pacifism, and which—in the case of Catholicism as Le Play suggests in his diary—influenced the spirit of French anarchism.

Moreover, the political expression of minority religions should be examined more closely: firstly European and American Judaism, but also Latin Protestantism which, for example, concedes to the state the role of pre-eminent arbiter which Anglo-Saxon Protestantism denies it.[36] The addressing of these questions would improve our understanding of these unexplored areas. Yet the old question remains: that of identifying in Western citizenship what is derived from the religious and what from values exterior to it.

[35] See G. Hermet, 'Les Fonctions politiques des organisations religieuses dans les régimes à pluralisme limité', *Revue française de science politique*, 23/3 (June 1973), 439–72.

[36] In France particularly, Judaism like early Protestantism was centralizing and Jacobin in nature. This is perhaps because it was the Revolutionary and, later, Napoleonic state which conferred full citizenship on these minorities.

7

Individualism and Citizenship

JEAN LECA

Michel Foucault made the following distinction between three accepted meanings of the term 'individualism':

(1) the individualistic attitude, characterised by the absolute value attributed to the individual in his singularity and by the degree of independence conceded to him vis-à-vis the group to which he belongs and the institutions to which he is answerable; (2) the positive valuation of private life, that is, the importance granted to family relationships, to the form of domestic activity, and to the domain of patrimonial interests; (3) the intensity of the relations to self, that is, of the forms in which one is called upon to take oneself as an object of knowledge and a field of action, so as to transform, correct, and purify oneself, and find salvation.[1]

It is the first meaning involving the problem of political rights and obligations and the individual as citizen which is the subject of the present chapter. The other two meanings will be referred to only in so much as they illustrate the first.

We shall not dwell for the moment on the status and attributes of this catch-all word 'individualism' of which Max Weber remarked that it covered 'the most heterogeneous things imaginable'.[2] We shall accept Foucault's definition with some modifications. Individualism cannot be properly understood, without proper qualification, as being restricted to those Western societies which resulted from the Reformation, the Renaissance, the Enlightenment, and capitalism. It is true to say, however, that it was within the material and cultural configuration which took place in these societies that the dual question of sociological individualism and state legitimation arose.[3] This configuration is

---

[1] M. Foucault, *The Care of the Self*, iii: *The History of Sexuality* (New York: Pantheon, 1986), 42.

[2] M. Weber, *The Protestant Ethic and the Spirit of Capitalism* (London: Unwin, 1967), 222.

[3] We shall take sociological individualism to mean here an attribute of the object studied, the practices, norms, and systematized general conceptualizations

doubtless less systematic, unitary, and coherent than a cursory reading of Louis Dumont's research would suggest. Dumont, moreover, is more concerned with 'predominant ideas' than with social practices, and he is at pains to point out the variations within both.[4] Having said this, we should note his cardinal distinction between two great 'apperceptions': 'holism', which 'valorizes the social totality and neglects or subordinates the human individual', and 'individualism', which 'valorizes the individual as a moral being, independent and autonomous, and essentially non-social[5] and thus neglects or subordinates social reality'. This individual, non-social in principle, is social in practice: he lives in society, 'in the world', as distinct from the renouncing Indian who becomes an individual by leaving society as such. 'Holism' is linked to the notion of 'hierarchy', an opposition between the whole and an element of the whole, difference within sameness, and the subsuming of opposites. It is also linked to 'value-ideas', that is, ideas which are inseparable from values. 'Individualism' is related, on the one hand, to the idea of 'conflict' between equal and opposed parts which cannot be reduced a priori to an overall unity and, on the other, to the segregation of values from ideas.[6]

This brings us on to the classical problem of contemporary political theory, that of the transition from the individual to the citizen. The problem is linked to the question of 'how a sociopolitical order which is based on its acceptance by individuals and is continuously judged by

('Individualist theories'), or diffuse cultures (*Zeitgeist*), which also incorporate political individualism. Only rarely will we refer to methodological individualism as an attribute of the approach of the researcher. We are not as convinced as Raymond Boudon and François Bourricaud that 'methodological individualism and individualism itself have the same relationship as the Dog Star constellation to the dog barking down the street, that is, no relationship at all' (*Dictionnaire critique de la sociologie* (Paris: PUF, 1st edn. 1982). See 'Individualism', p. 289). There probably is a connection between methodological individualism as a method, and sociological individualism as a climate favourable to this method, even though the favourable climate does not preclude approaches other than methodological individualism. However, methodological individualism is in a more natural affinity to certain aspects of sociological individualism, and it is at least plausible that they belong to the same world view (cf. Steven Lukes, *Individualism* (Oxford: Blackwell, 1974), 141).

[4] L. Dumont, *Essais sur l'individualisme: Une perspective anthropologique sur l'idéologie moderne* (Paris: Seuil, 1983), 68.

[5] We would rather say: an individual-subject who is in a relationship of distance to his social roles (to which he cannot be *reduced*, hence the concept 'role'), and between which he can consciously choose on the basis of his interests and opinions, and under constraints which are 'exterior' to him.

[6] Dumont, *Essais sur l'individualisme*, pp. 264–5 ff., and in particular, on value, pp. 222–63.

them is possible at all'.[7] Three questions result from this: (1) What is the basis of political obligation and what are its limits? (And what causes individuals to participate in public life in a 'civic' way and in the public interest?) (2) How is the extension of citizenship to be understood? The means of access of individuals to the status of citizen creates different types of political community (of owners, taxpayers, nationals, members of ethnic or religious groups, territorial residents whatever their nationality).[8] (3) How is citizenship to be understood? The nature and significance of rights and obligations linked to such status can vary considerably.[9] Does, for example, belonging to a particular religion allow an individual exemption from certain legal obligations such as military service?[10] Does belonging to an ethnic group justify a differential application of criminal law? Do the rights of the citizen and, more widely, of 'man' involve the right to reproduce?[11] Individualism is at the centre of each of these questions.

The question of political obligation is clearly the one which has

---

[7] S. N. Eisenstadt, 'The Basic Characteristics of Political Modernisation', in S. N. Eisenstadt (ed.), *Political Sociology* (New York: Basic Books, 1971), 339.

[8] This was the theme of a debate 'Citizenship without nationality', on immigrant groups in France. I have tried to offer an explanation of this claim in 'Questions sur la citoyenneté', *Projet* (1983), 171–2.

[9] T. H. Marshall's classic essay analyses the sequence of the extension of the rights of the citizen, from civil to political and then to social rights, T. H. Marshall, 'Citizenship and Social Class', in *Class, Citizenship and Social Development* (Chicago, Ill.: University of Chicago Press, 1977; 1st edn. 1963), 72–134.

[10] The study of legal decisions in the United States shows the progressive change in the status of religion, from the basis of the citizenship community, and the obligations which go with it, to the justification of the individual rights of members of 'religious minorities to receive the same treatment as members of the majority', if not to benefit from a 'privilege' (a private law which differs from the established rule in secular matters), on condition that their practices do not constitute a clear and real threat to law and order; John Burkholder, 'The Law knows no Heresy: Marginal Religious Movements and the Courts'; Leo Pfeffer, 'The Legitimation of Marginal Religions in the United States', in M. Leone and I. Zaretsky (eds.), *Religious Movements in Contemporary American Society* (Princeton, NJ: Princeton University Press, 1974).

[11] 20 Mar. 1985, before the Council of Europe in the context of the European conference on Human Rights, the French Minister of Justice declared that 'the right of all human beings to give life' implies 'freedom to choose the means by which life is given', which logically implies the availability of *in vitro* fertilization techniques for all human beings (at least females), married or single, living alone or as a couple, free and able to choose. One is not surprised to find in the Jesuit review *Études* one of the rare critiques of the 'individualist philosophy' of the sovereign individual, which grants absolute primacy to 'individual preferences over the *social good*, and particularly that of *children*', P. Verspieren, 'Un droit à l'enfant?', *Études* (May 1985), 623–8. The growing deregulation of interpersonal relations and the apparent growing regulation in the economic regulations of labour, referred to among others by Daniel Bell, is one of the interesting sociological puzzles of our time.

generated the most discussion in political theory, given that it is seen as a prerequisite to the two others, and involves more serious and wide-ranging issues. Political obligation even has a significance for those passive citizens who still do not possess the political franchise. In fact, the three questions are related not only in political philosophy terms but in political sociology terms. The way in which the community of citizens and the rights attached to it are conceptualized has effects upon the question of obligation *vis-à-vis* government and its legitimation. These conceptualizations are not dependent upon the (good) will of legislators and other political actors, but are themselves socially and politically produced. The issues raised, therefore, are not only ones of logic or normative theory, they depend upon the way in which disposable cognitive capital is constituted in a society. In this way, they are open to empirical investigation. Before analysing them more closely, we need to make several additional observations on the concept of citizenship, with which French political science in particular is relatively unfamiliar.[12]

The Construction of the Concept of Citizenship

The principal difficulty raised in any discussion of 'citizenship' proceeds from the lack of precision attached to the term, from the variety of spatial and operational dimensions ascribed to it (e.g. family, workplace, local community, or world citizenship), and from the empirical situations it refers to (its juridical status, which defines rights and obligations which themselves are very diverse, the private and the public, the totality of specified roles, attitudinal and behavioural traits). The difficulty stems above all from the status of the concept itself, which is always suspected of implying both a reality and a desired ideal: to speak of citizenship implies both the theoretician and the social reformer, the admonition of those who stray from the model, and the suggestion of types of education, punishment, and sanctions which should be applied to them. It is true that this

---

[12] Georges Burdeau is an exception here, and one whose distinction between the 'citizen' and the 'person in situation' (*l'homme situé*) is central to his theory of democracy. In thirty years, only two works have been directly concerned with civic attitudes: J. W. Lapierre and G. Noizet, *Recherche sur le civisme à la fin de la IVe République* (Gap: Ophrys, 1961); M. Grawitz, *Élèves et enseignants face à l'instruction civique* (Paris: Bordas, 1980).

approach exists,[13] and is no more scandalous than the approach of critical sociology which is placed, sometimes wrongly, in a different ideological camp. These are not the only possible approaches. We do not subscribe to the view that only jurists can speak empirically of citizenship and make an inventory of the attributes of the citizen as they are formally described by law or constructed by jurisprudence, or philosophers elaborate logically and normatively on what people should do if they wish to be reasonable, leaving to political science only the study of the more or less well-founded illusions that people make for themselves when they speak of citizenship. If there is a 'citizenship for itself', there is also a 'citizenship in itself'. The identification of these categories of analysis of the socio-political world (and of course of its representations) is no more, no less, difficult than those such as 'class affiliation', 'partisan identity', or 'ethnicity' which are usually taken as understood.

Arthur Stinchcombe defines the citizenship of a person in the normative system of a group as the proportion of his problems in life which are resolved on the basis of this normative system.[14] In other words, the citizenship of a person is the degree to which he can control his own destiny within the group. It is the degree to which a person is subject to the group multiplied by the degree of influence or representation which that person has in the government of the group. In spite of appearances, the public and political dimension of citizenship as a phenomenon with a particular status and role *vis-à-vis* an overall community — in Durkheim's terms — has not been forgotten: the degree of subjection to the group depends, in fact, on the degree to which the group possesses institutions to resolve the group's problems (its 'institutional completeness'), multiplied by the degree to which a person experiences these problems. Institutional completeness is precisely that which gives the group its overall 'political' dimension, and is the product of three factors: the 'aggregate ecological range' of a group of people, the 'ecological range' of the institutions of the group, and the number of areas regulated by the institutions of the group.[15]

---

[13]   e.g. Robert E. Lane, 'Good Citizenship: The Pursuit of Self-Interest', in *Political Man* (New York: Free Press, 1972), 299–318; Richard Sennet, *The Fall of Public Man* (New York: Knopf, 1977).

[14]   Arthur Stinchcombe, 'Social Structure and Politics', in Fred Greenstein and Nelson Polsby (eds.), *Handbook of Political Science*, ii: *Macropolitical Theory* (New York: Addison-Wesley, 1975), 602.

[15]   Ibid. 605, see also p. 602.

Stinchcombe's depiction poses certain difficulties which we shall just mention here. It gives to citizenship a purely instrumental (contractualist) dimension dependent upon the self-interest of the political actor. This is uncontentious if self-interest does not have any specific connotation attached to it, whether individualist or utilitarian; 'solving problems' does not mean solving them in terms of market individualism. What is more contentious is the idea of civic loyalty as a product of citizenship,[16] as a potential 'output'. The private dimension seems here to be overstressed, the 'loyal citizen' becoming synonymous with the 'trusted client'.

Overall, however, Stinchcombe's view is strikingly similar to the fundamentals of classical citizenship. It is, nevertheless, described differently, the merit of this being its ability to distinguish the concept from the various traits drawn from different cultural codes and to do so with different emphases according to different societies. What remain are the fundamental cultural traits without which the concept itself disappears.

The participation–subjection relation

The first characteristic is the liaison between participation in 'government' and subjection to it (the duality 'subject-influence or representation'). The Aristotelian citizen is defined, over and above the exercise of the military function, by the ability to exercise the two functions of magistrate in the legal order and member of deliberative assemblies, functions which the citizen is called upon to exercise either by election or lot, and these either continuously or for a limited period. All citizens have this right. Participation (*methexis*) is, therefore, the pre-condition of the political community. Of course, the Greek city had no 'sovereign people', and probably not even the concept of sovereignty, even less that of representation. All writers agree on this and rightly place great emphasis upon it.[17]

In the city-state the community, like the individual, is defined and is based upon a prerequisite philosophical order which is both legal and

---

[16] According to Stinchcombe, the loyalty of a person *vis-à-vis* the group depends upon the degree to which the person can control his own destiny through this action in the group, that is to say, by his degree of citizenship in the group, ibid. 605.

[17] See also Lucien Bescond, 'Remarques sur la conception aristotélicienne de la citoyenneté', and Jean-Paul Dumont, 'Le Citoyen-roi dans la République de Zenon', in *Cahiers de philosophie politique et juridique de l'Université de Caen*, 4 (1983). Jean Baechler sums up the generally shared view: 'For the Ancients, the citizen was a part of a whole, for the Moderns, he is a whole who incorporates himself into a super-ordered whole', *Démocraties* (Paris: Calmann-Lévy, 1985), 402.

physical. For Zeno, citizenship is the prerogative of the sage, who is capable of autonomous conduct, that is to say, able to interiorize universal law. Of course, 'no man is a slave by nature', as Philo reminds us, but we can say that there have been many fools and many slaves, whether by law or by accident.[18] This view bears little relation to the *Second Treatise on Civil Government* (and the notion of trust), even less to universal suffrage and to democracy without *telos*. There is, however, a common core in the Aristotelian idea that citizens share civil life, are by turns rulers and ruled, and have a legally guaranteed role in the creation and conduct of government (whether or not such 'government' is efficient or influences in a real way the concrete existence of individuals — and which individuals, and how it influences them, is another question). Citizenship is not a universal attribute of social life but a specific form of the division of political labour borne of the incorporation of the lower classes into political activity (irrespective of the constitutive principles of social stratification and the ways in which these classes are identified).[19] Citizenship does not exist when the separation between governors and subjects is total and permanent. As Morris Janowitz points out: 'By definition citizenship rests on a balance or rather, on an interaction of obligation and rights. Citizenship is a pattern and a rough balance between rights and obligations in order to make possible the shared process of ruling and being ruled.'[20]

'Non-citizenship' is not simply a 'corruption' of or a deviation from citizenship. Such a view would imply that citizenship was the only

[18] On the relationship of this to nominalism, and on the concept of the king-citizen as an analogical concept deduced from the cosmic order, see Jean-Paul Dumont's remarks, 'Le Citoyen-roi', pp. 42–5.

[19] Moses I. Finley, *Politics in the Ancient World* (Cambridge: Cambridge University Press, 1983).

[20] Morris Janowitz, 'Observations on the Sociology of Citizenship: Obligations and Rights', *Social Forces*, 59/1 (1980), 3. The conditions necessary to establishing this equilibrium are, of course, variable, if not fundamentally incompatible. Does recognizing and supporting an obligation of itself allow for the exercising of rights ('no representation without taxation', as it were), or does the exercising of rights create a sense of obligation? Stinchcombe, by making loyalism dependent upon the power of control, places himself in John Stuart Mill's camp. For the latter, to entrust political rights (the right to vote, for example) to the popular classes reinforces active citizenship, and thus a sense of obligation, by allowing the worker to transcend the limited horizon of the workplace, and enter into relations with citizens other than those he is in daily contact with, and makes of him a conscious member of a community. It is a way of cultivating public-spiritedness, political intelligence, and a sense of personal responsibility; John Stuart Mill, *Three Essays: On Liberty, Representative Government, the Subjection of Women*, ed. Richard Wollheim (London: Oxford University Press, 1975).

reasonable and rational form of social life and of government. The various forms of 'traditional' domination in the Arab world over a long period illustrate this point. The tribal leadership of Ibn Khaldun is, in certain respects, the abstract negation of citizenship: only those who do not themselves accept domination can dominate; only those who have an *esprit de corps* (*açabiya*) strong enough to withstand all subjugation can legitimately subjugate others. Domination is therefore based upon the refusal to be dominated. When the tribe, strong in its *esprit de corps*, and emboldened by the mission (*dawa*) it carries within it, takes control of the city, the seat of 'civilization', government is based upon the tribal connection, and is separate from urban society, the 'beneficiary' of government.[21]

In the patrimonial Ottoman model, an exemplary illustration of an imperial system, the dynasty creates an administrative élite whose members are individually recruited from among the slaves, the non-Muslims, or from members of the lower classes who are brought to and brought up in the palace.[22] It is a question, not of the government of citizens called upon to participate, but of subjects whose due is the justice expressed by the 'circle of equity': he who governs would have no power without soldiers, no soldiers without money, no money without the well-being of his subjects, and no subjects without justice.[23]

The citizenship membership–social membership distinction

The distinction between citizenship membership and membership of the social groups to which one belongs because of the prescribed rules they impose (and which are with greater or lesser difficulty internalized) is the second characteristic of citizenship. Such citizenship constitutes 'civil society'[24] as distinct from family, lineage, or seigneurial communities, and refers to a different 'ecological range',

[21]   Cf. E. Gellner, *Muslim Society* (London, Cambridge: Cambridge University Press, 1981). The fact that the tribe does not possess the concept of citizenship does not stop it from being often more egalitarian than the city. Citizenship and social equality are two completely distinct concepts. From a certain point of view, citizenship only has meaning as the weapon of the poor against the rich, or as the latter's means of obtaining the acquiescence of the former.

[22]   Gellner, *Muslim Society*, p. 73. See also Bernard Lewis, *The Emergence of Modern Turkey* (Oxford: Oxford University Press, 1968).

[23]   Norman Itzkowitz, *Ottoman Empire and Islamic Tradition* (New York: Knopf, 1972), 46 and 88.

[24]   'Civil society' in the sense given to it by the theoreticians of the social contract (Hobbes and Locke), that is to say, 'political' society subject to law.

which is characterized by aspiration to institutional completeness. The Weberian analysis of the Western medieval city offers an illustration whose sociological relevance remains as true as ever.[25] The essential quality of the medieval city was its associational form (*Verband-scharakter*), that is, its 'corporate' structure to which the individual was allied (sometimes by oath) over and above his allegiance to his professional corporation, guild, or tribe. The town-dweller had a special citizen status from the moment the city became a 'commune', and where an association (a juridical entity) representing the commune of burghers existed, and which was different from associations endowed with the power to address the specific problems of their members.

The essential characteristic of the Western city is not the combination of a market, a fortress, and a system of land law, as distinct from law relating to agricultural land, but a system of law for the people themselves and which forms them into a group with a juridically autonomous status. All towns were made up of immigrants who came from a statutorily rigid rural system. The medieval city, and herein lies its 'revolutionary' originality, undertook a conscious statutory policy in order to break down the relations prescribed by seigneurial law. *Stadtluft macht frei*, 'the town air makes us free': through this central and northern European saying, the master of a slave or a serf lost the right to reclaim him after a certain period of time. New sets of laws were formed creating a new social stratification which, different from non-urban stratification, maintained the specificity of the town as a political unit.

Weber notes also the weakness of religious ties related to lineage, clan, or caste. Ritual exclusivism, however, did not stop the establishment of cities as religious communities of 'individual' burghers (heads of household), which made of them 'secular foundations', even though a shared religion was still the necessary condition of citizenship.[26] The economic interest of the burghers in making the city an institution-alized association (*anstaltsmäßige Vergesellschaftung*) which was autonomous and self-governing was not hindered by the magical or religious divisions separating clans from one another, nor by a rational administration representing a wider association. Thus the Italian *coniurationes* developed from purely interpersonal and temporary

---

[25] M. Weber, *Economy and Society*, ed. G. Roth and C. Wittich, vol. ii (Berkeley, Calif.: University of California Press, 1978), 1212–65, in particular, pp. 1238–9.
[26] Ibid. 1247. Cf. the analysis of R. Bendix, *Max Weber: An Intellectual Portrait* (London: Methuen, 1966), 77–8.

associations into permanent political associations, as did, via a different and incomplete model, the *confraternitates* of northern Germany.

Why did such a type of city not develop in the Islamic world, whose abstract religion lent itself better to the emergence of citizenship ties? Weber's answer is close to that of Ibn Khaldun: the absence of military autonomy in the cities, due to the presence of other, more efficient centres of power which already occupied the site of physical force. He does not emphasize the military force of the tribes (on which he had apparently no documentation), but only that of the royal army which was recruited thanks to the resources of a powerful bureaucracy, and which was necessary for the implementation of the irrigation policy. The conscripted soldier financed by the royal quartermaster was different from the city-dweller who was not a soldier. In the West, on the contrary, the military were supplied by the communities who supported them, and provided knights and bourgeois militias. Because of this military autonomy, the king had to negotiate with those whose military and financial help he needed. The European bourgeoisie could develop autonomous communes, whereas the Arab bourgeoisie had to negotiate the king's, or his mercenaries', protection, or that of a tribe.

Recent research on Arab towns has not, overall, undermined the Weberian view.[27] It is true that there were cities of 'citizen-merchants' alongside the religious and the bureaucratic city, but these did not give rise to communes. It is also true that the Arab town bore many of the traits of the Western city: cosmopolitanism due to common membership of the territory of Islam, a relative social mobility, the existence of a 'Muslim public opinion' on what was right and wrong, and which was informed by reference to religious law.[28] All of this facilitated the emergence of roles distinct from those prescribed by primary groups and blood ties. As for patron–client relations and the domination of noble families, these were not exclusive to Muslim towns.[29] Essen-

---

[27] Ira Lapidus, *Muslim Cities in the Later Middle Ages* (London: Cambridge University Press, 1984; 1st edn. 1967); Ira Lapidus (ed.), *Middle Eastern Cities* (Berkeley, Calif.: University of California Press, 1969); Marshall Hodgson, *The Venture of Islam* (Chicago, Ill.: University of Chicago Press, 1974), ii. 105–35; Leon Carl Brown (ed.), *From Medina to Metropolis: Heritage and Change in the Near Eastern City* (Princeton, NJ: Darwin Press, 1973); Michel Seurat, 'La Ville arabe orientale entre J. Weulersse et I. Lapidus', in *Politiques urbaines dans le monde arabe* (Lyon: Maison de l'Orient, Presses universitaires de Lyon, 1984).

[28] On each of these points see Hodgson, *The Venture of Islam*, ii. 107, 108, 117, 120.

[29] See Moses I. Finley, 'Authority and Patronage', in *Politics in the Ancient World*.

tially, and this point is emphasized by Lapidus, the city was neither a point of reference nor a focus of political allegiance.[30] There was neither a common institutional structure nor the organization of free bourgeois who were defined initially by their belonging to the city. The city had no legal status recognized by the dynastic leadership, a status, moreover, which would be difficult to envisage in classical Muslim law which recognized first the legal character of physical beings and of the moral entities which were the natural extension of them (the family essentially).[31]

The army was made up of a garrison independent from the city-dwellers, drawing where necessary upon an additional power from its control of the agricultural economy.[32] The Muslim town did not develop in a feudal context where it might have become an auto-nomous power centre which would negotiate with other powers. It was the seat of government (which is suggested by the term *Medina*, the site where justice—*din*—is rendered, and where the government looks after law and order), but did not draw its strength from the town itself, as Ibn Khaldun has shown. Without an autonomous character, urban interests were not constituted in groups which were likely to impose a 'constitutional' constraint upon the power of the dynasties and their garrisons. The town was an intermittent political system which was most clearly defined against the external threat born of the fear of tribal 'pillage'.[33] It was segmented into groups which identified themselves sometimes by their living in separate parts of the town, which were closed off physically from one another especially when they possessed different 'tribal' or religious identities,[34] or by their membership of urban 'gangs', or *çoffs* in North Africa, which were in perpetual struggle with a power regarded as predatory and unjust, but

[30] Clearly, analysis becomes more nuanced and diverse as one focuses more specifi-cally on case-studies. Cf. e.g. Jean-Pierre Thieck, 'Décentralisation ottomane et affirma-tion urbaine à Alep à la fin du XVIIIe siècle', in *Mouvements communautaires et espaces urbains au Machreq* (Beirut: CERMOC (Librarie orientale); Paris: Sinbad, 1985), 117–68. Even in these cases, however, the general picture remains the same.

[31] Hodgson, *The Venture of Islam*, i. 344.

[32] Ibid. ii. 109.

[33] Ira Lapidus, 'Muslim Cities and Islamic Societies', in Lapidus, *Middle Eastern Cities*, pp. 47–74; see also the contributions of Shlomo Goitein, Nadav Safran, and Clement H. Moore, pp. 74–9.

[34] Hodgson, *The Venture of Islam*, ii. 116; Lapidus, *Muslim Cities*, pp. 49 and 51–2. On the identity of a residential quarter in the context of a civil war and a town seen as dominated by an outside power, cf. Michel Seurat, 'Le Quartier de Bâb Tebbané à Tripoli (Liban): Étude d'un "asabiyya" urbaine', in *Mouvements communautaires*, pp. 45–86.

almost never in the name of an autonomous urban identity.[35] These reflect very well the model of adversary participation which the modern advocates of urban movements proclaim in opposition to 'consensual' or 'co-operative' participation. They strengthened solidarity and the intransigence of neighbourhood groups, putting pressure on their leaders not to become more 'opportunist' (that is, less given to negotiation and to institutionalized deliberation).[36] Only the literate religious élites (*ulama*) and their schools constituted socially and religiously central sites, bringing together recruits from all the neighbourhoods and from all classes of the population around a shared law and judicial authority, and sharing the 'common services' of education and mutual support. From the eleventh century, the *ulama* emerge not only as religious but also as political and social élites, independent from the empire, and fulfilling the role of the old classes of administrators and property owners, before falling once again in thrall to external powers, as in the Mameluke period. A school, however, does not dominate a city. In fact, there were several schools, which often went beyond the city limits, or coexisted, sometimes in violent conflict, within them. These schools had neither fiscal power, nor military force, nor territorial jurisdiction and could not be (any more than brotherhood lodges) a substitute for the urban political community. Belonging to a school or a lodge does not constitute citizenship.

This long discussion of Western and Muslim cities demonstrates that citizenship is not an ideal category borne of the thought of the 'great writers', but is one element of a specific social configuration. Seeing this will enable us to place in its context the third element, 'citizenship for itself'.

'Citizenship for itself'

'Citizenship for itself', conscious of itself (which Stinchcombe calls, too generally, 'loyalism'), often appears under the too wide term of public-spiritedness or *civisme*. Conversely, it is sometime saturated

---

[35] The essential factor is not the existence of factions, but the orientation and identity of these: those which are segmented or transversal do not allow the integration of individuals in an urban community, those involving guilds or groups of merchants and artisans are weak and only rarely represent the autonomous interests of their members. Lapidus, *Muslim Cities*, p. 49.

[36] David Austin, 'Residential Participation: Political Mobilisation or Organisational Co-operation?', *Public Administration Review* (Sept. 1972), 409–20; Michael Peter Smith, *The City and Social Theory* (Oxford: Blackwell, 1980), 275 ff.

with so many characteristics that one questions whether it is a useful empirical concept, or simply useful as a supporting term for teachers of civic education.[37] Other definitions suffer from limiting citizenship to its modern liberal idea[38] or to its relationship to 'nation-building' where the modern citizen is a loyal practitioner of rational legal administration.[39]

We can, however, make three points here. The belief in the *intelligibility* of the political world to each citizen is logically linked to the first characteristic of citizenship: it is impossible to conflate subjection and government, the actual situation of the ruled and the imagined situation of the ruler, if we do not have a cognitive map of the 'system' as a mechanism (causal or effective) which is knowable or able to be mastered, at least in part or at certain levels. Its exact opposite, the idea of a hidden part, out of reach of ordinary mortals, whose workings only the initiated understand, in other words, the perception of the political world as a 'conspiracy' controlled by hidden élites, is shared by (marginal) populist ideologies, and (centrist) élitist ones. Schumpeter has argued, not without good reason, that in fact the citizen behaves precisely in this way because of his lesser ability to understand public affairs as opposed to his personal ones. This destroys the thesis of the rationality of democratic choices.[40] But the

[37] See e.g. Charles E. Merriam, *The Making of Citizens* (Chicago, Ill.: University of Chicago Press, 1931), 1–26, who lists (quite seriously) the following qualities as being in 'nearly all countries' necessary to citizenship: patriotism and loyalism, obedience to laws, respect for the government and civil servants, recognition of the obligations of political life, a minimum degree of self-control, an ability to respond to the needs of the community in periods of tension, honesty in social relations, knowledge and approval of the basic ideology of the regime, and the keeping of criticism of this ideology within reasonable limits, and often, a special belief in the quality of the people, compared to other peoples.

[38] See e.g. Mark Roelofs, *The Tension of Citizenship* (New York: Rinehart, 1957), 1–30, who identifies three basic attitudes: pride in participating in public events (the Greek tradition); defiance towards authority and insistence on the right to a private life (the Romano-Christian tradition); and loyalty and acceptance of sacrifice for the common good (the Hebrew tradition). Why is liberal market individualism not mentioned as an equally important source of the second attitude?

[39] See e.g. Alex Inkeles and his 'syndrome' of 'modern citizenship': 'Participant Citizenship in Six Developing Countries', *American Political Science Review*, 62/4 (Dec. 1969), 1112–23.

[40] Joseph Schumpeter, *Capitalism, Socialism, and Democracy* (London: Allen & Unwin, 1976), 256–68. In fact, Schumpeter criticizes not one, but three theses: (1) the idea that the desires of individual citizens constitute perfectly defined and independent givens; (2) the idea that democratic political decisions (achieved by the electoral process) please the greatest number; (3) the idea that the citizen maintains a 'sense of realities' when he 'becomes involved in politics'.

reality is different: to say that citizens are not (or not always, or not often) 'intelligent' does not deny intelligibility as a logical condition of citizenship. It is precisely because citizenship is considered a prerequisite, or distant mental horizon that the citizen can say that 'things are too complicated' or give in, as Schumpeter says, 'to extra-rational or irrational prejudice and impulse'. It would be impossible to term these prejudices or impulses irrational if one did not consider rationality or intelligibility possible. It does not follow, however, that only one intelligent choice is possible or that democratic choices are necessarily rational.

Intelligibility can be applied to two objects: overall collective affairs, and collective private affairs. The first is particularly emphasized by analysts of 'the democracy of antiquity', such as Moses Finley, and, in the modern context, by the theoreticians of 'participative democracy'. The advocates of 'liberal democracy' insist, on the other hand, on the ability of the citizen to understand his own affairs (along the lines of the Tocquevillian individualist). The difference between these two is great, but the 'weak' version also proposes a minimal understanding of the relationship between 'private' and 'public' and of the fashioning of the second through mastery of the first.[41]

Against this interpretation we can say that there is no obvious relationship between assumed intelligibility and citizenship: one can have an absurdist or surrealist view of the political scene and still participate actively in a given humanitarian cause (Amnesty International, for example) or in single issue group politics (saving baby seals, for example), although, in fact, the two cases are not the same: involvement in a given humanitarian cause demonstrates a (pretension to) certain understanding, but also a different view of important problems and of the ecological range involved in solving them. Such understanding only contradicts citizenship if it simultaneously rejects all other forms of behaviour. As for single issue group politics, in its extreme form, it has nothing to do with citizenship because it does not take into account anything outside itself: its (doubtful) relationship with political intelligence is therefore not relevant.

The second characteristic of 'citizenship for itself' is *empathy*, the ability (always limited by the rules of the political game itself) to put oneself in the place of other citizens in order to understand, not their

---

[41] Cf. Ellen Meiskins Wood, *Mind and Politics* (Berkeley, Calif.: University of California Press, 1972), 158–61.

strategies[42] and structures of preference, but their interests and justifications. Taken to its extreme, of course, this characteristic becomes absurd in that it makes of the citizen someone who understands everything and chooses nothing, or a god in whom is incarnated universal Reason, the only actor qualified to govern himself democratically. Empathy indicates neither complete understanding nor complete sympathy, but the ability to conceive of roles different from one's own and to adjust to this. The formula would not be, 'If I was in his place, I would probably do the same thing'[43] (this is the formula of 'scientific empathy' or of the bomber pilot machine-gunned by an enemy DCA), but 'I can modify my behaviour in order to come to a minimal provisional agreement'. Empathy authorizes negotiation and deliberation. It operates also between 'high' and 'low', between rulers and ruled, and is facilitated when the material conditions of the life of the citizen predispose him to put himself in the place of the ruler. If sufficient autonomy is allowed to the ruled to take 'political decisions' (not only the vote or the petition, but also participation which is neither politically controlled, nor pre-orientated towards collective activities), then the experience of the ruler is not completely alien to the citizen, and the citizen can imagine himself in the place of the ruler. Michael Walzer has noted, 'Because he can do that, and commonly does it, he engages in what I want to call ... anticipative and retrospective decision-making'.[44] It is doubtful, however, whether this is also true for 'historic decisions' where the statesperson commits once and for all the collective destiny at maximum cost.[45] Not all decisions are reducible to choices between local libraries and the sponsorship of a football team.

Civility, the third characteristic of citizenship, allows for the management of the tension between social differentiation and common membership. It is clearly related to empathy, but implies different situations: empathy is related to collective choice, civility to inter-individual recognition. As the term itself implies, it is 'civil',

[42] This is the basis of all strategies or 'heresthetic' behaviour which has nothing to do with rhetorical argument (which concerns convictions). This 'universal' behaviour transcends citizenship, cf. W. Riker, 'Political Theory and the Art of Heresthetics', in Ada Finifter (ed.), *Political Science* (Washington, DC: American Political Science Association, 1983), 47–68.

[43] Boudon and Bourricaud, *Dictionnaire*; see 'Action', p. 5.

[44] Michael Walzer, 'Political Decision-Making and Political Education', in M. Richter (ed.), *Political Theory and Political Education* (Princeton, NJ: Princeton University Press, 1980), 159.

[45] Raymond Aron, *Études politiques* (Paris: Gallimard, 1972), 192.

whereas empathy is more 'civic'.[46] Lloyd Fallers has made an apposite analysis of this: he defines it as 'a tolerant and generous recognition of common attachment to, and responsibility for, the social order, despite diversity'. Civility perishes when collective identities (whatever their sources and codes) oppose one another, not only in their 'official' political expression, in debates, votes, and demonstrations, but in all the circumstances of daily life:

Then the most routine acts of everyday life may become heavy with larger meaning. A song, a sporting event, an item of clothing or a church bell may become an incitement to conflict, the family car a sign board for slogans. Citizens come to regard each other warily and to make exorbitant demands upon each other's civility. Everyday interaction with neighbour and workmate becomes uneasy and harsh—a continuing negotiation of fresh social contracts. The common use of public space is threatened; insult, or even violence, lurks behind every misstep or misunderstanding.[47]

Such are the ingredients of what those who are protected from it by virtue of their social class or position of power condescendingly call 'the security ideology'. This ideology turns its back on civility because its supporters feel themselves threatened by incivility. It is nourished by the feeling that security is compromised by 'delinquents' who want to take individual and collective revenge on the ruling group (depending on the circumstances, the 'Whites' the 'imperialists', the 'Christians', the 'bourgeoisie', and so on).[48] Just as looting follows a revolt, or assaults or rapes precede ghetto risings, they are all only extreme forms of 'contact terrorism' where even clothes or hairstyles are perceived as a deliberate affront to the other's identity, and as an attack upon the system of which the other is the (real or perceived) beneficiary.[49] With the destruction of civility, all contact becomes an oppositional expression of non-negotiable identity. Citizenship breaks out in war, if not of all against all, at least of 'minorities' against

[46] On the modern distinction between 'civil' and 'civic' see George Armstrong Kelly, 'Who Needs a Theory of Citizenship?', *Daedalus*, 108/4 (Fall 1979), 21–36. The 'civil' is orientated more towards the private individual, and has a passive dimension which places emphasis on security and rights; the 'civic' is orientated towards public solidarity as a primary obligation, and has a more participative dimension.

[47] Lloyd Fallers, *The Social Anthropology of the Nation-State* (Chicago, Ill.: Aldine, 1974), 3–7.

[48] It is not, therefore, surprising that this ideology is widespread among those who themselves live in ghettos, in a culturally linked or closed community, or in the ghetto of their individual isolation.

[49] Erving Goffman, 'The Interaction Order', *American Sociological Review*, 48/1 (1983), 1–17, in particular, pp. 9–13.

'majorities', which the modern state tries virtuously to conceal with gestures of social and cultural events, and programmes against poverty or educational backwardness, whereas in the classical Muslim city one would simply have shut the gates of neighbourhoods, leaving to each community its own 'rehabilitation programmes'.

Civility, which is essential to citizenship, can, paradoxically, be better maintained when citizenship itself does not exist. In the Ottoman Crete of Kazantzakis's *Liberty or Death*, the Greek Metropolitan and the Turkish pasha were able to maintain courteous social relations, Nouri Bey and Captain Michaelis becoming blood brothers. But with the rise of nationalism, an incident in a café, or an illicit inter-ethnic flirtation, could break personal ties and provoke a blood-bath. In fact there is nothing paradoxical in this. When 'ethnic groups' are too separated culturally speaking, and later are too economically and politically unequal, civility cannot be strong enough to encompass everyone as citizens of the same political unit. On the contrary, the struggle for citizenship destroys civility, and civility itself is only maintained by the maintenance of each community with its own laws and social organizations, along the lines of the Ottoman *millet*, until nationalism is able to create political communities which are relatively homogeneous culturally, or which at least have élites which are relatively so, in order that civility becomes, once again, possible until the next manifestation of cultural pluralism arises, and asks yet more civility of its citizens.[50]

Intelligibility, empathy, civility. These terms do not, however, cover the totality of the meaning of 'citizenship for itself', which cannot be completely explained within a range of unambiguous, univocal attributes, because it is always an unstable combination of contradictory (or complementary) elements[51] which operate according to different criteria. As a feeling of *belonging*, citizenship operates according to three criteria: the first, the 'general-particular', expresses orientation towards the overall group, the 'political community', and relates to territory and to other more particular (interest group, class, professional association) or more universal groups (Church, *umma*, revolutionary International); the second, a 'community-society' (or communalization-societization in Weberian terms, which perhaps

---

[50] Fallers, *The Social Anthropology of the Nation-State*, pp. 5–6.

[51] This has been noted by Roelofs, *The Tension of Citizenship*, and well documented by non-directive interviews conducted by Robert E. Lane, 'The Tense Citizen and the Casual Patriot: Role Confusion in American Politics', in *Political Man*, pp. 227–98. Our interpretation is, however, different and far removed from a dimensionalization.

better express the process of affiliation) expresses membership of more flesh and blood, more prescriptive groups, and has more essential registers (the family, close-knit communities, classes, sects), and of more volatile and more contractual groups which normally operate on only one register (the market, sometimes labour relations, clientele relations, or the relationship to non-communitarian political groups); the third, the 'high–low' criterion expresses membership of local (the municipality, the committee), regional (the member state of a federal state, the region), national, and, sometimes, supra-national communities. As a feeling of *commitment* also, citizenship expresses itself according to three criteria: the 'public–private' criterion which goes from the 'civic' extreme ('one should be prepared to die for one's country') to the 'civil' extreme ('one must look after one's family and friends'); the 'conformity–autonomy' criterion which ranges from conformism ('stay out of trouble') to 'individualism' ('follow your conscience', 'criticize and damn the consequences'); and the 'claiming of rights–recognition of obligations' criterion which, in the latter case, involves the supplementary problem of the object of orientation — the city as society (a pact of association) or as state (trust of government) — and raises the question of civil disobedience.[52]

The notion of 'citizenship for itself' should not, however, be understood as possessing equally the first three criteria, or as being situated approximately midway amongst the second three. Such a view would simply make of the citizen an archetypal middle-of-the-roader. It is a view which would most likely emerge from any interview-based survey undertaken in a Western democracy. It would, however, give no idea of the variety of attitudes, nor of the presence or absence of syndromes (groups of related attitudes).[53] Such a view is barely more helpful than that portrayed by civic instruction. We can, however, make the purely abstract hypothesis that the positions taken on the basis of the various criteria of membership and involvement allow us to establish varying degrees and several types of citizenship. Without elaborating upon all of them, an impossible task given that any abstract classification which pretends to be exhaustive is a vain exercise, we can give several examples.

[52] Cf. Michael Walzer, *Obligations: Essays on Disobedience, War and Citizenship* (Cambridge, Mass.: Harvard University Press, 1970), in particular, pp. 16–17, and Kelly's critique, see 'Who Needs a Theory of Citizenship?'

[53] Lane, 'The Tense Citizen', p. 280 on the following referential image: a moral man, a good family man, a good member of the local community, a good member of the political community.

Types of citizenship

Activist (military) citizenship, with its exclusive membership of the city according to all the membership criteria (and the communalization of membership) and, in terms of the criteria of commitment, deferential public commitment, and dominant obligation towards the city as a state, can be contrasted with civil citizenship, which involves non-exclusive membership of the city, moderate and autonomous public commitment, and dominant obligation towards the city as an association, and which is combined with reservations concerning social conventions. The 'civic humanism' of the Renaissance, according to a contemporary, caricatures military citizenship thus: 'Thou knowest not how sweet is the *amor patriae*: if such would be expedient for the fatherland's protection or enlargement, it would seem neither burdensome and difficult nor a crime to thrust the axe into one's father's head, to crush one's brothers, to deliver from the womb of one's wife the premature child with the sword'.[54] This interesting character goes beyond the dutiful preacher so scorned by Thoreau: 'The broadest and most prevalent error requires the most disinterested virtue to sustain it. The slight reproach to which the virtue of patriotism is commonly liable, the noble are most likely to incur. Those who, while they disapprove of the character and measures of a government, yield to it their allegiance and support, are undoubtedly its conscientious supporters, and so frequently the most serious obstacles to reform.'[55] In the case of civil citizenship, government is viewed with suspicion because it is the obstacle to the fulfilment of conscience. According to Emerson's formula: 'Good men must not obey the laws too well', to which he adds, 'Wild liberty develops iron conscience. Want of liberty, by strengthening law and decorum, stupefies conscience ... The less government we have the better—the fewer laws, and the less confided power', because 'the law is only a memorandum' for the moral conscience.[56] This is the extreme point of civil citizenship. If suspicion of conventions is greater than a sense of group obligation (whatever it may be) then belonging disappears and social

---

[54] This eloquent little piece, from the 'humanist' Salutati, is quoted by E. Kantorowicz, *The King's Two Bodies* (Princeton, NJ: Princeton University Press, 1957), 245. With certain modifications to the vocabulary the quotation still keeps much of its relevance today.

[55] Henry David Thoreau, *On the Duty of Civil Disobedience* (1849; London: Housmans, 1980).

[56] Ralph Waldo Emerson, 'Politics', in *Complete Works* (London: Ward Lock & Co., 1889), 199, 203, 206, and 192.

citizenship gives way to isolated marginalization. In the same way, if the sense of obligation towards the city as a state becomes exclusive (that is to say that the state becomes a 'cause', 'right or wrong', transcending all other things), then activist citizenship triggers total depersonalization. Psychologically, it is not beyond the bounds of possibility to imagine that the exacerbating of an attitude of marginality towards the city itself becomes resolved in depersonalization to the profit of another city or membership group which can lead even to collective suicide.[57]

Another opposition is that of participative citizenship (involving a strong sense of belonging according to all the criteria, with special emphasis upon the communalized political city, a strongly dominant public commitment which is autonomous or deferential depending upon conservative or oppositional choice, and a recognition of duties as a normal means of claiming rights), as against private citizenship (involving a strong sense of belonging to the 'particular', 'low', and associational—with a possible exception for the family, deferential private commitment, and a sense of obligation towards the state inasmuch as it permits the exercise of private activity). Is this an effect of contemporary 'individualism'? The opposition 'activist (military)–civil' is often reduced to the participative–private duality, as if the participative were unaware of all civil duty, and as if the civil were devoid of all participative orientation. It is true that, just as the civil can become marginality, the private can be transformed into passive citizenship (a weak sense of belonging according to all the criteria, a totally deferential private commitment, a sense of the law which the state should recognize), and into negative citizenship (an extension of the former where exclusively private commitment combines with an acute sense of autonomy).[58]

Participative citizenship can become contestatory citizenship if the

---

[57] This psychological possibility is obviously not a logical continuum. The thought of 19th-century American 'individualists' is constructed to counter such a possibility. It is also excessive to qualify them as 'anarchists' (at least in the absolute European sense); for them, *if* the government is of such a type that it demands that you be the agent of injustice towards someone else, then, 'I say, break the law' (Thoreau). An unconditional adherent of the ethics of conviction is not *ipso facto* an anarchist. See George Kateb, 'Democratic Individuality and the Claims of Politics', *Political Theory*, 12/3 (Aug. 1984), 331–60.

[58] The expression used by Kelly 'Who Needs a Theory of Citizenship', p. 32, to indicate the attitude of people linked to the state for their subsistence and protection, like clients (that is, reclaiming 'social' and not only 'civil' rights), but who are basically not committed to public affairs and problems.

sense of belonging to the political city diminishes to the benefit of the other criteria of membership (for example, towards the more universal and/or the more particular, towards the higher and/or the lower),[59] or if public commitment is weak *vis-à-vis* established regime symbols and strong *vis-à-vis* substitution symbols, while remaining strongly autonomous. The most extreme form is substitution citizenship, which is nothing other than participative citizenship orientated towards a political city other than its own. In contrast to the opposition identified above, where marginality can encourage activist citizenship, it is psychologically implausible that negative citizenship can be resolved in substitution citizenship (except in cases of conversion like those of the French surrealists to the Communist Party). It is, however, sociologically plausible that the possibility of this is a significant obstacle to the development in groups of the syndrome of negative citizenship.

Such cursory observations are only valuable if their relation to the conditions of existence of the various categories is established, and in particular their relation to individualism. Here we meet the dominant paradigm of contemporary political science.

Individualism and Citizenship: The Dominant Paradigm

It seems to be generally accepted that individualism has a strong correlation with citizenship to the point where the modern individual and the modern citizen seem to constitute a single juridical and sociological unit. It is also generally accepted that individualism leads to (or is a symptom of) the 'crisis of citizenship', notably in terms of its legitimation of government, and acceptance of political obligation. The essential concepts, according to this view, are the following: individualism, as a manifestation of the individual's value (whatever its roots or affiliations), extends citizenship to all those who live in a given territory; as a claim by the individual to the control of his overall behaviour, notably in the cultural and private spheres, it lends to citizenship a growing number of rights and extends its scope; the combination of these two exigencies and the development of 'impersonal' mechanisms, such as the world market, the international division of labour, and large organizations,[60] produce a feeling of

---

[59] One can feel one belongs more to the workplace group (towards the particular) and to the *umma* (towards the universal), to the village (towards the low) and to a trade union or political International (towards the high).

[60] The best synthetic discussion of the notion of the 'corporate person' and his influence on relations between physical individuals seems to me to be that of James S.

powerlessness which leads to the decline of public-spiritedness. Loss of understanding or of control (even if illusory) of collective mechanisms makes the material limitations placed upon the satisfaction of demands intolerable (demands which are no longer normatively delimited by 'communitarian' internalization of the social structure). Because of this, the 'anticipated satisfaction' of the individual's demands (in fact the acceptance that these are not, or not yet, satisfied), which is one of the effects of civic participation, disappears. The 'amateur democrat' retreats to marginality or directs pressure towards satisfaction of one demand which is considered as taking priority over other demands (and over the demands of others).[61] The more that citizenship is demanded, the less it is perceived as efficient, and the more it is selectively exercised: the frontiers of the political are displaced and widened and its context is modified. From being a vision of the destiny of the city, the political becomes the system of mediation of the most divergent social demands, and the private takes precedence over the public as the goal of citizenship activity, as the public takes precedence over the private as a mode of resource allocation.[62]

Let us look again at the paradigm in order to examine in more detail its constitutive elements and to demonstrate that what are called 'corruption' and 'crisis' proceed from the fact that individualism and citizenship, although historically and socially assimilated, belong to two different logical (or systematic) domains: it is this 'incoherent' combination which has created the identity of Western political society and given it its coherence.

The procedures for identifying individualism–citizenship

These can be distinguished under three distinct rubrics: a historical thesis, an (ideo)logical thesis, and a sociological thesis.

1. *The historical thesis.* In the historical thesis the 'individual' has been so strongly identified with the 'citizen' that the individualism–citizenship relation seems tautological. Let us leave to one side the

Coleman, *The Asymmetric Society* (Syracuse: Syracuse University Press, 1982).

[61] James Q. Wilson, *The Amateur Democrat* (Chicago, Ill.: University of Chicago Press, 1966).

[62] Cf. e.g. Edward Shils, 'On the Governability of Modern Societies', *Notes et documents* (Institut international Jacques-Maritain, Rome) (July–Sept. 1984), 39–59, in particular, p. 49. 'L'action volontaire privée qui tendait auparavant à stimuler plus d'activités privées vise maintenant principalement à aiguillonner le gouvernement vers plus d'action.'

Greek city, 'Ionian individualism', and Hannah Arendt. The development of the individual in the feudal Middle Ages has been characterized by Walter Ullmann as the movement from 'subject' to
'citizen'.[63] Ullmann demonstrates the extent to which medieval corporatism diminished the notion of the physical individual endowed
with autonomous rights in the public sphere and having the right to
participate in government.[64] As a member of the corporation and of
the Church as the Body of Christ, the *fidelis* was subjected to a law
which was imposed rather than fashioned by the individual. Politically, this meant a 'descending theory' of government. Faith and not
consent was the fundamental component of law. Physical individuals
were hierarchically ordered and were entrusted, as a minor to a
guardian, to government which was not derived from the people as the
sum of individuals but from the divine, hence the importance of the
notion 'king by the grace of God'.[65]

The 'abstract' medieval thesis was to be countered by the 'practical
thesis', at least while it concerned the place of the individual as a
category, that is, as a citizen.[66] The 'lower part' of the rural periphery of
society, negligible from the point of view of government, took as given
the rights denied by the descending theory: villagers acted, as it were, as
complete citizens electing their local administrators. The towns benefited
from self-government and allowed the crossing of hierarchical barriers
(*Stadtluft macht frei*, as we have already noted). Customary law was
based upon the activity of individuals of low status who were considered as *idiota*, that is to say, devoid of the necessary *scientia*.[67]

---

[63] Walter Ullmann, *The Individual and Society in the Middle Ages* (London:
Methuen, 1967).

[64] Ibid. 6. The theme is treated in a similar manner by Georges de Lagarde,
'Individualisme et corporatisme au Moyen Âge', in *L'Organisation corporative au
Moyen Âge à la fin de l'ancien régime*, Collection of Historical and Philosophical Works,
2nd series, vol. 44 (Louvain, 1937), 3–59; Otto von Gierke, *Les Théories politiques du
Moyen Âge* (Paris: Sirey, 1914) (partial translation of *Deutsches Genossenschaftrecht*, 1891).

[65] Ullmann, *The Individual and Society*. 18–19. This can be compared with trust
(Locke) where government is entrusted to the king by the individual people in order
that he exercise it for their benefit, what Ullmann calls an 'ascending theory' and
Weldon a 'mechanical' theory of government: T. D. Weldon, *States and Morals*
(London: J. Murray, 1947).

[66] Ullmann takes care to emphasize that the 'abstract thesis' did not possess the
modern concept of the individual subject to autonomous and independent rights but 'by
virtue of its collectivist nomocratic character, it nevertheless firmly implanted the idea of
the supremacy of the law in the Western mind, not in spite of, but—the paradox is
merely apparent—because of the absence of any thesis of autonomous rights on the part
of the individual', *The Individual and Society*. 49–50.

[67] Ullmann over-assimilates the oppositions 'high (law)–'low' (custom), and

Above all, the feudal system itself gave rise to the idea of the individual and the citizen. By implying reciprocity of obligation, which was expressed by the *diffidatio*—the repudiation by the vassal of ties if the lord did not fulfil his part of the contract—feudal ties affected the lord as an individual person and not as the titulary of an institutional charisma, such as the Pope or the king. Article 39 of the Magna Carta was based upon this. The Magna Carta was a feudal document in which lord–vassal relations became merely contractual, and liberty, security, and the freedom of the individual were declared inviolable.[68] Feudal England of the fourteenth century thus reinvigorated the Ciceronian axiom of *consensus utentium. Voluntas populi dat jura* (which was engraved on a commemorative medal at the coronation of Edward III). Even though we should not confuse feudal community with the *populus* made up of individuals as citizens, feudal practice, as an unintended effect, gave a reality and significance to Ulpian's maxim. The rights and duties of a member of the feudal community were later to be transferred to the rights and natural obligations of the citizen-individual epitomized by the Virginia Declaration of 1776. Ullmann then goes on to show, in the 'humanistic thesis', the links with the theory of natural law, and with the political Aristotelianism of the fourteenth century, and differentiates the *fidelis*, the religious subject of the supernatural, and the *civis*, the political animal, which draws upon the idea of the natural in the work of Thomas Aquinas. Ullmann's journey ends with Dante's *humana civilitas* (who is inspired by Aristotle and is distinguished from the *christianitas*) and with the *universitas civium* of Marsiglio of Padua, who is endowed with the power to decree human laws, the only ones which can be called 'laws' because only they involve consent (which is not the case with divine laws). Marsiglio is probably the most 'modern' theoretician mentioned. He argues for: the freedom of interpretation of the Bible by

'descending theory' (holist)–'ascending theory' (individualism). Local custom does not prove the existence of an individual as possessing rights; as women and children know, the opposite is often the case. It remains true that custom presents a barrier to the supremacy of the law, but not always to the benefit of individuals. For an interpretation of English history based upon a strong monarchy and individual civil rights which derive not from local custom but from the 'common law of the land', cf., Marshall, 'Citizenship and Social Class', pp. 79–80. See also Blandine Barret-Kriegel, *L'État et les esclaves* (Paris: Calmann-Lévy, 1979), 106 ff.

[68] See Sidney Painter, *The Reign of King John* (Baltimore, Md.: Johns Hopkins University Press, 1949), 326–7; Ullmann, *The Individual and Society*, pp. 75 ff., for all the precautions necessary to precluding from the Magna Carta the modern democratic spirit.

the individual, and his argument evokes, perhaps unintentionally, the individualism of the Reformation; the universality of citizenship, which does not make distinctions concerning ability or *scientia*; the equality of citizens without consideration of the 'natural inequality' of men; and the rule of the majority between citizens of differing status.

Ullmann's thesis is intriguing because it links, at the level of structures of thought as social representations, what the history of ideas distinguishes or separates.[69] Ullmann bases the individual citizen on feudalism and not on its opposite, the monarchical state, as does the (ideo)logical thesis (see below). In spite of its ingeniousness, Ullmann's view is not completely convincing because it integrates into the individualization process born of the feudal world the territorial state of Marsiglio de Padua, with its single king, its body of administrators (including scholars), and its population of atomized citizens. The break with medieval corporatism is too stark here. More concerned with gradual developments as perceived by actors (and historians) than with clear breaks, Ullmann does not adequately define either 'individualism' or the medieval state. His work is, however, important for several reasons. First, it helps us better to specify European individualism (public, based on feudalism and on the separation of the religious and the political), and an Arab-Islamic individualism (private, based on the tribal and patrimonial context and on the liaison between the religious and the political, at least as an ideal). Second, it clarifies the distinction between several types of citizenship, that of continuity and the expansion of feudal communities, such as in Great Britain, that of discontinuity and rejection of both monarch and privileges, such as in France.[70] Third, and perhaps most importantly, it demonstrates how an 'individualist citizenship' is based, not upon the isolated individual, but on a communal system. This, in fact, is its chief difference from the (ideo)logical thesis.

2. *The (ideo)logical thesis.* This, more widely held than the historical thesis, more or less conflates the individual and the modern citizen. It does this, however, upon the basis of the sovereign state rather than feudalism. This thesis also appears to be tautological. Interest and will

---

[69] See the same approach in Joseph Strayer, *Les Origines médiévales de l'État moderne* (Paris: Payot, 1978). It would take another chapter to confront Ullmann or Strayer's approach to the history of ideas as advocated by Quentin Skinner.

[70] Lord Edward Acton, 'Nationality', in Talcott Parsons, Edward Shils, Kaspar Naegele, and Jesse R. Pitts (eds.), *Theories of Society* (New York: Free Press, 1961), 392–404, in particular, p. 400; Robert Nisbet, 'Citizenship: Two Traditions', *Social Research*, 41/4 (winter 1974), 612–37.

dissociated from all social ties (communitarian or corporatist) are the only sources of state legitimacy. It is, therefore, as a citizen that the individual emerges at the moment political obligation appears. If this can only be founded upon will and not upon some entity transcendent of it (the cosmos, God, an 'elect', a hierarchical organization), it follows that the individual is, by the same token, a citizen member of 'civil society', in, for example, the Lockian sense.[71]

On this point, the French republican tradition is not fundamentally different. It is true that 'the civil order excludes fundamentally the political order',[72] and indicates in legal language the opposite of both 'public' and 'criminal'. It retains, however, all the value of its Roman etymology: 'which concerns the citizens'. If civil and political rights are distinguished, one arrives at the idea that if man has rights as a social being this is precisely because he is—potentially and in fact—also a citizen.[73]

The individual citizen constitutes the state but is also constituted by it, because only equality before a common law allows the individual to be freed from 'particular' networks of solidarity and domination. There is no individual identity without the sovereignty of the state. The identity of the individual is borne of his common and equal subjection to a sovereign. Where there is hierarchical holism, there is neither state nor individual.[74] These latter share certain characteristics:

---

[71]   C. B. Macpherson has noted that this proposition of Locke goes with an opposite claim. Those who do not own property are not full members of civil society; having given their tacit consent, they are obligated by law and are citizens as subjects; only those who have property are full citizens. This second proposition, however, does not preclude the first, hence a logical contradiction; it does not posit the identification of the individual with the citizen, but reserves citizenship for a category of individuals. Macpherson draws the radical conclusion of the inability of the individualism of property owners to create modern citizenship (one of the symptoms of which is that the word 'citizen' does not even appear in the index of his book). C. B. Macpherson, *The Political Theory of Possessive Individualism: Hobbes to Locke* (Oxford, London: Oxford University Press, 1979; 1st edn. 1962), 248 ff.

[72]   Claude Nicolet, *L'Idée républicaine en France* (Paris: Gallimard, 1982), 330.

[73]   Ibid. 331. In Nicolet's interpretation of Rousseau as a representative of the republican tradition 'Society—that is to say individuals in association—and citizenship are conflated because the social relationship ... is only conceivable through and in freedom, a freedom which must, therefore, be guaranteed by a political relationship or "contract".' Ibid.

[74]   Larry Siedentop, 'Political Theory and Ideology: The Case of the State', in David Miller and Larry Siedentop (eds.), *The Nature of Political Theory* (Oxford: Clarendon Press, 1983), 53–73.

the state is the creator of new law (and rights);[75] because it is sovereign it is separate from 'states' (*stande*); in the same way, 'individualism' demonstrates a change in the relations of the self (*soi*) to its own roles, the abstract self (*moi*) never being reducible to the roles prescribed by the social structure. As a consequence, its will is morally sovereign and creative. It is therefore not surprising to see individualist theories of political obligation ('ascendant' theories in Ullmann's sense, 'mechanical' in Weldon's sense, or 'extrinsic' in Quinton's)[76] which are also theories of the sovereign state, whereas holist 'descending', 'organic', or 'intrinsic' theories are theories of the socio-political totality where the state does not emerge as such.

3. *The sociological thesis.* This is derived essentially from Durkheim and from Merton. Durkheim's view has apparently little in common with the (ideo)logical thesis in its contractualist form, and does not accept as a founding concept the individual of Hobbes or Locke, nor even of Rousseau (let alone Bentham). Hobbes's normative *tabula rasa*, which ignores (non-contractual) moral pre-conditions of civil society, is as alien to Durkheim as the epistemological *tabula rasa* of Locke and Rousseau which, ignoring the a priori social character of categories of knowledge, makes all social knowledge an abstraction. For Durkheim it is society itself which is 'the state of nature' and is differentiated analytically from the juridical order and from government of the 'civil state'.[77] Durkheim's thesis can be stated thus: citizenship is necessary to individualism in order that the latter is not

[75] Involved here is the whole controversy between the German (Jellinek), and French (Carré de Malberg) 'positivistes' and the Anglo-Saxons where 'common law' is basic and where law does not issue solely from *jus positum* via the state. The controversy is not always so stark: Marcel Waline recognized both the sovereignty of the state (and its submission to law on the basis of Jellinek's self-limitation idea), and the concomitant creation of customs; Marcel Waline, *L'Individualisme et le droit* (Paris: Domat-Mont-chrestien, 1945), 404ff., 304ff.

[76] Cf. n. 65 above, and Anthony Quinton (ed.), *Political Philosophy* (London: Oxford University Press, 1967), Introduction. We can note that these three classifications are not completely interchangeable. Ullmann would be reluctant to place Burke in his 'descending' theories, whereas Quinton would put him in his 'intrinsic' theories. Ullmann, in fact, is not convinced by the necessary relation between 'state' and 'individual'. Also the 'organic' theories have nothing to do with Durkheim's organic solidarity but, in fact, with its opposite on another level (cf. Louis Dumont's remark, *Essais sur l'individualisme*, p. 69n.). Conversely, Quinton divides Weldon's 'organic' category into two subcategories: 'intrinsic' (Burke), 'organic' (Hegel), to indicate in the latter a theory giving rise to the obligation of a fully moralized, and not utilitarian, individual.

[77] Émile Durkheim, *Montesquieu et Rousseau* (Paris: Rivière, 1953), 14–198. We refer here also to Reinhard Bendix's analysis which seems to us as apposite now as thirty years ago, 'Social Stratification and the Political Community', *Archives européennes de sociologie*, 1/2 (1960).

overwhelmed by the suffocating conformism of secondary groups (corporations), which are themselves necessary in order to resist the anomie which results from the atomization of individuals by the state. Durkheim's view seems to combine two incompatible theses, one which is, in fact, strictly speaking, sociological, and one which is normative and political. In the sociological thesis, the growth of the complex division of labour is the source of individualism: if collective consciousness becomes more abstract and permissive, the individual loses an identity clearly prescribed by group membership, and the individual becomes freer and more anxious.[78] Nothing in the sociological thesis predisposes the individual to citizenship.

It is at this point that the normative political thesis comes in: the 'secondary groups', in particular professional groups, provide the physical individual with internalized social norms, and enable him to avoid an isolation *vis-à-vis* the state which would lead to either anarchy or servitude. However, in order that the individual, individualized by the division of labour, does not become oppressed by corporate groups, these groups must be restrained from dominating and conditioning their members:

There must therefore exist above these local, domestic—in a word secondary—authorities, some overall authority which makes the law for them all: it must remind each of them that it is but a part and not the whole and that it should not keep for itself what rightly belongs to the whole. The only means of averting this collective particularism and all it involves for the individual, is to have a special agency with the duty of representing the overall collectivity, its rights and its interests vis-à-vis these individual collectivities. These rights and interests merge with those of the individual. Let us see why and how the main function of the State is to liberate the individual personalities. It is solely because, in holding its constituent societies in check, it prevents them from exerting the repressive influences over the individual that they would otherwise exert. So there is nothing inherently tyrannical about State intervention in the different fields of collective life; on the contrary, it has the object and the effect of alleviating tyrannies that do exist. It will be argued, might not the State in turn become despotic? Undoubtedly, provided there were nothing to counter that trend.

It is true that the state too can become 'levelling' and 'compressive', especially as it is more artificial, more vast, and more distanced from diverse interests, in which case individual diversity cannot come into

[78] Émile Durkheim, *The Division of Labour in Society* (New York: Free Press, 1964), 345–50.

play, and the state can become perceived as even more alien in that it does not 'envelop' or shape the individual in its own image, but instead forcefully denatures the individual:

The inference to be drawn from this comment, however, is simply that if that collective force, the State, is to be the liberator of the individual, it has itself need of some counter-balance; it must be restrained by other collective forces, that is, by those secondary groups. It is not a good thing for the groups to stand alone, nevertheless they have to exist. And it is out of this conflict of social forces that individual liberties are born.[79]

It is not certain that Durkheim's two theses are as different in status as Reinhard Bendix has claimed. The appeal to corporatism is less an aspiration than the recognition that a society made up of atomized individuals faced by a hypertrophied state is a 'veritable sociological monstrosity',[80] that is to say, is sociologically impossible. As for the appeal to the state and to citizenship against the tyrannies of corporatism, this too can be interpreted as an effect of the division of labour and of an individualization which increases the ability of individual citizens to modify their social (psychological and moral) characteristics, thanks to their participation in the action of the state in the interests of justice.[81] Individualism is clearly linked sociologically to citizenship.

The research of Robert Merton and those he has influenced is at first sight less pertinent to political theory inasmuch as the problem of political obligation is not really stressed. It does suggest, however, by implication, an affinity between individualism and citizenship. Interested, like Durkheim, by social structure as a pre-condition of the individual's perception of self-identity, Merton is less concerned with the effect of a complex structure of societization upon anomie and alienation. The latter are not causally linked to the former. Rather, the multiplicity of roles performed exposes the individual to contradictory obligations, and the variety of the individual's social attributes which are not related to one another by a single inflexible status (classically, being Jewish, American, a member of a university, born in Europe, a democrat, etc.) obliges the individual to make uncertain choices for which traditional models do not exist. This does, however, develop empathy, a sense of relativity and flexibility, and the propensity not to

---

[79] Émile Durkheim, *Professional Ethics and Civil Morals* (London: Routledge & Kegan Paul, 1957), 62–3.
[80] Durkheim, *The Division of Labour in Society*, preface to the 2nd edition, p. 28.
[81] Ibid. 396–409.

consider rules as being absolute, and to bring personal judgement to bear upon them, and to adopt an elaborate universalist language in order to be understood by those who are not intimates (as distinct from the particularist and coded language used in *Gemeinschaft*).[82] This 'individualist' resembles (perhaps overresembles) the ideal citizen, at least in terms of what we have called 'civil citizenship'. The complete individual resembles the perfect citizen, just as the perfectly civic citizen resembles the complete individual.[83]

The corruption of citizenship by individualism

The theme of the destruction of community life by individualism coincided with the appearance of the word itself in the French language. In 'traditionalist' thought, such as that of Joseph de Maistre and Lamennais, individualism atomizes, fragments, and corrodes all social groups and transforms the individual into 'the sovereign judge of all things'.[84] Individualism is linked here to 'anarchy' because it is opposed to 'society'. In the 'social' family subscribed to by Lamennais, Pierre Leroux, Constantin Pecqueur, or by activists such as Blanqui, individualism is related to the Hobbesian state of nature which is recreated by the capitalist economy, and makes of men ravening wolves, destructive of the physical individual. Here individualism is linked to exploitation and to the market and is the opposite of 'association', 'socialism', and 'fraternity'.[85]

A 'traditionalist' critique   The traditionalist critique does not directly concern us in the first analysis, inasmuch as it does not oppose individualism to citizenship, but rather rejects both by conflating them. This is the violently hostile position of Cochin:

[82] Robert K. Merton, 'Continuities in the Theories of Reference Group Behaviour', in *Social Theory and Social Structure* (New York: Free Press, 1968), 422–40. Cf. esp. Rose Laub Coser, 'The Complexity of Roles as a Seedbed of Individual Autonomy', in Lewis A. Coser (ed.), *The Idea of Social Structure: Papers in Honour of Robert K. Merton* (New York: Harcourt Brace Jovanovich, 1975), 237–63.

[83] Compare this e.g. with the qualities of citizen according to Merriam (see n. 37 above) and with the democratic individual who is, according to Baechler, ethically individualist, politically autonomous, and psychically individuated, Baechler, *Démocraties*, pp. 202–4.

[84] Ferdinand Brunetière, 'Après le procès', *La Revue des deux mondes*, 67 (13 Mar. 1898), 445, an eloquent anti-Dreyfusard defence to which Durkheim replied.

[85] This opposition–condemnation is not found in Fourier. Louis Blanc saw in it an opposition–transition, and speaks of the greatness and achievements of individualism (Lukes, *Individualism*, pp. 11–12) in terms reminiscent of Marx's attitude to the bourgeoisie.

In France the revolutionary catastrophe downgraded national sentiment, by degrees, from personal loyalty, and from earlier loyalty which gave everything without counting the cost, and which served without denouncing others, to legal solidarity, to social trade unionism which, on principle, responds to the highest bidder, which offers nothing in the way of risks, which always claims and demands, and never gives, and makes of France a society of shareholders, a socialism of economic interests, and of the nation a selfish trade union. It is the rule of the *citizen*, of social man by definition, the rule of unity, of indivisibility, as our Jacobins put it.[86]

Cochin's traditionalist critique is of major significance because it in fact illustrates the dominant paradigm through its apparent rejection of it. In general, the paradigm considers individualism as a threat to public-spiritedness and participative citizenship. Cochin, on the other hand, considers individualism as leading to a suffocating participation which destroys personal freedom (which the dominant paradigm would call 'civil'). Like Rousseau's citizen, a totally autonomous self and a member of a totally unified social whole, Cochin's citizen is free in opinion and the producer-product of a 'new consensus around a deified and constantly reaffirmed social whole'.[87] However, whereas the participating citizen of Rousseau has, or should have, divested himself of self-esteem through rational, individual calculation in the name of the general good, Cochin's activist participant operates according to a diametrically opposite logic. Here, it is the equally rational but selfish calculation of social man which is the basis of active participation. Cochin's argument is the following: solidarity is based in principle on a sense of justice which leads the individual to pay his dues, 'but all debts are loans and it is as loans that solidarity becomes effective. It is necessary to keep an eye on one's neighbour in order not to have to pay for him, and it is easy, in the case of fraud, to unleash against one's neighbour all the power of collective resentment: the cry against selfishness "which grows fat on the sweat of the people" is still heard. The basis of unity is the *interest* and not the duty of each person, *watchfulness*, and not conscience, constraint and *fear*, not

---

[86] Augustin Cochin, *La Révolution et la libre-pensée* (Paris: Copernic, 1979), 212–13 (texts written in 1898 and 1909). By 'social man', Cochin means man tied by a 'social tie', as distinct from personal and living ties. In the 'social tie' 'wrong doing by others releases me; and my obedience without theirs is completely gratuitous stupidity, and a good lost'. There is a symmetry here with Olson's paradox of collective action where the free rider could say, 'My disobedience, thanks to their obedience, is a behaviour which profits me, a good gained'.

[87] François Furet, *Penser la Révolution française* (Paris: Gallimard, 1978), 227.

enthusiasm and love.'[88] Activist citizenship is the result of individual-ism because this functions according to interest, that is to say, according to resentment and envy.

This surprising view, however (which would not, of course, surprise a Zinoviev), hides another, which is much more significant and logi-cally problematic: the social in Cochin's sense, that is to say, a social which is entirely conscious of itself via the morally and cognitively sovereign individual, cannot be the basis of community life. Conse-quently, citizenship cannot itself be based only upon the inter-individual contract without becoming its opposite, that is, material and intellectual subjugation:

> Orthodoxy rests on dogma and implies a *credo*. Society does not have one, precisely because it has replaced faith and loyalty by contract and solidarity. It is not to a particular article of its programme that it owes its unity, but to watchfulness and the argument for solidarity. It has all the rigidity of the faithless orthodoxies on which it is based: external and material unity without internal and moral unity.[89]

If we take away Cochin's spiritualist language and convert it into Durkheimian terms (bearing in mind the danger of misinterpretation at the level of each of their opinions), if the social subconsciousness of a collectivity is perceived as subconscious and, because of this, becomes suspect, the 'despotism of society' becomes intolerable, because it no longer constitutes 'the atmosphere which weighs upon the shoulders of each individual'.[90] The divine becomes (sociologi-cally) the 'camouflaged social': it ceases, in the instant it is named, to fulfil its function of personal identification. Generalized revelation and the 'disenchantment of the world' lead to personality disorders,

---

[88] Cochin, *La Révolution*, p. 155. We can note in passing how Cochin, anti-sociologi-cal individualist, can be just as good a methodological individualist as Rousseau.

[89] Ibid. 153.

[90] The expressions are Durkheim's own. When Cochin writes, 'An individual is a being freed from all moral authority, all ties of this kind being considered as purely *voluntary*', *La Révolution*, p. 149, he is expressing in his own language the Durkheimian idea that society as a moral entity becomes more permissive and less personalizing (that is less supplying of identity) because everything is held as being in principle *sub judice*. Cochin would object to such an assimilation, but it is an epistemological point. For the sociologist, only the social and the individual exist. But if these are objectified and reified (sociology was born with Cochin's 'social'), they cease to function. For personal-ist philosophy, only the 'person' and 'real society' exist (and God). All this cannot be reduced to the 'social'. Different epistemologies cannot construct the same object, but they can indicate the same problem by constructing it in a different though homologous way.

whether individual or collective, and to escape in the form of a search for conformity.[91]

The dilemma of democratic theory   To a certain extent it could be said that our discussion hitherto has been an extremely 'French' one which interprets both citizenship and individualism as Jacobin in form. The traditionalist critique too may be regarded as a blueprint of conservatism: 'Draw our prejudices around us, they keep us warm'. Such a phrase, however, is possible only inasmuch as prejudice has ceased to be part of us and has become part of an ideology. What we have here is the debate concerning the foundations of political obligation from the moment traditional beliefs were drowned in the 'icy waters of egoistical calculation'. Can authority exist unless it is taken as given, and incorporated, and not as external, and revisable?[92] Is an order of monks possible without a founding father, a group of believers without a founding (and non-social) Koran, members of a tribe without lineage, holy orders without founding saints? Similarly, are citizens possible without a basis other than possessive or, more generally, 'social' individualism?

We can describe the constant dilemma of modern democratic theory as follows: democratic citizenship is either founded rationally upon the self-interest (even well-understood or enlightened interest) of each individual. If this is the case, how does one avoid the conclusion that this interest leads to a 'culture of subjects' orientated towards outputs, which in turn leads to the degeneration of public spirit which 'substitutes more and more particular interests for sentiments, opinions, and shared ideas'?[93] Or else it is a 'culture of participation' orientated towards inputs, such civic loyalism having to find its origin elsewhere than in individual interest which leads naturally, at the level of behaviour, to Olson's 'free rider', the clientelist vote, or to social corporatism, depending on the circumstances, and, at the level of structures, to the impersonal exploitation of the labour market. In this case, democratic citizenship has no sociological base. How can participative democracy be encouraged if paternalistic authoritarianism

[91] 'As Durkheim pointed out, it is conformity which replaces the old arguments of reason, sentiment or interest. Such is the will of the people. Such is the new and only argument.' Cochin, *La Révolution*, p. 153.

[92] The overall problem is (exhaustively) treated using the whole range of sociological theory in Roland Robertson and Burkart Holzner (eds.), *Identity and Authority* (Oxford: Blackwell, 1980). Ibn Khaldun, who was not a specialist of the complex division of labour, put it more elegantly: no power without identity, no identity without cohesion.

[93] Speech by Alexis de Tocqueville to the Chamber of Deputies, 27 Jan. 1848.

and/or an 'amoral familism'[94] seem more effective? We should note that the dilemma remains formally the same if we introduce into the democratic scenario not the utilitarian and quantitative individualism of the market orientated towards comparability, but the qualitative individualism of German romanticism, orientated towards the incomparability and incommensurability of individuals. As Simmel has noted, 'this individualism (in which liberty is reduced to its purely internal sense) evolves easily into an anti-liberal tendency'.[95] For reasons substantially opposed to the reasoning informing the individualism of the Enlightenment or of utilitarianism, romantic individualism is part of the dilemma of citizenship, the former only being able to base citizenship on a 'mechanical unity' of atomized and indistinct individuals, the latter on an organic unity of individuals to each of whom the totality assigns a role. Such an interpretation places 'descending' or 'holistic' theories in an individualist context.

An individualism conscious of itself and constitutive of a *Zeitgeist* can only give to citizenship a moralist and voluntarist foundation whose contemporary version is the somewhat overused appeal to a 'social project'. Lindsay, the author, over forty years ago, of a remarkable work, *The Modern Democratic State*, raised the question of revealed legitimacy. Lindsay showed the extent to which the theory of monarchical divine right, by transferring the religious duty of obedience from law and the Church to the monarch, maintained the authority of God to the benefit of the absolute sovereign, who nevertheless claimed religious authority. He noted that this formula had the advantage of legitimating government better than could the rational calculation of individual advantages; the latter being unable to provide the stability and universal obedience which a political society requires: 'Reasoned individual selfishness is not enough ... A sense of interest has somehow to be translated into a sense of obligation.'[96]

There are several answers to this dilemma. The first is that in this precise context nothing can be the sociological basis of citizenship.[97]

[94] E. Banfield, *The Moral Basis of a Backward Society* (New York: Free Press, 1958).

[95] G. Simmel, 'L'Individu et la société dans certaines conceptions de l'existence du XVIIIᵉ siècle: Exemple de sociologie philosophique', in *Sociologie et épistémologie* (Paris: PUF, 1981), 137–60, in particular, p. 159.

[96] A. D. Lindsay, *The Modern Democratic State* (New York: Oxford University Press, 1962), 74 ff.

[97] C. B. Macpherson maintained that possessive individualism cannot be the basis of political obligation from the moment that property owners no longer constitute a united and hegemonic class. Let us remind ourselves of the eight principles of possessive individualism: (1) There is no authoritative association of work. (2) There is no

Stirner demonstrates this negatively by the absurdity of his own position. He conceives individualism as being a utilitarian and amoral attitude whereby the self sacrifices nothing to the well-being of 'human society', but only uses it. However, in order to be able to do this, he must make society his own property and shape it, that is to say, annihilate it and replace it with 'the union of egoists'.[98] The citizen himself is not possible in such a view, indeed, nor is Stirner's own individual, because in order for him to profit from society and not suffer from frustrated egoism, it would be necessary that others should not behave in the same manner, that is to say, be egoistical in a different way: no stowaways are possible without a boat that others sail. It is true that the 'union of egoists' can function, but only in order to produce individual goods or exclusive collective goods. However, citizenship is involved among other things in the production of inclusive collective goods.[99] Stirner's individualism, therefore, excludes citizenship. This is why, according to him, the French Revolution did not emancipate the individual but only the citizen, not real men, but only one form of the human species, the *genre* of citizen. And it is only as such, and not as a person, that the individual was liberated. Henceforth, it is the nation, and not the individual, which becomes the agent of history.

Marx says more or less the opposite: the individual was 'freed' in the form of the bourgeois (with his necessary corollary, the worker, able to sell his labour power in the market). This individualism, however, also excludes citizenship.[1] In bourgeois society, 'the individual' and 'the citizen' are in a necessary (in the sense that neither could exist without the other) and antagonistic relation. *Homo oeconomicus* and *homo politicus* are radically distinct. It is assumed that the first will behave according to needs and selfish interests, the

authoritative provision of rewards for work. (3) There is authoritative definition and enforcement of contracts. (4) All individuals seek rationally to maximize their utilities. (5) Each individual's capacity to labour is his own property and is alienable. (6) Land and resources are owned by individuals and are alienable. (7) Some individuals want a higher level of utilities or power than they have. (8) Some individuals have more energy, skill, or possessions than others. *Possessive Individualism*, pp. 53–4.

[98] Max Stirner, *The Ego and its Own: The Case of the Individual against Authority* (1844), quoted in Lukes, *Individualism*, p. 19.

[99] Cf. M. Olson, *The Logic of Collective Action* (Cambridge, Mass.: Harvard University Press, 1965), in particular, pp. 36–43.

[1] Karl Marx, *The Jewish Question*, in *Early Writings* (Harmondsworth: Penguin, 1975); *The Holy Family* (London: Lawrence & Wishart, 1957). See also Shlomo Avineri, *The Social and Political Thought of Karl Marx* (London: Cambridge University Press, 1968); Wood, *Mind and Politics*, pp. 147 ff.

second according to universal criteria, an example being the emancipation of the Jews, proof of the separation of state and religion and of the triumph of citizenship. According to this view man has thus a double life, celestial and terrestrial, not only in thought but in reality: he leads the universal life of the species ('generic being') as a member of the political community, and a material life as a private individual, where he treats other men as means, reduces himself to a means, and becomes the toy of outside powers.[2] Real individuality[3] is destroyed on both sides: in 'civil society', here the individual appears real to himself and to others, he is an illusory phenomenon; in the 'state', where he appears as a member of the species, he is only an imaginary member of an imagined sovereignty, turned away from his real individual life and endowed with an unreal universality.

We can observe that, for Marx, it is only bourgeois individualism which has this relation of constitution–negation with citizenship; only a fully realized individuality would enable the individual to become a true citizen. When the real individual has attained for himself the status of the abstract citizen, when he has become, in daily life and in work, a universal man (that is to say not separated from the species) and has been enabled by material life to recognize and exercise his own powers as social powers unseparated from political powers, only then will his 'human emancipation' be complete.[4] In this case, however, we are no longer dealing with the same 'individualism', and the notion of 'citizenship', even the notion of the 'political', changes its meaning, if not disappears. At this point, Marx takes a leap into the unknown future, just as Cochin makes a leap into the unknown past (because no longer lived). Each can only imagine or reinvent what led them to a critical sociology of their actual object, but cannot establish a positive sociology of something else ('human emancipation' for Marx, 'real society' for Cochin). It is true that subsequently we have

---

[2] T. H. Marshall illustrates this point by showing that the ephemeral institution of 'social rights' in England at the beginning of the 19th century (the Poor Law, and the Speenhamland System analysed by Karl Polanyi) was based upon an earlier model which was neither individualist nor related to citizenship: the poor were to be protected from the labour market as members of a community of the medieval type and, because of this, were excluded from the rights and responsibilities of citizenship, Marshall, 'Citizenship and Social Class', pp. 87–90. The true individual had to be a 'free' individual, without social protection, selling and buying freely labour power in order to be a citizen endowed with rights.

[3] Real individuality (which is not that of the individual of civil society) can be assimilated in Marx's work with the term 'independence'.

[4] *The Jewish Question*.

had certain information on Leninist-Stalinist 'human emancipation', but this 'something else' is 'another story' which perhaps has something to do with individualism (if we are to believe Zinoviev and Louis Dumont), but certainly nothing to do with either citizenship or 'real individuality'.

The negative thesis (or the non-solution of the dilemma) is very strong. One does not need to subscribe to Marxism as a global system (and in particular to its scorn for political rights) to recognize this. Even if one considers that the political emancipation of the citizen not only is 'formal', but is precisely what saves the real individual from being dissolved, as it were, either in the market or in some romantic community (or denied by the total state), the empirical situation which the thesis refers to is no less problematic. This can be illustrated directly by 'evidence' compatible with the construction of the thesis itself, but also indirectly by 'incongruous' evidence which does not fit into the framework of the construction, but which illustrates in a different way the problem posed by it.

First, the 'compatible' evidence is provided (at least in part) by micro-sociology and the study of behaviour. Sombart's 'bourgeois' offers examples. Here is 'one of the initiators of high German capitalism' whose 'only ambition … in undertaking the construction of the railways was to make enough money to be able to buy a large property, give up business and, *when the occasion arose, obtain a parliamentary seat in order to devote himself entirely to parliamentary activity*', and who, 'driven on by circumstance', 'expanded more and more the sphere of his activities, moving further and further away from his original plan, and, thinking only of how to realize his ideas for the greatest good of the workers, ended up by devoting himself to business'. Doctor Strousberg is clearly here more 'Weberian' than 'Marxian', but the description of this type of 'isolated' man for whom 'the Fatherland becomes … a foreign land, a land of exile', for whom 'nature, art, literature, the state, friends, all disappear … into a mysterious nothingness', because 'he no longer has "time" to be involved in all of that',[5] is a striking example of the uncivic (*incivique*) force of 'civil society'.

The ordinary man is just as divided: Marcel Waline has noted that, after the introduction of obligatory military service in France in 1872, the 'bourgeoisie and sadly the intellectuals [*sic*] managed to restrict

[5] *Dr Strousberg und sein Wirken von ihm selbst geschilder* (1876), quoted by Werner Sombart, *Le Bourgeois* (Paris: Payot, 1928; republished 1966), 333, my italics, and 335.

privilege to themselves especially in the form of the one year voluntary service. When these privileges were suppressed in 1889, there was a real outburst of anti-militarism by the intellectuals.'[6] He has also noted examples of resistance to fiscal measures,[7] and concludes that the 'individualist spirit contributed to the neglect of the most crucial national interests'. Are these illustrations of the strength of 'civil society' or of the sense of the alien and extraneous character of the state which has less to do with individualism than with 'traditional' behaviour, a good example of which would be the fiscal revolts in Arab countries, in Tunisia among others, in the nineteenth century? Resistance to citizenshp is not all 'civil' or 'individualist'. Bourgeois France, nevertheless, can be classed among civil societies, as can be, *a fortiori*, the United States: Robert Lane's in-depth interviews, long before the Vietnam crisis and the permissive society, are all the more striking given that they involved good, white, lower-middle- and working-class citizens, the conscientious pillars of their local communities, all ideal game for Merton's sociology. Lane, nevertheless, highlights a conflict and an ambiguity of roles between the civic citizen and the man trying to lead his private life, a situation which creates feelings of unease and disquiet for approximately one-third of those interviewed, the essential point being that: 'the vague and unstructured area of duty implied in the concept of citizenship invites a variety of guilty feelings, each reflecting some more basic problem faced in other areas of life by the "guilty party".'[8]

Lane's observations can be interpreted in two and, in our opinion, non-contradictory ways: classically, one would say that the individual who is little integrated into 'civil society' is likely to be a 'tense' citizen, but we can note also that the abstraction of the life of the citizen makes this role more vulnerable to the tensions which affect the individual in his private life.

It is not necessary to fall back on Ronald Inglehart's thesis on the

---

[6] Waline, *L'Individualisme et le droit*, p. 328.

[7] 'Fiscal legalism' is still not doing too well in France, particularly among the young (18–24-year-olds). The statement, 'A good citizen pays his taxes, without trying to defraud the Inland Revenue', received positive response from 20% of them in 1976, and 18% in 1983, against, respectively, 49 and 44% of the 65s and over. This did not stop 75% (in 1976) and 71% (in 1983) of the same 18–24 age group from declaring virtuously that 'it is important to be a good citizen'. To this question, the number of negative replies and did not answers is striking (25% in 1976 and 29% in 1983), Olivier Duhamel, 'L'Évolution du dissensus français', in SOFRES, *Opinion publique, 1984* (Paris: Gallimard, 1984), 137.

[8] Lane, 'The Tense Citizen', pp. 280–1 and 282. Interviews conducted in 1957–8.

'silent revolution' of post-materialist values,[9] on the ideas developed
by Christopher Lasch on 'the culture of narcissism',[10] on the increased
need for 'transparency', autonomy, active wealth, and roots as
opposed to membership of large, abstract entities such as 'France',
and on the development of ideas such as 'personal expression', 'less
attachment to the established order', 'less sexual differentiation', as
complacently put forward by the Cofremca,[11] to see that the point
emphasized by Marx was not, after all, held in such disdain.

Inglehart's views appear at first sight directly contrary to Marx's
(though not to Stirner's) because they attribute to post-materialist
individualism values which are almost the opposite of those of the
individualism of industrial society: hedonism instead of Puritan egoism, denigration instead of the cult of science, the quest for community life instead of fierce competition, a concern with the quality of
life rather than with growth and consumption. However — assuming
these views are justified[12] — they, in fact, create a new 'civil society'
which widens the gap between the individual (the ex-bourgeois, now
middle manager-intellectual), who has become more and more concrete (and illusory), and the citizen, who has become more and more
abstract. Inglehart's findings are undoubtedly outstanding examples of
'incongruous evidence'.

The macro-sociological theses which arrive at similar conclusions
are too numerous to be properly dealt with here. We can note,
however, the classic theme of dualism or of disjunction between, to
paraphrase Weber, the kingdoms of the 'constellation of interests' and
of 'the moral order of authority'. Weber identified, in modern capitalism, the development of an ethic of responsibility which allowed for
the motivation of individuals in economic life (according to Sombart's
'bourgeois' model). Weber did not, however, elucidate a comparable
cultural resource which provided motivation for the political

---

[9] Ronald Inglehart, *The Silent Revolution: Changing Values and Political Style among
Western Publics* (Princeton, NJ: Princeton University Press, 1977).

[10] Christopher Lasch, *The Culture of Narcissism* (New York: Norton, 1978).

[11] Cofremca: Compagnie française d'études de marché et de conjoncture. We can
judge the interpretations these results can give rise to if we consider the phrase:
'Television makes the people it shows relatively transparent', Alain de Vulpian,
'L'Évolution des mentalités: Conformisme et modernité', in Jean-Daniel Reynaud and
Yves Grafmeyer (eds.), *Français, qui êtes-vous?* (Paris: La Documentation française,
1981), 307.

[12] C. Wilensky's critique: Harold L. Wilensky, 'Le Corporatisme démocratique, le
consentement populaire et la politique sociale: Quelques Considérations sur l'évolution
des valeurs morales et la "crise" de l'État protecteur', in *L'État protecteur en crise* (Paris:
OCDE, 1981), 215–28.

rationality of citizenship, given that the state was culturally differentiated from the nation.[13] Daniel Bell, in the context of advanced capitalism and an interventionist state economy, has argued that 'Western society lacks both *civitas*, the spontaneous willingness to make sacrifices for some public good, and a political philosophy that justifies the normative rules of priorities and allocations in the society'.[14] In Parsonian[15] terms, one could argue that 'societal community', that is to say, shared moral commitments which allow a society to define its criteria of membership and to support political and economic activities essential to its self-maintenance, and to base itself upon instrumental values of self-interest, can no longer support the polity (collective organization for the achievement of aims) at the point at which it most needs it. These general observations, however, are less pertinent than the analyses of James Coleman arguing from a completely different sociological perspective.

James Coleman, analysing the development of corporate persons, that is, impersonal actors who are not the prolongation of physical individuals but only the aggregate of specialized roles which individuals must play, emphasizes that individualism is exacerbated by new structures of influence born of commercial marketing: 'the interests that are most easily nurtured and strengthened by advertising are interests of self-indulgence. It is especially easy to convince a person to spend money on the self.' He points out that the term 'duty' has practically disappeared from current usage for, in a social structure made up of new impersonal actors, only 'duties of office' are relevant, and never duty towards another person.[16] The resources of citizenship—empathy with and civility towards 'fellow-citizens' (and not only members of his 'group')—are affected by this, in that its abstract

[13] See Richard K. Fenn, 'Religious Identity and Authority in the Secular Society', and Roland Robertson, 'Aspects of Identity and Authority in Sociological Theory', in Robertson and Holzner, *Identity and Authority*, pp. 119–44, 218–65. See also David Beetham, 'Class Society and Plebiscitary Leadership', in *Max Weber and the Theory of Modern Politics* (London: Allen & Unwin, 1974), 215–49, and Jeffrey Prager, 'Moral Integration and Political Inclusion: A Comparison of Durkheim's and Weber's Theories of Democracies', *Social Forces*, 59/4 (1981), 918–50.

[14] Daniel Bell, *The Cultural Contradictions of Capitalism* (London: Heinemann, 1976), 25. This is a good example of the 'incongruous evidence' of Marx's intuition, not only because Bell interprets his information in a 'conservative' way, but above all because 'civil society' has become strongly 'public', even though the dualist structure remains the same.

[15] T. Parsons, *Societies: Evolutionary and Contemporary Perspectives* (Englewood Cliffs, NJ: Prentice-Hall, 1966), 13–19.

[16] Coleman, *The Asymmetric Society*, pp. 131–3.

and imaginary character can only be accentuated. In a fascinating reflection on the education of children, Coleman reminds us that the family, one of the only impersonal actors still existing which is a prolongation of physical individuals, was, in the past, an overall structure of physical, economic, and social reproduction: it prescribed personalized roles, and constituted a community and a unit of production or employment allocation. All this is uncontentious enough since Le Play. The consequences are all the more unexpected: in the traditional family, the child is, in economic terms, a 'private good', an investment which the parents would profit from in their old age.[17] This is no longer the case: the child is no longer a private good which is taken care of, but an obstacle to the roles which parents must occupy in impersonal organizations and professions. The child becomes a 'public good' and 'as with every public good, the fundamental question arises, who will pay the cost of the public good? That is, who will take the responsibility for rearing children and for investing resources in them? The question must increasingly be answered, "no one", as parents see it less and less in their interest to make such investments,[18] and there is no actor at a level below the state other than the family in whose interests such an investment lies.'[19]

The state must, therefore, intervene, as it does in areas such as care for the old and the sick. In order to do this it needs money and, of course, citizens able to contribute such money. These, however, are more and more abstract for the very same reason that individuals have more and more need of money. And the reason is simple: the individualist individual of civil society externalizes costs and internalizes gains, not because he is more selfish than his 'holist' cousin, but because this is the rational strategy of possessive individualism. There is no reason

[17] We should point out that these 'private' goods are often members of a 'whole' in terms of lineage. The community is the normative basis which allows children to be treated as a 'private good' that one sells second-hand.

[18] Coleman shows, against the economists of human resources, that investment in children has decreased, even though qualitative investment has increased (*The Asymmetric Society*, p. 127 n.). This may be true but there is a much easier way of scaling down investment, which is not to have children. These disappear as a good (private or public). It is, therefore, quite possible that economists see, in their graphs, investment per child increase; Coleman is, nevertheless, basically right.

[19] Coleman, *The Asymmetric Society*, pp. 127–8. One cannot but be struck by the fact that occasional and useless 'natalist' campaigns usually have the theme 'Who will pay your pension?', as if the naming of an 'individualist' reason for reproduction (assuming it were empirically founded) had ever globally modified practices which were in another context (that of community) legitimate. One can consume because one is convinced that this serves the individual, one cannot socially reproduce for the same reason.

182   *Jean Leca*

why the maxim 'socialize losses, privatize profits' should belong only to 'private' entrepreneurs. Public entrepreneurs and ordinary individuals behave in the same way.[20] There is little modification here of the fundamental principles of possessive individualism. However, of Macpherson's eight principles, only the sixth, 'land and resources are owned by individuals and are alienable', has been modified, and the second, third, and eighth, 'there is no authoritative provision of rewards for work', 'there is authoritative definition and enforcement of contracts', 'some individuals have more energy, skill, or possessions than others', have been contested or eroded, without, however, having disappeared altogether.

Each person is a conscious and intelligent owner of his own abilities and desires in a game where the impersonal 'system' is more and more important (whether one plays the game or 'cheats', from evading tax to pinching things in the supermarket), and the political community more and more suspect and thus exposed. The more one is 'alienated' from the political community, the more one is a 'gambler' in civil society; and one has a greater need of the public-spiritedness of others the less one needs to practise it for oneself. Stirner is not, after all, all that obsolete in his absurdist reasoning. The imagined universal citizen remains a necessity for the individual of civil society (here Marx's opposition still holds), but the individual has perhaps dug his own grave by 'exposing' the citizen and depriving him of his universal community basis, given that he has been reduced to the position of consumer in the political market-place.

There is a slightly different way of telling this story, namely, by referring to the thesis (equally Marxian, but which Marx did not use in this way) according to which explicit justifications are different from (because unaware of) the non-perceived determinants of social institu-

---

[20] This explains among other things the sociological puzzle we mentioned earlier: 'private' individualism in life-styles, marriage, bringing up children, etc., and 'social' collectivism (or solidarity). For examples see, respectively, Émérencienne de Lagrange, 'La Crise de la famille, le législateur et le juge', *Mélanges Weill* (Paris: Dalloz-Lifec, 1983), 353, and also Edmond Bertrand, *L'Esprit nouveau des lois civiles* (Paris: Economica, 1984), which notes the infiltration of the family, the importance of moral and collective aspects 'even if they are limited principally to the immediate family in the home and to the children', pp. 49 ff., and François Ewald, *Assurance-prévoyance-sécurité: Formation historique des techniques de gestion sociale dans les sociétés industrielles* (Paris: Ministère du Travail et de la Participation, 1979). Coleman would probably see in this evidence that the 'structures of relation' between an individual and 'corporate actors' (in the case of 'social collectivism') are different from structures of relations between physical individuals (in 'private individualism'), and that it is this

tions. Fred Hirsch has argued that the success of the market and the civil society individual were due, not to a calculating individualism, as Marx thought, but to its opposite: a social ethos which predated the market. Respect for truth, trust, self-discipline, a sense of obligation, all these 'social virtues', rooted in religious beliefs, have played a role in the functioning of a contractual individualist economy.[21] Western religion, however, is 'disenchanted' and has become a 'private' affair, and subject to the rational judgement of *Zweckrationalität*, that is to say, in Weberian terms, instrumentalized, or, in Cochin's terms, 'socialized',[22] that is, has undermined its own role in providing a social ethos. The moral foundations of the market, therefore, have been shaken while its behavioural norms (self-interest) have attained a quasi-hegemony.

It is possible that citizenship has enjoyed the same fate: officially based on the contract between 'rational' and 'universal' individuals, it was perhaps based on the 'pre-contractual' element of ethnic and religious communities and displaced on to the state, a situation which would allow for the play of 'opinions'.[23] As the explicit norms of citizenship gained the ascendant (while modelling themselves on the norms of market individualism via the idea of 'free access' to the political community and to the goods offered by it, via 'opinion' as an expression of demand, and via the vote as strategy and response to electoral supply), its social foundations were eroded, and this at the moment it was all the more necessary to the functioning of civil society, now deprived of its social ethos. Citizenship was not only indispensable to bourgeois society in order to maintain the abstract idea of an unreal universality, and to legitimate class domination under cover of the state, as Marx maintained; it is even more necessary to the Welfare State in order to support civil society by increasing the social rights of individuals and by orientating their actions towards the needs

which produces the illusion of two incoherent systems, see James S. Coleman, *Power and the Structure of Society* (New York: Norton, 1974), 36.

[21] Fred Hirsch, *Social Limits to Growth* (London: Routledge & Kegan Paul, 1977), 12, 141. We can see how much this thesis owes to Weber.

[22] At the other end of the spectrum, individualized religion produces 'irrational' and romantic religion based only upon the emotions of feeling.

[23] We can interpret in this sense the two apparently incompatible Durkheimian theses according to which the democratic state encourages the critical spirit, liberated from unchecked prejudices (which implies a flexible and modifiable self (*moi*)) and presents itself as a kind of sacred manifestation of collective consciousness, a form parallel to the divine principle governing religions. See Prager, 'Moral Integration and Political Inclusion', pp. 936–7.

of the community.[24] The paradox is that a citizenship which has explicitly this aim of prothesis of individualist society can only become all the more 'disenchanted'. The process of disenchantment of society thus makes the enchantment of the citizen necessary at the same time as it undermines him.

The solutions to the dilemma and their inadequacies   'Eppur, si muove ...' at least for a while. The Keynesian state and the Welfare State developed around a combination of civil society and citizenship, the effects of which are far from exhausted.[25] There are, therefore, other answers to the dilemma. We shall mention two: the alchemy of the community of small groups; the effect of predisposition resulting from the possibilities opened up to individual strategies.

The first is proposed by Saint-Just:

The *patrie* is not the earth but the community of feelings which means that because each person fights for the safety and freedom of what each holds dear, the *patrie* is itself defended. If each person comes out of his cottage with a rifle in his hand, the *patrie* will be saved. Each person fights for what he loves: that is what is called speaking in good faith. To fight for everyone is only the effect.[26]

This is clearly in the Roman vein of the labouring citizen, and is reinforced by the pastoral image of the cottage. We should note, however, that the idea could be applied in its entirety to the mobilization of a ghetto against the police in a city or inner city. Active citizenship is enhanced here by the notion of the love of each for his kith and kin (those who are like him. Saint-Just forgets to add 'and from resentment against those who are different from him'), civic mobilization ('to fight for everyone') being 'only the effect'. This does

[24] This problem is at the centre of discussions on the economy of collective goods and on the orientation of individual action towards collective needs. Cf. Hirsch, *Social Limits to Growth*, pp. 145–51.

[25] This is in particular Harold Wilensky's thesis ('Le Corporatisme démocratique', n. 12, p. 179). See also *The 'New Corporatism', Centralisation and the Welfare State* (London: Sage, 1976). The great bulk of recent literature on neo-corporatism can be interpreted as a social-democratic version of Marx's distinction supplemented by the organization of interests in representative corporations, and the negotiations between these and the state, Gehrard Lehmbruch and Philippe Schmitter (eds.), *Patterns of Corporatist Policy-Making* (London: Sage, 1982).

[26] Quoted by Gerard Mairet, 'Peuple et nation', in François Châtelet (ed.), *Histoire des idéologies* (Paris: Hachette, 1978), ii. 74.

not stop Saint-Just from advocating the reinforcement of this civic disposition by proposing compulsory conscription for the young,[27] although the basis for it is attachment to the 'little *patries*'. Instead of withdrawing peacefully with his family and friends, like his Tocquevillian equivalent, the individualist of Saint-Just takes his family (those old enough to fight) and takes up his gun. The first makes a living from trade, the second makes war. This, however, is not the real difference between them. Saint-Just's citizenship is possible because the individual is a member of a community of communities, a situation which allows us to see in this 'society', in Durkheimian terms, 'a moral entity, or rather an ethical one'.[28] The 'pre-contractual' element is maintained, not by an anachronistic delaying effect (the survival of traditional holist elements in an individualist context), but by a synchronic transferring on to a new object. However, can a community be based only on the loyalty 'of free men under a shared law', in Marshall's terms (Saint-Just would add 'virtuous'), or else does it posit a pre-existing entity?

Stinchcombe's individualist thesis faces a similar problem.[29] The institutional plenitude of the group, the superimposing of the ecological ranges of individuals and group, and the possibility of resolving individual problems in the framework of the group are the three requirements which, together, predispose the individual to loyalism, that is to say, to identifying his interest with that of the group and, consequently, to sacrificing his individual interest to the profit of the group's interest. Each individual taken in isolation can be tempted to become 'a free rider', but the composition of individual wills probably produces an identification with the group if the latter satisfies three requirements. Loyalism is an output of the operation of the group, but thus becomes an input within the system, which comes not from each individual but from the collective identity of the group, and produces in its turn the additional incentive required by Olson for collective action (or at least ensures that this is not hampered by too great a

---

[27] 'The young should, instead of wasting their lives in the delights and idle vice of capital cities, wait to reach majority in the fighting army. One should achieve the right of citizenship only after four years' army service. Then would we see a more serious youth and love of the patrie become a public passion', 'Esprit de la révolution et de la Constitution de la France' (1791), in *Théorie politique*, texts compiled and commented by Alain Liénard (Paris: Seuil, 1976), 83.

[28] Mairet, 'Peuple et nation'. We should remember, however, that for Durkheim it is the state rather than the people which is the ethical entity in individualist society.

[29] Stinchcombe, 'Social Structure and Politics', p. 163 n. 2.

degree of passivity).

Stinchcombe's argument could be placed alongside the 'procedural' thesis in spite of his apparent distance from its recognized advocates: it is the validity of a procedure (in this case, the three requirements) which constitutes the basis of political obligation and predisposes individuals not to close themselves off by withdrawal or violent secession. Of course this procedure is not based directly on the self-interest of the 'new contractualists',[30] but is mediated via a structure of communication and cultural unification which makes the group other than an aggregate of isolated individuals, and makes loyalism other than the product of a synallagmatic contact ('I support you because you — the group — help me'). Nevertheless, the procedure governs. There can, however, be different procedures for different problems according to the position of the individual within the social structure. He can be both alienated and politically excluded even though 'succeeding' economically. He will therefore give his loyalism to a group (the 'Algerian nation', for example) while 'resolving [some of] his problems' in the framework of the group from which loyalism has been withdrawn (by buying goods in 'France' or choosing to go there and set himself up in business or send his children to be educated). These are, of course, constrained strategies (like most strategies), which produce 'incoherences of status', but which are necessary to combine the honour of the life-style with the interest of the economic actor. Because of this, loyalism itself will not always be the result of the three requirements but a predisposition to find that, on a problem (that of political identity), one group fulfils the requirements, even though on another problem (that of economic possibilities) it does not fulfil them as well. It is therefore possible that, as Stinchcombe puts it, the more a person sees the problems in his life resolved within the framework of the institutional order created by the political system, the more that person will identify the system with his own life.[31] However, the way in which the person judges whether his problems are 'resolved' can depend in its turn on his pre-existing identification with the group. This is not a problem of procedure but of affinity of life-style and of the internalization of substantive norms which define a type of ration-

---

[30] See Scott Gordon, 'The New Contractarians', *Journal of Political Economy*, 84 (1976), 573–890. See also Georges Lavau and Olivier Duhamel, 'La Démocratie', in M. Grawitz and J. Leca (eds.), *Traité de science politique*, ii: *Les Régimes politiques contemporains* (Paris: PUF, 1985), 91–5 (on Hayek), 95–100 (on Rawls and Nozick).

[31] Stinchcombe, 'Social Structure and Politics', p. 615.

ality.[32] Thus, accepted and loyal citizenship can be the result, not of success in the pursuit of individual interests, but of a weakening of the barriers of status and of a greater communication between life-styles, all of which modify the conditions of calculation.

It does not therefore appear possible to resolve logically the dilemma if we start from individualism nor, consequently, to establish the basis of a citizenship within a society operating upon the basis of individualism. The present crisis of citizenship is possibly only the continuation of a long history begun with the appearance of the modern individual. It does not, however, follow that citizenship remains abstract and empty, nor that individualism is purely and simply self-destructive. It is possible that a dilemma which cannot logically be overcome is, at the same time, sociologically necessary to the functioning of a society: the combination of two contradictory principles, the private and calculating individual, optimizing on the market, and who is both the producer and product of a new type of class inequality, and the individual, participating in a community of rights, equal to others, exchanging rights and obligations for the common good and investing a loyalism in the city, is perhaps the non-logical spring of contemporary societies. The individual of the economics of politics and the individual of political economy are both part of the same society, but not of the same 'system', and that is why the citizen is not simply the falsely generic, necessary abstraction of the bourgeois-individual. The tension between them, borne of belonging to two different systems, is the basis of democratic society, which is always informed by the civil, liberal, and inegalitarian principle on the one hand, and by the civic, interventionist, and egalitarian principle on the other.[33] The present extension of the civil principle is clear: interventionism is no longer justified in Western democracies, as it was at the beginnings of the Keynesian state, by the necessary politicization

[32] Harold Wilensky has made the following observation: it is not the level of imposition and social expenditure that best explains the 'taxpayers revolt', but the taxes themselves which have *'visible* repercussions which are particularly unpleasant', 'Le Corporatisme démocratique', p. 225. He attributes this to the visibility of technical choices (direct tax on physical people, property tax). This strengthens the individualist thesis (in order that rational citizens do not protest, it is better that they remain ignorant of what is happening to them). But nothing here contradicts the assumption that there are also social and cultural conditions to visibility: one often sees what one's symbolic universe predisposes one to see. This would make an abstraction of the idea that the 'balance-sheet' of a government or state can be the object of a 'rational' appraisal.

[33] Ernest Gellner has argued that market liberalism can only be 'betrayed' by democratic governments, 'A Social Contract in Search of an Idiom: The Demise of the Danegeld State?', *Political Quarterly*, 46 (Apr.–June 1975), 127–52.

of the economy in the interest of social justice, and even less by the extension of citizenship to industry and the struggle against 'the private use of public money', but is justified by state support for the demands of individual autonomy.[34] It is true that these demands are more easily legitimated when they emanate from private individuals in the domain of morals and the environment, and from ethnic groups in the cultural domain, than from businesspeople in the economic domain. But a new tendency is appearing, born of the view that the civic principle and its corollary, the intervention of state power, produce effects as inegalitarian as the competitive market. It is in this spirit that appeals to the market are made, not only to increase the efficiency of the public services, but also to restore the sense of 'civic' responsibilities and obligations to citizens who have become passive and negative, and to public servants who have become 'patrimonial'. There is an intriguing paradox here in that market individualism is being asked to revive a failing public-spiritedness, a new variation indeed on the relations between the Puritan ethic and capitalism.[35]

These interesting social and ideological developments should not make us forget, however, that if market individualism can, just about, be based on an individual free from any social attachment and from community ties,[36] and therefore can operate as a self-maintaining mechanism, the same is not true of citizenship: the citizen individual is its agent and its aim, he cannot also be its social base (nor, because of this, its sovereign actor) whether by the magic of a voluntarism creative of community, such as that of Rousseau or Saint-Just, or by the subtle play of Stinchcombe's life-mastering strategies. The 'structures of mediation', claimed by social reformers of all ideological camps as filling the space between the isolated individual and organizations,[37] demonstrate a simple sociological truth: without community of some

[34] This is reminiscent of the theme of the 'silent revolution' and its ambiguities. Cf. the analysis of Bernard Cazes, 'L'État protecteur contraint à une double manœuvre', in *L'État protecteur en crise*, pp. 175–91 esp. pp. 184–6.

[35] M. Olson, *The Rise and Decline of Nations* (New Haven, Conn.: York University Press, 1982), 174–5.

[36] Defences of the market are now innumerable, but the most paradoxical contribution was made by a Catholic philosopher showing that the market has its roots in the community spirit of individuals and that it contributes to shape it towards more responsibility and solidarity, Michael Novak, *The Spirit of Democratic Capitalism* (New York: Simon & Schuster, 1982).

[37] See e.g. Peter L. Berger and Richard J. Neuhaus, *To Empower People: The Role of Mediating Structures in Public Policy* (Washington, DC: American Enterprise Institute, 1977). For some observations on the ambiguities of structures of mediation as generative of socio-cultural cleavages, see Nathan Glazer, '"Superstition" and Social Policy',

kind, there can be no citizenship, because a 'political community' is not a summation of individuals.

We have developed and clarified the dominant paradigm of the relations between individualism and citizenship, but only a part of the road has been travelled. We have taken individualism as being, for the clarity of our exposition, (1) a relatively precise and universal notion, (2) a characteristic of Western modernity. These two propositions are not as incontestable as they seem and should be analysed more closely in the light of historical documentation. Only such an analysis will allow us to refine the relationship of the individualisms and citizenships which we have identified, and to isolate better the pre-contractual social elements which govern individualist societies. The present study is only therefore an ensemble of the prolegomena necessary to a much wider enquiry.

Regional Studies, 12/5 (1978), 619–29; 'Des rôles et responsabilités en politique sociale', in *L'État protecteur en crise*, pp. 279–97, in particular, 293–5; 'Individual Rights against Group Rights', in *Ethnic Dilemmas 1974–1982* (Cambridge, Mass., London: Harvard University Press, 1983), 254–73.

PART III

INDIVIDUALISM AND COLLECTIVE ACTION

8

Individual Mobilization and Collective Action

CHARLES TILLY

What's the Problem?

The scholarly literature on popular collective action contains plenty of good descriptions and numerous general models, but leaves a gap between the two. Analysts who want to build serious theoretical foundations for the treatment of concrete social movements and real revolutions must work with defective theoretical apparatus, while theorists who start with models must adopt simplified, conventional accounts of well-known events, without developing new insights into the events. While our theories will always gain from new, insightful descriptions, at present we have a greater need for superior models and theories. Here are the chief conceptual and theoretical difficulties:

1. *Gaps within models.* Existing models supply more or less satisfactory accounts of the reasons for which a set of persons who share an interest undertake concerted action, treat less precisely the reasons for which individuals join collective action, and fail to establish convincing connections between the individual and collective decisions.

2. *Single-actor models.* Since real collective action generally consists of strategic interaction among groups and within groups, models that analyse the behaviour of a single actor miss their targets, especially when they assign the actor a unified orientation and a unique strategy.

Another version of this paper appeared as 'Models and Realities of Popular Collective Action', *Social Research*, 52 (winter 1985), 717–47, which translated and adapted the article's original French version. The National Science Foundation (USA) supported the research reported in this article. I have omitted the citations of archives and newspapers for the events of 1906; for more detail and full citations, see C. Tilly, *The Contentious French* (Cambridge: Belknap Press, 1986), 313–18.

3. *Static models.* Since collective action is dynamic, and since its consequences depend on the course of strategic interaction, static models that deduce the behaviour of a group from its character or from the consequences of its action represent the process badly.

4. *Emphasis on causal rather than purposive accounts of action.* Although it would be desirable to improve causal explanations and eliminate essentialist explanations (those that deduce action from the character of the actor), for the time being theorists do not have the means of creating causal, multi-actor models of such complex phenomena. At present models imputing ends, means, and decision rules to actors deal more effectively with collective action.

As we shall see, some theoreticians escape one or another of these difficulties: we have some interesting efforts to fill the gaps, some valuable multi-actor models, and so on. But in general theorists only achieve partial solutions to one of the problems by aggravating the others: they build, for example, purposive analyses of popular collective action by postulating single actors with unified dispositions. And no one escapes from all four difficulties.

The four problems help explain a peculiarity of writing about collective action: the sharp contrasts among lively models of different aspects of action, rich accounts of some types of action, and flaccid efforts to build comprehensive accounts of action. The complaint extends to my own efforts to build comprehensive accounts.

This essay will not resolve the theoretical difficulties presented by collective action. It will try merely to facilitate their resolution in two ways: by examining a few cases of collective action in which the connection between the individual and collective levels is clearly problematic, and by studying carefully the theoretical problems those cases present. The examination of a concrete set of collective actions rather than a fabricated example will complicate the analysis, but clarify the weaknesses of current models. With those ends in mind, let us examine conflicts that occurred in France during the spring of 1906 before considering the various possible ways of analysing the collective action involved in those events.

My analysis will emphasize conflict and discontinuous collective action, contestation rather than stability. The evidence comes from an inventory of strikes, collective violence, and 'contentious gatherings': moments in which people assemble in a publicly accessible place and make collective claims on others which would, if realized, touch the interests of those others. Contentious gatherings include almost all events that authorities, ruling classes, and badly informed scholars call 'riots', 'disorders', 'troubles', and the like, as well as many meetings, marches, and other gatherings for which all observers commonly use less derogatory terms.

For the period around 1906, my research group drew its calendar of events from a number of sources: the *Statistique des grèves*, correspondence and reports of the Justice and Interior ministries, local administrative archives, political annuals, and newspapers. The catalogue falls short of being comprehensive or even representative, but it does provide a large, rich picture of the action, the issues, and the consequences of popular collective action at a critical early moment of the twentieth century.

A Turbulent Spring

The spring of 1906 found France worried. Government workers were demanding the right to organize, labour unions were flexing their muscles, and the defenders of the Catholic Church were mobilizing. The CGT called for a series of giant demonstrations on May Day, a general strike, and the launching of the long-delayed campaign for an eight-hour day. For the elections of 6 and 14 May, furthermore, a recently unified Socialist Party was fielding candidates almost everywhere for a vigorous campaign.

At the same time, Catholic activists reacted to the separation of Church and state, which had been enacted at the end of 1905. All religions were to have the same legal status; duly registered religious associations were supposed to run church institutions. The government chose February to start inventories of church properties preliminary to their transfer to the control of the religious associations. On 1 February, activists opposed the inventories by barricading the Parisian churches of Sainte-Clothilde and Saint-Pierre-du-Gros-Caillou, driving away the agents sent to conduct the inventories, and forcing those who sought entry to batter down the church doors. The people arrested at Sainte-Clothilde included Counts Louis de Bourbon and Guy de la Rochefoucauld; clearly aristocratic legitimists were joining the resistance of the ordinary faithful.

The battles at Sainte-Clothilde and Saint-Pierre started a series of battles in Paris and the provinces. The most serious event took place in Boeschepe (Nord) on 6 March. There the son of the agent responsible for the inventory defended his father by shooting, and mortally wounding, a demonstrator. The parliamentary discussion of Boeschepe's struggle brought down the government, and ten days later the new government advised its agents to suspend inventories where open resistance seemed likely. During April such confrontations became less frequent, but did not disappear.

The springtime of 1906 likewise brought a number of conflicts between workers and employers. In Toulon, for example, café waiters went on strike at the end of March. On Saturday 31 March, striking waiters marched through the streets and broke windows of cafés that had stayed open. On Sunday 1 April, they began demonstrating again, and that night the wine steward of the café de la Rotonde, surrounded by jeering strikers, pulled his knife and stabbed Jean Bruno, a waiter at Hyères; Bruno died almost immediately. Fearing a united front of militant arsenal workers and waiters and faced with the socialist mayor's refusal to ban demonstrations, the prefect intervened. Three days later, strikers took hostage the police officer sent by the prefect; they demand the right to demonstrate. Similar struggles continued in Toulon throughout the month.

Industrial conflicts likewise spread through northern France. After the Courrières disaster (10 March), in which 1,101 miners died as a result of an explosion and ensuing underground fires, most of the Pas-de-Calais minefield went out on strike. Georges Clemenceau, Interior Minister of the new government, soon sent troops to the mines; for about 60,000 strikers, he sent in 20,000 soldiers. The soldiers soon found themselves protecting both mine property from workers' destruction and non-strikers from their fellow-workers' attacks.

Mining struggles continued through April. In the Pas-de-Calais and the Nord, miners barricaded their pits, beat up workers who stayed on the job, and stoned trains bringing in Belgian blacklegs. On 2 April, a thousand workers, with red flags, broke into Billy-Montigny and demanded the freeing of miners arrested during earlier conflicts. On the fourth, the 557 men and 40 boys who worked the mine at Ligny-lès-Aire joined the thousands of strikers in nearby cities. On the fifth, women gathered at the pithead of Courrières no. 4, close to Billy, despite the presence of a military detachment; they stoned the personnel who entered or left, and then tried to break through the barricades in order to search for miners who were still buried underground. On the ninth, miners' wives from Billy marched with black, red, and tricolour flags.

Other confrontations, some complemented with explosions of dynamite, occurred almost every day in April. Clemenceau called out the cavalry, and had some forty union officials jailed; Clemenceau, the implacable Jacobin and nemesis of governments, became Clemenceau the strikebreaker.

In addition to miners, many other workers of the north of France joined April's action. On the fourth, for example, a crowd in Roubaix attacked the carriage of Jules Méline, the former minister, who had come to confer with the city's industrialists. On the sixth, strikers in Fressenneville (Somme) sounded the 'Marseillaise' and the 'Carmagnole', broke the windows of the lock factory in which they worked, went to break the windows of non-strikers, then sacked and burned their boss's house.

That was not all. In Grenoble, Alès, Limoges, Lavelanet, Lorient, Brest, Châtelguyon, Marseilles, and Paris itself strikes led to other struggles, while Catholic militants, conservatives, and socialists took the opportunity to fight elsewhere. France seemed ready to crack.

The Meaning of 1906

At first glance, these conflicts give an impression of chaos. Yet on a closer look some more or less regular features appear. First, the events involve a limited variety of actors: over and over, we find the same organized workers, political activists, militant Catholics, and few others. In general, the same actors maintained extensive social ties outside of moments of conflict, and their action depended on those social ties. The forms of action they deployed were few: strikes, meetings, demonstrations, and a few others. Finally, the events of that turbulent spring appeared in bunches: the problem of power in the minefields, over the Church, and in the National Assembly extended far beyond any individual confrontation. In 1906, the struggles in question took place on a national scale.

From 1905 to 1907, France went through one of its greatest political crises of the nineteenth and twentieth centuries: ending of the Concordat, resolution of the Dreyfus Case, arrival of socialists and organized workers on the national political scene, emergence of national strike waves orientated to Paris, appearance of southern winegrowers as a political force, varied and extensive contestation throughout the country. The rise of those conflicts raises new questions. In terms of everyday life, most of the actors and interests that the conflicts activated had existed for a long time; why and how did they enter national struggles for power at that point in time? Knowing in 1900 the map of French social structure and individual interests, what further evidence would have allowed us to predict which of the thousands of possible groups would actually begin to make claims in the following years, and what forms their claim-making would take?

The question is not fantastic, nor even ahistorical. On 26 April 1906, a remarkable report to the Interior Minister presented a *pronostic* of May Day in Paris. (The report now resides in Archives nationales F7 13267.) In 1906, the government was not dealing with an ordinary workers' holiday, since May Day was to come in the midst of an electoral campaign in which socialists hoped to gain a number of seats. Many people were aware, furthermore, of the recent failed revolution in Russia. That was why Clemenceau, the new minister, called for information.

That synthesis of many reports from *commissaires de police*, fed by many observers and spies, predicted the action of each important group of workers during the time in which the great struggle for the eight-hour day was supposed to begin. The report said of the carriage-makers, for example, that 'they will take the First of May off and will start to strike. They won't ask for the eight-hour day, since they're sure they won't get it, but they will demand an increase in pay.' The report estimated their contribution to the general strike at 25,000 to 50,000 workers, 'if the wheelwrights and mechanics join the carriage-makers'.

Electricians, on the other hand, seemed 'too divided, and they know it; they say themselves that they're not ready. They can only be successful if all their plants go out at once, which is impossible for the time being. Small groups may persuade a few of them, no more than 500, to strike.' The predictions continued: navvies would have 30,000 strikers, of whom a few were thinking of dynamiting tunnels in order to block railway traffic, while food workers would stay out of the movement, and so on. The predictions later turned out to be relatively accurate.

Taken together, the reports to the minister portray the possibility of a large movement against the government, based in Paris but spread through the country. The possibility seemed more real because the north of France had already experienced an important series of strikes and demonstrations after the Courrières disaster. Clemenceau and his police prefect, Lépine, took precautions: detention of Griffuelhes, secretary of the CGT; banning of parades and public meetings; recall of 45,000 soldiers from the provinces to Paris; deployment of armed forces throughout the capital. The greatest French strike wave so far—and the first national strike wave truly centred on Paris—began. But, despite almost 200,000 strikers in Paris, the demonstrations and meetings of 1 May 1906 stayed within limits, never becoming a general rebellion.

The files of the Interior Minister would have surprised an *ancien régime* police official. They involved rather effective, continuous surveillance, anticipating rather than simply reacting to collective action. Unlike pre-revolutionary repression, which was sometimes ferocious but almost always reactive, the government of 1906 sought to anticipate, control, and channel popular collective action, and often succeeded in doing so. That anticipatory policing of ordinary people's collective action took shape with the Revolution and the Empire. A century later, it had reached an impressive scale.

In addition, the police analysis displayed some understanding of the conditions and mechanisms of workers' action. At a time when Le Bon was describing the madness of crowds and Sorel was laying his hopes on the catastrophic effects of a general strike, police *commissaires* and ministerial officials were calmly dissecting workers' organization and strategy, developing a clear enough picture to allow for useful predictions and effective repression.

Not that the police of 1906 were theorists of their subject. They knew it as direct participants in many public actions of workers, and thanks to a network of informers who conveyed to them the practical lore of activists. An important gap existed, in fact, between this insiders' understanding of popular collective action and the theories implicit in the language of state officials. On one side, knowledge of working-class life, of the organizational bases of action, of workers' strategies. On the other, a vocabulary of order and disorder, of attitudes, of good workers and bad. Faithful servants of the state, police used the language of the powerful. Yet despite weak theories, the police of 1906 could follow and even anticipate workers' action. Can theorists of our own time do as well?

The analysis from above has roughly the same defects as current theories of popular collective action:

1. leaping unjustifiably from individual attitudes to group orientations without laying out a valid account of the process linking the two;

2. concentrating on the behaviour of single actors, presumably unified behaviour, that of the person or group who are protesting, rebelling, demanding, or attacking, thus ignoring interaction;
3. remaining static, without specifying the means by which collective action changes and creates its consequences;
4. adopting causal and/or essentialist explanations rather than purposive ones, even though practical knowledge of the events in question regularly takes strategy into account.

We can understand that participants in action whose principal concern is to anticipate and control popular collective action might adopt such perspectives. But for theorists of the same action, they raise insuperable obstacles to effective analysis.

Gaps in Our Models

If we assume that any collective decision flows from multiple individual decisions, how do thousands of individual decisions accumulate into a large social movement? In what way could one infer the forms of individual participation from the character of collective actions? Can we, for example, take the demands made in a group's name as evidence of the motives for individual involvement? Does the process of mobilization itself predictably transform individual motives? All these questions link the individual and collective levels. The slope between the two levels is slippery; theorists often fall in trying to scale it. Since the challenge of Mancur Olson which blocked any direct, simple, and immediate translation of individual interests into collective action (and, even more so, any direct, simple, and immediate translation of collective interests into individual action), theorists have often addressed the question. They have so far had little success.

The analysis of industrial conflict, for example, entails the relationship of individual to collective objectives. On the individual level, we can easily imagine the formation of workplace grievances by everyday experience; by extension, we move easily to the decision to join a strike. At the level of a firm or even of a whole industry, we likewise find it easy to attribute common grievances to most workers; given a certain intensity of organization, we arrive at an explanation of strike activity. Yet the correlation between the degree of individual discontent and the extent of worker organization, on one side, and the amount of industrial conflict, on the other, is quite imperfect. That very imperfection calls for an analysis of the process linking an interest or a shared attitude to collective action. In that regard, existing models of industrial conflict lack substance.

The same is true of general models of mobilization. Standard models of mobilization divide roughly into two rather different lines of reasoning: *cumulative* and *constructive*. On the one hand, a reasoning we might call cumulative because of its initial conception of a set of individuals, each having interests, who decide more or less consciously, one by one, to attach themselves to others with whom they share interests, a process that promotes the development of common consciousness and finally of concerted action. The process takes something like the form of Fig. 8.1. In the first stage, separate individuals;

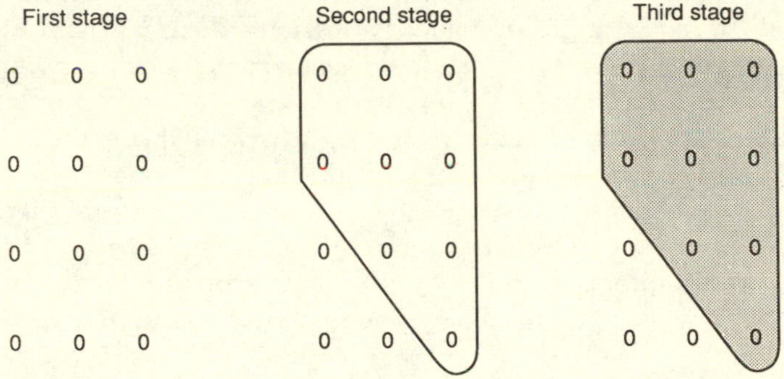

FIG. 8.1

in the second, some of those individuals integrated into a common framework; in the third, shared consciousness and collective action — except for the individuals who remain outside the frame.

The idea of a development of consciousness often marks this mode of analysis. In summarizing her studies of 'Messianic movements' in the Third World, for example, María Isaura Pereira de Queiroz declares that:

Messianic belief and Messianic movement, two distinct social facts, are two aspects of Messianism that one can not separate entirely; the first can exist without the second, but the second always requires the first. Without the inspiration of the myth, the collectivity cannot organize; nevertheless, the myth can endure a long time without the formation of any movement. The movement depends on the formation of a group, on the gathering together of individuals having some function to fulfil.[1]

Thus we arrive at a sharp separation of the stages, a separation depending at once on the development of consciousness and the creation of social ties as a consequence of a new shared belief.

Such reasoning immediately raises two serious objections: first, that it does not explain how and why an individual ignores his individual interest in security and minimization of effort; and second, that it lacks specification of the social process that produces the movement from one stage to the next. Alteration of consciousness coupled with some form of social creativity? Spiral accumulation of beliefs and of social ties embedded in those beliefs? Here, as is often the case, the reasoning runs backward, from the fact of a movement to a search for the necessary conditions of its appearance.

The second line of reasoning presumes the prior existence of a social structure that already connects most individuals, a structure that changes and elaborates as a result of repeated communication among individuals. Thus we may call it constructive reasoning. In that line of thought, ties may well multiply and reinforce each other in the course of collective action, but previously existing ties form the main base for mobilization and collective action. Furthermore, the divisions of interests that motivate collective action rest especially on social cleavages that already inform workaday social life. Schematically, we might represent the constructive line of thought as shown in Fig. 8.2. The

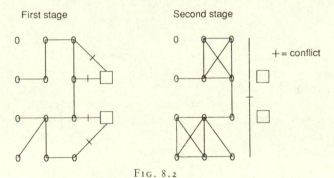

FIG. 8.2

diagram portrays a mobilization process activating existing social net-

[1] María Isaura Pereira de Queiroz, *Réforme et révolution dans les sociétés tradition-nelles: Histoire et ethnologie des mouvements messianiques* (Paris: Anthropos, 1968), 291.

works, extending those networks, forming coalitions, and generalizing established oppositions. Thus Michael Schwartz bases his analysis of the movement pitting tenants and landowners in US cotton regions against each other from 1880 to 1890 directly on the social relations established by the region's agriculture, and treats the creation of the Southern Farmers' Alliance (the tenants' defence organization, which achieved impressive, if temporary, success) at once as a product and as a crucial transformation of struggles that preceded and succeeded the SFA's days of glory.[2]

Often, it is true, analysts represent collective action as a direct expression of the common interest of a fully formed social group—a social class, community, ethnic group, union, party, or something else—without asking seriously what connection exists between the acting group and the base population it claims to represent. This theoretical short circuit suppresses the first stage of the cumulative model (Fig. 8.3). The short circuit avoids the problem of individual

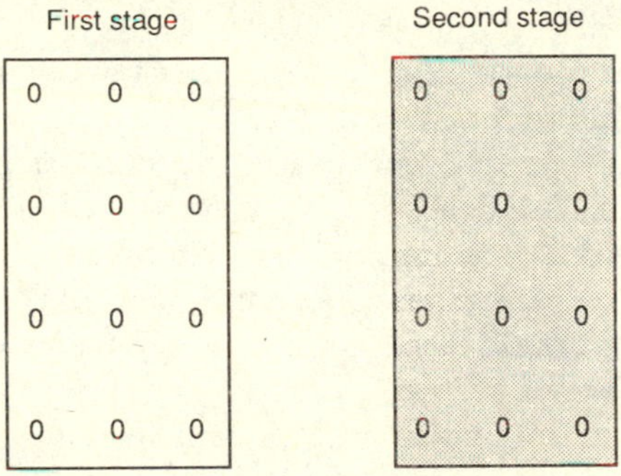

FIG. 8.3

mobilization without resolving it. Only the full cumulative and constructive arguments sketch continuous circuits from individual to collective action.

Single-Actor Models

Although constructive models, as I have sketched them, accommodate relations of conflict as well as of co-operation, at bottom they describe the change of state within a single actor. What is more, they ordinarily

[2] Michael Schwartz, *Radical Protest and Social Structure: The Southern Farmers' Alliance and Cotton Tenancy, 1880–1890* (New York: Academic Press, 1976).

assume that the actor has a unitary disposition—a single utility function, no internal division, no significant change in boundaries. Applied to French strikers of April and May 1906, they would at best give us the means of explaining which sets of workers mobilized more quickly and fully for confrontations with employers and officials. They say almost nothing about the relationships among actors, and especially about changes in those relationships.

Most users of accumulative and constructive models, indeed, set up their analyses on the analogy of epidemiology: they define a population at risk to some form of collective action, then try to discover the conditions determining susceptibility to that condition. Strike propensities, riot propensities, social-movement propensities, and other propensities to collective action become the variables to explain. Studies of participation have their value; without them, for example, riff-raff theories of involvement in rebellions and revolutions would no doubt be even more prevalent than they are. But they strengthen an illusion: that the explanations of such events lie in the characteristics of rebels and revolutionaries.

Consider the treatment of industrial conflict, where formal modelling has gone quite far. Analysts of industrial conflict customarily treat strikes as workers' actions, representing the action of management or of government officials as an influence external to the decision to stop work. Official collections of strike data reinforce such an interpretation; they emphasize characteristics and actions of the workers, and neglect both characteristics of employers and relations between workers and employers.

To be sure, such authors as Orley Ashenfelter and George Johnson, Walter Korpi, Douglas Hibbs, and Paul Edwards have laid out different kinds of power-struggle interpretations for strike activity. Business-cycle analysts such as Albert Rees have interpreted the generally negative effect of unemployment on strike activity as a consequence of changes in the relative bargaining positions of employers and workers. Still, their formal modelling, measurement, and estimation have characteristically taken the form of single equations describing the frequency, size, and/or duration of strikes, and implicitly conceiving of those features as aspects of workers' behaviour. By concentrating on the incidence of strike activity, furthermore, they have ruled out any representation of the interaction between workers and employers. Meanwhile, in real life, the beginning, the development, and the end of a strike always take place within a continuous stream of bargaining that includes repeated, mutual assessment of the relative strength of the parties, and often depends on strategic and tactical considerations that are distinct from the probability that workers will gain or lose their objectives. An adequate model would take direct account of mutual interaction.

Eric Batstone, Ian Boraston, and Stephen Frenkel stand out among analysts of industrial conflict for their attempt to fill the gap between individual and collective action by looking directly at the mobilization process. Their results are promising. Yet notice how they set up the problem:

There are a number of factors which have to be taken into account in any satisfactory and total explanation of strikes. First, it is essential to recognize that strikes, as an expression of individual conflict, reflect the subordination of workers within industry and, indeed, society more generally. Second, the institutions of collective bargaining, forms of social and political integration more generally, and management and trade union organization all have some relevance to the probability of strike action. However, the extent to which strikes do actually occur will be most immediately determined by processes of negotiation among workers themselves. For this reason an understanding of the distribution of power among workers and the sorts of vocabularies employed is crucial to an analysis of strikes.[3]

Thus the problem of explaining strikes becomes chiefly a problem of accounting for the behaviour of workers. With a few concessions to management and the outside world, the basic model remains that of a single actor undergoing changes of state.

The same theoretical habits also appear in other domains of collective action. Consider something so mundane as a demonstration. We have the habit of representing it as expressing the unified will of a fairly well-defined group: a demonstration of veterans, students, local residents, or something of the sort. That representation obscures the reality in two important ways: first, because—as every organizer of demonstrations knows—the action of demonstrators results from an effort at construction, often painful, that itself often involves the striking of bargains; second, because every demonstration involves not one but at least four parties: the people who gather in the street, the object of their attention (ordinarily a symbol, an organization, or an important person), the immediate spectators, and the social base the demonstrators claim to represent. Furthermore, authorities ordinarily pay

[3] Eric Batstone, Ian Boraston, and Stephen Frenkel, *The Social Organization of Strikes* (Oxford: Blackwell, 1978), 4.

attention to demonstrations, even when the demonstrators are attacking or supporting someone else.

Several of those parties are commonly present at the action; in MacCannell's study of 'protest demonstrations' in the United States around 1970, 'protest targets are encountered by demonstrators 60% of the time ... bystanders are present in 94%, police in 89%, media in 54%, and organized counter-demonstrators in 36% of the demonstrations.'[4] The interaction is not incidental, but integral to the collective action. Here again we need models with multiple actors.

Current models of social movements present similar problems. Available models almost uniformly portray movements as the expressions of particular groups. Many models, to be sure, assign those groups unusual structures: dispersed, composite, and fluid. More sophisticated models, furthermore, divide the participants into several concentric circles: the social base from which the movement draws, people who support the movement but remain inactive, rank-and-file movement activists, leaders, and so on. Nevertheless, the normal theoretical procedure consists of identifying a more or less coherent set of persons, and then explaining the movement's action as a consequence of the social characteristics of those persons—in short, the classic sociological procedure. When Alberto Melucci analyses what he regards as a profound transformation of social movements in the post-industrial era, for example, he sticks to the same kind of argument; he characterizes the new social movements as:

segmented, reticulated, polycephalic structures. The movement is composed of diverse, autonomous units that expend an important part of their resources on internal solidarity. A network of communication and exchange keeps the cells in contact with each other; information, persons, and models of behaviour circulate in the network, moving from one unit to another and thus promoting a certain homogeneity of the whole structure. Leadership is not concentrated but diffuse; it is limited to specific aims, and different people can assume leadership roles, depending on the function to be fulfilled.[5]

The image of a special sort of group, but a group nevertheless, informs Melucci's description. His portrayal, in fact, makes an implicit contrast with a party or a trade union.

There lies the problem. The proper analogy to a social movement is

[4] Summary from Clark McPhail and Ronald T. Wohlstein, 'Individual and Collective Behaviors within Gatherings, Demonstrations, and Riots', *Annual Review of Sociology*, 9 (1983), 586.

[5] Alberto Melucci, 'Mouvements sociaux, mouvements post-politiques', *Revue internationale d'action communitaire*, 10 (1983), 14.

neither a party nor a union but a political campaign. What we call a social movement actually consists of a series of demands or challenges to power-holders in the name of a social category that lacks an established political position. Although we sometimes apply the term to *ancien régime* conflicts, the social movement really appeared as a way of doing collective business in Western countries during the nineteenth century. Its demands and challenges depend on groups, as electoral campaigns depend on parties. But in both cases the interaction among actors constitutes the identity and unity of the movement.

The analysis of the workers' movement presented by Alain Touraine and his collaborators half-recognizes this fact. They require, say Touraine and company, that the study of social and political institutions be complemented and even governed by an analysis of working-class action itself, 'of the working class as an actor in the central conflicts of industrial societies, that is, of syndicalism as a social movement,' to which they add the obligation 'to consider the workers' movement as a social actor defined at once by conflict relations and by a positive reference, shared with its adversary, to the cultural orientations of industrial society'.[6] The language, mixing references to actor and action, manages to hide the object of the analysis, which turns out later to be a changing system of relations among workers, managers, unions, government officials, and the public.

The reality of social movements hides behind a veil of mystification, shared by both sides of the conflict, that identifies the current actors with a broad base of support at the very moment when the self-styled spokespersons of the movement rush to create coalitions, eliminate rival leaders, solidify their own bases, avoid visible breaks, and organize public displays of unitary will. That preparatory work does not belie the sincerity, seriousness, popular support, or efficacy of many social movements. It builds the structure of the social phenomenon bearing that name. Such a phenomenon requires a model of interaction with multiple actors rather than a single-group model.

Static Models

If theoretical disarray with respect to connections between individual and collectivity in the course of collective action results in part from

---

[6] A. Touraine, M. Wieviorka, and F. Dubet, *Le Mouvement ouvrier* (Paris: Fayard, 1984), 22.

the application of models of unitary action to realities involving multiple actors, it also results from the static character of current models of collective action. Having generally abandoned natural-history models postulating stages for revolutions, social movements, or other forms of collective action, investigators have been unable to substitute other models giving the same sense of internal change. Even Manuel Castells, for all his knowledge of and sympathy with urban social movements, proposes a model that serves mainly to match the aims and composition of a social movement with the social structure surrounding it. As for the process that produces movements, he settles for the declaration that 'the production of the structural formula leading to urban social movements is specific to each national-cultural context, and any attempt to find a general formulation is to resort to metaphysics'.[7] In trying to avoid metaphysics, however, Castells sends us to cultural history, without telling us what features of cultural history to explore.

Castells's abdication resembles that of other analysts. Neither familiarity with concrete collective action, readiness to make comparisons, nor theoretical imagination suffices to overcome the obstacles to dynamic representations of popular collective action. To the extent that we adopt single-actor models with unitary dispositions, and lodge the explanation of action in those dispositions, we commit ourselves to dynamic models in which changes of disposition occur at each new phase of the action. To the extent that we also insist on causal accounts of those changes — for example, by trying to root each successive action in the actor's material interests — we take on a task that is impossible in the present state of knowledge.

Yet we do have some clues about dynamics. At the level of micromobilization, Mark Granovetter, Clark McPhail, John Lofland, and other researchers have formulated useful models of the communications processes that transform a passive aggregate into an acting group. William Gamson's research team, for example, conducted a series of experiments on resistance to unjust authorities. The central experiment exposed its subjects to a supposed researcher who systematically and progressively violated the group's initial agreement by seeking to influence their testimony. According to Gamson's analysis, open resistance to that violation, when it occurred, resulted

[7] Manuel Castells, *The City and the Grassroots: A Cross-Cultural Theory of Urban Social Movements* (Berkeley, Calif.: University of California Press, 1983), 324.

from the coalescence of three kinds of actions. Organizing actions increased the group's collective capacity, divesting actions neutralized ties to the authority, and reframing actions created a new context for the interpretation of the authority's actions; in this case the new frame labelled the authority as unjust.

A successful rebellion against unjust authority, in this model, results from a sequence of organizing, divesting, and reframing acts. But the experiment simplifies its analytic problem by giving the authority very little room for manœuvre; he reveals and reinforces his injustice without really being able to bargain or change strategy. Strategic interaction remains poorly represented. The model therefore achieves at best a specification of the necessary antecedents for certain consequences of interaction. It is not actually a dynamic model of the interaction itself.

Mark Granovetter has edged in on the dynamics of micromobilization from another angle. His 'threshold models of collective behavior' postulate a distribution of actors each having his own calculation of costs and benefits for participation in a particular action, a calculation that depends strongly on the proportion of others who are already acting or committed to act. Activation of the entire group, if it occurs, depends on the successive arrival of different actors at their thresholds—for example, 20 per cent of the rest, 40 per cent of the rest, 90 per cent of the rest—as others join the action. In these models, two groups with identical average propensities to act (e.g. two groups in which the average member is prepared to join the action when 40 per cent of the rest are already involved) can differ significantly in their collective propensity to act, depending on the distribution of individual thresholds. Granovetter's models lend insight into the information-gathering about other people's commitment that commonly precedes a risky action: milling about, comings and goings, reviews of tactics, recollections of previous encounters, appeals to solidarity, striking of bargains among pairs of participants, and so on.

Granovetter achieves that much dynamism and verisimilitude by deliberately adopting a purposive frame. As he puts it:

These models treat the aggregation of individual preferences; they do not consider how individuals happen to *have* the preferences they do ... Most existing literature, by contrast, channels its main effort into determining how norms, motives, and preferences are caused and assumes that nothing more need be done to explain collective behavior. I maintain instead that once these are known, there is still a great deal to be done, and that outcomes cannot be determined by any simple counting of preferences. This will be particularly clear in cases where a very small change in the distribution of preferences generates a large difference in the outcome. Analysis focusing only on determination of preferences could not explain such a phenomenon.[8]

It is only a step from this reasoning to an analysis in which responses to antagonists operate simultaneously with the responses to potential allies that Granovetter represents directly.

Nevertheless, it takes two steps or more to reach analyses in which actors are not simply deciding whether to join an action but also which of any array of actions to take, and in which antagonists likewise make choices. Models of micromobilization lack at least two elements of a truly dynamic analysis: (1) description of the transition from one stage to the next; (2) representation of the interaction of parties in opposition or coalition. For these purposes we ought to construct models of strategic interaction in which each displacement of one party incites more or less calculated responses on the part of the others. We therefore need to adapt and improve models of rational action.

Causal v. Purposive Models

Ideally, it would be useful to create models taking as their starting-point the structure of social relations characterizing a set of actors, cataloguing the means of action open to individuals and groups, allowing for the creation of new social ties, and centring on strategic interaction. In the present state of knowledge, we have no way to make such an analysis strongly causal. It will have to be purposive; that means taking the actors and decision rules as given at the start of the interaction. Most likely the analytic programme will have to break into two parts: (1) a causal analysis determining which actors are available for collective action, what decision rules their action will follow, and within what constraints they will operate; (2) a purpose analysis taking actors, decision rules, and constraints as given. For the latter, we need models not just of rational action but of rational *inter*action.

Models of rational interaction generally assume a fixed set of actors with a specified amount and type of information about each other's identities, actions, and interests. They usually require specifications of (1) the actors, (2) their interests, (3) the decision rules adopted by each actor, (4) current values of the elements of those decision rules. Those

---

[8] Mark Granovetter, 'Threshold Models of Collective Behavior', *American Journal of Sociology*, 83 (1978), 1421.

elements, in their turn, typically concern (5) probable costs of the various sequences of action that are available to each actor, (6) probable benefits of each of those sequences, (7) the capacity of each actor to sustain the costs of each sequence. Thus, crudely speaking, we explain a single actor's participation in a social movement as a function of a choice among multiple alternatives whose relative attraction depends on a product:

(expected benefits − expected costs) × (capacity to act)

A single actor may, of course, consist of an individual or a connected set of individuals.

In order to convert such a model of rational action into a model of rational interaction, we make the expected benefits and costs (and possibly some of the other variables listed above) for each actor depend on the actions of other actors, and institute communication among the actors. Within this framework, specifying relevant actors, interests, decision rules, costs, benefits, and capacities—not to mention the relations among them—sets the theoretical challenge.

To see the nature of the challenge, take the intelligent synthesis of Guy Caire, *La Grève ouvrière*. After giving a comprehensive summary of research on strike activity, Caire finds himself at a loss when he arrives at the actual initiation and internal development of strikes. He makes an essential distinction himself: 'Cost–benefit analysis has an *ex post* inspiration; in contrast, gaming analysis takes an *ex ante* position. In that domain, alas, almost everything remains to be done.'[9] He resorts to the fifty-year-old model of Hicks, which represents the crossing of a concession curve on the part of management and a resistance curve on the part of workers, both as a function of a strike's duration—which comes down, as Caire himself remarks, to a static model of the threat of conflict rather than a dynamic model of battle or bargaining.

Furthermore, Hicks's model assumes a group of workers who are already organized and decided; it thereby finesses the essential problem instead of resolving it. When he returns to the problem of strike strategy, Caire borrows a military analogy and proposes the stages of outbreak–battle–settlement; although he has intelligent comments to make on each stage, he is unable to order them according to an explicit logic. From a theoretical viewpoint, the analysis reaches a dead end.

[9] Guy Caire, *La Grève ouvrière* (Paris: Éditions ouvrières, 1978), 156.

There is nothing unusual about that dead end. That is the point. Caire finds himself in the normal position of students of collective action. Two formidable obstacles block the road: the complexity of strategic interaction and the difficulty of dynamic modelling.

Games and Strategic Interaction

Yet we have at our disposal two related analytic traditions that permit dynamic modelling of strategic interaction: game theory and simultaneous-equation modelling of mutual-influence processes. To adopt either one, we must be prepared to use purposive models, at least to the extent of attributing decision rules to each actor, and must specify actors, interests, decision rules, costs, benefits, and capacities to act. (We may still, to be sure, derive each of these from empirical description and/or causal analysis.)

Robert Axelrod's studies of the prisoner's dilemma show that the specifications may be crude and yet yield illuminating results. In its elementary form, the dilemma characterizes an interaction in which the self-interested action of both parties leads to undesirable outcomes for both, yet a combination of self-interested and co-operative action on the part of the two participants leads to an even more desirable outcome for the self-interested party and an undesirable outcome for the co-operator. Many real-life situations resemble the prisoner's dilemma: environmental pollution, arms races, legislative bargaining, and even the natural encounters of organisms having the possibility, but not the certainty, of symbiosis. In the course of a single interaction, both parties have strong reasons to avoid co-operation and to pursue their individual interests without regarding the interests of the other.

If, however, the parties enter into frequent interaction, the situation changes. During repeated encounters, even entirely egoistic parties tend to gain from strategies combining initial co-operation with sharp discrimination among responses depending on whether the other party co-operates or continues to serve his individual interest. The strategy of tit for tat—I start by co-operating in our first encounter, and then imitate your response faithfully—tends to win over every more egoistic strategy. The advantage of a strategy of initial co-operation, furthermore, grows with (1) the probability of further encounters, (2) the sharpness of discrimination among responses, (3) the certainty of the other party's identity, his actions, and their consequences. Even in the midst of a population of irremediable egoists, a cluster of tit-for-tat players tends to win. So the analysis demonstrates, among other things, the advantages of coalition.

In that regard, Axelrod's findings recall Mancur Olson's analysis, in *The Rise and Decline of Nations*, of the probability that small groups and groups having access to selective incentives will form 'distributional coalitions'. Industrial employers, craft unions, and producers' associations serve as examples. Such groups, according to Olson's scheme, gain from their organizational advantage by influencing the production and distribution of goods. In the long run, that influence leads to sclerosis, or at least to pronounced deviation from classic market rationality. Whence a cycle following each great national struggle: first a relatively open expansion during which those who have the capacity to form distributional coalitions start to do so, then slowdown as a result of the coalitions' actions.

There exist, according to Olson, two ways of escaping from that silting up: either smash the coalitions from time to time, or assure the formation of global coalitions whose particular advantages also serve the general interest. In the schemes of Axelrod and Olson, the certainty and continuity of social relations facilitate the formation of stable coalitions serving the mutual interest of actors who continue to follow their particular interests and global coalitions serving the general interest.

Axelrod's theoretical and experimental results immediately suggest analogies to legislative bargaining, military and diplomatic alliances, and collusion among industrial firms. These analogies, in turn, suggest the possibility of generalizing the foundations of game theory to the level of large-scale structural processes. That is, in fact, the project proposed by Jon Elster, and pursued (in rather a different direction from Elster's) by Andrew Schotter.

Some assurance that the effort is worth it comes from two sources: from analyses of international conflict, in which interesting and crudely plausible models based on game theory and simultaneous-equation modelling are proliferating, and from scattered but promising applications of similar approaches to domestic conflict. One example of the latter is Richard Berk's application of a game-theoretical analysis to a 1972 confrontation at Northwestern University. Another is Barbara Salert and John Sprague's simultaneous-equation simulation of the conditions for 'police riots' and other sequences of violent encounter given an initial episode of crowd violence.

Nevertheless, game theory alone will not suffice. Eventually we will have to place the character of ties among persons at the centre of the analysis. Many ties that constitute and shape social life involve so little strategic interaction as to require other modes of analysis. Communications networks, daily relations among bosses and workers, circulation of tax money, paths of disease, movements of capital, chain migrations, and promotion ladders all sometimes involve strategic interaction. But their crystallization in durable structures and their incessant transformation call for specifically structural analyses.

Even within the zone of strategic interaction, none of this is easy. In popular collective action, the number, identity, and boundaries of relevant actors change frequently. Identifying the actors and the stakes, not to mention the rules of the game, often requires profound analyses of class structure and political process. Confronting such complexity, we will either have to employ simplifications or to build very complex models. Thus we return to constructive models of collective action.

Reflecting on rational interaction adds two elements to constructive models. First, we must consider each of the social ties, and especially those between antagonists, as a site of more or less continuous communication and negotiation following a strategic logic whose consequences transform the structure and the content of its ties. Thus a dynamic model of strikes should take into account at least the negotiations occurring within these pairs:

workers–unions
workers–bosses
workers–government officials
unions–bosses
unions–government officials
bosses–government officials

Often a fifth participant enters the picture: some sort of public. The problem is complex, but at least it is explicit, and draws attention to stakes, forms, and consequences of each of these relationships.

Finally, reflection on models of rational interaction suggests the value of a separate analysis of the established forms of interaction. For each pair of interlocutors adopts and modifies a rather limited set of means of negotiation—what one may call the characteristic repertoire of the pair. In the case of the pair workers–bosses, for example, the strike, the lock-out, the lay-off, the firing, the plant meeting, sabotage, absenteeism, and a few other forms of action which vary by region, industry, and period, have constituted the standard repertoire in many Western countries for close to a century. In our French conflicts of 1906, we saw some of these routines replaying, with strategic variations, in encounter after encounter. As the events of 1906 suggest, a limited repertoire is quite compatible with manœuvre and change. While there are many variations and combinations, and while each party seeks to gain the advantage by innovating within each established form and by insisting on its own interpretation of custom and law, in general the parties know and support the rules of the game.

Sometimes an important innovation, such as the occupation of workplaces, comes into being despite the resistance of at least one of the parties. Most of the time the repertoire remains in place and serves as a well-defined frame for interaction. Recognizing that frame simplifies the theoretical task, for what seemed at first an unlimited range of possibilities shrinks to a constrained choice among relatively well-defined courses of action. Our next theoretical step consists of the construction of models of strategic interaction among multiple parties within the framework of action repertoires that are specific to each pair of interlocutors.

At first glance, this programme looks like an abandonment of historical concreteness for theoretical abstraction. At second glance, however, it brings us back to history. For it forces us to ask precisely the questions entailed by a sound historical understanding of such events as the conflicts of 1906: who were the actors, how were they organized, what relations of power, conflict, and solidarity did they maintain with other actors, what were their interests and strategies, with whom did they interact, within what limits, with what outcomes. Historians, too, need to turn from static, strictly causal, single-actor models that leap uncritically from individual interests to collective action.

9

Individualism, Mobilization, and Collective Action

FRANÇOIS CHAZEL

Because of its polysemic nature, the coherence of the notion of individualism in the domains of ethics, politics, and the social sciences generally is questionable.[1] In sociology, the notion of individualism denotes both a particular social phenomenon and a methodological approach. On the one hand, we understand by individualism a well-defined system of values which confers full autonomy on the actor and, by the same token, allows for the development of 'possessive egoism',[2] and the modes of conduct which apply to such criteria. In this sense, individualism is a major component of modernity and, as such, is often taken as an essential characteristic of modern Western societies, as opposed to traditional societies which are depicted as 'holist'. On the other hand, individualism also indicates a way of approaching problems, that is to say, in the most general sense of the term, a method. This is why one speaks generally of 'methodological individualism'. It is difficult here to summarize methodological individualism. It can be expressed in a variety of ways, but it is based on the primacy of individual action (at this level of generality, the distinction, in itself significant, between agent and actor can be ignored), and attaches great importance to alternative courses of action between which individuals must choose. Whether applied to social reality to define types of values and modes of conduct, or else to a methodology, individualism thus has two distinct meanings. It is tempting, of course, to confer upon it a unity by affirming that

---

[1] In his book *Individualism* (New York: Harper & Row, 1973) Steven Lukes has attempted, by examining the multi-faceted phenomenon of individualism, to draw up an overall picture.

[2] This expression is close to that used by Crawford B. Macpherson for the title of his book *The Political Theory of Possessive Individualism: Hobbes to Locke* (Oxford: Oxford University Press, 1964).

'methodological individualism' is only appropriate to the study of 'modern' societies dominated by an individualist value system, to the exclusion of other societies to which an approach of the holist type would be appropriate.[3] It would be wrong, however, to restrict, a priori, the heuristic potential of methodological individualism[4] (just as it would for any research orientation) by such systematic association of a predetermined methodology to a given type of society. And it is with the latter we shall be primarily concerned in this chapter.

As is known, methodological individualism gave rise, in the Anglo-Saxon world, to a rich and complex debate.[5] Our task here is not to add a tardy contribution to this, nor to draw up a critical balance-sheet. Rather, we shall attempt to assess the contribution of methodological individualism to the understanding of two social phenomena which, although analytically distinct, are often related to one another, namely, mobilization and collective action. Two points should be borne in mind here. First, we shall treat methodological individualism here in a highly specific way, that is, in relation to the application of the economic paradigm and, more generally, to utilitarianism. This is characterized by the rationality of individuals, as defined by the search for personal interest. Nothing, however, precludes—at least in principle—the association of methodological individualism and irrationality.[6] And this possibility must be seen as even more relevant, in that 'irrational individualism', if we can make such a conflation, focuses upon, in particular via the fascination for 'crowds' as witnessed by Tarde, Le Bon, and their followers, certain aspects of mobilization, if not of collective action.[7] Of course, in terms of themes addressed, we can still ask to what extent this current of thought conforms to the canons of methodological individualism. However, there is little doubt about its fundamentally individualist nature. We shall examine, therefore, one variant of individualism, but

---

[3] This is the position adopted by Louis Dumont in his *Essais sur l'individualisme: Une perspective anthropologique sur l'idéologie moderne* (Paris: Seuil, 1983).

[4] A whole current of research has grown up in recent years in an attempt to apply the principles of methodological individualism to pre-capitalist collectivities. Samuel Popkin's study of the Tonkin peasants, *The Rational Peasant* (Berkeley, Los Angeles, Calif.: University of California Press, 1979), is perhaps the best illustration of this.

[5] John O'Neill has compiled the main contributions to this debate in his edited book *Modes of Individualism and Collectivism* (London: Heinemann, 1973).

[6] Brian Barry notes this in passing in the conclusion of his book *Sociologists, Economists and Democracy* (London: Macmillan, 1970), 181.

[7] Serge Moscovici's *L'Âge des foules* (Paris: Fayard, 1981) is in the mainstream of this tradition. See also Yvon Thiec and Jean-René Tréanton, 'La Foule comme objet de science', *Revue française de sociologie*, 24 (1983), 119–35.

also—and it is appropriate to add this—its most significant and strongest contribution to the dual sociological problem of mobilization and collective action. These two notions themselves call for certain clarification. To begin with, we shall limit ourselves here to a general classification which will allow us to develop an overall idea of what are often complex phenomena. We shall include in collective action all common action involving shared aims,[8] and take mobilization as being a rallying of a relatively important number of actors with a view to undertaking a collective action.[9]

Olson's book *The Logic of Collective Action* is now well enough known for us to dispense here with a detailed explanation of it. Part of its importance lies in its forceful questioning of a kind of sociological good conscience. Olson puts forward in fact 'the impertinent proposition'[10] that, in the framework of an unorganized group, the existence and the recognition of a common interest are not sufficient to create a collective action designed to satisfy this interest. The proposition applies, in accordance with the economic paradigm, to 'rational, interested' individuals who, Olson claims, 'would not act to achieve their common group interests'[11] in the absence of 'particular dispositions' (which we shall come back to below). The proposition is taken up again, through an explicit borrowing by Olson from the theory of state spending, in the language of 'collective goods', that is to say, of all goods whose enjoyment, once acquired by a member of a given group, cannot, in practice, be refused to its other members.[12] All persons belonging to the same group can, therefore, take advantage of a collective good (this is the Olsonian version of common interest), but this concordance of interest, though clear, is not sufficient to make them compete for its production. Each one, in fact, will benefit from the collective good, once produced, whether or not he has participated in the efforts necessary to obtain it. Each one, however, has an interest in leaving the other members to pay the price, which will possibly be

[8] Charles Tilly subscribes to this elementary characterization in his book *From Mobilisation to Revolution* (Reading, Mass.: Addison-Wesley, 1978), 7, 55.

[9] I have suggested a more elaborate definition in 'La Mobilisation politique: Problèmes et dimensions', *Revue française de science politique*, 25/3 (June 1975), 516. A simpler, less contentious definition is more suitable to our argument here.

[10] This expression is used by Raymond Boudon in the illuminating preface of the French translation of Olson's book, *Logique de l'action collective* (Paris: PUF, 1978), 8.

[11] M. Olson, *The Logic of Collective Action* (Cambridge, Mass.: Harvard University Press, 1965), 2.

[12] Ibid. 14.

higher inasmuch as it will necessarily involve, in the case of a group which is unorganized or 'latent', organization costs.

This logic is strengthened at the individual level by the fact that his personal contribution will affect only negligibly the chances of obtaining the collective good, and whichever conduct is adopted will probably go unnoticed. In these conditions, numerous actors might be tempted by the strategy of the 'free rider', which is based upon the hope of a benefit without costs. Such a view, however, in its extreme form, implies a kind of generalized waiting game and, ultimately, the failure to obtain the collective good. To a certain extent, Olson's explanation applies to the entire domain of collective action, an argument initially applied by Anthony Downs to voting behaviour.[13] It also upsets the false certainties behind which many sociologists and political scientists hid, both pluralists and Marxists. The pluralists developed, from Bentley to Truman, and with growing conviction, the idea that all groups are capable of organizing and exercising an effective political pressure as soon as interests deem it necessary. However, it is precisely the importance given to the 'potential group', which 'could and allegedly would organise and act'[14] each time the situation requires it, and the optimistic, if not Utopian, idea of an equilibrium of interests, which Olson's analysis calls radically into question.[15] However, the good pluralist conscience is not the only one to be scrutinized; the good Marxist conscience—which one should not necessarily ascribe to Marx, whatever Olson says—is also undermined in its perpetual underestimation, if not avoidance, of the question of the movement from class in itself to class for itself.[16] The virtue of Olson's argument is that it illustrates starkly, and at the level of its own analysis, the existence of important obstacles to mobilization and to collective action, neither of which can be held as occurring automatically, even in critical situations.

[13] We should remember that Anthony Downs had 'already fully grasped the logic of collective action in the context of one of the most commonplace of public goods: electoral victory', to take the expression used by Brian Barry and Russell Hardin in their introduction to the first part of their excellent compilation of texts, *Rational Man and Irrational Society?* (Beverly Hills, Calif.: Sage, 1982), 23.

[14] Olson, *The Logic of Collective Action*, 128.

[15] In fact Olson's argument (ibid. 131) is directed less against the equilibrium of interests than against its basis, that is to say, the claimed ability of all big groups to organize, as soon as the need is felt. The term Utopian, not used in the English, nevertheless illustrates Olson's view; he reproaches the 'analytical pluralists' with committing an error of judgement analogous to the anarchist fallacy.

[16] Poulantzas's position here is very revealing: he tended disdainfully to avoid the issue as one not worthy of Marxian structuralism.

Olson invites sociologists to show more realism in their analyses, and the invitation is worth responding to. We can, however, ask whether it is possible to account for phenomena of non-mobilization from a different perspective and in different terms. It is from this angle that we shall examine the syndrome of 'amoral familism', which is, according to Edward Banfield, fundamental to the inhabitants of Montegrano, a rural community in southern Italy.[17] Such an illustration can, first of all, seem foreign to our analysis, but, in fact, it is not without a certain ironic significance, inasmuch as Olson himself enjoyed emphasizing the pertinence of his theory for this culture so distant from the American world.[18] We should not, in any case, be surprised at Olson's interest in an analysis whose explanatory model is constructed around the hypothesis that 'the Montegranesi act as if they were following this rule: Maximise the material, short-run advantage of the nuclear family; assume that all others will do likewise.'[19]

We can leave aside the question of knowing whether this radical absence of co-operation, in the context of a profound misery, evokes rather the condition of men in the state of nature described by Hobbes, whose famous quotation is given at the beginning of the book, or whether, through their reliance upon egoism, and the refusal of all generosity and all humanity on the part of others, the inhabitants of Montegrano should on the contrary be likened, as Alessandro Pizzorno cruelly suggests, to the English bourgeois of the eighteenth century at the time of the rise of capitalism.[20] Whichever is the case, Banfield's first sub-hypothesis and the important observation which accompanies it conform perfectly to the Olsonian view: Banfield writes in effect that in a collectivity of this type no one would try to promote the interests of the group or of the community unless it were in his personal interest to do so, and adds that such a principle is of

[17] Edward Banfield's book *The Moral Basis of a Backward Society* (New York: Free Press, 1958) is devoted entirely to demonstrating this thesis.
[18] Olson, *The Logic of Collective Action*, p. 162 n. 97: 'A detailed study of a community in Southern Italy, an area with a political culture profoundly different from that of the United States, suggests however that the theory offered here fits that culture very well': see Banfield, *The Moral Basis of a Backward Society*.
[19] Banfield, *The Moral Basis of a Backward Society*, p. 83. See 'A predictive hypothesis' at the beginning of ch. 5.
[20] A. Pizzorno, 'Amoral Familism and Historical Marginality', *International Review of Community Development*, 15 (1966), 55–6. Pizzorno refers explicitly to a passage in Adam Smith's *The Wealth of Nations* (New York: Cannan edn., 1937), 14, in which he illustrates his argument by means of an example drawn from daily life: 'It is not from the benevolence of the butcher, the brewer or the baker, that we expect our dinner, but

course consistent with the complete absence in Montegrano of civic or even charitable organizations.[21] This, however, is not all. Starting from the assertion that it is almost impossible, in the context of a society characterized by 'amoral familism', to create or even maintain organizations, Banfield uses, and this constitutes his fourth sub-hypothesis, aspects foreign to Olson's argument, to explain how their absence on Montegrano territory is related to the inhabitants' fundamental inability to undertake a concerted action. These aspects are, in the order of presentation adopted by Banfield: identification with the objectives of organization, interest directed at its activity, a certain degree of mutual confidence on the part of its members, and, finally, a minimum of loyalty towards an organization.[22]

Banfield thus places emphasis upon an ensemble of variables that we could term 'the moral bases' of organization. The last two seem to us to be the most important, and, in terms of these, we can assume that social actors would not have a strong chance of displaying such confidence or such loyalty, indispensable to the success of an organization, even to its creation, unless they have already had experience of it elsewhere within real networks of solidarity. One of the distinctive traits of Montegrano, according to Banfield's description, is deprivation of such networks of solidarity. Here, Banfield places particular importance on the absence of the extended family, and even regards this as one of the factors which has contributed to the emergence of 'amoral familism'.[23] The absence of collective action is thus inscribed into the social structure specific to Montegrano, and Banfield's analyses are orientated towards a type of interpretation which evokes Oberschall rather than Olson, giving priority to the characteristics of the referential collectivity and, thereby, to the structural context of a case of non-mobilization.

It is in this sense, which accords well with Anthony Oberschall's model designed to demonstrate the social conditions of mobilization,[24]

---

from their regard to their own interest. We address ourselves not to their humanity but to their self-love, and never talk to them of our own necessities but of their advantages.'

[21] Banfield, *The Moral Basis of a Backward Society*, pp. 87–8.

[22] Ibid. 89.

[23] Ibid. 144–52.

[24] In his book *Social Conflict and Social Movements* (Englewood Cliffs, NJ: Prentice-Hall, 1973), Anthony Oberschall constructs what he calls a 'sociological theory of mobilisation' by conflating two dimensions: a 'horizontal' dimension, which concerns the nature of the social ties within a given collectivity, and a 'vertical' dimension, which concerns the relations maintained by the referential collectivity with the rest of society, in particular with other collectivities, pp. 118–37.

that Oberschall himself chooses to read Banfield's study, using it as a major illustration of one of his types, type B, which defines a collectivity by two related properties, the poverty or scarcity of its internal relations on the one hand, and a strong vertical integration towards centres of power on the other, both of which militate against mobilization.[25] The first property suits Montegrano, as it is described by Banfield, the second is less obvious, and it is therefore useful here to examine the analysis. According to Oberschall, we need to remind ourselves how vertical integration is established in cases of this type: it is based on a specific form of subordination which passes via the necessary mediation of the upper classes and leading citizens who occupy the positions of command. However, according to Banfield, there are in Montegrano no real leaders surrounded by their supporters. Clientelist relations have not acquired this characteristic even though they do exist at a less developed level. Can we, therefore, speak, in the absence of this authoritarian mediation of the upper classes, of a real vertical integration? The overall description established by Banfield implies the question, but we have to look twice before providing an answer. We can suggest first, with Pizzorno, that clientelist relations have in fact played a relatively important role at the political level, expressed in particular by sudden electoral fluctuations for one party or another.[26] And in Banfield's book there is an abundance of references, whether to the deference of the godchild to the socially superior godfather, or to the paternalist relations of members of the privileged classes with the peasants, which indicate the social control exercised by the privileged classes over the, essentially peasant, mass of the population. We can, therefore, speak here of vertical integration, even if the characterization which Oberschall puts forward conforms better to southern Italy as a whole than to the specific case of Montegrano.

The type of non-mobilization demonstrated by Banfield can thus be interpreted in the light of Oberschall's model of general application, which privileges, as we have just seen, two structural dimensions, the range of relations internal to a given collectivity, and the mode of liaison of this latter with the central authorities of society. The attention given to even the characteristics of the social context in which 'amoral familism' has developed has, at the same time, taken us a long way from the Olsonian problem which was our starting-point.

[25] Ibid. 122.
[26] Pizzorno, 'Amoral Familism', p. 62.

One might be tempted to minimize this divergence of perspective by pointing out that Oberschall presents his own theory of mobilization as a 'simple extension' of the analytic framework created by Olson, and which allows for its application to the study of the modes of political protest and mass movements.[27] But, as he himself recognizes, Oberschall is drawn to modify — and not simply to complete — this analytical framework, and in one essential aspect in particular: his theory is constructed around the central claim that 'group structure and solidarity do enter directly into mobilisation theory',[28] even though this claim was formulated later in an article where he distances himself from the utilitarian model.[29] There is, however, in the 1973 work, an important point on which he is in agreement with Olson: he adopts the postulate of rationality of action, underlining in this way his radical opposition to theories of collective behaviour, in particular, of course, Smelser's. From this angle, he situates himself in the Olson tradition, and it is this which made him momentarily underestimate, although not ignore, a fundamental difference in their respective views of society.

It is worth remembering this partial concordance of views when one attempts to explain the non-mobilization of Montegrano using Oberschall's model: such an interpretation is a long way, it is true, from the Olsonian perspective, even in terms of its scale of analysis. It, nevertheless, remains compatible with one of its premises, that of the postulate of the reasonable actor. One can privilege as explanatory factors the scarcity of links of solidarity in Montegrano and its dependent integration in the wider society, while maintaining that its inhabitants adapt to this context by virtue of a rationality of an instrumental type; and it seems that a reading of this type corresponds well with Banfield's study and argument, when considered in a general way. It is perhaps not, however, sufficient to account for the Olsonian resonances of some of the hypotheses, which leads us to believe that an important aspect of Olson's scheme is present here in an implicit way. A further examination seems necessary, therefore, and one which implies a level of more general analysis and which, because of this, will seem to be something of a diversion.

The preceding remarks should allow us to identify, over and above

[27] Oberschall, *Social Conflict*, pp. 102, 118.
[28] A. Oberschall, 'Theories of Social Conflict', *Annual Review of Sociology*, 4 (1978), 308.
[29] Ibid. 307.

the consideration of a particular case, a real research orientation, which consists in specifying the internal relations of a collectivity (or of a specific group or aggregate) in order to account for the degree of mobilization (which can in fact be nil, as in Montegrano) of the members of the collectivity, group, or aggregate under scrutiny. Yet in order to do this, it seems to us important to use a distinction suggested by Raymond Boudon between two types of system: systems of inter-dependence, and systems of interaction. Systems of interdependence are characterized by the fact that the behaviour of each individual affects the overall behaviour of all the others: these are, to restate Boudon's definition, 'systems generative of external effects in the absence of interaction between individuals'.[30] The sociologist is, of course, more used to treating systems of interaction, such a notion bearing full significance for him. It seems, however, that Boudon is somewhat reductive here in assimilating systems of interaction and systems of roles. Even if it is true that interaction is often crystallized in roles, it manifests itself in all social relations — formal and informal — as in the case of a plurality of individuals: 'the action of each takes account of that of the others and is orientated in these terms'.[31] This distinction is especially important in that it is immediately applicable in the framework of a system of interdependence: the choice by each person of a waiting strategy means for everyone the unwelcome conse-quence of not being able to enjoy a collective good. It is equally clear that Oberschall's interpretation leads him to recognize that, in the case of a system of strong interaction, there is a communitarian or associat-ive basis to it, one of the two conditions propitious to mobilization in a given collectivity. It is also the case, as we have seen, that a feeble and loose network of interactions is accompanied by a lack of mobilization.

What can we now say in the Montegrano case, when it is viewed in this new light? Montegrano, like all local collectivities, certainly does not correspond to a pure system of interdependence. Outside even the nuclear family, there are some exchanges, some social relations, both inside the social groups and between them. These relations, however, are very limited, in particular between the peasants who constitute the great majority of the population. According to Banfield, neighbour-

---

[30] R. Boudon and F. Bourricaud, *Dictionnaire critique de la sociologie* (Paris: PUF, *1982*), see 'Système', p. 551.

[31] M. Weber, *Economy and Society*, ed. G. Roth and C. Wittich (New York: Bed-minster Press, 1968), i. 26.

hood relations are dominated by distrust, true links of friendship out of the question, and solidarity fundamentally absent, to the point of appearing unenvisageable to the actors themselves. At this level, at least, the system of interaction is distended and without consistency. Not only does it not constitute an eventual basis for mobilization but it has only minimal influence on the orientation of conduct. In the absence of a strong attachment to the group or to an identification with community, the logic of self-interest, more particularly the interests specific to each nuclear family, can thus operate without opposition and without checks. Ultimately, everything happens as if, through the very fragility of the system of interaction, the inhabitants of Montegrano were in some way in a system of interdependence. This is why we can risk suggesting, for cases of this type, the expression 'system of approximate interdependence', while specifying that such a phenomenon needs, in order to develop, the favourable terrain of a network of interaction which is both loose and restricted. One is thus able to explain the Olsonian character of a hypothesis put forward by Banfield as well as the stress placed by the author on the predominance and the quasi-exclusive pursuit of self-interest in the peasant world, but also, to a less marked extent, in the other milieux of Montegrano.[32]

By a kind of paradox, we come back to Olsonian elements through our re-examination of the Montegrano case, which led us first and foremost to a different frame of reference which privileged more specifically sociological factors. But just as a paradox should not be confused with a contradiction, the recognition of this Olsonian dimension does not imply, at an overall level, a return to this type of approach. It seems to us that phenomena of non-mobilization can be divided into three principal types. The first includes all the cases which apply neither to groups nor to collectivities but to simple categories (consumers, for example): these involve systems of interdependence in which Olson's view applies fully. The second concerns the group of cases defined by a network of weak interaction: when this weakness is accentuated, systems of approximate interdependence are involved. Here we can transpose Olson's logic although, in a more general way, it is perhaps better to retain Oberschall's proposition that the collectivity under consideration is strongly predisposed by the poverty of its internal links to an absence of all mobilization, and this all the more because it is in relations of dependent integration with power centres.

[32] Banfield, *The Moral Basis of a Backward Society*, pp. 115–18, 129, 158.

Finally, the third type groups cases which cannot be envisaged in the framework of Olson's approach: these are, in fact, strong systems of integration (outside small groups, Olson could only take account of these with difficulty) which, furthermore, are well integrated in the overall society, and therefore do not need to commit themselves to energetic movements of opposition to make known the legitimacy of their claims or the justification of their aspirations. The perspective represented by Olson appears thus as fully pertinent in the treatment of the first type, partially applicable to the second, and quite inadequate to the third. In spite of its generality, it neglects important obstacles to mobilization which cannot always be reduced to 'perverse effects' which proceed from the logic of individual actions.

We should not forget, however, that even if Olson is first and foremost the destroyer of false sociological certainties concerning the passage to collective action, we can also identify, through a simple modification of his premises, positive reasons why actors mobilize. If, normally, in the cases of 'latent groups', the well-understood self-interest of individuals deters them from collective action, it is possible that this same interest encourages them to it. Two cases here can be envisaged, depending on whether the refusal to contribute to collective action is penalized or whether, on the contrary, the participants see themselves granted specific advantages, independently of the collective good sought. It is, therefore, always the logic of interest which is at work here, but the positive or negative 'selective incentives' modify sufficiently the cost–benefit ratio for a waiting game to give way to participation; the 'latent group' thus becomes — but only in this type of case according to the paradigm — susceptible to mobilization.

The importance of this argument is undeniable. First it has the merit of underlining the fact that, even in the case of a system of inter-dependence where individuals are, in some way, juxtaposed, collective action is possible when certain conditions are met. It also offers multiple possibilities of application at the level of professional organizations and economic pressure groups[33] even though, at this level, Olson only illustrates his thesis with appropriate examples, instead of proceeding to a systematic investigation.[34]

For Olson, recourse to selective incentives represents, therefore, an

---

[33] These applications are presented in ch. 3 ('The Labour Union and Economic Freedom'), and ch. 4 ('The "By-Product" and "Special Interest" Theories') of Olson's book.

[34] A critique as thorough as Brian Barry's does not fail to raise this point in his discussion of Olson's book, Barry, *Sociologists, Economists and Democracy*, p. 29.

elegant and sometimes illuminating way of accounting for various observable forms of collective action inside his own paradigm. However, as we shall see, this is a mode of explanation which should not be abused and whose value should not be overestimated.

One is immediately confronted with a crucial problem which touches upon the very application of the notion: what can be put into the category of selective incentives? Is it appropriate to opt for a strict meaning or, on the contrary, for a flexible usage, which would allow for the incorporation of very diverse motivations? Olson did not avoid the problem and exposed clearly the well-circumscribed principles which he used in his treatment of selective incentives. Nevertheless, even this formulation is not free of a certain ambiguity. On the one hand, he points out that next to monetary incentives and those which are of a specifically social order, such as the desire to be accepted in a group, there are also 'erotic incentives, psychological incentives, moral incentives'. There is, according to him, a multiplicity of types of incentive which can be analysed according to the same logic. On the other hand, as he himself points out, there is no place in his argument, even as illustrative examples, for these moral, erotic, and psychological motivations, whose existence he admits.[35] It is as if Olson dissociated the two questions asked at the beginning of this paragraph: the category of selective incentives is conceived as very wide, even unlimited, Olson extending the erotic incentives, psychological incentives, and moral incentives by 'and so on'. However, although these various modes of selective incentive all proceed from the same type of analysis, they do not offer the same guarantees from the point of view of explanation. Olson abstains, in his analysis, from appealing to moral incentives because, in his view, this would render the theory undemonstrable, would uselessly weigh down the explanation, and, furthermore, would be inappropriate to the organized pressure groups which are his principal interest.[36] He himself adopts, then, a tempered use of selective incentives but seems to leave the door open, for other objects of study, to a wider application of the argument which proceeds from his own theory.

He makes no mention, however, of the major vice to which all research based upon an indiscriminate use of selective incentives is exposed, that of tautology. Starting from the postulate that all participation in a collective action is based on selective incentives, one can

[35] Olson, *The Logic of Collective Action*, p. 61, n. 17.
[36] Olson, *The Logic of Collective Action*.

put in this category the motives, whatever they may be, which have pushed actors to mobilize effectively. In the case or cases studied, if the analysis does not demonstrate a clear benefit of a social or economic kind which results from participation, the researcher then turns to moral satisfaction, the maintenance of self-esteem, or to any other conceivable motive in the observed situation in order to make this play the role of substitute selective incentive.[37] In these conditions, if one treats it as a specific mode of selective incentive, one can always show an apparently susceptible motive as accounting for the emergence of collective action. In reality, however, no progress has been made in the explanation of the phenomenon. An authentic explanation implies the formulation of hypotheses which must be submitted to the test of empirical reality, and which will only be valid under certain conditions. But we have here a pseudo-explanation which 'will always work' and thus does not satisfy the criterion of falsifiability, as Louise White correctly points out.[38] White also observes that this kind of interpretation is purely *post factum* and cannot, therefore, unlike a true explanatory theory, serve as the basis for specific predictions made within the framework of hypotheses.[39] It seems, then, appropriate to quote here, in the form of a final appraisal, a formula of Brian Barry, whose general value should not let us forget that it is aimed specifically at systematic and therefore misplaced recourse to selective incentives: 'The constant danger of "economic" theories is that they can come to "explain" everything by merely redescribing it.'[40]

We should point out, in order not to distort Brian Barry's intention, that he elaborates upon this point. He adds that such a tautology, when it is used conjointly with propositions of empirical content, can produce interesting observations. Louise White also emphasizes this when she states that arguments based on a wide interpretation of selective incentives organize observation; she therefore ascribes a heuristic function to them.[41] However, it is still the case that, on its own,

---

[37] Bruce Fireman and William Gamson have put forward the expression 'soft selective incentive' to account for substitution incentives, in their excellent chapter 'Utilitarian Logic in the Resource Mobilisation Perspective', in Mayer Zald and John MacCarthy, *The Dynamics of Social Movements* (Cambridge: Winthrop Publishers, 1979).

[38] Louise White, 'Rational Theories of Participation', *Journal of Conflict Resolution*, 20 (1976), 271.

[39] Ibid. 272.

[40] Barry, *Sociologists, Economists and Democracy*, p. 33.

[41] White, 'Rational Theories of Participation', p. 272.

this tautology, like all tautologies, is, by definition, powerless to produce the least explanation.

From our examination, we can draw certain conclusions concerning research. It is important, in the first place, to remember that the specialist in the social sciences has a certain latitude in the definition and manipulation of his categories. By the same token, he can choose between a strict and a wide meaning of selective incentives. We should not be surprised if the researcher, used to working in an 'economic' perspective, prefers to adopt a flexible, even loose, interpretation of selective incentives. He will thus translate into the more familiar language of utility, observations or results which proceed from other currents of thought. Such a transposition is quite acceptable on condition that it does not pretend to explain the phenomenon or phenomena in question. It seems preferable, therefore, as we widen the explanation itself, to restrict the range of the category of selective incentives. From this point of view, we subscribe whole-heartedly to Fireman and Gamson's suggestion which limits selective incentives 'to inducements or constraints, that is, some positive or negative sanction that is added to the situation of the actor'.[42]

To conform to the logic of self-interest consists, first of all, in taking account of the advantages and inconveniences associated with the situation one finds oneself in, and defining one's strategy accordingly. Ultimately, the researcher, authorized to choose between the plurality of languages (and logics) of analysis, should be aware that a simple reformulation into the language of his choice does not generally, of itself, have explanatory value; the category of 'selective incentives' is a very good illustration of this recommendation of elementary vigilance.

We shall leave there our remarks on the acceptability of the argument of selective incentives and the various uses to which it is put by the advocates of the economic paradigm. We have not exhausted, however, the theme of incentives, which has been used to different ends, and from a different perspective, namely, that of the theory of organizations. Olson refers, moreover, to representatives of this view in order to note their contribution to the treatment of an important form of selective incentives, namely, social incentives.[43] Yet by seeking to interpret their contribution in the light of his own theory, he

---

[42] Fireman and Gamson, 'Utilitarian Logic', p. 21.

[43] Olson, *The Logic of Collective Action*, p. 61 n. 16. Olson mentions the names of Chester Barnard, Peter Clark, James Q. Wilson, and Herbert Simon, along with their respective works.

proceeds in a rather reductive way and undrestimates the value of their approach. It is, in fact, to a very specific problem, that of the maintenance of an organization as a system of specific co-operation, that these authors, since Chester Barnard, have addressed themselves. They have, Clark and Wilson in particular, looked for an answer in the analysis of the range of incentives (or stimulation) to which diverse organizations are likely to appeal. Their analysis proceeds from organizations or, more precisely, from the supply—which is at the same time partly a manipulation—of an ensemble of incentives by their leaders, and not from the individual actors and their motives, even though these last cannot, of course, be neglected, given that the stimulations put into play by an organization aim either to awaken motives or to support them. It is certainly true that Clark and Wilson create an elementary classification of types of incentives, which appear side by side with those of a social and a 'material', that is to say, a specifically monetary type, or ones easily evaluated in such terms. And their insistence on both the limits and fragility of incentives which legitimize adherence to the explicit objectives of organization—their third type—seems to comply well enough with the spirit of the Olsonian interpretation.[44]

It is appropriate, however, to point out two important differences. The first concerns the treatment of incentives themselves: can these be truly characterized as selective, in the sense that Olson gives to the term? Whatever the nature of the incentives considered, one can, by definition, distinguish two categories of actors: the individuals who are, on this basis, recruited by the organization, and those who remain at a distance from its activities. But, continuing the analysis, one is led to make other observations of a different kind: it could be the case that, contrary to a central proposition in Olson's argument, certain incentives are not specifically individual benefits but collective advantages, which the members of an organization enjoy conjointly. This is recognized by James Q. Wilson in his book *Political Organizations*, where he refines his own and Clark's earlier classification by distinguishing a category of incentives which can only be identified by

---

[44] In their article 'Incentive Systems: A Theory of Organizations', *Administrative Science Quarterly*, 6 (1961), 129–66, Clark and Wilson distinguish three major types of incentive: material incentives, 'solidary' incentives, a term which may surprise given that these include incentives as different from one another as the anticipated acquisition of a statutory, or honorary, position in the organization and the enjoyment of participation in activity, and purposive incentives linked to the aims of the organization, and which are related to sharing its objectives and the satisfaction of contributing to a 'just' cause.

their collective enjoyment.[45] Incentives cannot, in these conditions, be interpreted in the sole light of the logic of self-interest, as Olson would have it. Wilson draws this logical conclusion when he writes that he will not postulate any liaison between an incentive and personal interest, nor encumber himself with a definition of this last notion, which appears to him to be ambiguous.[46] In this way, the analysis of incentives no longer rests on theoretical bases borrowed from the economic paradigm; it is the explicit dissociation of the theme of incentives from an argument based upon this paradigm—so strongly interwoven in Olson's book—which it is important to note here.

The second difference—just as important—proceeds directly from the strategy of research adopted. To explain the maintenance of an organization, it is helpful to account for both the range of incentives it possesses and their efficiency in recruitment. In order to do this, it is indispensable to identify the principal factors which affect the organization's disposition towards a particular type of incentive and the receptiveness of the public concerned. Such an approach reveals factors of a structural order. Wilson's book *Political Organizations* is an excellent example of just such an approach and of certain of its results.

The author emphasizes that in the case of voluntary formal associations of a political nature, their access—more or less wide-ranging—to diverse types of incentive depends upon the nature of the political structure. More precisely, he formulates, on the basis of comparisons between nations, between towns in the same country, and between different periods in the history of the same city, the proposition that the decentralization and dispersal of political power facilitates access and, because of this, creates conditions propitious to the development of associations.[47] In terms of receptiveness to incentives, he maintains

[45] More precisely, James Q. Wilson replaces the global category of 'solidary' incentives, whose heterogeneous character was a source of ambiguities, by two clearly distinguished subcategories; specific solidary incentives, linked to a particular position of responsibility or honorary role within the organization, and collective solidary incentives, such as conviviality, a sense of belonging to a specific group, or the prestige of the organization, *Political Organizations* (New York: Basic Books, 1973), 33–4. We can note in passing that the term 'solidary' does not fit well in the first subcategory, which refers to individual advantages which are normally only accessible to a restricted number of people.

[46] Ibid. 33, 52 n. 9.

[47] Wilson devotes a whole chapter of his book, ch. 5, 'Political Structure and Organizations', to the effects of the political structure on associative activity and arrives at this conclusion after a long discussion of the problem, ibid. 89.

that this is influenced by the social structure. He emphasizes the differential modes of participation in associations according to social class; the advantages in terms of time, money, reputation, and competence from which the privileged classes benefit, and their sensitivity to a wider range of incentives, whereas the members of disadvantaged classes tend to claim, whatever the incentive offered, 'immediate, substantial and personal' advantages. He is thus led to the conclusion that, inasmuch as the privileged classes take a larger part in the life of associations, the importance and internal diversity of the associative world depends upon the relative weight of these groups.[48]

This is not the place to undertake a detailed critique of these propositions and of the studies which support them. We would argue, though, that they allow us to establish that the theme of incentives is not exclusive to analyses undertaken from the individualist and utilitarian perspective and that it can involve approaches which, far from reducing the role of structural factors—only the size of organizations is taken into account in Olson's argument—give to them a large place. Thus, even on a theme as strongly associated with the economic paradigm as that of incentives, taking into account dimensions other than the rationality of individual actors can be fruitful.

In order to complete our examination we must return once again to the argument of selective incentives, as formulated and used by Olson. It is not sufficient, in fact, simply to discuss the conditions of the argument's admissibility, as we did earlier; we must circumscribe its degree of relevance, that is to say, indicate the limits of its explanatory significance. Yet if we envisage it from this angle, the argument presents a major weakness, as Brian Barry and Russell Hardin have pointed out. It can, of course, serve to indicate—to a certain degree—adherence to or participation in an already existing organization. It leaves, however, completely unanswered the creation of an organization and, more generally, it throws no light on the process by which numerous groups have endowed themselves with an organization.[49] As empirical analysis of the first attempts at—and forms of—organiza-

---

[48] It is in ch. 4, 'Social Structure and Organizations', that Wilson develops these various points and comes to his conclusion. He has, however, already formulated his assertion by p. 32, thus forewarning the reader of the results of his analysis.

[49] Barry and Hardin, *Rational Man*, pp. 28–9. Hardin develops the same idea in his book *Collective Action* (Baltimore, Md.: Johns Hopkins University Press, 1982), 34, which is one of the most ambitious efforts to analyse this problem from the perspective of 'rational individualism', and which brings out both the strength and the limits of this approach.

tion indicates, whether in the world of work, or the liberal professions, the pursuit of collective goods through the creation of an organizational structure preceded—and did not follow—the distribution to its members of various individual advantages constitutive of selective incentives. This anteriority is fundamental here because it concerns the question—and relation—of causality. As Samuel Gompers has shown in the context he was concerned with, 'the union shop naturally follows organization', rather than is its source.[50] These observations are of capital importance. If one goes from organization to the collective actions it is supposed to serve, one can reverse the Olsonian proposition and state that, in numerous cases, selective incentives should be seen as a result, and not as a condition, of collective action, that they can even constitute the fruits of its success. Even if it is possible, on the basis of selective incentives, to illuminate the modes of participation in an already established organization, this type of argument does not really allow us to understand, even less to predict, the emergence of a collective action and the process of mobilization which underpins it. This is not surprising because the argument is more appropriate to the understanding of continuities than to what can overturn them; in that it only allows for the adding together of individual commitments, it is of very little relevance in the analysis of the processes of mobilization.

With this observation our examination of the Olsonian argument ends, and we would have willingly closed our critical discussion on a note of this kind, if we did not have to consider a final argument inspired by the economic paradigm. Certain commentators, belonging to the same current of thought as Olson, have been conscious of the limits of application of his analysis. Thus, in his review article of Olson's book, Richard Wagner has proposed, in order to overcome these difficulties, the concept of the 'political entrepreneur'.[51] In the interests of his political career, the political entrepreneur undertakes to procure collective goods for specific groups; the provision of collective goods is still explicable on the basis of self-interest, but, in this new formulation, the intervention of a clearly defined category, the leaders, would be indispensable. In fact, the argument has taken two distinct forms. The first, mainly put forward by Wagner himself, is hardly worthy of attention because the groups concerned remain in this case unorganized and only accede to collective advantages by

[50] See Barry and Hardin, *Rational Man*, p. 29.
[51] Richard Wagner, 'Pressure Groups and Political Entrepreneurs: A Review Article', *Papers on Non-market Decision Making*, 1 (1966), 161–70.

giving their electoral support to entrepreneur-candidates who are likely to provide them.[52] The second, on the other hand, presented by Frohlich, Oppenheimer, and Young in their work, *Political Leadership and Collective Goods*, is more interesting to our analysis because here political entrepreneurs devote all their efforts to creating and developing organizations capable of providing collective goods for those who are part of them, inasmuch as it is upon the power and vitality of these organizations that their success depends.[53] The argument is not without value, but it has the same fundamental weakness and therefore invites the same criticisms as that of selective incentives. The argument can only be used with great difficulty to account for the appearance of new organizations capable of providing collective action. It is much more acceptable, as a possible — though not single — explanation in the case of already established organizations.[54] Ultimately, the individualist and utilitarian perspective seems more able to illuminate certain important obstacles to collective action — even if, as we have seen, it does not allow us to understand all of them — than to explain its creation. In spite of the partial illustration it provides, it does not seem to offer an adequate basis for an elaboration of a theory of mobilization.

The limits imposed by this chapter prohibit us too, of course, from engaging in such an undertaking, and it would be presumptuous on our part to offer simply a rough outline, especially as there have been many theoretical elaborations in this area, the best known being those of Oberschall and Tilly.[55] Perhaps, however, it would not be superfluous to clarify, with reference to these different works, certain aspects which seem to us essential in a study of mobilization, and to

[52] Brian Barry illustrates well the weaknesses of this argument in *Sociologists, Economists and Democracy*, pp. 37–9.

[53] This work was published in Princeton by the University Press in 1971. After having demonstrated, in their view, the limits of Olson's argument and earlier articles — like Wagner's — which used the concept of the political entrepreneur (pp. 14–20), the three authors, on the basis of a brief 'Reconsidering [of] the Problem' (pp. 20–5), elaborate an elementary model (pp. 26–32). We should note that Mancur Olson comments on the various works devoted to the role of political entrepreneurs in the acquisition of collective goods at the end of the appendix which he wrote for the second edition of his *The Logic of Collective Action* (1971), 175–8.

[54] Barry and Hardin, *Rational Man*, pp. 30–1.

[55] Other than the works of Oberschall and Tilly, it is perhaps worth pointing out here, for their relevance to our argument, the counter-model sketched by Fireman and Gamson, 'Utilitarian Logic', pp. 21–32, and the kind of analysis undertaken by Kenneth Wilson and Anthony Orum in their article 'Mobilizing People for Collective Political Action', *Journal of Political and Military Sociology*, 4 (1976) 187–202. These are certainly, however, not the only works worth mentioning.

suggest directions of research which, though not necessarily new, need to be further exploited:

1. The first aspect involves both the degree and the modes of social liaison between the potentially mobilizable actors. By generalizing from Oberschall's interpretation but without limiting ourselves to the relatively well-circumscribed framework of a collectivity, we can determine whether in the cases analysed there exist constant and significant social relations which form the frame of what we might call real social networks. We need, in particular, to take into account the presence of organization(s) and to evaluate its (their) strength. Yet, important as this variable is, it should not be overestimated. As Oberschall himself has demonstrated, lively community structures constitute a terrain as propitious to mobilization as strong formal organizations. And we should further note, with Kenneth Wilson and Anthony Orum, that strong social links make up a substratum that is particularly favourable to mobilization precisely because of the absence of former commitments regarding specific political organizations (although we recognize that collective action can be greatly facilitated by organizational support).[56]

2. The second aspect concerns the orientations of action which always possess a cultural constituent and can, because of this, be treated as culturally defined. The first crucial question—for the observer as well as the actors—is that of collective identity. Let us point out first, however, so that our reference to culture is not misunderstood, that such identity is not necessarily given once and for all, but is susceptible to evolutions, even, in extreme cases, transformations. Sometimes it is even in a state of creation or constitution. This last notion is particularly interesting for our study in that mobilization can create the opportunity to affirm, in a visible and public way, an identity which is still not fully recognized or established. To these statements or restatements of identity, ideology can contribute a particular vigour. Yet we cannot reduce the analysis of such a crucial factor to this sole aspect. Ideology serves to define priorities for action and thus to invest the resulting movement which carries them with objectives and tasks which go well beyond the personal interest of the participants.[57] It can also make the actors even more convinced of the urgency of collective action by bringing them the hope of early victory.

[56] Wilson and Orum, 'Mobilizing People', p. 198. More precisely, we refer to their second proposition and to the qualification which accompanies it.
[57] It is in similar terms that Brian Barry characterizes ideology: 'a set of beliefs

3. The third and last aspect which we should mention takes into account social and political conduciveness in its multiple forms. Conduciveness is perceived here as structural, as in Smelser's use of the term, even though it is no longer associated with a chain of processes (of which it was the first stage) constructed on the model of the logic of added value.[58] The conditions of permissiveness vary considerably from one social system to another. Because the modalities of such a phenomenon are diverse and complex, the relevant variables will depend upon the specific object of research. Probably even these will be different, according to whether the analyst is attentive to the emergence of a mobilization, that is to say, to its genesis or its eventual success or outcome. This is why it would be pointless and illusory to attribute, at this level, a truly general significance to a specific list of variables. It is, nevertheless, possible to identify the particular importance of some of these. Thus the conditions of entry into a political system will be of great importance. When these become more flexible, they often provide 'new' groups with the opportunity to force their entry into the system on the basis of a strong mobilization. The strength of the state—which of course represents a combination of variables—is also worthy of attention, but its effects are complex. By using and abusing its forces of repression, a state can suffocate all forms of mobilization. However, a 'strong' state, through its very visibility, is one of the principal targets of social movements, and it is easier to do battle with a state than with a market.[59] Finally—and negatively—one should expect little vigorous collective action from groups which are themselves represented and therefore do not 'speak for themselves'. We have here the mechanisms of dependent integration, whose significance has been well illustrated by Oberschall.

Such are, in our view, the essential aspects which it would be appropriate to privilege in the study of mobilization and collective action. The approach which we have just sketched suggests points of reference and proposes tools very different from those which the application of an individualist and utilitarian perspective would imply. It is not, however, on this affirmation of divergence, significant though

attributing to the movement some significance over and above the self-interest of the participants', *Sociologists, Economists and Democracy*, p. 39.

[58] Neil Smelser, *Theory of Collective Behaviour* (New York: Free Press, 1963), 15.

[59] On the relationship between mobilization and state, see, in particular, P. Birnbaum, 'La Mobilisation contre l'État', in *Dimensions du pouvoir* (Paris: PUF, 1984), ch. 7, and 'A chaque État ses mouvements nationalitaires', in *La Logique de l'État* (Paris: Fayard, 1982), 173–89.

that is, that we wish to conclude. It seems to us, in fact, worth stressing, at this point in our argument, that if the kind of analysis based on the economic paradigm throws only a partial light on the associated phenomenon of mobilization and collective action, it had — and continues to a certain extent to have — critical virtues through its ruthless exposure of false sociological proofs. We shall not go over once again the paradox of collective action which has undoubtedly helped sociologists better to measure the importance of obstacles to mobilization which has too often been taken as given from the moment common interest sees its desirability. Nevertheless, it is worth pointing out that, through its insistence on the rationality of actors, this mode of argument has contributed to the rehabilitation of the idea of collective action. This is at least how it has been understood by researchers belonging to an important theoretical current, that of 'resource mobilization'. It is perhaps permissible — in the longer term — to have certain doubts on the fruitfulness of analyses which are so preoccupied, not to say obsessed, wtih the antithesis rationality–irrationality. We should also recognize that the adoption of the postulate of the rationality of actors has constituted a useful counterweight to explanatory schemes which too easily associate collective action with a form of deviancy. Finally, at a more general level, by its ironical repudiation of a form of sociological pseudo-reasoning — even though such reasoning constitutes in fact a gross distortion of the spirit of the discipline — which implies 'programmed actors' or which involves the invocation 'of structures which work by themselves', the individualist perspective has encouraged, if not a 'return to the actor', at least a renewal of interest in his action and in the strategic capacities it implies. Such a concern with action, and especially with individual action, is quite legitimate, on condition that it is not exclusive and does not therefore preclude taking into account the structural conditions the actors involved confront.

In an attempt to summarize our appraisal of the 'economic' analyses of social or political phenomena, we could perhaps draw inspiration from Anthony Heath's description of his own intellectual journey in relation to 'rational choice theories' based upon the economic paradigm; he went from scepticism to interest, then from interest to enthusiasm.[60] As far as we are concerned, it is clear that we have

---

[60] Anthony Heath, *Rational Choice and Social Exchange* (Cambridge: Cambridge University Press, 1976). It is perhaps worth pointing out that Heath's book remains one of the best on the subject.

stopped somewhere *en route*. Starting from indifference, we have not passed the second stage—that of interest. Such a position will of course irritate the dogmatic, but, and this is the most important point, lack of allegiance to a paradigm has never precluded concerted attention being paid to the works it inspires, nor the undertaking of a constructive discussion.

10

Individual Action, Collective Action and Workers' Strategy

PIERRE BIRNBAUM

Paradoxically, Lenin and Olson, proceeding from diametrically opposed theoretical positions, reach the same conclusion concerning the working class's disinclination to commit itself to a movement of collective mobilization. This identical finding is explained in opposing ways. For Lenin, it is the dominant ideology in the service of the bourgeoisie which encourages workers to prefer automatically the raising of their standard of living, and which, by alienating them, deflects them from any true consciousness. This situation thus necessitates the creation (in capitalist countries too) of a party of professional revolutionaries who 'from the outside' will detonate this collective mobilization of the working class, which otherwise would be extremely improbable. According to Lenin, the working class prefers spontaneously to adopt a trade-unionist strategy, that is to say, an action for the collective maximization of its interests, instead of committing itself to revolutionary action. Action remains, therefore, instrumentalist and utilitarian, taking place at a pragmatic level, and does not produce collective action even though this exists.

For Mancur Olson, the overall view is the same, but rests upon very different analyses: it is because each worker acts to maximize his own interest that he refuses to engage in a collective movement, because he knows that the extra cost in money, time, etc. which he would have to pay will always be higher than the marginal profit received from the gains which result from the collective involvement of other workers. If each worker reasoned in this way, logically no action would take place. There would be no trade-union action of the kind Lenin so derided, let alone a revolutionary movement. Collective non-action is, in this view, the consequence of rational behaviour, not of alienated behaviour. In order to overcome this refusal of commitment, the trade union professionals, just like Lenin's professional revolutionaries, must wield power over the workers, by which means they can force them to participate in collective action.

In both cases, a theory of the absence of voluntary mobilization justifies the determining role of a professional élite which is the only actor able to derive a specific benefit: professional politicians can develop their party organizations, hold locally and nationally elected salaried offices, be the editors of newspapers, be a power on the public stage which the mass media will accentuate, and play an essential role in the organization of society. The trade-union élite in their turn can hold office within the trade-union organization, at the national or local level, in a word, live for and from trade unionism as professional politicians live, according to Weber's expression, for and from politics.

We should note that Lenin and Olson's observations both concern Anglo-Saxon societies, that is to say, systems profoundly marked by individualism, where the market developed early, the state remained weak, and where the ideology of social Darwinism and equality of opportunity gave rise to a real belief in social mobility, where utilitarianism and pragmatism became a social philosophy, and where socialism and, *a fortiori*, Marxism had only minor influence, particularly on the working-class movement. In these societies, systematic and closed ideologies had only a minor impact, and the belief in social mobility itself was transformed into a collective myth, destructive of collective solidarities. In the United States, Darwin has been more influential than Marx, and the model of the struggle for life, of the survival of the fittest, and the stories of Horatio Alger bear witness to the faith in the possibility of individual social ascension.[1] The generalized economization of society encourages not collective action but individual strategies. According to Albert Hirschman,[2] the workers, following the example of other American citizens, prefer to adopt exit strategies rather than the more costly actions of using their voice. The functional character of the 'exit' in a society where social barriers are less crystallized (Lenski), where, for a long time, the frontier made horizontal mobility possible (Turner), and where Protestantism legitimated action of an individualist type explains the weakness of the

---

[1] On the myth of mobility, see P. Birnbaum, *La Structure du pouvoir aux États-Unis* (Paris: PUF, 1971); Jean Heffer, 'Pourquoi n'y a-t-il pas de socialisme américain?', *L'Histoire* (Mar. 1980).

[2] A. Hirschman, *Exit, Voice and Loyalty* (Princeton, NJ: Princeton University Press, 1970).

collective action of the working class, which came to see more and more of its networks of sociability destroyed by the geographic separation of workplace and residence.[3] This destroyed still further the possibility of mobilization, diminished collective identification, and limited the influence of a universalizing perspective such as socialism. In a society so profoundly individualist, the strength of utilitarian behaviour, which aims at the maximization of gains by the adoption of strategies relevant to each actor, is noticeable. We can see why, in such circumstances, so many models of political theory were based upon utilitarian economics. Among these, we must pay particular attention to that of Mancur Olson, inasmuch as he attempts to demonstrate the great improbability of any collective action by social groups of any size (latent groups) in a society based upon individualism.

Utilitarianism and collective ethics or action do not seem at all compatible. This is in fact what other American Marxian authors also claim, that rational calculation leads each worker to prefer an individual strategy to the hypothetical results of a collective socialist action which, because of the upheavals it would cause (flight of capital, lowering of the standard of living, the possibility of violence), seems too costly an undertaking.[4] For some supporters of 'analytical Marxism', it is therefore rational, in a society based upon utilitarianism, to turn away from socialism. In this sense, to criticize Olson's perspective by saying that his model cannot really apply to social groups which are structured by a strong sociability, which is itself due to the solidarity of internal networks within which actors act according to the solidarity which unites them as a group, and in response to the interwoven psychological links which shape their own personality,[5] does not really provide effective criticism of the model. This is precisely because such collective primary ties would have largely disappeared within an American working class increasingly deprived of communitarian structures, and where each worker finds an individualist strategy more useful. Again, instead of accusing the leaders of the American

[3] Jérôme Karabel, 'The Failure of American Socialism Reconsidered', *The Socialist Register* (London: Merlin Press, 1979); Ira Katznelson, *City Trenches* (New York: Pantheon Books, 1981).

[4] See A. Przeworski and M. Wallerstein, 'The Structure of Class Conflict in Democratic Capitalist Societies', *American Political Science Review*, 76 (1982); Bertel Ollman, 'Towards Class Consciousness Next Time: Marx and the Working Class', in Ira Katznelson *et al.*, *The Politics and Society Reader* (New York: David MacKay Co., 1975).

[5] Bruce Fireman and William Gamson, 'Utilitarian Logic in the Resource Mobilisation Perspective', in Mayer Zald and John MacCarthy, *The Dynamics of Social Movements* (Cambridge: Winthrop Publishers, 1979).

working-class world of treason,[6] as others have accused the leaders of the British Labour Party, it is more helpful to look for a rational interpretation of the behaviour of American workers. The intentionality of these actors allows us better to understand the weakness of socialism in the United States, like the strengths of labourism in Great Britain, than do explanations of conspiracy and alienation. In this sense, methodological individualism applies particularly well to the analysis of the mode of action of American workers inasmuch as they seem less integrated into networks of sociability than were, for a long time, their British or French counterparts.

The force of the market and of individualism explains the weakness of socialism within the working class. We know, moreover, that the rapid expansion of the market is often in a correlation with a state which remains weak. For Marx himself, the state 'changes with a country's frontier. It is different in the Prusso-Germanic Empire from what it is in Switzerland, it is different in England from what it is in the United States. "*The* present-day State" is, therefore, a fiction.'[7] Consequently, Marx emphasizes strongly the determining role of feudalism in the creation of the state which then differentiates itself, and becomes itself an autonomous actor, and against which, in France, for example the workers' movement orientates its activity. He deduces that in a country where the state cannot structure itself, and where there is such a complete economization of society in the framework of a liberal democracy, no collective movement can develop.[8] Into the twentieth century, this interpretation remains constant in Marxian thought in its attempt to understand the reasons for the exceptional character of the United States, the most industrialized society, where no working-class movement of any significance ever really developed.[9] Even in the United States, this hypothesis has been assumed, especially in terms of the nature of the political regime, where the early gaining of political rights explains the absence of socialism. Such a view is

[6] Philip Foner, *History of the Labor Movement in the United States* (New York: International Publishers, 1955), vol. ii.

[7] Karl Marx and Friedrich Engels, *Critique of the Gotha Programme*, quoted in T. Bottomore and M. Rubel, *Karl Marx: Selected Writings* (Harmondsworth: Penguin, 1974), 260–1.

[8] 'Unpublished Letters of K. Marx and F. Engels to Americans', *Science and Society*, 2 (1938).

[9] See S. M. Lipset, 'Why no Socialism in the United States?', in S. Bialer and S. Sluzar (eds.), *Sources of Contemporary Socialism* (New York: Westview Press, 1977). See also S. M. Lipset, *The First New Nation* (New York: Doubleday, Anchor Books, 1967).

shared by authors as different as John Laslett and Robert Dahl.[10]

At the other end of the spectrum from economistic explanations, as early as the 1950s Louis Hartz, in his classic book *The Liberal Tradition in America*, declared: 'It is not accidental that America which has uniquely lacked a feudal tradition has uniquely lacked also a socialist tradition'.[11] As American society was, at this time, both profoundly individualist and liberal (with the exception of course of its treatment of the Black question), it was hostile to the idea of the strengthening of the state. Thus it prevented in advance the creation of a socialist movement. It has perhaps not been sufficiently noted that this view was already held by Sombart himself. Sombart himself takes into consideration the political factor, arguing that: 'among American workers one therefore finds none of the opposition to the state that is to be found in continental European socialism'.[12] The American workers' movement does not have to oppose a state which is not strongly differentiated. Rather, it tries, like other groups, to make its voice heard, to negotiate, to bargain, in order to get decisions taken which are favourable to it. In this sense, the fact that the American state remains 'incomplete'[13] has major consequences for the mode of action of the working class by creating a type of political regime which does not favour the expression of collective interests of a universalist type. Whence the decentralized character of political life, the specific structure of a system of parties grouping coalitions of heterogeneous interest, their adaptation to these conditions in the form of political machines functionally apt at getting, wherever this is possible, votes (catch-all parties according to Otto Kirchheimer's formula), and the preponderant role of local bosses who have been able to weave a clientele network that aggregates the diverse interests which do not express themselves via a strongly structured universalist ideology. American political science, from V. O. Key to Robert Merton, has shown how 'the political machine does not function through a

---

[10] John Laslett, *A Short Comparative History of American Socialism* (New York: Harper & Row, 1977); Robert Dahl, *Polyarchy* (New Haven, Conn.: Yale University Press, 1971).

[11] Louis Hartz, *The Liberal Tradition in America* (New York: Harcourt, Brace & Co., 1955), 6.

[12] Werner Sombart, *Why is there no Socialism in the United States?* (New York: M. E. Sharpe, 1976), 19. See John Laslett, 'Sombart and After: American Social Scientists Address the Question of Socialism in the United States' (unpublished article); R. Boudon, *La Logique du social* (Paris: Hachette, 1979).

[13] Theodore Lowi, *American Government: Incomplete Conquest* (New York: Dryden Press, 1976).

generalized appeal to broad political concerns, but through quasi-feudal relations between the local representatives of the machine and the electors of the neighbourhood. Politics is transformed into personal ties.'[14] Intellectuals, who often play an essential role in the construction of a socialist movement, cannot easily operate in such a localized and clientilist framework.[15]

The type of state influences, therefore, via a particular political regime and party system adapted to it, the conditions of emergence of a socialist movement. As we have noted, the types of French, British, and American states act as essential variables in the conditions of the emergence of socialism. This point is stressed by S. M. Lipset who has analysed, rather than the type of state, its favourable or hostile attitude to the working class in countries as different as the United States, Australia, Germany, France, Spain, and Italy. He has shown how, in the latter three countries: 'trade union organizations were harassed by the state institutions that claimed to represent the electorate democratically. Because the unions were weak...intellectuals or other upper-class radicals came to dominate the labour movements.'[16]

In Canada, faced with a very structured state with a long interventionist tradition, a socialist movement did establish itself.[17] This suggests that the political specificity of the United States involves more than just the nature of the regime, its presidential and non-parliamentary character which determines particular electoral strategies, its federal dimension which leads to a localization of conflicts, and a heterogeneity little compatible with universalizing ideologies like socialism.[18] In reality, as Lowi observes, it was because no rational

[14] Robert Merton, *On Theoretical Sociology* (New York: Free Press, 1967). See V. O. Key, *Politics, Parties and Pressure Groups* (New York: Crowell, 1964); F. Sorauf, *Party Politics in America* (Boston, Mass.: Little Brown, 1973). And, more recently, A. B. Callow, *The City Boss in America* (New York: Oxford University Press, 1976); M. Johnson, 'Patrons and Clients, Jobs and Machines: A Case Study of the Uses of Patronages', *American Political Science Review* (June 1979), 385–98.

[15] Stanley Rothman, 'Intellectuals and the American Political System', in S. Lipset (ed.), *Emerging Coalitions in American Politics* (San Francisco, Calif.: Institute for Contemporary Studies, 1978).

[16] S. M. Lipset, 'Radicalism for Reformism: The Sources of Working Class Politics', *American Political Science Review*, 77/1 (1983), 1–18.

[17] S. M. Lipset, 'Radicalism in North America: A Comparative View of the Party Systems in Canada and the United States', *Transaction of the Royal Society of Canada*, Ser. 4, 14 (1976), 25.

[18] More than Sombart, Selig Perlman had already noted the importance of this factor. *A Theory of the Labor Movement* (New York: Augustus, Kelley, 1966). See John Laslett, 'The American Tradition for Labor Theory and its Relevance to the Contemporary Working Class', in Irving Horowitz, John Legett, and Martin Oppenheimer (eds.), *The*

system of law, of legitimation, or of repression existed which would have made the socialist critique convincing that the latter failed to develop into a collective movement: 'in the American context, it is Madison not Marx who seems to be having the last word'.[19] The weakness of the state and the success of individualism as collective representation account for the quasi-non-existence of socialism in the United States. This is why sociologists talk in terms of strata rather than classes. From Warner to Lipset and Bendix, the social structure is portrayed as an immense staircase of strata superimposed one upon the other.[20] In this way, the individual can change stratum, mobility is individual and not collective, and the 'exit' of the actor, and more particularly that of the worker, takes place via his personal strategy and not via commitment to a collective movement. Strata do not constitute historical groupings with their own nature and will and a role to play in history. There are no strata struggles as there are, in other historical perspectives, class struggles.

We can understand, in these conditions, the success of nominalist Weberian sociology with its particular emphasis on individual actions. For Weber 'classes are not communities', that is why it is wrong to consider them as communities because 'the passages from one class situation to another are very numerous, easy and diverse, and "class unity" is a very relative element'.[21] Rejecting all collective class psychology, Weber refuses, as a true nominalist, to consider class as a real whole with its own will and specific history. It is worth noting here also Schumpeter's influence in the United States, where he taught from 1913 onwards and ended up living permanently between the two wars. Emphasizing that a social class is both more and other than a sum of individuals, and is felt as being and is perceived as a whole, and stressing that the relations between social classes can remain constant, Schumpeter arrives at the idea of permanent 'circulation'. Ultimately, for him, a class can be compared for all of its collective life, that is to

American Working Class: Prospects for the 1980s (New Brunswick, Transaction Books, 1979).

[19] Theodore Lowi, 'Why is there no Socialism in the United States? A Constitutional Analysis' (unpublished article).

[20] Lloyd Warner, Marckie Meeker, and Kenneth Eells, *Social Class in America* (Chicago, Ill.: Social Research Associated, 1949); S. M. Lipset and R. Bendix, *Social Mobility in Industrial Society* (London: Heinemann, 1959); Peter Blau and O. Duncan, *The American Occupational Structure* (Englewood Cliffs, NJ: Prentice-Hall, 1969); Richard Coleman and Lee Rainwater, *Social Standing in America* (London: Routledge & Kegan Paul, 1979).

[21] Quoted in G. Gurvitch, *Le Concept des classes sociales* (Paris: CDU, 1954), 79–80.

say during the time it remains identifiable, to a hotel or a bus, always filled up, but always filled up by different people.[22]

The image of the 'lift' is also used by Schumpeter to illustrate the importance of the mobility of individuals who 'in the sphere of their own real interest', which does not include politics, adopt a form of behaviour which corresponds to the possibility of movement from one class to another whose demarcation lines are neither 'rigid' nor 'thick'.[23] These interpretations of social classes were particularly appropriate to the analysis of American socety, and many sociologists have used the notions of strata and mobility within this individualist framework as against that of class in its holistic sense.

Taken together all these factors seem to encourage the search for 'private happiness' as opposed to the betterment of the 'public good' through, for example, commitment to a collective action. Nevertheless, even though for a whole series of reasons American workers are profoundly 'divided',[24] there have been, contrary to Olsonian logic, a great many strikes throughout the history of the United States. The comparative analysis of strikes has shown that they were particularly long, that more often than not they had no explicitly political dimension, and that they formed a stage in the process of bargaining which particularly characterizes American society.[25] Many authors have invoked the decentralized nature of the American political system to explain the distinctiveness of American strikes, which are always longer than those of other Western industrialized countries, and whose duration does not seem to have changed, whereas in France and Great Britain their length has altered between the nineteenth century and today.[26] As P. K. Edwards observes, 'there is a virtually automatic tendency for strike frequency to be lower in centralised than in

---

[22] Joseph Schumpeter, *Imperialism and Social Classes* (New York: Meridian, 1955).

[23] Joseph Schumpeter, *Capitalism, Socialism, and Democracy* (London: Allen & Unwin, 1976).

[24] Herbert Gutman, *Work, Culture and Society in Industrializing America* (New York: Knopf, 1976); David Montgomery, 'To Study the People: The American Working Class', *Labor History* 21/4 (autumn 1980) 485–512; David Gordon, Richard Edwards, and Michael Reich, *Segmented Work, Divided Workers: The Historical Transformation of Labor in the United States* (Cambridge: Cambridge University Press, 1982).

[25] E. Shorter and C. Tilly, *Strikes in France* (Cambridge: Cambridge University Press, 1974), 306–30; J. T. Dunlop, 'Structure of Collective Bargaining', in G. G. Somers (ed.), *The Next 25 Years of Industrial Relations* (Madison, Wis.: Industrial Relations Research Association, 1973); H. A. Clegg, *Trade Unionism under Collective Bargaining: A Theory Based on Comparison of Six Countries* (Oxford: Blackwell, 1976).

[26] See e.g. A. M. Ross and P. T. Hartman, *Changing Patterns of Industrial Conflict* (New York: Wiley, 1960).

decentralised bargaining systems'.[27] In this society, with its weak state, the workers also adopt a pressure-group strategy and can apply considerable pressure thanks to their resources. Such action is not aimed at destroying the system and does not presuppose a strong class-consciousness but allows strikes to take place at the local level, and be explained in 'costs and benefits' terms.[28] In such a context, therefore, when collective action occurs, it retains a utilitarian dimension.

In the British system, also with a weak state, many of the same characteristics can be found. In Britain, strikes are for the most part devoid of an explicit political dimension. As in the United States the workers are not faced with a strong state, and industrial relations therefore involve confrontation between workers and employers,[29] the institutionalization of conflicts, and strong unionization conferring once again an essential role on the unions which appear as functional organizations representative of workers. Olson's interpretation seems more fruitful than Lenin's to an understanding of the strategy of British workers. Their near-indifference to Marxism and to ideologies in general explains their adherence to trade unionism, which privileges 'loyalty' as opposed to the collective 'exit' strategy. Moreover, 'the Labour Party in Parliament was not merely a political party, it was the parliamentary emanation of the Labour Movement'.[30] It is true that, unlike in the United States, the workers organized themselves into a party and not simply into pressure groups, but here too the perspective remains deliberately gradualist and cannot be explained simply in terms of alienation.[31] British workers, unlike American workers, consider themselves as belonging to a social class with a collective dimension to it and, for a long time, preserved forms of community life widely favourable to collective action. Their strikes conform, nevertheless, to referential values and do not normally lead to political mobilization.

[27] P. K. Edwards, *Strikes in the United States 1881–1974* (Oxford: Blackwell, 1981), 225–7.

[28] Ibid. 229.

[29] Shorter and Tilly, *Strikes in France*, pp. 317–29; Edwards, *Strikes in the United States*, p. 234; Gérard Adam and Jean-Daniel Reynaud, *Conflits du travail et changement social* (Paris: PUF, 1978); James Cronin, *Industrial Conflict in Modern Britain* (London: Croom Helm, 1979); Neville Kirk, *The Growth of Working Class Reformation in Mid-Victorian England* (London: Croom Helm, 1985).

[30] R. T. McKenzie, *British Political Parties* (London: Mercury Books, 1964), 13.

[31] I. Taylor, 'Ideology and Policy', in C. Cook and I. Taylor, *The Labour Party* (London: Longman, 1980); H. Drucker, *Doctrine and Ethos in the Labour Party* (London: Allen & Unwin, 1979); P. Birnbaum, *La Logique de l'État* (Paris: Fayard, 1981).

It is true that strikes have been numerous and often intense; resistance in the defence of jobs and workplace control has also been permanent, creating even a strong activism at the base, and a resurgence of conflict which often appears as the negation of trade-unionist action on the part of workers' organizations.[32] But this resistance within the framework of the workplace does not undermine the Leninist view on the question of worker spontaneity, in that it 'has fitted well with the dominant cultural (and institutional) traditions in Britain',[33] which can be interpreted not as the sole result of alienating practices but as a reaction which is better adapted to the British political system itself. Consequently, even if the British workers have a strong sense of constituting a specific social grouping, they remain more often than not 'loyal', and their radicalism is less than French workers'.[34] Even if they have a real consciousness of their social identity, British workers do not oppose, as a quasi-holistic reality, other social groups or political authorities. So to understand their action, English sociologists and historians turn more and more to autobiographical works, towards stories of working-class life which have little in common with the broad overall visions which have been widespread on the continent.[35] Rejecting Marxism, they too are interested in the possibility of social mobility, and in the social hierarchy in terms of status and prestige.[36] Classes are conceptualized, therefore, by Anthony Giddens, for example, as an aggregate of individuals, the absence of mobility being the condition of the eventual structuration

[32] C. Crouch and A. Pizzorno (eds.), *The Resurgence of Class Conflict in Western Europe since 1968*, vol. i (London: Macmillan, 1978); Theo Nichols and Huw Beynon, *Living with Capitalism* (London: Routledge & Kegan Paul, 1977); Leo Panitch, *Social Democracy and Industrial Militancy* (Cambridge: Cambridge University Press, 1976).

[33] Richard Price, 'Rethinking Labour History', in James Cronin and Jonathan Schneer, *Social Conflict and the Political Order in Modern Britain* (London: Croom Helm, 1982), 210.

[34] Michael Mann, *Consciousness and Action among the Western Working Class* (London: Macmillan, 1973); Arthur Marwick, *Class: Image and Reality in Britain, France and the USA since 1930* (New York: Oxford University Press, 1980); Duncan Gallie, *Social Inequality and Class Radicalism in France and Britain* (London: Cambridge University Press, 1983).

[35] From this point of view it is helpful to contrast the school interested in stories of working-class life which has formed around Raphaël Samuel; R. Samuel (ed.), *People's History and Socialist Theory* (London: Routeldge & Kegan Paul, 1981), and the structuralist Marxist view influenced by Althusser (P. Anderson, T. Nairn, and B. Jessop), which is perhaps more concerned with accounting for the type of consciousness of British workers belonging to a more pragmatic society in which values and culture play an essential role as described by the work of E. P. Thompson.

[36] David Glass (ed.), *Social Mobility in Britain* (London: Routledge & Kegan Paul, 1954).

of a class.[37] Such a view recognizes the central role of classes, but does so on the basis of an interpretation which is compatible with the realities of British society. We can thus say that the notion of social mobility appears widely 'underestimated', and that the idea of closure is debatable. Given the existence of such processes which British, like American, workers profit from,[38] a purely holistic approach to the working class appears to be more and more inoperable.

In France, on the contrary, the working class has often been considered as a unified actor having its own will and specific values. That is why a more structural Marxist interpretation has exerted a strong influence in the analysis of the working class. Scorning the few texts in which Marx insists on the crucial role of class-consciousness, contemporary French Marxist authors reason in purely structural and quasi-holistic terms which are perfectly in tune with a particular socio-historical view of reality which always speaks of the State, the Nation, the People, the Working Class, and the Revolution, as the actors in the history of a French society ill-disposed towards market individualism. It is true that the ideologues from the eighteenth century to today have played a central role in French history, precisely because, on the right (de Bonald, Taine, Renan, Maurras) as on the left (Rousseau, Robespierre, Michelet, Jaurès, Sartre), they reason unceasingly in holistic terms, with the People, the Army, the State, the Working Class clashing like beings endowed with their own will. These globalizing visions of the world, deaf to and scornful of all Benthamite utilitarian interpretation, hostile also to any preoccupation with individual psychology, and preferring the idea of the soul of the people, the destiny of the nation, the will of the state, or of the working class, seem, at first sight, better adapted to the specifics of French society where, from feudalism to the present day, allegiances to peripheral structures of territory or of class have remained strong, and have clashed incessantly with a state which claims to incarnate legitimacy. Hence the conflicts between these various entities which encourage closed and systematic ideologies, strikes directed against the state, the important role given to the party, the weakness of the trade unions, and the refusal of voluntarism.[39]

[37] Anthony Giddens, *The Class Structure of Advanced Societies* (London: Hutchinson, 1973).

[38] See e.g. John Goldthorpe with Catriona Llewellyn and Clive Payne, *Social Mobility and Class Structure in Modern Britain* (Oxford: Clarendon Press, 1980), 42–62.

[39] Shorter and Tilly, *Strikes in France*; Adam and Reynaud, *Conflits du travail et changement social*.

Seen as solid communities, the People or the Working Class have almost always been portrayed in the literature in this unanimist way, as an actor who is but the living expression of a moving social entity.[40] One can, therefore, understand the extreme hostility of French sociologists to what appears to them as psychologism: the analysis of the values of workers, of their own consciousness, and, *a fortiori*, of their individual projects. Up to a point, it could be said that, for a long time, French sociologists of the working class simply ignored the questions asked by Lenin and by Olson, because social reality seemed to them different, and very different from that of the Anglo-Saxon countries. The working class has often been presented as a single actor, collectively organized via its parties and trade unions, whose role is determined by its place in the relations of production. As André Gorz notes:

The political imperatives of the class struggle have hindered the working-class movement from analysing the basis of the desire for autonomy as a specifically existential exigency ... proletarian activists have generally fought against the desire for individual autonomy as a residue in the worker of *petit bourgeois* individualism. Autonomy is not a working-class value.[41]

Nevertheless, even if we say, as Gorz does, 'Farewell to the proletariat' we are still imagining it as an actor, as a single and holistic entity, and can, then, displace globalizing interpretations on to the New Working Class,[42] the presumed 'spearhead' of social change.

Without embarking on a rigorous sociology of the sociology of the working class (which would, however, be extremely useful), we can compare briefly two contemporary French sociologists who represent very different intellectual traditions. Nicos Poulantzas condemns the 'problematic of the subject' according to which

the agents of a social formation, 'men', are not considered, as by Marx, as the supports of objective instances which act upon these through the class struggle, but as the genetic principle of levels of the social whole in the form of 'concrete individuals'; hence the view of social actors, of individuals as the origin of 'social action'. In this way, research is orientated not towards the study of co-ordinated objectives which distribute agents among social classes and the various forms of the class struggle, but towards ultimate explanations based on the behavioural motivations of actor-individuals.[43]

[40] One need only think of Brunet, the worker, in Sartre's *Roads of Freedom*.

[41] André Gorz, *Adieux au prolétariat* (Paris: Galilée, 1980), 44.

[42] Serge Mallet, *La Nouvelle Classe ouvrière* (Paris: Seuil, 1969).

[43] Nicos Poulantzas, 'Sur l'État de la société capitaliste', *Politique aujourd'hui* (Mar. 1970), 68.

Condemning 'the anthropologism of the subject',[44] he believes, like Althusser, that the agents of production occupy places 'inasmuch as they are bearers of its functions' integrated into the relations of production.[45]

Similarly, according to Manuel Castells, 'one speaks of places and not of individuals', because 'analysis which proceeds on the basis of concrete actors and their strategies necessarily shuts itself into an impasse'.[46] Ultimately, for Nicos Poulantzas 'social classes are not empirical groups of individuals', because the 'places [they occupy] are independent of the wills of these agents'.[47] It is understandable that he condemns 'the inanity of the bourgeois problematic of social mobility', and strategies of social ascension which demonstrate only the persistence of 'petty-bourgeois individualism'.[48] In this view, as with Lenin, individualism, which can also be found in the workers, is simply evidence of their alienation. However, contrary to Lenin's conclusions, this individualism has little influence, given the structural character of the determination of the position and the action of the whole working class whose movement and collective action is no longer dependent upon an outside party.

The Marxian interpretation of the French working class assumes, therefore, the ability to ignore the question of the values of the workers themselves. It analyses structures, not actors, and, from this point of view, condemns, in particular, empirical works of the Anglo-Saxon type. It is thus surprising and all the more unexpected to find in the work of Alain Touraine, with very different theoretical preoccupations, a language which is often just as globalizing and quasi-holistic. For him it is a question of studying the transformations in 'working-class consciousness' and 'the working-class movement'. The working-class movement 'is that aspect of working-class action which questions the relations of production in the name of production itself. The working-class movement is not only a class movement, but is the working class in action.'[49]

Distinguishing certain stages which the working class goes through

[44] Nicos Poulantzas, *Pouvoir politique et classes sociales* (Paris: Maspero, 1968), 65.

[45] Louis Althusser, *Lire le capital* (Paris: Maspero, 1965), ii. 157.

[46] Manuel Castells, *La Question urbaine* (Paris: Maspero, 1972), 314–34. See also Daniel Bertaux, *Destins personnels et structures de classe* (Paris: PUF, 1977), 47–9.

[47] Nicos Poulantzas, *Les Classes sociales dans le capitalisme d'aujourd'hui* (Paris: Seuil, 1974), 16, 19.

[48] Ibid. 37, 312.

[49] A. Touraine, M. Wieviorka, and F. Dubet, *Le Mouvement ouvrier* (Paris: Fayard, 1984), 53.

as part of its insertion into a technological framework, and a more or less accentuated division of labour, Alain Touraine has emphasized how the working class adheres to different values, those found, for example, in the building industry, the steel industry, and, lastly, the gas and electricity industries where the workers become white-collar supervisors. For him, the working class has a class-consciousness only during intermediary moments such as the creation of the large-scale factories at the end of the nineteenth century where Taylorism predominated. After this, the working class has no class-consciousness, even though workers' consciousness remains. This gives rise to questions concerning the future of the workers' movement in post-industrial society. 'After this period of crisis, worker consciousness is situated within the system of labour, where, although it does not lose its sense of dissatisfaction on the bases of its demands, it loses all its absolute principles of opposition.'[50] Henceforward 'class-consciousness is situated at the beginning of industrial society as the thunderclap which heralded its birth'.[51] The working-class movement still continues its action but is no longer based on class-consciousness, and no longer occupies such a central position in society.[52]

What interests Alain Touraine, therefore, is the problem of changes in collective consciousness. He emphasizes strongly the importance of the study of 'personal satisfaction' or of 'the evaluation of life chances', but, for him, these perspectives only involve 'the individual', and the individual's 'strategies', and remain 'on the margins' of his own work of analytical sociology.[53] He recognizes the 'usefulness' of the 'economistic' approach according to which the workers too 'act in a so-called rational way, that is to say, attempt to maximize their individual advantages', but declares his own intention to move from 'analysis of the individual to that of the organization or system of social relations'.[54] The work of Alain Touraine on the French working class throws into relief the essential role of values and of consciousness which is crucial to an understanding of workers' strategies. Might we suggest cautiously that it remains, nevertheless, structure-based by making the state of the workers' collective consciousness dependent upon the nature of the organization of the production system. And that, therefore, it does not give sufficient attention to the problems

[50] A. Touraine, *La Conscience ouvrière* (Paris: Seuil, 1966), 118.
[51] Ibid. 331.
[52] A. Touraine, *La Société post-industrielle* (Paris: Denoël, 1969), 50, 90–101.
[53] Touraine, *La Conscience ouvrière*, pp. 336–9.
[54] Ibid. 13–14.

raised by Olson, precisely at the level of the behaviour of individual actors? For Alain Touraine: 'Trade unionism is not only a coalition formed to obtain "collective goods", as Mancur Olson and Anthony Oberschall claim, but is a movement which is defined by its position within the power relations of the production process of industrial society.'[55]

Because, in France, the working class appears to be a collective actor which does not hesitate to mobilize, Olson's conclusion is assumed to be wrong since it cannot explain the action 'of a category which contests relations of domination'.[56] One can ask, however, if this specificity of the French working class should not be examined comparatively. Olson would thus be able to explain the behaviour of American workers in an individualistic society, with a market and a weak state; Lenin and contemporary English sociologists would be able, from different starting-points, to explain the reasons for the functional character of reformist trade unionism; French sociologists of the working class would, on the other hand, be able to illustrate the apparently more collective character of a working class organized in a more structured way, and how the parties and unions related to it willingly provoke, in the name of this social grouping conceptualized in a quasi-holistic way, mobilizing, collective actions against employers but also, and above all, against a state which itself is conceptualized in an equally holistic way.[57] The various sociologies would thus become particularly well adapted to the specific nature of each society and each type of state.

[55] Touraine, Wieviorka, and Dubet, *Le Mouvement ouvrier*, p. 22.
[56] Ibid. 30.
[57] It is clear that such overall correlations are always fragile. Today, there are many structural sociological analyses of the working class in the United States, e.g. Erik Olin Wright, *Class, Crisis and the State* (London: New Left Books, 1978), or, in Britain, Barry Hindess and Paul Hirst, *Mode of Production and Social Formation* (London: Macmillan, 1977); J. Bloomfield (ed.), *Class Hegemony and Party* (London: Lawrence & Wishart, 1977) — or the journal *Capital and Class*. Conversely, one finds in France works more concerned with the values of workers: Maurice Halbwachs, *La Classe ouvrière et les niveaux de vie* (Paris: Alcan, 1913). Today, Paul-Henry Chombart de Lauwe, *La Vie quotidienne des familles ouvrières* (Paris: Éditions du CNRS, 1977), and Jacques Rancière, *La Nuit des prolétaires* (Paris: Fayard, 1981). We should note, however, even among those who are attentive to values and ways of doing things, the continuing presence of an opposite view *vis-à-vis* the study of actors, and one which presupposes a necessary solidarity. Thus, for Luce Giard and Pierre Mayol 'to be a worker is less to be harnessed to a specific task, than to participate, and this is fundamental, in a popular urban culture, in which values of essential identification predominate and which involve principally *practices of solidarity*', Luce Giard and Pierre Mayol, *L'Invention du quotidien* (Paris: UGE, 10/18, 1980), 64.

We can, however, raise the question of the validity of such correlations which encourage us to identify anew a particular method of analysis of the real (methodological individualism or holism) with the type of object one proposes to analyse. What would be more fruitful would be to blend methodologies or objects of analysis, and apply the methodological individualism perspective in an examination of the actions of French workers, just as it would be equally desirable to use a more holistic point of view to illustrate other aspects of the reality of the American workers' world which Olson's approach cannot on its own account for.

Is it the case that, as social actors, French workers too have strategies for the maximization of their individual interests which distance them from participation in collective action? Does the analytical approach of methodological individualism offer a different perspective on working-class reality by not assuming its holistic nature from the outset? We can note straight away that at each end of its history, in the middle of the nineteenth century and in the contemporary period, individual strategies seem to be so strong that they appear to undermine the status of class solidarity. We need only read the memoirs of workers to see the reality of their individual 'exit' strategies which diminish 'loyalty' by diminishing, at the same time, the intensity of the collective 'voice' and mobilization. Martin Nadaud describes, for example, the importance he attached to achieving professional and social ascension: 'a little vanity was born in his mind. This growing ambition was a good thing, a kind of lever inside, which stirs a young man's consciousness.'[58] As a specific social actor, Nadaud hopes to better himself,[59] and this future leader of the workers' world, having made his 'fortune', has only one worry: 'Where can I hide my savings?' he cries.[60] Even though he participates in the struggles of the people, he does not forget to apply his own strategy for social ascension, and he notes how 'jealousy and hatred' reign between the workers.[61] As Efrahem, a shoemaker, emphasizes in the same period, the workers are 'isolated, scattered': 'Stop our stupid jealousies, smother our hatreds, let us build ties of friendship, kindness and fraternity', let us not fall into 'individualism and the selfishness of isolation'. Ultimately, the

---

[58] Martin Nadaud, *Léonard, maçon de la Creuse* (Paris: Maspero, 1982), 122.
[59] Ibid. 194.
[60] Ibid. 154. Georges Duveau shows how, in Lorraine and Lyon, the workers had a taste for 'speculation', buying shares, and so on. Georges Duveau, *La Vie ouvrière en France sous le Second Empire* (Paris: Gallimard, 1946), 408–9.
[61] Nadaud, *Léonard, maçon de la Creuse*, p. 119.

workers must constitute 'a body' to affirm their 'solidarity'.[62] In an explicit way, what he notes is the strength of individualism; what he calls for, as is illustrated by his organicist metaphors, is the creation of a holistic structure. As one tract claimed, 'Cease, oh bourgeois, to drive us from your bosom ... if it is evil for the worker to free himself and become bourgeois in his turn, whose fault is that?'[63] However, in the heat of the events of 1848 and all the political mobilization, the workers' newspaper, founded by the worker delegates at the Luxembourg, declared in its first issue of 4 June 1848: 'The work we are undertaking today is not and will never become an individual work ... Individual undertakings only bring disappointment and ruin. Collective undertakings are inexhaustible.'[64]

What a perfect illustration of the theses of Albert Hirschman: the inadequacy of the purely individual project, and the inadequacy of collective commitment.[65] These workers want both individual success, which leads apparently to 'disappointment and ruin', and the success of a movement of collective solidarity; they are aware of its fragile foundations but not of its being the source of other disappointments. As Jules Leroux notes: 'Class does not exist, only individuals',[66] and to establish real 'fraternity' between them is not easy while the attachment to 'independence', and the need 'to present an image of oneself', hold such sway. The typographer Vasbenter once wrote in a letter to Flora Tristan: 'We must appeal to material interests, not to devotion; all ears will remain deaf. Appeal to selfishness',[67] a selfishness not uncommon among the 'real workers': 'The real worker rarely mixes with his workmates. He has few friends and does not make friends easily ... There are many workers, but they are trying to set themselves up ... he has the right and legitimate hope of all workers: ownership.'[68]

We can add that, at this time, many were the corporations of workers which rivalled one another, defended their privileges, if needs be by force, and appeared to be structures which resulted from individual choices, and which deliberately encouraged protection and

[62] In *La Parole ouvrière 1830–1851*, ed. J. Rancière (Paris: UGE, 1976), 160, 163, 166.

[63] Ibid. 215–17.

[64] Ibid. 298–301.

[65] A. Hirschman, *Shifting Involvements: Private Interest and Public Action* (Princeton, NJ: Princeton University Press, 1982).

[66] In *La Parole ouvrière*, p. 95.

[67] Rancière, *La Nuit des prolétaires*.

[68] See Denis Poulot, *Le Sublime* (Paris: Maspero, 1980), 139–41.

secretiveness, such a community of working people serving as a structure of collective protection to all those who are part of it. In this way corporatism as object becomes corporatism as subject.[69]

But how can one reconcile collective action, that is, planned fraternity, with 'egoism'? This question is crucial because it indicates not only the difficulties but also the possibilities for collective mobilization on the basis of a multiplicity of individual 'egoistic' decisions. But the transition from one to the other in a situation where mobilization now depends, not on the reified will of a holistic social structure, but on individual interests, does not go without saying. Here is a startling illustration of this from *L'Atelier*:

We know that communists say that there is true moral happiness to be gained from devotion to the cause. We do not share this view. It is doubtless a great moral satisfaction to have shown devotion; but the effort involved, compared with the pleasure gained, is always greater. To be devoted to something, some motivation stronger than moral happiness is necessary.[70]

One could be reading—and this by a French worker—a perfect replica of Bentham's materialist and utilitarian critique of Rousseau. It was the satisfaction of their own interests which procured for the old French workers an egoistical pleasure and not the moral search for happiness *à la* Saint-Just. As if following the British theoretician of utilitarianism, invoked by authors today such as Olson, the French workers of the nineteenth century calculated their 'pleasures' and their 'pains'. As has been noted, liberals like Bentham or James Mill adopt a purely individualist idea of interest which precludes the idea of a collective interest, such as that of social groups and, *a fortiori*, social classes. It is the individual who must calculate rationally where his happiness is. In such a context one cannot speak of the interest of the working class, even less of its happiness. Happiness does not proceed from the public domain as in Rousseau or Saint-Just but clearly from the private.[71] The workers should not, therefore, be tempted by an entry, even a provisional one, in Hirschman's sense, into the public domain. As convinced utilitarians, the French workers, like the British workers, would not know the Hirschmanian cycle, unless tempted

[69] Denis Segrestin, *Le Phénomène corporatiste* (Paris: Fayard, 1985).
[70] Quoted in Rancière, *La Nuit des prolétaires*, p. 281.
[71] Jack Lively and John Rees, *Utilitarian Logics and Politics* (Oxford: Clarendon Press, 1978); Ghita Ionescu, *Politics and the Pursuit of Happiness* (London: Longman, 1984).

even further away from their true interests by the siren calls of idealism.

The search for private happiness seems to be a constant factor in the nineteenth century, and this, ironically, in a society where the holistic representation of social structures is so dominant. Long is the list of workers' memoirs which, throughout the nineteenth century, bear witness to the strength of this utilitarian and individualistic attitude.[72] Today, at the other end of the history of the working class, as it were, individualistic motivations seem to be one of the main causes of workers' action. And it is worth noting that the individual workers themselves become ever more different from one another. Pierre Dubois is perhaps right when he says that the '"working class" remains a mobilizing myth which is referred to in phases of struggle, and which allows temporarily for the masking of internal differences; it is only a myth'.[73] This would mean, though, that even as a myth this notion facilitates mobilization and, therefore, that mobilization is itself created on mythic and thus quasi-holistic bases, and not as the ultimate result of an aggregation of rationally decided individual choices. However, in terms of our argument we must turn to analysis of the values of workers themselves, rather than to the significance of mythologies. Just as in the first part of the nineteenth century, the individual search for an 'exit' strategy seems today to play an important role: especially as it can now base itself on a significant and growing inter- and intra-generational working-class mobility. As Claude Thélot demonstrated in 1977, 31 per cent of the sons of French workers were, at 40–59 years of age, white-collar workers or cadres; in 1953, there were only 21 per cent.[74] In the same way, intra-generational mobility of workers is relatively great: nearly 12 per cent of workers in 1965 were, five years later, in a different profession; 2.5 per cent of them had become small businesspeople.[75] In the year 1960–70, we see also a strong rise 'in working class households who adopt the "fewer children/educational success of children" model'.[76]

Today, as in the nineteenth century, French workers aspire, through

[72] See also Agricol Perdiguier, *Mémoires d'un compagnon* (Paris: Maspero, 1978).
[73] Pierre Dubois, *Les Ouvriers divisés* (Paris: Presses de la Fondation nationale des sciences politiques, 1981), 117–18.
[74] Claude Thélot, *Tel Père, tel fils?* (Paris: Dunod, 1982).
[75] Nonna Mayer, 'Une filière de mobilité ouvrière: L'Accès à la petite entreprise artisanale et commerciale', *Revue française de sociologie*, 18 (1977), 28–30.
[76] Jean-Pierre Terrail, 'Familles ouvrières, école, destin social (1880–1980)', *Revue française de sociologie*, 25 (1984), 430.

a strategy of mobility, to achieve an increase in personal satisfaction without waiting for the hypothetical results of collective action. Hence the strong allegiance to Benthamite values. If we compare, for example, two SOFRES opinion polls concerning possible measures which made creating a business and starting up on one's own more difficult, in 1976, 58 per cent of workers were alarmed by the possibility; in 1983, 72 per cent thought the same.[77] Conversely, they regarded, more or less in the same proportions from one date to the other, the idea of abolishing political parties (27 per cent and 32 per cent), or even trade unions (46 per cent and 44 per cent), with alarm. We can see, therefore, the very strong attachment of French workers to individual strategies such as the creation of business, perhaps the most pertinent illustration of market logic over class logic, and their relative indifference to or greater tolerance of the idea of abolishing even the instruments of collective mobilization. The attachment of workers to liberalism is, moreover, explicit: 57 per cent of them had, in 1985, a favourable opinion of it, 69 per cent of them were favourable to competition, only 16 per cent to significant state intervention, and 39 per cent to nationalizations.[78]

Today, as in the nineteenth century, the logic of the market, the strategies of personal wealth creation, the betterment of careers, even the hope of creating a business and 'being one's own boss' exert a strong attraction on a great many French workers, a certain number of whom have been able to translate these dreams into reality. Fifty-eight per cent of workers believe it acceptable eventually to profit from the surplus-value linked to the rise in house and land prices,[79] 62 per cent of workers hope to be able to own their own home, and we know that this last 'distances the working-class family still more from the centre of things'.[80]

Few French workers are unionized or ascribe much importance to union action. They even consider the general strike as the 'wrong means' to change society (53 per cent),[81] and only 12 per cent (9 per cent in 1983) considered that in order 'to be a good citizen' one should join a union. This proportion falls to 6 per cent for joining a political party. We should note that between 1976 and 1983, the proportion of workers who believed it was necessary to join a party falls from 6 per

[77] SOFRES, *La France de 1983: Une nation ou des classes?* (Mar. 1983), 26.
[78] SOFRES, *Le Classement idéologique des Français* (Feb. 1985).
[79] SOFRES poll, *Le Nouvel Observateur* (Mar. 1984).
[80] Michel Verret, *L'Espace ouvrier* (Paris: Colin, 1982).
[81] SOFRES, *Dépolitisation des Français: Mythe ou réalité?* (1972), 12.

cent to 2 per cent.[82] This shows the extent to which workers tend to give preference to individual action over collective action. Even if the working class remains in France in a situation of profound exploitation, the workers, as individual actors, seem to subscribe strongly to the liberal and individualist ideology and perceive their professional or even educational future[83] only in terms of the maximization of their own chances within a system which they know to be particularly unjust and strongly structured into a social hierarchy, difficult of access, and comprising many 'barriers'.

It is not only, therefore, conservative workers who reject commitment to collective action.[84] It is true that the majority of the French working class still has a strong class-consciousness, but most, nevertheless, attempt to join, as far as they can, the 'haves', rather than try to change their situation by an act of collective mobilization.[85] Andrée Andrieux and Jean Lignon stress the will 'to escape' as a characteristic of the contemporary French worker who, for a long period, maintained the specificity and culture of the group. The authors go on to point out that 'the worker who seeks escape undertakes an activity in the true sense of the word. It is, however, a purely personal activity, the pursuit of a plan of escape. It does not link the worker to other workers in a common cause. On the contrary, it isolates him.'[86] In the contemporary period, many 'elements which erode the level of class-consciousness' have appeared, and workers seem to participate less readily in collective action, the numbers of disputes having declined in

---

[82] SOFRES, *La France de 1976* (1976), 33.

[83] R. Boudon, *Effets pervers et ordre social* (Paris: PUF, 1977), 99–130.

[84] J. Capdevielle, E. Dupoirier, G. Grunberg, E. Schweisguth, and C. Ysmal, *France de gauche, vote à droite* (Paris: Presses de la Fondation nationale des sciences politiques, 1981).

[85] P. Birnbaum, *Le Peuple et les gros: Histoire d'un mythe* (Paris: Coll. Pluriel, 1984). 36% of workers voted for Reagan in 1984 and only 22% for Mondale; and 40% of them favoured a reduction in the state's role, SOFRES, *Opinion publique 1985* (Paris: Gallimard, 1985), 257, 263.

[86] Andrée Andrieux and Jean Lignon, *L'Ouvrier d'aujourd'hui* (Paris: Gonthier, 1966), 163. See also Jacques Frémontier, *La Vie en bleu* (Paris: Fayard, 1980), 313. 'There are lovely jobs everywhere, said a worker, it's just a question of finding them; with a little effort, you can make your little niche', in P. Molyneux and C. Merinari, *La Parole au capital* (Paris: UGE, 10/18, 1978), 148.

[87] Jacques Kergoat, 'Combativité, organisation et niveau de conscience dans la classe ouvrière', *Revue française des affaires sociales* (Apr.–June 1982), and 'De la crise économique à la victoire électorale de la gauche: Réaction ouvrière et politiques syndicales', in Mark Kesselman (ed.), *1968–1982: Le Mouvement ouvrier français* (Paris: Éditions ouvrières, 1984), 353–5.

class country, in Lorraine, 'the man of iron' also seems to seek isolation. Here too 'individualism is winning'.[88] In Lorraine, where the supposedly united working class was born, acting collectively, conscious of itself, and organized, Gérard Noiriel has illustrated the importance of 'strategies of individualization' which grow as the present crises grows. The opening up of possibilities for upward employment mobility has become 'ways of mobilizing, on an individual basis, the energy of those who are not satisfied with their lot'.[89] If there is mobilization then it is individual and not collective. And even when real mobilization is created, as in May 1968 at Bulledor, in the Paris region:

solidarity is no longer the natural expression of a specific social class as in the case of traditional skilled workers, but is justified in terms of its function in relation to 'individual needs'. As a worker said on this occasion, 'I went on strike, the masses gained something. No single person can win a war.' It is, therefore, because he knows that collective commitment will maximize his 'benefits' that each worker can decide to take part in a collective action which is not, in this case, the result of the holistic will of a class which is supposedly united and the master of its own destiny. It is, in this case, 'a utilitarian view of strike action'.[90]

Ultimately, whether it is purely individual or else the result of the commitment of a plurality of individuals in a collective action designed to increase the rewards of each, mobilization shows itself today as often having a utilitarian character.[91]

Thus, in the contemporary period, either the workers attempt individually to escape, that is to say, to 'get out', or they decide to take part in an action which is perhaps better described as common rather than collective, given that it is the result of the accumulation of individualist and utilitarian behaviour. One can understand, from this, that many authors have tried to assess the 'embourgeoisement' of French workers who transform themselves into contemporary Benthams by adapting to the increasing pre-eminence of the rules of the market, and by abandoning an earlier and supposedly more collective

---

[88] Serge Bonnet, *L'Homme de fer, 1960–1973* (Nancy: Presses universitaires de Nancy, 1984), 375.

[89] Gérard Noiriel, *Longwy: Immigrés et prolétaires 1880–1980* (Paris: PUF, 1984).

[90] Danielle Kergoat, *Bulledor ou l'histoire d'une mobilisation ouvrière* (Paris: Seuil, 1973), 195–6.

[91] Many strikes, in the 1970s for example, had as their aim, in a disparate way, the maintenance of the standard of living. 'Les Grèves', *Sociologie du travail*, 4 (1973).

commitment to oppose, above all, the state. At this time of dominant anti-statism, the growing individualism of French workers also seems to suggest the lesser relevance of holistic models, whether applied to the state or the working class. It is not necessary here to dwell upon the exact terms of the debate over the 'embourgeoisement' of the working class; we can note simply that even the term itself seems to indicate the victory of the Anglo-Saxon model over the apparently more collective traditions of the French working class. Let us note, however, that if the 'new workers' baulk at committing themselves collectively, the same applies, *a fortiori*, for all workers who work in areas where the working-class bastions have been bypassed.[92] Where modern industries have been set up, as in Normandy, and stripped of all culture and traditions reminiscent of the old areas of industrialization, such as Lorraine and the Nord, the working population is recruited especially from among women, the young, and immigrants. Each salaried worker, often employed by agencies, works in several businesses at a time: 'the employees are strongly individualized, only know each other through working teams, and have no collective dimension which would facilitate a collective defence'. The 'man of iron', the Fordian worker, white, and male, who incarnated the great moments of workers' struggles at the turn of the century, has been replaced by other categories of workers, and the destruction of working communities which were apparently strongly welded together by their history and interests is accelerating. To the 'solitude' of this new working class, moreover, is added the fact that the new generation of salaried workers has had, since the 1960s, more of a 'self-consciousness', than a 'class-consciousness'.[93] The picture is clear enough: at, as we called it earlier, the other end of the history of the French working class, individualist strategies and the refocusing of attention on the individual actor seem to be the rule; and we witness the shattering of old solidarities and the weakening of the will to commit oneself in a collective movement. And this especially because the workers are more and more 'divided'[94] into a large number of distinct categories with multiple interests: from the qualified, white-collar, 'new working class' to the new model army of 'temps'.

Therefore, independently of the successive stages of the division of

[92] Thierry Baudouin and Michelle Collin, *Le Contournement des forteresses ouvrières* (Paris: Méridiens, 1983).

[93] Ibid. 42, 106, 128.

[94] Pierre Dubois, *Les Ouvriers divisés* (Paris: Presses de la Fondation nationale des sciences politiques, 1981), 79–81.

labour, the working-class movement seems — in the nineteenth century, like today — to have been faced with the individualist strategies of workers whose attitudes differ markedly from received opinion.[95] By analysing these two great moments of workers' history, comparison is often made with the intermediary stage, that of the end of the nineteenth century and the first half of the twentieth, which, in the usual presentations of the working-class movement, corresponds to the idea of a community in action and ready to mobilize collectively to defend its group interests. The works of historians of the working class often present us with such an image of this social group at this moment of its existence. Given this perspective, it is almost impossible to assess behaviour of an individualist type.[96]

In this intermediary stage in the big iron and steel concentrations and in the motor industry a working class seems indeed to have existed, and to have been defended by the trade unions and represented by its own political parties. As Michelle Perrot shows, the strike was often 'a clamour borne of a collective gesture ... they grouped themselves together, made claims *en masse* and in one voice, so as to avoid reprisals'.[97] As a collective act, the strike crystallized the workers into a united grouping, and police intervention simply 'welded the unanimity together; the strike was like a collective celebration. Hence the procession, the songs, almost instinctive forms of denunciation, all ways of staying grouped together and making a noise.'[98] 'Proletarian dialogue' took place especially in cafés, taverns, and eating-houses, all of which were places of worker sociability,[99] which reinforced the social ties favourable to collective mobilization.[1] Lorraine, with its heavy industry and its blast furnaces, saw the development of what seemed to be the traditions of the real working class. And it was here in the cafés that the solidarity and consciousness of strikers was strengthened: as Serge Bonnet notes: 'the café in the working-class quarter replaced the village tavern. It encouraged the maintenance of com-

[95] Michel Verret, 'Mémoire ouvrière, mémoire communiste', *Revue française de science politique* (1984), 415–16.

[96] For Rolande Trempé, 'The miners had acquired, as early as 1869, the consciousness of belonging to a specific group, but it was only when they were raised to a class-consciousness in the 1890s that this group constituted a truly homogeneous whole', Rolande Trempé, *Les Mineurs de Carmaux, 1848–1914* (Paris: Éditions ouvrières, 1971), ii. 928.

[97] Michelle Perrot, *Les Ouvriers en grève* (Paris: Mouton, 1974), i. 256.

[98] Ibid. ii. 554.

[99] Ibid. ii. 591.

[1] P. Birnbaum, *Dimensions du pouvoir* (Paris: PUF, 1984).

munity links; the processions, the celebrations, and the dances were all, in one way or another, linked to the cafés, the source of "elementary" social life.'[2] In the Toulouse region[3] as, soon after, in the Lyon region, 'the mobilization of the working masses', and the spread of strikes in the 1890s, led to the zenith of a mass union movement.[4] The history of the CGT was linked to this type of mobilization, the best expression of which was the action of steel industry workers, and the solidarities formed as a result of working patterns which produced strongly welded communities.[5] However, even in this context which was particularly favourable to collective action and which seems to refute, for this specific period of the history of the working class, the usefulness of the methodological individualism approach, and which excluded, moreover, all utilitarian action by the workers themselves, one can legitimately question the validity of such a univocal interpretation of the strategies of workers always supposed to act solely within the framework of their community. As Denis Segrestin has pointed out:

It was essentially a unitary approach and was at least tendentially majoritarian, if not unanimist. It was also an undertaking which operated at the level of immediately felt solidarity which had little to do with real personal commitment. It was an approach which was psychologically both inexpensive and not very profitable. The worker who joined the union did not alter or improve his relationship to the community. The worker who was not in the union or had let his membership lapse did not endanger his status within the community.[6]

It is clearly the 'inexpensive' and 'not very profitable' character of trade-union commitment which explains its weakness, even at a time when community and work-based solidarities remained very strong. Pushing this analysis to its limits one could almost conclude, in Olsonian terms, though here in the context of a 'community', that each worker who was a member of a network of solidarity might be tempted to apply the 'free-rider' strategy, inasmuch as the overall price

[2] Serge Bonnet, *La Ligne rouge des hauts fourneaux* (Paris: Denoël, 1981), 122, 226, 253. See also Noiriel, *Longwy*, p. 84.

[3] Ronald Aminzade, *Class, Politics and Early Industrial Capitalism* (Albany, NY: State University of New York Press, 1981), 197.

[4] Yves Lequin, *Les Ouvriers de la région lyonnaise: 1848–1914* (Lyon: Presses universitaires de Lyon, 1977), ii. 146, 147, 296.

[5] G. Adam, 'Les Structures syndicales', in G. Adam, F. Bon, J. Capdevielle, and R. Mouriaux, *L'Ouvrier français en 1970* (Paris: Presses de la Fondation nationale des sciences politiques, 1970), 31.

[6] Denis Segrestin, 'Pratiques syndicales et mobilisation: Vers le changement?', in Kesselman, *1968–1982: Le Mouvement ouvrier français*, p. 263.

of collective action is paid for by the other members of the working community. This approach has had little impact on historians of the working class of the late nineteenth and early twentieth centuries, attached as they have been to their quasi-holistic vision of a united working class, mobilizing in collective action. The material is missing to us which would demonstrate whether there were 'cost–benefit' calculations of a very utilitarian type during this crucial moment of the history of the workers' movement. However, if it is possible to demonstrate the existence of individual strategies even in the framework of a village of peasants which cannot be understood simply as a holistic reality,[7] then, *a fortiori*, such behaviour can take place even at the time when workers form a working community welded together by a common culture. The real problem, therefore, is to know what secures the solidarity of workers without assuming that solidarity is a naturally given phenomenon resulting from the shared work experience which gives rise to a social community. In this respect it is necessary to consider Michaël Hechter's iconoclastic view: 'What is there inherent in a structural explanation to inhibit actors from being free-riders? The answer is clear: there is nothing.'[8]

From a methodological point of view, it is crucial to break with the practice whereby research links method and object, and each stage of the history of a social phenomenon must be analysed with a specific method.[9] Even in the framework of a working community which corresponds to the myth of a united working class, the Olsonian approach is still valuable. Whether the observer is looking at a caste or at a class, it must be assumed that the actors have a particular point of view. Class members might simply consider that loyalty, in this type of structure, and in terms of the choices offered in a rigid society, appears as helpful and less costly whereas, as members of a stratum, they would probably not hesitate to 'get out'. Such an approach would be necessary, moreover, to explain the solidarity which might exist between the members of a workers' collectivity at a moment in its history: instead of having recourse only to interpretations in terms of social control, of the reproduction of norms, or of 'working-class culture', all of which can, in fact, exercise an often important role, one can see also in solidarity the result of a chosen adherence by those who

---

[7] S. Popkin, *The Rational Peasant* (Berkeley, Los Angeles, Calif.: University of California Press, 1979).

[8] M. Hechter, 'A Theory of Group Solidarity', in M. Hechter (ed.), *The Microfoundations of Macrosociology* (Philadelphia, NJ: Temple University Press, 1983), 19.

[9] Birnbaum, *Dimensions du pouvoir*, ch. 10.

express such solidarity. It would be extremely useful to use such an approach to analyse this crucial moment of the history of the working class. It is just as indispensable in the present period to understand more fully the shared character of the behaviour of workers, given their apparent adherence to a more individualist and utilitarian attitude. Guy Michelat and Michel Simon's research demonstrates, for example, the maintenance of a communist culture in a part of the 'embourgeoised' working class which, from the inter-generational mobility point of view, comes from a communist working-class milieu.[10] This means that the sons of workers, who have effected an 'exit', often prefer, contrary to Olson and Lenin's hypotheses, to remain in solidarity with their original milieu.

It is not a question here of returning to a holistic interpretation, but of attempting always to understand the link between the nature of the milieu, the more or less community-orientated or individual-orientated context, and the choices of actors. We should add that the behaviour of workers also varies enormously according to their relation to the public or private sector. For example, in the public sector, there is a greater frequency of class-based trade unionism linked to the more explicitly political character of the working environment.[11] It is worth noting here that collective behaviour is in a relation to its place within a highly institutionalized state, and becomes more overt as the state extends its public sector. Thus the determining role of the state in working-class mobilization takes on a new character. This is true, for example, of France, but tomorrow may be true of the United States where, confronted by facets of a strong state, worker mobilization may increase. As Theodore Lowi points out: 'In the American context, it is Madison not Marx who seems to be having the last word. This, of course, can change. As the American national state has expanded and federalism in the economic domain has now disappeared, one of the conditions that seems to have systematically inhibited socialism is no longer present.'[12]

---

[10] Guy Michelat and Michel Simon, *Classe, religion et comportement politique* (Paris: Presses de la Fondation nationale des sciences politiques, 1977). However, as Claude Thélot notes, 'Leaving the working class to become a white-collar worker does not have much effect upon voting behaviour; leaving it to set up on one's own has a dramatic effect', Thélot, *Tel père, tel fils?*, p. 215.

[11] Claude Durand, *Conscience ouvrière et action syndicale* (Paris: Mouton, 1971), 219.

[12] Theodore Lowi, 'Why is there no Socialism in the United States? A Constitutional Analysis' (unpublished article).

PART IV

INDIVIDUALISM AND DEMOCRACY

Is the Voter an Individualist?

GEORGES LAVAU

On the stockmarket of ideas in France certain values have for some years been quoted very highly: liberalism, deregulation, the market (for its gentle and precise adjustments), and a certain inequality (the indispensable motor of innovation). In this basket of highly quoted stock, we should include another value which, in the 1940s and 1950s, was the most derided there was (in both 'Vichyite' and socialist/communist thought): individualism.

Unfortunately, those who today celebrate and welcome the 'return of individualism' are actually referring to a wide and not very homogeneous range of attitudes and behaviour subsumed under the term 'individualism'. It should be stated, however, that this individualism has little in common with other 'individualisms' whose meanings are established and relatively precise (the philosophical individualism of the Enlightenment, the individualism of classical economic theory, methodological individualism, and so on). In fact, what is usually meant by the term 'the new individualism' is the rejection of group solidarity, and the abandonment of beliefs and a sense of heritage. What else is Gilles Lipovetsky describing in *L'Ère du vide: Essais sur l'individualisme contemporain?*: Post-modernity in Western societies is characterized by the destruction of the old social disciplines, by the narcissism of the individual, by an era of listless emptiness, and an absence of the sense of the tragic. The post-modern individual has cut his moorings from the institutions which provided collective values, and no longer believes the lessons of the great stories of the past.

With a different approach and another vocabulary, the creative psychosociologist Bernard Cathelat has drawn up a topography of French life-styles where we find several profiles of the post-modern 'new individualists': the adventurers, the realigned, the profiteers, the wait-and-seers, the showmen, the sensualists, and so on.[1] The question

[1] B. Cathelat, *Les styles de vie des Français: 1978–1998* (Paris: Stanké, 1977).

is not whether these portraits are accurate or not, but whether other radically different behaviour could not also be termed 'individualist'. Whatever the case, our concern in this chapter is whether there has also been, in the domain of electoral behaviour, a momentous increase of individualism. Would this not account for, for example, the weakening of class voting, the weakening of partisan allegiances, electoral instability, the emergence of a 'volatile' electorate which calculates its surprises more independently than before, and seems to have voting 'strategies' based upon a cost–benefit rationality? What is the reality of these changes? And if they have really taken place, to what extent can they be seen as evidence of the rise of electoral individualism?

From the Captive to the 'Individualist' Vote?

New findings on voting behaviour

Since antiquity, it is of course individuals, in the physical sense of the term, who have been the empirical subjects involved in the opinions and decisions expressed by the vote (even if the vote was taken by order and not individually). It was not, however, solely as individuals that they had the right to vote, but as part of a *universitas* (later a *societas*), or as member of a city, order, village, or corporation.

In the contemporary period, moreover, being an individual is never, strictly speaking, a necessary and sufficient qualification: it is citizenship which allows for the exercise of the political vote. And citizenship always requires several supplementary attributes to the 'naked' individual (nationality, age, registration, non-privation of civic rights). Yet it is true that the two notions, individual and citizen, have almost become one. This could only begin to happen from the moment life ceased to be seen, before the social contract, as solitary, poor, nasty, brutish, and short, and the individual could be considered as a moral, independent, and autonomous being, and as such endowed with the ability to judge and orientate his action to this 'free' judgement.[2] In this way, the right to vote as a right *of man* emerged.

However, as universal suffrage in the old democracies became widespread, this individualist voting theory was put under increasing strain

---

[2] In 1759 in his *Moral Sentiments*, Adam Smith claimed the existence in each person of deep moral sentiments of approval of or repulsion by good and evil, truth and falsehood.

by empirical evidence. Now emancipated from the most oppressive religious and institutional constraints, now apparently endowed with free will and the ability to elaborate a moral law of universal value, this citizen-elector was revealed, nevertheless, under sociological examination, as not always behaving morally, and just as disinclined to use his autonomy, freedom, and ability to judge. It is usually political manipulators who are blamed for this, but the conclusions nevertheless affect substantially our interpretation of the elector himself. What are the main complaints against him? He does not—and cannot—use his reason, he allows himself to be seduced, his behaviour obeys social determinations, or illusions, or follows false identifications with parties or groups, or responds to either aggressive impulses or a vague desire for woolly reconciliation.[3] To these complaints we can add the observation that many voters are apathetic. This inevitably brings us to the conclusion that, from the sociological point of view, there are no reasoning electors, but only electorates characterized by collective determinations: the working-class electorate, the bourgeois, Catholic, Protestant, young, old, male, female, Tuscan, Sicilian, and so on.

Towards the end of the 1960s, therefore, political sociology arrived at the point where it explained both the voters who had no well-established opinion and were uninterested in the electoral game, and open-minded voters with no declared, stable, partisan identification or identification with a community (class, ethnic, religious, cultural, or territorial group), in negative and pejorative terms such as 'unstable', 'floating', 'versatile', or 'middle-ground' voters.

An influential book on voting behaviour in the United States, published in 1960 by the researchers of the Survey Research Centre at the University of Michigan, emphasized the lack of interest in politics of the majority of American citizens, their inaptitude in forming individual political opinions from abstract principles,[4] and the contingent, superficial, and incoherent nature of their opinions on numerous political issues. Conversely, it seemed that the attitude of

---

[3] Philippe Braud, for example, brought many of these ideas together in *Le Suffrage universel contre la démocratie* (Paris: PUF, 1980). Let us just quote several formulae from the conclusion: 'The citizens like to believe that they can influence the state powers'; 'candidates and elected representatives must hide from the public their quest for a following or for power'; 'all those who identify with the overall structure of constraint need this liturgy of explicit consensus'; 'the suffrage functions first and foremost on the basis of illusions', pp. 241–2.

[4] Cf. D. Klingeman, 'Measuring Ideological Conceptualisations', in Samuel H. Barnes and Max Kaase (eds.), *Political Action* (Beverley Hills, Calif.: Sage, 1979).

the majority of these voters was as if guided by their generally strong and stable identification with one of the two big political parties.[5]

It is true that a certain 'school' (much better represented among economists than among sociologists) has never ceased to analyse the behaviour of the voter—his vote, abstention, and choice—while considering him as a calculating individual and rational strategist,[6] whose calculation can, moreover, operate just as well on the basis of individual utility to the voter as on the basis of non-'egoistical' utility. This type of very formal analysis, most of which is dominated by the utilitarian paradigm, has, however, been so refuted by empirical studies on voting behaviour that it is considered by most sociologists and political scientists as, at worst, a pure logical game and, at best, a model which can sometimes identify some pertinent questions, but which provides only inadequate answers, and which remain unsubstantiated even by the most apparently rigorously controlled empirical observations.

However, in the 1970s, electoral analyses became more sophisticated, and new questions were raised by what seemed to be (and perhaps was) a significant modification in the behaviour of certain voters, not only in the United States but also in Britain and in France.

The results of electoral sociology research raise the question of whether strong and durable party identification by a large majority of

[5] Angus Campbell, Philip E. Converse, Warren Miller, and Donald E. Stokes, *The American Voter* (New York: Wiley, 1960). See also Philip E. Converse, 'The Nature of Belief Systems in Mass Publics', in David E. Apter, *Ideology and Discontent* (New York: Free Press, 1964); David Butler and Donald Stokes, *Political Change in Britain: The Evolution of Electoral Choice* (London: Macmillan, 1st edn. 1969, 2nd edn. 1974). This is a more complex and refined adaptation to the British context of *The American Voter*.

[6] It is true that this school has been less often concerned wth voting for representation to elected assemblies than with votes within committees and with the problem of the decision of the majority between diverse practical alternatives. From the abundant literature on the subject we can list here several of the major works: Kenneth J. Arrow, *Social Choice and Individual Values* (New York: Wiley, 2nd edn. 1963); Duncan Black, *The Theory of Committees and Elections* (Cambridge: Cambridge University Press, 1958); J. M. Buchanan and G. Tullock, *The Calculus of Consent: Logical Foundations of Constitutional Democracy* (Ann Arbor, Mich.: University of Michigan Press, 1962); Robin Farquhason, *Theory of Voting* (New Haven, Conn.: York University Press, 1969); A. Downs, *An Economic Theory of Democracy* (New York: Harper & Row, 1957). More recently, A. Breton, *The Economic Theory of Representative Government* (Chicago, Ill.: Aldine Publishing Co.; London: Macmillan, 1974); B. Barry, *Political Argument* (London: Routledge & Kegan Paul, 1965) (a work which criticizes, from a philosophical point of view, the works of this school). The most interesting work, in my view, is W. H. Riker and P. C. Ordeshook, *An Introduction to Positive Political Theory* (Englewood Cliffs, NJ: Prentice-Hall, 1973) (esp. chs. 2, 4, and 11). See also James H. Enelow and

electors was only a passing phenomenon, or at least was particularly noticeable in the 1950s and 1960s. A lot of research shows, in fact, that partisan identification is transmitted less frequently than in the past from generation to generation, that over a period of about fifteen to twenty years, two-thirds of voters change their vote at least once,[7] and that in France, over a shorter period (10 May 1981–17 June 1984), one voter in two was 'unstable'.[8] It has also been discovered, notably in the United States, that 'partisan dealignment' is above all the result of a younger generation which attained voting age after 1960. These new voters have a tendency not to adopt 'prefabricated' partisan identification, they are less passive and less 'captive' than before, have more coherent ideological attitudes, express their views on political issues and questions, rather than simply on the names of candidates and parties, are more 'rational' and calculating, and decide their vote on the basis of a complex bundle of factors, amongst which are calculations of personal utility, an evaluation of the worth of existing parties in relation to political questions which they consider pertinent (the salient issues effect), the state of electoral supply, and the general orientation of voters towards a particular party.[9] Without pushing this observation too far for the moment, we can, however, note that these new findings on electoral behaviour have reduced, although not

Melvin J. Hinich, *The Spatial Theory of Voting: An Introduction* (Cambridge: Cambridge University Press, 1984).

[7] This has been shown in the case of Great Britain for the six general elections from 1964 to 1979, by H. Himmelweit, *How Voters Decide* (London: Academic Press, 1984).

[8] See Gérard Grunberg, 'L'Instabilité du comportement électoral', in Daniel Gaxie et al., *Explication du vote* (Paris: Presses de la Fondation nationale des sciences politiques, 1985). See also Marie-France Toinet and Françoise Subileau, 'Un refus du jeu partisan', *Le Monde*, 31 Aug. 1984. These two studies show that instability results especially from the movement from abstention to participation and vice versa.

[9] See, in particular, on the United States: Walter D. Burnham, *Critical Elections and the Mainsprings of American Politics* (New York: Norton, 1970); Gerald Pomper, *Voter's Choice: Varieties of American Electoral Behaviour* (New York: Dodd Mead & Co., 1975); see esp. Norman H. Nie, Sidney Verba, and John R. Petrocik, *The Changing American Voter* (Cambridge, Mass.: Harvard University Press, 2nd edn. 1979); on Great Britain, see I. Budge, I. Crewe, and D. Fairlie (eds.), *Party Identification and Beyond: Representation of Voting and Party Competition* (London: Wiley, 1976); Himmelweit, *How Voters Decide*, p. 305 n. 1; B. Sarlvik, I. Crewe, and D. Robertson, *A New Conservative Electorate* (Cambridge: Cambridge University Press, 1983); Richard Rose, 'From Simple Determinism to Interactive Model of Voting; Britain as an Example', *Comparative Studies*, 15/2 (July 1982), 145–68. In French we can mention three good general studies: Daniel Gaxie, 'Mort et résurrection du paradigme de Michigan', *Revue française de science politique*, 32/2 (Apr. 1982), 251–69; Grunberg, 'L'Instabilité du comportement électoral'; Alain Lancelot, 'L'Orientation du comportement politique', in M. Grawitz and J. Leca (eds.), *Traité de science politique* (Paris: PUF, 1985), iii. 367–428.

removed altogether, the distance separating formal individualist models from empirical studies of electoral sociology.[10] Attention has been focused in particular on two points which, even though related, must be distinguished from one another analytically.

On the one hand, greater attention has been focused on observing, measuring, explaining, and understanding better the 'volatility' of voters who are neither 'apathetic', nor ill-informed and incoherent, nor simply 'versatile', but who (as much as one can measure) are capable of forming their preferences in an autonomous way and of developing a strategy at election times (which implies that this can change according to their assessment of the situation). On the other hand, attention has been focused on the ability of these 'changing' voters to relate their view of a 'crisis' of an economic system to that of the social system, and to evaluate their personal interests accordingly;[11] such a dual interpretation could explain calculated defection from parties judged as not having (or as no longer having) a satisfactory answer to particular salient issues.

These changes in the attitudes and behaviour of voters can be explained both by societal changes affecting the cultural and social system and as an indirect consequence of modifications in the personality of individuals.[12] This 'new' electoral behaviour, which is more willingly 'unfaithful', and more independent and calculating, depending upon the importance attributed to the issues involved, could therefore be the result, observed at the individual level, of the retreat of certain values which privileged the collectivity, and of the weakening of traditional forms and mechanisms of social identification. These two general factors would contribute to weakening the framework within which social behaviour is set, and, because of this, would increase the effects of contingent and conjunctural events. Thus, it becomes tempting—especially so, given the modishness of individualism—to draw a profile of a new type of voter, the individualist voter, and to put forward the hypothesis that individualism has become, more than partisan identifications and socio-cultural determinations, one of the principal motors of the voter's choice.

However, independently even of the value judgements that this idea

---

[10] See in particular I. Budge, 'Electoral Volatility: Issue Effects and Basic Change in 23 Post-War Democracies', *Electoral Studies*, 1/2 (Aug. 1982).

[11] This is the result in particular of James Alt, *The Politics of Economic Decline* (London: Cambridge University Press, 1979) and of the report presented by Ivor Crewe to a workshop organized by the ECPR, 'Electoral Volatility in Britain since 1945'.

[12] Cf. Lancelot, 'L'Orientation du comportement politique', iii. 375–8.

inevitably raises (and which can differ widely: for some, the 'individualist' voter is the liberated voter, for others he is the non-citizen), it seems to me that nothing is gained in terms of clarity by using the far too polysemic concept of 'individualism' to analyse these very real but complex phenomena, and that there is a real risk of confusing several very distinct issues.

The polysemic nature of 'individualism'

In everyday language the word 'individualist' denotes two dimensions which are almost opposites of one another. On the one hand, there is the egoistical and self-centred person, and on the other, there is the autonomous individual who defends this autonomy. Within these two poles of meaning, the term can designate serious defects of character (the individualist who refuses collective disciplines, the general interest, or even coming to the aid of other people), as well as highly laudable attitudes (the individualist who, while respecting otherness, recognizes each other individual as another version of himself, and who does not allow himself to impose judgements and actions contrary to good sense and moral imperatives). Specialized use of the term does not, in fact, differ very much from its everyday meaning. Here too there are several 'individualisms' whose meanings and contents can hardly be reduced to a few shared characteristics.

Let us look at several of these 'individualisms' in terms of their relation to and implications for electoral behaviour. This will help us properly to evaluate the notion of the 'individualist voter'.

1. The individualism of the movement of the Enlightenment saw man's intellectual emancipation and his refusal thenceforth to submit his faculty to judge to any other authority: *sapere aude* (dare to use your judgement!). The image of this particular individualism is long-standing, though is far from always presenting a perfect unity of views. At the level that we are interested in here, the behaviour which would correspond to it would doubtless be that of the voter deciding in the 'freest' manner possible, being concerned to inform himself, and not hesitating to enter into constructive argument with those whose opinions and interests are different from his own.

This particular individualism excludes the 'calculating' and 'strategic' voter no more than it excludes the voter loyal to the same party, or loyal to the political solidarities of a class or group. The point is, however, that neither of these behaviours is necessarily called into being by this form of individualism. Such a view would impoverish

considerably the spirit of the Enlightenment if it were to argue that the
true inheritor of the Enlightenment was the voter who declared himself as being 'very' or 'quite interested in politics', voted 'regularly' and
'independently', and was of stable, partisan identification.

2. A second individualism is that of the utilitarians. The individual
has the right to, and is naturally drawn towards, the search for his
greatest happiness and greatest utility. Appropriate electoral
behaviour would be that of the calculating voter, egoistical and
rational, who grades and weighs up the utility and expected cost of his
abstention or choices with reference to electoral supply and the information at his disposal.

3. It would be futile to imagine to what kind of voting behaviour—
systematic electoral abstention?—Stirner's individualism, or rather
integral egoism, would lead. It would also be pointless (and even more
ridiculous) to try to ascertain how a voter who was inspired by the
individualism of Nietzsche would vote.[13]

4. It might be said, on the other hand, that one could understand
infinitely more about individualism and voting behaviour from the
ideas of de Tocqueville, especially from his *On Democracy in America*.
I, however, have my doubts. Unlike egoism, 'the oldest vice in the
world', 'a passionate and exaggerated love of oneself', individualism,
says de Tocqueville, is recent and 'of democratic origin': 'It is a
considered and peaceful feeling which encourages each citizen to
withdraw from the mass of his fellow-men and enjoy the company of
his family and friends; so much so that, having created a little society
of his own, he willingly abandons wider society to itself.'[14] As Lamberti has shown,[15] de Tocqueville does not condemn individualism as
do Bonald, Royer-Collard, or Guizot. Nor does he praise it as does
Benjamin Constant. He is not insensitive to the private virtues for

---

[13] 'Ultimately, however, it is indifferent whether the herd is commanded to have one
opinion or permitted to have five. Whoever deviates from the five public opinions and
stands apart will always have the whole herd against him' (*The Gay Science* (New York:
Random House, 1974), s. 174, p. 202). One might interpret this as being in support of
abstentionism if, in the same work, there were not other infinitely more 'activist'
aphorisms, such as the following for example: 'We now need ... more endangered
human beings, more fruitful human beings, happier beings! For believe me: the secret
for harvesting from existence the greater fruitfulness and the greatest enjoyment is—to
live dangerously! Build your cities on the slopes of Vesuvius! Send your ships into
uncharted seas!' (Ibid. s. 283, p. 228).

[14] A. de Tocqueville, *De la démocratie en Amérique* (Paris: Garnier-Flammarion,
1972) vol. ii, part ii, ch. 2, p. 125.

[15] J.-C. Lamberti, *Tocqueville et les deux démocraties* (Paris: PUF, 1983), in particular, p. 127.

which this kind of individualism acts as a refuge, and he does not ignore the fact that, arising as it does from political equality, it expresses 'that instinctive desire for political independence',[16] and he knows that its more disastrous political consequences can be remedied.[17] For de Tocqueville, individualism is a vice of the spirit because of its isolation, its retreat to the 'private', to the detriment of the 'public',[18] and its forgetting of the virtues of citizenship. Above all, however, de Tocqueville constantly links individualism to its natural consequence, apathy, the source of anarchy and despotism.[19] One can ask here whether he was referring particularly to electoral individualism.

By condemning apathy, de Tocqueville conceivably had in mind abstentionist voters, but, more likely, is talking of much more than this, his conception of civic virtues going well beyond simply the election of representatives. If one insists, however, on finding from de Tocqueville answers to our false problem, the harvest is meagre: certainly the habitual abstentionist is an 'individualist' (but above all an 'egoist'), but hardly more so than the 'ritualist' voter who believes himself acquitted of all the duties of the citizen once he has put his vote in the ballot box in accordance with some weak but habitual partisan identification. And who, having made the gesture, chooses to 'withdraw ... and enjoy the company of his family and friends ... [and] willingly abandons wider society to itself'. In other words, on the basis of 'Tocquevillian' individualism, one can deduce nothing just from electoral behaviour understood in its strictest sense. Whether the voter abstains or votes in a conformist, ritualist way, or as a rational calculator, or as a convinced partisan, or whether he was a habitual abstentionist ten years before he became, from the 1970s onwards, a 'calculating strategist', none of this authorizes us to cover ourselves with the authoritative mantle of de Tocqueville and claim that the voter is individualist or is not. We can only use these terms (in the sense de Tocqueville gives to them) by considering the ensemble of other behaviour (and perhaps not only political behaviour), and the overall attitudes of the voter.

Let us try to draw a conclusion from this long digression. One could

---

[16] Tocqueville, *De la démocratie en Amérique*, vol. ii, part iv, ch. 1, p. 354.

[17] The remedies the author observed in America: local democracy, the associative movement, 'the doctrine of self-interest, of course'.

[18] 'Only the closest are of interest', *De la démocratie en Amérique*, ii. 126.

[19] Nothing is clearer on this point than the note which concludes ch. 6 of part iv of vol. ii, ibid. 408, the closing lines of which are, 'It is important to combat, not so much anarchy and despotism as apathy, which can easily create both of the other two'.

conceivably give to the term 'individualism' a definition strictly limited to voting behaviour, and which would signify a behaviour which the observer could with certainty claim involved decisions taken as the result of a personal strategy and only weakly orientated to altruistic values. This definition, however, would either be arbitrary (why should the activist, convinced since adolescence that it is good for the world, if not for himself, to try to attain victory for the party, not be considered just as 'individualist'?), or else completely tautological.

This terminological and conceptual convention is not, then, acceptable. And if one wishes to use the terms 'individualism' and 'individualist' in a less rigorous sense, this simply indicates the abundance of their meanings. But I have tried to show that the attempt to use the terms in this way is unhelpful. We must therefore try to reformulate the problem and first, perhaps, reduce it to more modest proportions.

Of Collectives and Individuals

Electoral sociology

What has been known as 'the Michigan paradigm'[20] (that is to say, the observation according to which the best predicator of the vote of the majority of individuals is their partisan identification, which is usually stable and very often 'inherited'), and all the electoral studies which illustrate the weight of 'religious', 'social', 'professional', and 'cultural' determinations on voting, have been unquestionably modified by the discovery of the 'volatile voter'. The reasons for this increased volatility, its conditions, degrees, and explanation await elaboration.

It should be remembered that, although research indicating the determinants of voting behaviour has used formulations which suggest that the voting subjects were collectives ('the working-class vote', 'the Catholic vote', 'the "youth" vote', and so on), these works have never forgotten (1) that these determinants were relative (the variability explained by the totality of the heaviest variables never being great);[21]

[20]   See the article by Daniel Gaxie, 'Mort et résurrection du paradigme de Michigan'.
[21]   As an example, in the various segmentations shown in the work edited by Richard Rose, *Electoral Behaviour: A Comparative Handbook* (New York: Free Press, 1974), the total variation explained by segmentation in the various countries studied occasionally reaches 50%, but is situated most often between 15% and 35%. We can also note, following Alain Lancelot, that even though in France the correlation between practising Catholicism and the right-wing vote seems to be established and to have varied little, this real correlation nevertheless masks a more important (numerical) phenomenon: when one takes into account the respective statistical bases of 'practising Catholics' on the one hand and 'non-practising Catholics' and those who do not subscribe to any

(2) that the weight of external determinants varied according to the nature of the election, electoral demand, and the importance of certain issues at the moment of the election; and (3) that at least a section of the voters usually considered as stable could modify its vote either occasionally (but at a significant moment for those who were 'changing'),[22] or in a more durable way at times of crisis and realignment.[23]

In the middle of the 1960s, V. O. Key, in a collection of studies published after his death,[24] had already shown, reviewing the evolution of voting behaviour in the United States in the course of the previous generation, that the voter could be unstable, but not in a mindless way; that his 'decision' was never entirely devoid of 'rationality'; and that, for example, the voters who changed camp by moving over to the party which had attained governmental power did it probably 'to support governmental policies or outlooks with which they agree, not because of subtle psychological or sociological peculiarities'.[25] Arthur Goldberg, studying the maintenance or abandonment by children of the partisan identifications of their parents, viewed this in relation to the level of education of the two generations, and showed that this transmission — whether or not 'successful' — was to be explained, not only by social determinants, but also, in part, by rational calculation.[26]

If we wish to rectify some of the omissions and errors of the electoral sociology of the 1950s and 1960s, we must begin by two remarks.

First remark The relative lack of attention paid to the individual voting strategy of the voter, in France at least, was perhaps due to the fact that relatively little work has been done on the interaction

religion on the other, it becomes clear that in 1978 almost half of the right-wing voters (and 80% of those of the left) came from non-practising Catholics and those not subscribing to any religion, see Lancelot, 'L'Orientation du comportement politique', iii. 392.

[22] We can give characteristic examples: the 1.5 million left-wing voters who, in 1958, forsook their usual allegiances and showed their support for General de Gaulle, mainly because of the Algerian issue; the defection of Republican voters in 1964 in the United States to the detriment of Barry Goldwater, who was considered too conservative, especially on internal affairs.

[23] See V. O. Key, jun., 'A Theory of Critical Elections', *Journal of Politics*, 17 (1955), 3–18; 'Secular Realignments and the Party System', *Journal of Politics*, 21 (1959), 198–210.

[24] V. O. Key, jun., *The Responsible Electorate: Rationality in Presidential Voting: 1936–1960* (Cambridge, Mass.: Harvard University Press, 1966).

[25] Ibid. 104.

[26] Arthur S. Goldberg, 'Social Determinisms and Rationality as Bases of Party Affiliation', *American Political Science Review*, 63 (1969).

between the strategies of the parties and candidates to maximize their electoral gains, and the strategies of the voters. On the one hand, there was research on the parties—the pioneering work of Maurice Duverger was of a rather different order—which was relatively uninterested in voters' strategies at the time of an election. On the other hand, there was some rare, little-known research on political marketing. And, of course, there was research on electoral sociology. However, once again, in France at least, there was very little response to the work of Lazarsfeld and his collaborators,[27] and even less to Anthony Downs's work published in 1957.[28] The question of the play of strategies between the parties and the voter, the interactions between political supply and demand, and questions concerning loyalty and exit, partially escaped attention, or else were only referred to in a historical, if not anecdotal, context.[29]

Second remark   The general probabilist pronouncements of electoral sociology were much more interested in collectives (socio-professional, religious, regional, and generational groups, and so on) into which the voting population under analysis could be 'divided' than in questions concerning voter psychology and rationality at the moment when, as an individual, he makes a decision. This was the case, not only because one of the aims of these studies was to predict the aggregated results of millions of decisions of the individual units of the population, nor because this type of probabilist pronouncement lends itself better to empirical statistical verification of 'collective' representative samples (it is obviously easier to construct samples of socio-professional category, age range, religious practice, and so on, than samples of diverse 'rationalities'), but, more generally, because this is one of the gentler slopes of sociology where some of the warnings of 'methodological individualism' can be ignored.

However, these two observations in no way refute the results of an electoral sociology however preoccupied it might be with the social and psychosocial determinants of electoral behaviour. They simply raise the question as to why less attention was paid to the 'freedom' of

---

[27]   P. F. Lazarsfeld, B. Berelson, and H. Gaudet, *The People's Choice* (New York: The University of Columbia Press, 1948); B. Berelson, P. F. Lazarsfeld, and W. N. MacPhee, *Voting* (Chicago, Ill.: University of Chicago Press, 1954).

[28]   Downs, *An Economic Theory of Democracy*.

[29]   We should remember, however, that the various *Cahiers* of the Fondation nationale des sciences politiques on the legislative elections of 1956, 1958, 1962, 1965, and 1967 contained studies on the strategies of the parties and the electoral campaigns.

the individual actor.

No one could ignore the fact that in the last more or less dramatized days of an election campaign the usually loyal and stable voter could become a 'new' voter, that he could move from the intention to vote to abstention, or vice versa, that he could either renew an old allegiance, or decide to be 'disloyal'. In spite of the 'sociologism' of electoral studies, it was always clear that the voter who sometimes abstained did not do so only because he was indifferent or because he had not resolved the 'cross-pressures' weighing on him, but that this could be also a result of his interest in certain political problems which he thought were not being properly taken into consideration by the parties and candidates that he would probably have voted for.[30] Though assumed, it was considered hardly worth saying that the normally stable voter who changed his vote might do so for many reasons, certain of which were clearly linked to strategic calculations, and others not—at least not directly. This might be, for example, the result of a conjunctural calculation involving both opportuneness and effectiveness, or because the structuration of political demand changed.[31] It might, however, also be the result of the erosion of a former allegiance (from 'very' close to the party, the voter becomes 'not very close'),[32] or because the dislocation of the modal behaviour of his membership group has made control of group members less strict, or because the 'membership collectivities' no longer show in tn the characteristics they had in $t1$, $t2$, and $t3$.[33]

All this was known but because it was considered of little interest relatively little attention was paid to it. This lack of interest was misplaced because such findings were an integral part of sociology (and not of 'individualism' in the sense we examined above).

The action of the voter and methodological individualism

Could these 'insufficiencies' and 'omissions' have been better avoided if researchers had adopted more rigorously the paradigm of

---

[30] This was shown, more than twenty years ago, by I. de Sola Pool, R. P. Abelson, and S. L. Popkin, *Candidates, Issues and Strategies* (Cambridge: MIT Press, 1964), 76 ff.

[31] e.g. a different position in tn of one or several parties, a drop in the electoral level of a party such that it encourages a part of its usual voters to transfer their vote more usefully to another party, modification of the system of alliances, the effects of a new electoral system, and so on.

[32] As Gérard Grunberg points out, the verification of this hypothesis requires the use of surveys by panel, sadly all too rare in France, 'L'Instabilité du comportement électoral'.

[33] e.g. increasing average age of the collective, a greater feminization, improvement

methodological individualism? Would it not have been more fruitful to see abstention, the distribution of electoral choices between parties, electoral stability or instability, and the socio-cultural 'determinants' of voting as 'the result of an ensemble of individual actions'?[34]

The individual act of each voter can be understood as a rational action adapted to his personal situation in a given system (such as he subjectively perceives it). Personal situation in the system, however, is defined, among other things, by socio-professional status and other characteristics (shared with many other individuals who are, at least as regards status and characteristics, in similar personal situations). The personal situation of the rich or poor 'farmer', of the 'worker' working in a small construction company or in a large chemicals factory, is itself a function of an ensemble of given macro-sociological phenomena (level and nature of unionization in the firm or the industry; level of education in the context of socio-professional status; the place of such status in social stratification, culture and subculture of the group, etc.). It is not therefore surprising that the aggregation of the individual adaptive choices of millions of individuals of similar status — determining groups of similar situations, themselves linked to near-identical macro-sociological factors — produces strong correlations between the voting behaviour of individuals and the groups which denote the social 'situations' of these individuals.[35] Nor is it surprising that the correlation becomes stronger when the personal situation of these voters is characterized by an accumulation of indices related to membership of this 'status'.

In the framework of this paradigm, it is clearly pointless to ask questions concerning the 'individualist' character of the vote according to whether or not it generally conforms to the correlation resulting from the aggregation of individual choices: whatever the case, the choice made by each individual is always an action of rational adaptation to his situation.

We can raise a very simple objection to this approach: where is the evidence that each voter, before making a choice, deliberates, however little, upon his decision, and calculates his vote in order to get the best rational adaptation of this choice to his personal situation, taking into account the information he has, the degree of salience for him of both

or deterioration of the position of the group in the status scale, and so on.
[34] R. Boudon, *La Place du désordre* (Paris: PUF, 1984), 39.
[35] I am using here as closely as possible the approach of Raymond Boudon, ibid., in particular, pp. 40, 46, 53, 58, and 67, and in the hope that I have not distorted his view.

the outcome of the elections and the programmes of the candidates, and, finally, the way in which electoral supply has been structured? Against such a view, moreover, there are many works of electoral sociology which show that, whether rationally 'deliberated' or not, the electoral choices of individuals are more often than not the same as the aggregated choices of the other members of their membership or reference group. In the same way, there is a lot of evidence that an individual who, several months before an election, positions himself spontaneously on the right side of the left–right axis will probably not change this allegiance at the moment of voting.[36]

Moreover, the notion of 'adaptive action' is not itself without problems. The notion is perfectly understandable when it is a question of the actor adapting his voting decision to his personal situation, to maintain it or improve it. This is a rationality orientated to an objective. The notion becomes far more problematic when it is a question of the voter orientating his choice in relation to a situation which is not personal to him (for example, on the question of aid to the Third World, the promotion of peace, or the blocking of a policy he judges harmful, even though it does not affect him, and so on). In this case, rationality is orientated towards values, and, in my view, the notion of adaptation here is inadequate. This is why the idea of adaptive action seems unnecessary to the paradigm of methodological individualism.[37] It is sufficient simply to assume that the individual interest of the actor can be either 'egoistic' or 'altruistic'.

Methodological individualism reminds us that, like any other action, voting action obeys not only processes of causality which condition it, but also those of intentionality,[38] where the actor, within the limits created by those conditions, seeks to adapt himself to his situation, and attain objectives. Or, to put it slightly differently, methodological individualism reminds us that the action of actors must be taken seriously. Action is not only the passive interpellation of objective causes; it must be understood on the basis of the structures, determinants, and antecedents informing it, but also on the basis of the motivations of actors and their search for 'rationality' (see above).

[36] This has been well analysed regarding voters classed as 'stable' by Colette Ysmal in her chapter, 'Stabilité des électorats et attitudes politiques', in J. Capdevielle *et al.*, *France de gauche, vote à droite* (Paris: Presses de la Fondation nationale des sciences politiques, 1981), in particular, pp. 118–24 and Table 62, p. 291.

[37] Raymond Boudon's use of this idea in *La Place du désordre* is justified because he is studying principally social change.

[38] This is one of the leitmotivs of Jon Elster's book *Ulysses and the Sirens*

Homo oeconomicus and *homo politicus:* the same action model?

For reasons of brevity, it is not possible to summarize, even succinctly, the theoretical models of voting behaviour which are based upon models of economic action. We shall confine ourselves, therefore, to some relatively simple illustrations of certain questions treated in these models and to several critical observations.

The basic hypothesis is that the rationality which guides the voter (or the candidate, or the party) rests on the expected utility of the action. Each maximizes his preferences in terms of its utility. Authors like James Buchanan and Gordon Tullock in *The Calculus of Consent* (1962) apply rigorously Pareto's optimality principle to elections. In terms of this, Anthony Downs[39] (with some reservations) and, later, Buchanan and Tullock raised the problem of the *voter's paradox*. If the voter is a calculating or rational egoist, he has few reasons for voting. If we put as an equation the utility of the decision of the voter, we get:

$$R = PB - C + D$$

where: R = the action of the voter (vote and seek information);
  P = probability that utility will be maximized if R is undertaken;
  B = benefits expected for action R;
  C = cost of action;
  D = private advantages complementary to action (moral, intellectual, material satisfaction, for example).

Except perhaps for the voter whose status shelters him from the collective consequences of the vote, whose level of education lowers the cost of information, or whose political commitment is strong, the consequence is very simple: it is 'irrational' to vote. The average voter will understand only with difficulty the differences which separate the parties on the political issues of the moment (which he will discern only with difficulty anyway, and in a context where his preferences will probably be relatively fixed). Moreover, he lacks information on both the past performances of these parties and the soundness of the 'products' on offer. He can only overcome these handicaps by collecting information, but this collecting presents a direct cost (time, effort ...) and an indirect one (frustration, a feeling of incompetence, an indecision unresolved by the information collected). If, as is probable, these costs are felt as exceeding the potential benefits of action, and if he has

(Cambridge: Cambridge University Press, 1979), in particular, pp. 137–41.
  [39] Downs, *An Economic Theory of Democracy*, chs. 11 and 14.

the feeling that the outcome is already decided, and that his single voice is negligible in the overall result, and that at the end of the day, whether he votes or not, he has the same ultimate chances of obtaining the advantages to be gained from the victory of one party or another, and that the additional personal benefits (D) to be gained from voting are non-existent or negligible, he will 'rationally' abstain.

Without getting into too profound a discussion, we can note that this approach completely disregards Herbert Simon's observations concerning economic entrepreneurs, who usually content themselves with a 'limited rationality' and rationally satisfying choices. The voter would not look for the most complete information (and not only for reasons of cost and access), and would not search indefinitely for the purest rationality, but would stop at the moment he judged himself satisfied, taking into account, first of all, what he wants to do, and then what he supposes to be the information of the voters who are comparable (in his eyes at least) to himself.

The 'voter's paradox' has often been criticized, in particular by Brian Barry,[40] and by William H. Riker and Peter C. Ordeshook.[41] Riker and Ordeshook in particular stress two groups of factors which greatly limit this 'rationality' of abstention. The first is that, in most democracies, the vote is automatically perceived by the majority of electors as a duty more than as a 'rational' action. The second is that, even in terms of the strict framework of 'rationality', the voter's paradox underestimates the value to the actor of these 'additional' satisfactions (the D of the equation) which he can obtain by not abstaining, even though he expects no material benefits from the fact of going and voting, and his action is a drop in the ocean.[42] However, this kind of 'satisfaction' is very important in the political world.

Another example of the logical problems raised by this type of analysis concerns the strategies of the parties more than those of the voters (even though it concerns the interaction between them). It is the

[40] Barry, *Political Argument*, pp. 281, 328–30.
[41] Riker and Ordeshook, *An Introduction to Positive Political Theory*, in particular, pp. 57, 63.
[42] Riker and Ordeshook (p. 63) enumerate some of the marginal satisfactions: (1) the pleasure of feeling part of the democratic ethic; (2) the (perhaps transitory) pleasure of stating a strong or average political allegiance; (3) the pleasure of having the chance to 'decide', or to be more actively interested than usually, to inform oneself (doubtless this is a cost for some, but for others, the satisfaction obtained is well worth the cost); (4) the satisfaction of escaping from the feeling of uselessness in the political system because, for most citizens, going to the polling station is the only chance to show that they and their actions can have a political meaning.

theorem of the so-called median voter. In the dual hypothetical condition that nearly all voters vote and that the distribution of opinions is
of a unimodal type,[43] the theorem would have it that each of the main
parties needs, in order to optimize its gains, to gravitate towards the
position of the median voter. With this aim, party A can be tempted —
like a firm trying to attain a section of an 'uncommitted' clientele — to
add to its initial programme several extras or 'products' designed to
seduce some of the voters of party B, its principal rival. This is a *spatial
model*. This invasion of a rival's territory, however, exposes party A to
the risk that those of its habitual voters who are furthest away from the
median voter will show their dissatisfaction by choosing abstention or
by giving their vote to a third party, C (theoretically, if the preferences
of voters were transitive, this third party would be even further away
from the median voter than they are — although, even then, not too
far). If, to reduce this risk, party A forms a coalition with this third
party, C, it will pay the cost either by not going far enough towards
party B's coveted territory, or by giving ally C various hostages to
fortune.[44] It is incontestable that these models correspond to a strategic and rational logic which is evident in the real actions of parties
and voters (it would be easy to give illustrations drawn from political
life).

   The main weakness of this type of reasoning is that it is too
dependent on one model of rationality, that of the economic actor,[45]
which supposes, on the one hand, transitive, coherent, and stable
preferences, and on the other, the overriding logic of the maximization
of utility. However, outside the domain of economic activity, human
actions follow 'rationalities' or 'quasi-rationalities' which are infinitely
less simple. One of the characteristics of man is that he knows how to
distinguish between his actions and his satisfactions, and has recourse
to indirect strategies. He can incorporate into one rationality of action
'altruistic' preferences, as well as loyalty and defiance (it would be

   [43] If the distribution is pluri-modal, the demonstration of the theorem is more
complicated, but the argument remains the same.
   [44] See W. H. Riker, *The Theory of Political Coalitions* (New Haven, Conn.: Yale
University Press, 1962). He shows that, as a general rule, the 'minimal' coalition is the
most rational and the most profitable.
   [45] Without taking into account all that Jon Elster, often not without humour, puts in
the categories of 'problematic rationality' (for example, altruism, sufficient rationality),
and 'imperfect rationality' (for example, Ulysses having himself tied to the mast of his
ship to protect him from his own future weakness *vis-à-vis* the sirens, Pascal recom-
mending blessing oneself with holy water if one wishes later to believe 'rationally', the
decision of travellers lost in the forest to walk always straight ahead to get to the edge of

interesting to reflect on the question of trust as a factor in a person's voting activity).

Until now, most of the economic analogy models incorporated very poorly 'political' and 'ideological' logics. For different reasons—reasons which are not always 'errors'—a party cannot aim for the median voter at any cost (cf. the Republican Party in the 1964 American presidential elections, the British Labour Party in 1979, for example), because this would expose it to internal crisis, or because its incumbent leaders wish to give the party a more coherent image, or because it would indicate an unacceptable renunciation of a position of principle.[46] Loyal voters for a party—if the structure of electoral supply allows it (if the regime has a two-round majority voting system)—can, for reasons which have nothing to do with pure calculation of utility, accept or refuse the 'spatial displacements' and alliances entered into by the party. The only truly foreseeable behaviour is that of acquired and 'distant' voters—that is to say, those who are in principle not 'calculating'. As for 'potential' and 'fragile' voters—that is to say, those who could be either won over or lost as a result of the new strategy adopted by the party for which they have a second-choice attraction, or that adopted by the party for which they have a first-choice preference[47]—the 'reasons' which could lead them to change sides are often so contradictory that the strategic innovations of parties will have very little influence on change. A model of political marketing must take into consideration both 'interests' and 'passions' (to use the title of Albert O. Hirschman's book). And although it would be naïve to believe that, in the political sphere, interests are less decisive

---

the forest, irrespective of the direction or the distance to travel), see chs. 1 and 2 of *Ulysses and the Sirens.*

[46] This is not what the German Social Democratic Party did in 1959 by adopting its Bad-Godesberg programme, but there are many contrary examples. In the same way a socialist party can, through its acts, effect its own Bad-Godesberg but without proclaiming as much, as in the case of the French Socialists after 1982. There is also the case of parties which, in spite of the dislocation caused by the 'class vote', cannot or do not wish to avoid appealing to it. See e.g. Jonathan Kelley, Ian McAllister, and Anthony Mughan, 'The Decline of Class Revisited: Class and Party in England, 1964–1979', *American Political Science Review*, 79/3 (Sept. 1985), 719–37.

[47] On these notions of committed, distant, potential, and fragile voters, see Denis Lindon and Pierre Weill, *Le Choix d'un député* (Paris: Minuit, 1974), 104 ff. The book shows that even the Communist Party can count on very few 'committed' (*acquis*) (9% of the whole of the French electorate) and only reached its scores at the time thanks to 13% of 'fragile' voters, that is to say, susceptible communist sympathizers who, depending on the circumstances, would desert, but who, at the time (1973), did not desert on polling day.

than passions, they are, nevertheless, rarely simple; and it can be in one's 'interest' to conform to one's passions ... or even to create them.

Is Voting a Political rather than a Sociological Phenomenon?

The questioning of the 'Michigan paradigm', of the central hypothesis of the stability of political orientations, and of the sociological quasi-determinants of voting, the new light being thrown on questions concerning electoral disloyalty and variations in the behaviour of certain voters depending upon the political issues of the moment, the structuration of supply, and the strategies of the parties; none of these, I believe, allows us to draw firm conclusions on the rise of 'individualism' among the voters of the 1970s and 1980s. Conversely, one can draw a more limited, though firmer, conclusion, which is that voting behaviour is linked much more to the political and to politics than it is to sociology, even if this last still tells us a great deal about voting.[48] We should not be carried away by the importance of this 'rediscovery', and should attempt, rather, to measure its significance and illuminate some of its implications.

Partisan proximity and 'sympathizers'

The hypothesis that the stability of electorates represents a general tendency presupposes that a large majority of voters have a strong attachment to one party. However, the indicators measuring this strength are usually rather crude. One asks, for example, of the US voter if he considers himself 'strongly' or 'weakly' Republican or Democrat, or if he classifies himself as 'independent'; of the French voter whether he is 'very close to', 'quite close to', 'not very close to', 'not at all close to', or 'far from' a party.[49]

We should note, however, particularly in France, that displacements of the vote from one election to another are few (although they nevertheless do take place) among the two groups 'very far away' and 'very close' (which are both a very small part of the whole of the

---

[48] This is no surprise for anyone who has read the three volumes of François Goguel's *Chroniques électorales* (Paris: Presses de la Fondation nationale des sciences politiques, 1981), which represent a great tradition.

[49] These are the findings of the wide post-election survey done in March 1978 by the Fondation nationale des sciences politiques and SOFRES and which is analysed in *France de gauche, vote à droite*, n. 36. The survey used also a different means of measuring which involved not attachment to party but the self-positioning of the voter in seven cases ranging from the extreme left to the extreme right.

electorate, see Table 11.1), whereas they are clearly more frequent among the 'quite close', 'not very close', and 'not at all close' (which in 1978 represented 73 per cent of the electorate, see Table 11.1).

TABLE 11.1. *Stable and unstable French voters between 1973 and 1978 according to the degree of partisan proximity* (%)

Partisan proximity	Left stable	Right stable	Unstable left→right	Unstable right→left	Total of electorate
1 Very distant	2	7	14	15	12
2 Not at all close	13 ⎫	23 ⎫	28 ⎫	30 ⎫	21 ⎫
3 Not very close	16 ⎬ 68	21 ⎬ 82	28 ⎬ 81	21 ⎬ 79	20 ⎬ 73
4 Quite close	39 ⎭	38 ⎭	25 ⎭	28 ⎭	32 ⎭
5 Very close	30	10	3	6	13
6 No reply	0	1	2	0	2

Source: Table based on Table 57, p. 285 of J. Capdevielle *et al.*, *France de gauche, vote à droite* (Paris: Presses de la Fondation nationale des sciences politiques, 1981). Even if we exclude the 'not at all close' from the grouping of 'weak' proximities, groups 3 and 4 still represent about half of the 'unstable' voters, whatever their allegiance.

A further interesting point to note is that these unstable voters who have changed their vote, sometimes even crossing the left–right divide, are overwhelmingly voters who position themselves in the central blocks of the left–right axis, and who often provide answers in discordance with the programmatic positions of the parties to whom they claim to be relatively close.[50] Certainly, in the communist electorate, the proportion of 'very close' respondents is greater than among sympathizers of the centre-left and the centre-right, although here too partisan proximity varies: among the 'very close' only 9 per cent voted for Mitterrand in the first round of the 1981 presidential elections, but this percentage rose to 17 per cent for the 'quite close' and 23 per cent for the 'not very close'; as regards the vote for the Le Pen (National Front) list in the 1984 European elections, the percentages were 0 per cent among communist 'sympathizers' 'very' or 'quite close' to the French Communist Party (PCF), but 5 per cent among those who declared themselves 'not very close' (SOFRES exit poll, 17 June 1984).

[50] In the French municipal elections of 1983, for example, 69% of those who said they were 'disappointed' by Mitterrand were on the central blocs of the axis (see J.-L. Parodi, 'Dans la logique des élections intermédiaires', *Revue politique et parlementaire* (Apr. 1983), 42–71; Jérôme Jaffré, 'Les Déçus du socialisme?', SOFRES, *Opinion publique 1984*, pp. 67–71). The 'stable voters of the left' were 72% 'in favour of the extension of (Paris: Gallimord, 1984) the public sector' whereas only 35% of those who between 1973 and 1978 went from the left to the right were in favour.

Even though in France there is a tendency towards 'centrism' by a large fraction of voters moderately 'close' to the PS (socialists), UDF (centre-right), and RPR (neo-Gaullists), the ultimately small proportion of voters who express a proximity to or great distance from parties calls for some remarks.

The first, which concerns the French situation, is that the quasi-disappearance since 1970 of an autonomous political centre might explain why voters who used to be drawn to the centre (radicals, Christian-democratic MRP) only have a relative proximity to the PS, UDF, and RPR, which are a 'second choice', a choice constrained by the structure of supply.

The second remark has a more general significance. Relative and constrained partisan proximities obviously encourage electoral instability and volatility. The causal sequence involved, however, is perhaps more complicated. Might it not be the desire, on the part of certain habitual voters (even those of the PCF), to have a less captive relationship with their party, a desire for a more independent and 'conditional' relationship which is translated into 'weak' proximities? And might this not indicate, in a more general way, the desire for a 'different' relationship to politics? The question has probably no decisive answer; but it is worth asking in order that researchers be more aware of what respondents have in mind when they answer that they 'are not very interested in politics' or that 'politics is too complicated . . .'. These kinds of answers, generally interpreted as an indication of an admission of incompetence and of a 'self-delegation' to the supposed experts, does not, however, stop those who provide such answers from seizing the opportunity, for example (and not just any opportunity which would indicate that they are not as 'incompetent' as one might think!), to inflict either on their party or on the government 'warning votes' and 'sanction votes'.

The structure of electoral supply: the nature and outcome of the election

On the question of voting behaviour Alain Lancelot says quite rightly that it is not a totally autonomous and expressive behaviour, but rather — whatever the desire of the voter — a 'constrained behaviour' because it is solicited and subject to constraints over which the voter has no power.[51]

Imagine a country where, for various reasons, there have existed for

[51] 'L'Orientation du comportement politique', iii. 412.

about a century two big parties sharing almost equally between them 80–95 per cent of votes cast, and where the voting system has always been, in all types of election, a 'first-past-the-post' system. The voters can only express their dissatisfaction with this situation in one of three ways: by abstaining periodically or perpetually, by voting hopelessly for the independents or small parties, or by voting for candidates of different parties according to the nature of the election (presidential, legislative, regional, local). Conversely, if they are unhappy with the policies of the party for which they voted in the preceding elections, they can at the following election change their vote to the profit of the rival party.

Now let us imagine a different country where the voting system is a two-round majority one (offering, therefore, a first-choice vote and, if the first-round winner has not got an absolute majority of votes cast, a second-choice one) where the parties are not only more numerous but more likely to be created and/or disappear, where the parties ally with one another, make and break coalitions with each other, stand down for each other, and where a high abstention rate can lead indirectly to the elimination of a party on the second round. Such a situation provides the voter, even if he is not particularly strategically minded, with a wider range of possibilities to express his dissatisfaction than in the first case, because electoral supply is infinitely richer and less rigid.

In an election, therefore, the voter, just as when he 'chooses' a school for his children, his leisure activities, his newspaper, or his television viewing, clearly makes a choice which is to a degree 'conditioned' by his social situation, religious practice, level of education, earlier socialization, and so on. He must also, however, take into account all the elements composing electoral supply at the time (the right-wing French voter between 1945 and 1947 had little choice but to vote MRP, the British communist sympathizer is almost always obliged to vote Labour). However, among these elements can be found not only those that we have suggested, but others too: the level of the election, the fame of the party or the candidate, the results of the preceding election, the time elapsed since it took place, and so on.[52]

Factors other than the structure of political supply also contribute significantly to making the voter's choice a political decision. The

---

[52] This is analysed in detail by Grunberg, 'L'Instabilité du comportement électoral'. This is the kind of analysis found in journals such as *Pouvoirs* and *Revue politique et parlementaire*.

'protest vote', like the so-called 'fear vote' of June 1968 in France, has had a bad press. However, such votes, like 'rallying' votes to the party in power, and 'warning votes', even though these are sometimes passing infidelities, are none the less political acts inspired by the wish to get a message across to the political authorities; such voters express a judgement which is linked, implicitly or explicitly, to the political situation of the moment. It is true that the 'warning vote' or the 'warning abstention' is expressed more easily at 'intermediary' elections (mid-term elections, by-elections, local elections), and at elections with no great immediate significance (European elections): the voter knows that government and party leaders will be very attentive to these 'polls', as it were; and the voter himself will feel little guilt if he abstains or votes for a party other than 'his own' (although we have seen how few are those who consider themselves 'very close' to or 'very far away' from a party).

Voting is finally 'decided' on the basis of certain questions which can be salient issues for voters, and which, because of this, justify for some of them a change of 'allegiance'.[53] Many examples spring to mind (the Algerian War for French voters, the crisis of 1930, the Vietnam War, and Watergate for American voters, the crushing of the Budapest insurrection, and the invasion of Afghanistan for certain French communist voters, etc.). At certain times 'new problems' arise which, whether real or imagined, can have far-reaching effects: law and order, the crossing of 'tolerance thresholds' of immigrant communities, and so on.

Even more important are the effects of the economic crisis and unemployment on electoral instability and on the varying degrees of change in partisan orientation.[54] The question has been studied in depth in the case of Great Britain,[55] where between 1964 and 1979 the hardening of views of Conservative sympathizers on questions such as the power of the trade unions, public expenditure, and new nationalizations was symmetrical to a 'deradicalization' of a proportion of

[53] The upheaval is often identifiable in advance, by means of opinion polls, when one takes stock of the changing priorities of those polled concerning the importance for them of certain questions, and when the number of 'discordant' opinions *vis-à-vis* 'their' party increases.

[54] See the studies of Dominique Schnapper, 'Chomâge et politique: Une relation mal connue' and Jean-Dominique de Lafay, 'Chomâge et comportements politiques: Bilan des analyses économiques', both in *Revue française de science politique*, 32/4–5 (Aug.–Oct. 1982), 679–702.

[55] Especially in Alt, *The Politics of Economic Decline*, and Ivor Crewe's Report, see n. 11 above.

Labour sympathizers on these same questions.[56] The developments can be explained, in part, by the effects of the crisis.[57] The crisis also partly explains why, on certain issues such as the 'climate of insecurity' or hostility to immigrants (issues which are not automatically perceived by voters as belonging clearly to a programmatic 'patrimony' of any one party), the upheaval of loyalties due to the crisis is accompanied by a 'demand' for law and order, and a repression which profits, in some cases, a more 'radicalized' conservative party, in others, a populist movement of the extreme right.

Passing instability or long-term drift?

Regarding the electoral effects of salient issues and, even more so, of the current economic crisis, it is difficult to know if what we have identified are transitory, though frequent, variations of an indeterminate nature, or slow, continuous changes of fundamental significance, or perhaps a combination of the two (which makes analysis even more difficult).

Over and above the salient issues effect and the effects of the crisis, we can make certain generalizations concerning all that we have examined so far. Are the relative decrease of partisan loyalties, the greater volatility of electorates, the apparently more 'strategic' behaviour of many voters, only passing accidents and conjunctural adjustments 'on the margins' provoked by small crises in the parties and between the parties and by events which temporarily upset alignments? Or are we witnessing the emergence of the desire for a greater individual autonomy which transcends *homo electoralis*, a desire to be less the captive of the instructions and mobilizing calls of the big party machines, a desire to have a say and to experiment (even at the risk of making a mistake)? Are changes observed in voting behaviour the reflection of these shifting involvements, of these alternating cycles of investment in 'public happiness' and 'private happiness', cycles punctuated by the crises of disappointment so acutely analysed by Albert Hirschman?[58] The present 'individualist' phase expresses a cyclical, though ambiguous, rejection of certain deceptive forms of the old recurring ideal of the *vita activa* to the profit of a return, not to the *vita*

[56] See Grunberg, 'L'Orientation du comportement politique'.
[57] We should note, nevertheless, that before the world crisis (although Great Britain was already in economic difficulties), from 1960 to 1970, there had already been a continuous displacement of the British electorate from the left to the right.
[58] A. O. Hirschman, *Shifting Involvements: Private Interest and Public Action* (Princeton, NJ: Princeton University Press, 1982).

contemplativa, but to a modern form of it: unbelief and strategic calculation.[59]

However, if we are at present in a 'private' cycle, this does not necessarily mean that the so-called 'individualist' voter will always seek to optimize the individual benefits of collective actions and spare himself the costs (see above). Here again Hirschman is right: 'The benefit of collective action for an individual is not the difference between the hoped-for result and the effort furnished by him or her, but the *sum* of these two magnitudes'.[60] It is true that these two magnitudes are reconciled only if the voter has some sense of there being still a new 'public good' to produce, which will dissuade him, therefore, from speculating on a 'free ticket' (and perhaps involve him, the next time, in being 'disillusioned'). I wait for it to be proven that such an attitude can be definitively destroyed.

[59] Take e.g. the following advertising in the Paris Metro in 1986 for a consulting agency: 'I am abandoning my security. I'm starting my own business.' In the same place, several decades ago, we would have read 'Assure your future: join the gendarmerie.' Does the shift from the imperative to the personally responsible 'I' demonstrate the shift to individualism?

[60] Hirschman, *Shifting Involvements*, p. 86.

12

On Rationality and Democratic Choice

ALESSANDRO PIZZORNO

Introduction

Received opinion on democracy carries within it a certain number of presuppositions: each individual acts according to his own interests; the individual is the best judge of these interests, in the economic as in the political sphere; because democracy allows citizens to choose between several 'policies' it is the most efficient way of satisfying interests. These presuppositions are the basis of a general theory of politics which is now hegemonic in the Anglo-Saxon world and widespread throughout continental Europe. It sees itself as a positive theory because it creates predictive models: the behaviour of individuals can be deduced once their intended aims are known (aims which can be deduced from their interests). And it is assumed that individuals act rationally, that is to say, choose the means adequate to the aims they are trying to achieve. It also sees itself as a normative theory: if it can be assumed that the possibility for each person to pursue his interests is a value, then the political procedures which will allow the greatest number to pursue the satisfaction of their interests can be prescribed. Thus the old dilemma of democracy is transcended, that is to say, whether political liberties are ultimate values, and therefore ends in themselves, or else means to other ends, for example, to a better satisfaction of social needs. If the new theory is valid, then liberty and efficiency, egoism and collective usefulness can combine harmoniously as they do in market theory. The theory can therefore claim to be realist (it recognizes egoism), while presenting itself as a legitimation of democracy through its recognition that the interests of everyone can only be satisfied by submission to certain procedures.

These theories[1] are worthy of serious discussion not only because they correspond to a widespread way of imagining politics, but also because they are an important attempt at systemization. We shall deal with these in the first part of this chapter.

To assess the value of a theory, we can examine whether the hypotheses on which it is based are realistic, or assess whether, on the basis of its premises, it explains properly the phenomena it purports to explain. One must therefore determine whether the phenomena are pertinent as regards the intentions of the theory, and whether the explanations are better than those provided by other theories. This second approach is generally considered as the more correct: hypotheses which are apparently not realistic can, in fact, allow us to formulate highly explanatory propositions. Of course, the two approaches are not exclusive of one another, and if, having taken the second approach, the theory being examined does not seem convincing, there are good grounds for then employing the first.

The empirical propositions contained in neo-utilitarian theories involve phenomena such as voting behaviour, the various forms of party competition, the operations of the representative system, the various means of allocating public expenditure (the tendency for governments to encourage producers rather than consumers, and redistribute income to the benefit of the poor, or the lower middle classes). The analysis of empirical forecasts deduced from neo-utilitarian theories has shown that they do not differ from the forecasts

[1] All these theories can be called 'neo-utilitarian'. One also speaks of 'economic theories of democracy', or 'rational-choice theories'. I shall normally use the term neo-utilitarian, but sometimes use the other two interchangeably. The problem was first elaborated by A. Downs, *An Economic Theory of Democracy* (New York: Harper & Row, 1957). The most recent and systematic discussion is Riker's. D. C. Mueller, *Public Choice* (London: Cambridge University Press, 1979), has made a general summing up of this but without developing any critique. If the reader wishes to consult a manual, a good one is D. Whynes and R. Bowles, *The Economic Theory of the State* (London: Oxford University Press, 1981), which is both useful and original. A. Breton, *The Economic Theory of Representative Government* (Chicago, Ill.: Aldine Publishing Co.; London: Macmillan, 1974); J. M. Buchanan and G. Tullock, *The Calculus of Consent: Logical Foundations of Constitutional Democracy* (Ann Arbor, Mich.: University of Michigan Press, 1962); N. Frolich, J. Oppenheimer, and O. Young, *Political Leadership and Collective Goods* (Princeton, NJ: Princeton University Press, 1971); B. Frey, R. Lau, and J. Lawrence, 'Toward a Mathematical Model of Government Behaviour', *Zeitschrift für Nationalökonomie*, 88 (1968), 355–80, have all elaborated original works inspired by this same idea. There is also a synthesis of theories of democracy in J. R. Pennock, *Democratic Political Theory* (Princeton, NJ: Princeton University Press, 1979). In Italy, apart from the early discussions of G. Sartori, *Théorie de la démocratie* (Paris: Colin, 1973), neo-utilitarian theories have mainly been debated in relation to the neo-contractarians.

we can deduce from other theories—this is the case, for example, for the claim that governments tend to favour producers—that the variables put forward by them cannot be translated into quantifiable indicators, or quite simply, that they are wrong.[2]

In spite of its weak empirical success, the theory is popular, probably because its premises seem plausible and its conclusions ideologically desirable. That individuals act politically to satisfy their interests, and that the procedures based on freedom of choice—procedures which vary according to various constitutional forms—produce the policies most likely to satisfy these interests, seems at first sight sufficiently plausible for one to be able, upon such premises, to elaborate sophisticated models for the interpretation of political phenomena. Others have already assessed the empirical tenor of these theories; I shall, therefore, adopt a different strategy and examine whether these models can explain political behaviour, in particular electoral participation, and the decision to commit oneself to activism or to undertake a political career. I shall not therefore discuss the realism of the premises (this has already been done)[3] but their logical coherence (this has never been done). I shall, therefore, examine the consequences of the assumption that individuals act to satisfy their interests.

In the second part of this chapter, I shall examine whether theories other than the neo-utilitarian can offer more convincing explanations of the same phenomena. I shall then try to sketch a view of politics which not only can account for selected phenomena, but will also enable us to answer the following questions concerning 'democratic choice': is it possible to justify the preference for democracy in terms of the rationality of representative democratic procedures?; is this the same rationality as that of the 'economic theory of democracy', itself based on the idea that individuals act to satisfy their interests? Such will be the themes addressed in the pages which follow.

Neo-utilitarian Theories

Schumpeter, an ambiguous precursor

Even though Wicksell can rightly be considered as the real precursor of economic theories of democracy, the most interesting forerunner is

---

[2] Cf. Mueller, *Public Choice*, and above all the convincing critique put forward by J. F. J. Toye, 'Economic Theories of Politics and Public Finance', *British Journal of Political Science*, 6 (Oct. 1976), 433–47.

[3] Among the numerous critiques of the realism of the premises, the reader can

without doubt Schumpeter.[4] Nevertheless, it has not been sufficiently appreciated that Schumpeter's views, though at the origin of the principal economic theories of democracy, cannot, in fact, be assimilated by these. To demonstrate this we need only remind ourselves of the main lines of Schumpeter's thought in this area:

1. Schumpeter maintains that, because individual utilities are not comparable, an optimum of collective satisfaction is not conceivable; the use of the concepts of 'common good' or 'collective utility' has only a rhetorical value.

2. Because, in a democracy, those who govern have to present themselves periodically to their electors, and because the latter are ill-informed, and their opinions fickle, a coherent political programme over time is not possible.

3. It is not true that each individual is the best judge of his interests; he could, perhaps, assess correctly what are his own immediate interests, but does not possess the knowledge necessary to determine his interests in the long term.

4. Because even experts cannot agree on the expected consequences of a policy, it is illusory to think that the citizens can choose properly between different policies.

5. Policies chosen democratically are not necessarily 'right' or rational simply because the majority want them: they can be 'bad'; the majority can, for example, choose to hound heretics, oppress a minority, declare an unjust war, etc.... The existence of a procedure allowing choice does not of itself make the content of that choice desirable or just.

6. For Schumpeter, democracy is distinct from other regimes because the political personnel only accede to power after having won a competition in which the voters are the judge; the voters decide who will occupy power but do not control the decisions taken by those they have put into power.

This last of Schumpeter's theses is the one which gave birth to economic theories of democracy. Schumpeter perceives democracy as a

consult the very general book by C. B. Macpherson, *Democratic Theory: Essays in Retrieval* (London: Oxford University Press, 1973), and the more subtle work of J. P. Cornford, *The Political Theory of Scarcity* (University of Edinburgh, Inaugural Lecture no. 50, 1969).

[4] Joseph Schumpeter, *Capitalism, Socialism, and Democracy* (London: Allen & Unwin, 1976), chs. 21, 22, 23.

system analogous to a free market: the voters are the buyers who, from among the programmes which the political entrepreneurs offer them, buy with their votes what they prefer; the political entrepreneurs acquire or retain power (governmental positions) by selling their programmes. The analogy was convincing, realistic, and systematic, and it is not surprising that it inspired political economists. It was not, however, coherent with Schumpeter's other views which were themselves so critical of classical utilitarian ideas. These voters are, in fact, very strange buyers, deprived of knowledge of the goods they buy, and incapable, therefore, of appreciating their value. And the political entrepreneurs are very strange sellers who work, not in order to make a profit (a category of income which in itself is not clearly defined but which is at least known to be easily convertible into other incomes), but to accumulate power. Power to do what? given that, by definition, they cannot be interested in the effects of their policies. In order to introduce a certain plausibility, we would have to assume that the voter, when he chooses his representatives, is capable of understanding the policies offered to him. His behaviour could then be considered as rational, and as determined by a calculation of maximized profits and minimized costs. This is effectively how Downs[5] proceeded when he constructed his model in which values are produced by means of policies, and only by means of policies. In the Downs model, voters act rationally because they are capable, directly or via their representatives, of foreseeing the effects of a policy on their interests. In the utilitarian tradition so scorned by Schumpeter, Downs maintains that a system of free choice can lead to efficient decisions. What is the truth?

Voting and political participation as irrational acts

If the voter is a rational agent, why does he go and vote? Why does he undertake such an irrational act? To go and vote has no utility, or very nearly none; the probability that a single vote decides the election of a candidate is infinitesimally remote, as is the probability that the election of a candidate results in the satisfaction of the expected utilities. It is true, of course, that the cost of going out to vote is practically zero; and as the cost goes up (when the weather is bad, if the polling station is a long way away, or if people are working) electoral participation indeed goes down. This empirical observation, however, demonstrates

[5] Downs, *An Economic Theory of Democracy.*

the opposite of the utilitarian hypothesis. Because certain external conditions have an effect on electoral participation and are therefore to be considered as costs, and because a large part of the electorate goes, nevertheless, even in such costly conditions, it follows that this part of the electorate does not vote by calculating the utility of an action. The costs, moreover, can in fact become very high, when, for example, those who go to vote are threatened physically or professionally, or in some other way, by opponents. Even in these circumstances, there will be people who vote. Why?

And that is not all. The theories we are discussing consider that informing oneself also has a cost. In this they are consistent with their premises: only the benefits which one can expect from governmental measures have a value in this model. Informing oneself about political questions can only therefore be considered as a means to accomplishing an informed choice. However, in the period between two choices—between two elections—the time devoted to informing oneself (reading, listening, conversing) varies according to individuals: some devote several hours, some hundreds or thousands of hours. In both cases, the cost will be disproportionate to the probability of expected benefits. Moreover, the effects of the act accomplished by those who will have devoted hundreds of hours to informing themselves will be no different from the effects of the act accomplished by those who will only have devoted several hours. One can, moreover, reasonably assume that the time of the former—probably individuals with a higher level of education and with higher incomes—is more costly than that of the latter. How can one claim that a system in which investments have such disparate productive effects tends towards equilibrium?

In the specialized literature, this problem is known as the 'voter's paradox'.[6] To raise such a paradox without resolving it should suffice to discredit a theory. The questions it raises can be stated as follows: can political action really be analysed in terms of costs and benefits? Can it seriously be claimed that only the decisions of state institutions produce political values? Are activities like going to vote, seeking

---

[6] I use the term paradox differently from that used by S. Brams, *Paradoxes in Politics* (New York: Free Press, 1976), which reflects his research into the paradoxical consequences of rational-choice theory (the impossibility of forming majorities, for example). What I mean here is that it is paradoxical for a general theory of democracy to be unable to explain political phenomena as significant as why people go and vote or become involved in politics.

information, the effort to persuade others, and political commitment, really to be considered as costs? Are there not other sources of the production of value in the political system?

The voter's paradox has not passed unnoticed.[7] But the solutions proposed are generally unsatisfactory. Most are simple, *ad hoc* explanations but they are worth examining because they will help us bring together the elements of an alternative theory. Among the arguments which attempt to escape the paradox, let us look at those put forward by Downs on the one hand, and Riker and Ordeshook on the other.[8]

According to Downs: 'Rational men in a democracy are motivated to some extent by a sense of social responsibility relatively independent of their own short-run gains and losses'.[9] In this way the citizens feel themselves responsible for the conservation of a system whose functioning can be a source of personal benefits in the long term. The argument is clearly inadequate: the probability that one single vote can have a positive effect on the survival of the democratic system is no greater than the possibility that one single vote decides the victory of the party for which one has voted. In other words, the argument that considers a system of procedures as a public good is exposed to the notion of the free rider.[10] It is interesting, nevertheless, that this solution, in spite of its logical weakness, was put forward by a partisan of economic theories of democracy. Because of the inadequacies of the theory, one is forced to introduce a distinction between interests in the short term and interest in the long term. Schumpeter himself was obliged to introduce just such a distinction.

According to Riker and Ordeshook, the voter votes in order to affirm his solidarity with the party of his choice. If this were the case, solidarity would be an end in itself. It would be, therefore, a source of value, an expression of political choice. But how does one compare an action motivated by solidarity with one that is determined by the maximization of utility? Such claims throw the whole theory into

[7] For a critical appraisal see B. Barry, *Sociologists, Economists and Democracy* (London: Macmillan, 1970), 14 ff.

[8] W. H. Riker and P. C. Ordeshook, 'A Theory of the Calculus of Voting', *American Political Science Review*, 62 (Mar. 1968), 25–42.

[9] Downs, *An Economic Theory of Democracy*, pp. 267 ff.

[10] It was formulated first in theories of public finance before being integrated into the political science debate by M. Olson, *The Logic of Collective Action* (Cambridge, Mass.: Harvard University Press, 1965). Since then it has been the object of a great deal of literature.

question. The same is the case where electoral participation is perceived as a duty.[11]

The voter's paradox has been discussed in great detail elsewhere. The same cannot be said of another paradox, which we can call 'the paradox of the professional politician'.[12] It can be formulated thus: if only governmental decisions produce goods which have value, politicians as such do not profit from them, being 'producers' and 'sellers', not 'buyers', of policies. The nature of the benefits which their activity should procure for them remains indeterminate, whatever these may be called, let us say, 'power' or 'professional satisfaction'. What is certain is that there is no question here of goods being convertible (corruption excepted) into goods produced by the system. Two interpretations of 'power', one belonging to common sense, the other given by the theory itself, have hidden the paradox.

In common sense terms, power is an end in itself, a value which one desires for its own sake. But if this is accepted, then the application of a policy is no longer the only source of value in the system; political activity is in part orientated towards the accumulation of a good called 'power'. The theory must be reviewed entirely in order to accommodate an explanation of what produces the value of a good called 'power'.

The other interpretation is that of neo-utilitarian theory. Here, power is defined as analogous, in the political sphere, to profit in the economic. Without mentioning the problems raised by the use of the concept of profit in economics, we can note that at least profits are conceived as being convertible into utilities (as consumable goods). Since this cannot be the case with power, the model includes two

[11] It seems that Pennock, *Democratic Political Theory*, remains unaware of this when he analyses these theories.

[12] Mueller, *Public Choice*, pp. 97 ff. raises this paradox when he recognizes that the definition of objectives striven for by the politician remains very vague. Barry, who ignores the question completely in his *Sociologists, Economists and Democracy*, talks about the issue in a recent work, B. Barry, 'Methodology versus Ideology: The "Economic" Approach Revisited', in E. Ostrom (ed.), *Strategies of Political Inquiry* (London: Sage, 1982), 123–47, and proposes considering politicians as acting for the satisfaction they gain from the feeling of having done something worth while. But for whom? I. Budge, 'What is Rational Choice: Shift of Meaning within Explanation of Voting and Party Competition', *Electoral Studies*, 2 (Apr. 1983), suggests somewhat maliciously that politicians, like citizens, are interested as private individuals in the public goods they produce. It can be shown (but there is no space here to develop the argument) that the consequences of this thesis are the opposite of what these authors assume. Indeed, they would lead us to the conclusion that the action of politicians has as its aim the creation of a collective identity. Such a conclusion would coincide with our own.

kinds of actions which are defined by objectives which cannot be measured by the same criteria.

Wittman[13] is the only writer who has tried to resolve the problems raised by the paradox of the politician. In the Downs model, parties (groups of politicians) seek only to maximize votes; they are uninterested in the utilities produced by the application of their programmes. Wittman proposes two other models. In both, the aim of party activity is the realization of their programmes, victory in elections being only a means to this end. In the first model, the parties are in competition and have no interest distinct from those of their electors. The parties are, therefore, unmediated expressions of their electors, the mediation of politicians being simply denied. In the second model, the parties tend to ally themselves with one another in an oligopolistic way to the detriment of the interests of their electors. A system with several parties, therefore, tends to behave as a one-party system. Thus we can understand why the American parties have failed, on several occasions, to choose as a candidate the man whom the opinion polls had designated as having the best chance of winning the election, choosing instead the man most likely to apply the party's programme. However, if, with Wittman, one assumes that the activity of politicians has as its aim the realization of their programmes, either one makes politicians a direct expression of their electors, in which case one faces the objection, even more acutely than in the Downs model, of the free rider, or else one assumes that politicians are directly interested in the application of policy, in which case we abandon the idea of utility for that of symbolic interest. The realization of the programme would then be conceived as the symbol of the victory of a group, the affirmation of a collective identity. The way is thus open to an alternative theory in which the concept of symbolic interest plays the main role. We shall examine this below. We need first to analyse a different aspect of the voting process.

How to ground trust

Others have shown that the predictive power of neo-utilitarian theories is weak. We have shown that these are also unable to account for the most significant political behaviour without creating paradoxes they are then unable to resolve. Let us show how neo-utilitarian presuppositions cannot explain even the basis of political choice in a

[13] D. A. Wittman, 'Parties as Utility Maximizers', *American Political Science Review*, 67 (1973), 490–8.

democracy.

Let us consider, in the simplified version of the Downs model,[14] the case of a voter who must choose between two parties. He will choose the party which, when it is in government and applying its policies, will procure for him the maximum of utilities: the voter must, therefore, deduce the probability of future events from the information he possesses. The information he possesses is the promises which the two parties make to voters, to which must be added, in the case of the party in power, the policy it has applied. The credibility of promises cannot be judged in the same way as an already applied policy. The fact that the party in power can be judged on what it has already achieved authorizes the voter to attach less importance to promises, and, indeed, opposition parties often are forced, more than the parties in power, to develop an ideological and programmatic discourse to shore up their promises, given that they have less policy result to show.

However, the calculation the voter can make concerning the utility which the future action of a candidate can bring about is one thing, the reasons for trusting him, another. Someone can make mouthwatering promises to me without my having any confidence in him. And given that all the parties can make mouthwatering promises, if the voters vote for one party rather than another, it is not because it promises them more utilities but because it inspires more confidence in them. A theory of political choice, rather than a study based on the utilities which might result from political party programmes, should be based on the reasons for citizens' confidence. A relation of trust must logically precede the relation of exchange between favourable votes and useful governmental measures.

In order to see whether neo-utilitarian theories have something to say on this question, we shall examine Fiorina's response,[15] one of the most recent and most elaborate. In order to explain voters' choice, Fiorina constructs a four-factor equation. The first, already put forward by earlier theories, is the anticipation by the future voter of the utility of the effects of policies proposed to him. When a vote is motivated solely by this factor, it is called 'issue voting', the vote of the rational voter *par excellence* (Fiorina completely ignores the voter's paradox).

[14] Downs, *An Economic Theory of Democracy*, pp. 58 ff.
[15] M. P. Fiorina, 'An Outline for a Model of Party Choice', *American Journal of Political Science*, 21/3 (Aug. 1977), 601–25; 'Economic Retrospective Voting in American National Elections: A Micro-analysis', *American Journal of Political Science*, 22/2 (May 1978), 426–43.

This sole factor, however, does not explain the results of empirical research which seem to show that voters' choice is not the result of checking the promises made, but rather the result of a judgement on the action of an incumbent government. Analyses and opinion surveys seem to prove that, on the one hand, when certain economic indicators (especially income per head, the rate of inflation, and the unemployment rate) are bad, the party in power tends to lose votes, and that, on the other hand, individuals who consider that their economic situation has improved during the period preceding an election will vote in greater numbers for the party in power.[16] It is no longer a question here of a calculation concerning expected utilities. The voter does not appraise the credibility of the promises made to him, but rather sanctions or rewards a past action. According to Fiorina, he acts as 'a rational God of vengeance and reward'.[17] The voter, in a symbolic act, praises or blames his public servants. Fiorina calls this type of vote: 'simple retrospective voting'.

However, because the combination of the 'issue' vote and the 'simple retrospective' vote does not account for all the empirical results of voting behaviour, Fiorina also integrates a third and fourth factor into his equation. The third factor is what is traditionally called 'party identification', a notion alien to economic theories of democracy. Identification with a party cannot be explained by a rational calculation of utilities, indeed, can induce behaviour which seems to be its opposite. The voter can go on identifying with a party and giving it his vote even if his interests lie in voting for another party. In order to avoid the horror that such a voter would provoke in the neo-utilitarian theorist, Fiorina attempts to subsume this traditional factor under the concept of 'complex retrospective voting', a vote which is worked out by the isolated voter from the totality of his experiences with a party since he began voting.

In order to explain the strong persistence of the hereditary voter, Fiorina invokes finally a fourth factor, which he calls the 'initial bias'. This is an attribute of the individual entering the political arena, and one can presume that it is a direct function of socialization, but indirectly a function of the past political experience of the socializing

---

[16] Fiorina, 'Economic Retrospective Voting'. I refer to the literature on the electoral cycle which, since the article by W. D. Nordhaus, 'The Political Business Cycle', *Review of Economic Studies*, 42 (1975), 167–90, is expanding rapidly. For an account of it see E. R. Tufte, *Political Control of the Economy* (Princeton, NJ: Princeton University Press, 1978). For a critical analysis, see Barry, 'Methodology versus Ideology'.

[17] Fiorina, 'An Outline for a Model of Party Choice', p. 604.

agents.[18] Such a model could only be empirically verified if one could measure, on the one hand, the experience accumulated by an individual in all the elections in which he has participated and, on the other, the influence on this individual of the socializing agents. The difficulty of such an undertaking is obvious, and the author himself openly admits this. Fiorina's work, however, shows us that if one attempts to explain an individual's trust in a party by the evaluation of the advantages which he can hope to gain from it, this involves the extension of the notion of the 'calculating individual' to include that of the 'judging individual'. This idea is not entirely consistent with the assumptions of a rigorous neo-utilitarian theory. It is, however, compatible with the idea of a democracy in which those who govern are responsible before the citizens, and can therefore be rewarded or punished. Empirical research[19] seems to confirm that people vote, at least in part, on the basis of a 'general judgement' on the ability of those who govern. If this were the case it would mean that those who govern are led to favour certain economic policies rather than others according to whether these can produce positive signs in an electoral period. This will certainly be no advantage to the economic system itself. Schumpeter himself had worried about this. The citizens have neither the information necessary nor the competence to impute with certainty the state of the economy to a particular governmental policy. Even the economic experts are rarely unanimous on this, as is well known. This means that a political vote cannot be based on a competent assessment of the general consequences (that is to say, of value to the national collectivity as such) of a certain governmental policy, when such an assessment is part of a domain of specialized knowledge such as economic policy (although it is difficult to imagine any which is not). Traditional liberal theory implies that the voter is competent. This is possible, according to the theory, inasmuch as the vote is given on the basis of a calculation by each person of the (probable) consequences of the choice concerning his own private interests. The vote given, on the contrary, on the basis of a general judgement is the vote of an incompetent who is influenced by representations both produ-

---

[18] Ibid. 610.

[19] D. Kinder and R. Kiewet, 'Economic Discontent and Political Behaviour', *American Journal of Political Science*, 23/3 (Aug. 1979), 495–527. D. Sears, R. Lau, T. Tyler, and H. Allen, 'Self interest vs. Symbolic Politics in Policy Attitudes and Symbolic Voting', *American Political Science Review*, 74 (1980), 670–84; S. Weatherhof, 'Economic Voting and the "Symbolic Politics" Argument: A Reinterpretation and Synthesis', *American Political Science Review*, 77 (Mar. 1983), 153–74.

ced and orchestrated by the creators of political spectacle. Such a vote is but the applause of the spectator. We can say, therefore, that the only empirical evidence which seems to support the utilitarian model of political voting, namely, the correlation one finds in certain countries between a good or bad state of the economy and a favourable or unfavourable vote for the parties in government, leads us not to a rational, but rather to a symbolic, if not theatrical, model of politics.

Symbolic Theories of Politics

The theories which we shall call here symbolic are the most radical alternative to neo-utilitarian theories[20] even though they do not constitute a coherent corpus which has developed in a cumulative way. In order to discuss them let us address, therefore, three of their central themes.

The first is the theme of solidarity in which political choice is influenced by sentiments of solidarity, of loyalty, and not by the desire to obtain personal advantages. It is determined by the social affiliation of the individual and not by a calculation of utilities. Social solidarities pre-date political choice, are expressions of the social structure, and are consequently related to an ethnic, linguistic, religious, class, territorial, or other identity. The decision to vote for a party is a symbolic supplement which reinforces pre-existing ties of solidarity. In his famous article, Parsons[21] defended this idea thus: because the voter cannot but be ignorant of which policies can increase the well-being of the country, it is impossible to imagine electoral choice as a rational choice determined by a calculation of utilities. The voter is faced with a decision which is presented as serious, but over which he has no control. Political choice becomes, therefore, an act of faith. In order to attain the reassurance which this uncertain situation threatens, the voter chooses to strengthen solidarity ties which unite him to a social group.

This model can explain why people vote even though they know

[20] This distinction between neo-utilitarian theory and symbolic theory is different from the distinction made by Barry, *Sociologists, Economists and Democracy*, between economic theory and sociological theory. It is different also from J. C. Harsanyi's interesting distinction 'Rational-Choice Models of Political Behaviour', *World Politics*, 21 (1969), 513–38.

[21] T. Parsons, 'Voting and the Equilibrium of the American Political System', in *Sociological Theory and Modern Society* (New York: Free Press, 1967), 223–63.

that their own vote decides nothing. It also explains the hereditary nature of electoral choices, and their relative stability. Yet there are phenomena this model cannot explain. In fact, in order to explain changes in electoral behaviour, this model can only refer to transformations in the structure and distribution of social groups, or else to phenomena such as social mobility. Such transformations, however, are slower and less erratic than brusque electoral changes, the shift of a vote from one party to another, or the sudden recovery of lost votes. The theory is also inadequate in that surveys seem to prove, as we have seen, that displacements of the vote are linked to the judgements of voters on the state of the economy. The model also does not explain why a homogeneous group chooses one party rather than another. It explains the choices of individuals, but not the choices of the group, which, according to the model, precede those of individuals. Nothing tells us that the choices of the group are not determined by a calculation of utilities.

The notion of solidarity this model rests upon is the product of social and cultural situations to which politics simply responds. If this is the case, why do politicians try to persuade citizens of the rightness of their views? Why is there debate over aims and values, why are there opposing ideas concerning the common good? Do not such political exchanges, and the activist or organizational activity indissociable from them, influence, are perhaps even the basis of, the identities referred to in the theory?

A model which takes into consideration action orientated towards solidarity certainly constitutes an advance on neo-utilitarian theories in that it explains facts these theories cannot explain. It fails, however, to explain other phenomena, above all the choice of a particular policy, and its effects on the citizens' trust in their representatives. It also fails to explain the meaning of a political discourse orientated towards the creation of collective identities, and demonstrates, by its presence, that these are not given once and for all by the social structure.

The second theme which we shall examine refers to the interpretation of political activity in terms of its relation to the concept of rite.[22]

---

[22] Here I refer especially to M. Edelman, *The Symbolic Uses of Politics* (Urbana, Ill.: University of Illinois Press, 1964); J. R. Gusfield, *Symbolic Crusade* (Urbana, Ill.: University of Illinois Press, 1963); J.-P. Sironneau, *Sécularisation et religions politiques* (The Hague: Mouton, 1982); and to the debate between S. Verba, 'The Kennedy Assassination and the Nature of Political Commitment', in B. S. Greenberg and B. Parker (eds.), *The Kennedy Assassination and American Politics* (Stanford, Calif.: Stanford University Press, 1965), 348–60; and L. Lipsitz, 'If, as Verba Says, the State Functions as a

Politics is full of rites: ceremonies, festivals, and solemn public occasions present themselves overtly as rites. It is difficult to imagine these phenomena in terms of the concepts of utilitarian theory, as means to an end. First, one would have to determine the aim of a rite as such. Other political activities do not appear as rites because officially they aim at outcomes over and above any ritual function they might appear to have. If, however, it can be demonstrated that they do not produce these outcomes, these activities too can be placed in the category of rituals. This is true of elections if it is the case that they do not have as part of their effect the realization of the programmes proposed for the choice of the voters. It is the same for meetings, demonstrations, and other activities of this kind. Very subtle rites may be also hidden within political activity: take, for example, meetings, the setting up of commissions, the appearance of MPs before parliamentary committees, even the application of certain governmental measures, apparently orientated towards outcomes, but in fact, in practical terms, completely sterile.[23]

Scholars, emphasizing the role of rites in political life, perceive them as offering to the individual a symbolic sense of reassurance in moments of uncertainty and anxiety. It seems more important to see rites as a means of reinforcing a solidarity which they, in fact, help create and sustain. Rite, indissociable from repetition, is the sign of the continuing existence of consensus within an enduring collectivity, and the sign of the permanence of the identity of the group. Rites are also characterized by the use of a particular language. The repetition of the same formulae and the same words endows them with specifically political meanings as distinct from their usual meanings. They can thus acquire meanings which are only comprehensible by a particular collectivity (party, movement, nation, etc.), and in this way reinforce the latter's identity. The discovery of the ritual aspect of certain kinds of political behaviour takes us beyond the notion of the influence of feelings of solidarity on political choices. Through ritual enactments and the use of a ritual language, political activity and political discourse appear to be constitutive of enduring collective identities.

Religion, what are we to do then to Save our Souls?', *American Political Science Review*, 62/1–2 (1968), 527–35. On the 'theatrical' model see C. Geertz, *Negara* (Princeton, NJ: Princeton University Press, 1980): his model seems to have been elaborated to distinguish between Bali and Western politics, although the implications for a general theoretical model are clear.
[23] See Edelman, *The Symbolic Uses of Politics*, ch. 2.

These observations still do not explain, however, the significance of the distribution of real benefits which traditionally, and especially since major intervention by the state in the economy, has been seen as one of the aims of political activity.

Those who introduce the concept of rite in the analysis of political reality find themselves at a half-way point between those who put solidarity at the centre of the analysis and those who see politics from a theatrical point of view. This is the third theme I wish to examine. Who has not experienced politics as spectacle? When the great majority of the population of democratic countries follows a political debate in the newspapers or on television, it does not behave differently from when it reads the reporting of a football match or watches it on television. We see what is going on, we are 'there' without really being participants, we get enthusiastic about a particular player, and we know that we cannot really help him in any way other than by urging him on and applauding. Elections can sometimes seem to be nothing but clapometers which simply expel the most maladroit actors and make way for more able ones. We have not had to wait for an actor to become the leader of the most powerful nation on the planet to know that politicians must also be actors. This, like our comments above, though illuminating, remains metaphorical. We must, therefore, address ourselves to more specific phenomena and apply the theatrical model to them.

Let us return to the neo-utilitarian view. A particular interest seeks satisfaction via political channels; if the majority agrees, the state replies by taking the decisions which can satisfy the claimants. The request having been granted, we return to equilibrium (the 'loss of interest' of interest). In fact, things only rarely take place in this way. When the claims of a group are satisfied, the group becomes more demanding, not less; or, when a claim emanates from a majority of the population, the state can take symbolic measures which do not respond effectively to the claims made, but are sufficient to cause a drop in enthusiasm, and eradicate the claim, even though it remains unfulfilled. In this case, equilibrium has been re-established, not because tangible goods have been distributed, but because symbolic measures have been enacted. Because the first case seems to be more likely when the interests of small organized groups are at stake, and the second when the claimants are mass movements, the political system can be described thus: on stage, in front of the public, characters formulate their claims within the framework of the rules and formulae of democracy; goods are distributed to them which seem to the public to be real, but which in reality have only a symbolic value. Behind the scenes other characters move about, almost imperceptibly. Theirs is the political power, and they fight over real, not just symbolic, goods.

This, then, in relative detail, is a sketch of the 'theatrical' model of politics. Is it simply an allegory or can it explain important realities? It is true that it explains the phenomena for which it was introduced, phenomena which neo-utilitarian theory could not explain. It takes into consideration the incompetence and powerlessness of the public, the non-satisfaction of claims which have been apparently accepted yet bogged down in institutional inertia. It can explain cycles of enthusiasm and indifference for certain political themes, and collusion between parties. Furthermore, unlike analyses which concentrate solely on ritual or on solidarity, a model which sees politics as spectacle does not neglect the specific function of policies—at least of the content of certain governmental decisions—in the relation between citizens and their representatives. Such a model, however, only takes policies into account from the point of view of their symbolic meaning, and not as a means of the distribution of real benefits.

By including the model, or metaphor, of political spectacle, symbolic conceptions of politics seem to achieve brilliantly their attempt to elaborate an alternative theory to those of neo-utilitarianism. In fact, what they propose is not a real alternative, rather a simple complement to the other theory. Symbolic goods are added to material goods,[24] and both circulate in the political market. The theory suggests a division of labour between those concerned with the managing and distribution of material goods and those who produce and distribute symbolic goods. In an optimistic, or perhaps paternalistic, interpretation, experts (administrators, or the relevant political leaders) are concerned with material goods; whichever party they belong to, they work for the common good, by choosing the means adequate to its fulfilment. They believe it useless to discuss the significance of these means with an inevitably ignorant public. Symbolic goods are instead distributed by the representatives, and facilitate the identification of the public with the national community, and the avoidance of the disorder which could occur through mass intervention in collective decisions.

[24] For an analysis of this distinction see R. E. Goodin, 'Symbolic Rewards: Being Bought Off Cheaply', *Political Studies*, 25 (1977).

In a more cynical view, the representatives of the dominant interests look after material goods, and politicians play their role of democratic representatives in order to divert public attention from the operations of power. These two versions of a theory of democracy are doubtless more realistic than neo-utilitarian simplifications. Are they, however, enough?

In the 'optimistic' view, the effort of experts and administrators to achieve the common good cannot always be crowned with success. Whatever indicator we choose to measure the effectiveness of their work, it will always consist of failures as well as successes. These failures are not without consequence for the material goods which can be distributed. And if fewer material goods can be distributed — when purchasing power diminishes, for example — it could become necessary to distribute more symbolic goods: to have, for instance, a prestigious success on the international scene, or extend participation to more numerous sections of the population. But at what value can material goods be exchanged for symbolic ones? And even, quite simply, how can we distinguish them from one another? Imagine the case of an ethnic minority, protesting because it does not feel that it has been properly recognized by the national community: government can increase investment in the region, or integrate the ethnic language into the education system. Which of these two is the material good, and which the symbolic? Which of these measures would have the greater influence on its position in the national community?

In other words, those who use the concept of symbolic goods seem to make the same mistake as the neo-utilitarian theorists: analysis stops at the individual enjoyment of a symbolic good, without reflecting on the structural conditions which make this enjoyment possible. The use of the symbol concept also raises the question of what a symbolic good represents to an individual if the symbol is not recognized by others? What is a medal if others do not understand its symbolic meaning? All symbols imply inter-subjective recognition. Is it really a different case for utility?

Rationality, Representation, Conflict

Our discussion leaves us with three unsolved problems: the determining of the conditions of the rationality of individual choice; the nature of political roles (of citizens and politicians) and their relationship to one another; and, finally, the establishing of distinctions between political identities (parties, groups, or factions, etc.). We shall examine these problems in turn.

The rationality of individual choices

We have seen that the concept of rational choice proposed by neo-utilitarian theories does not help us understand why an individual goes out to vote, informs himself of political debates, is an activist in a movement or a political party, or takes up a political career. The inability of neo-utilitarianism to account for such significant political behaviour is the result of its having to extend the notion of cost, an extension which is implied by its use of the notion of utility. Anything which is not the enjoyment of benefits created by the application of the decisions of the political authority must necessarily be seen as a cost. From this we must conclude that in a political system only governmental measures are sources of value, and that political values and social values are not comparable.

Consider the case of an individual who wishes to improve his social position in a society based on a certain scale of values. First, he can choose to act individually, work harder or become more enterprising. Second, he can decide to act politically by associating with other individuals who share his aspirations, and try to obtain from the government measures which improve the position of the members of the group. Third, he can attempt to transform the scale of values which determines his social position by modifying, for example, the status of manual work, or by overturning particular ethnic prejudices. From a utilitarian perspective, this individual, in order to choose the most rational method, should compare the costs of these three approaches. How is it possible, however, to do this without some form of common measurement, some shared value which makes comparison possible?

This example demonstrates the inadequacy of applying traditional equilibrium theories to political analysis. These theories seek to establish how equilibrium is reached, given a certain hierarchy of preferences. In the eyes of a political analyst, however, all means of re-establishing equilibrium cannot be of equal value. Independently of the empirical findings we referred to above (that the satisfaction of a claim is not sufficient to re-establish equilibrium because the claim disappears without the needs which created it being satisfied), the example we have chosen reminds us that there are at least two processes of satisfying a claim, the consequences of which are very different.

One leaves intact the structure of needs, the other transforms it. Political action is more often orientated towards a modification of needs than towards the satisfaction of existing needs.

In order to explain this quality of political action it is necessary to re-examine not only the obvious idea that needs are socially induced, but also the less obvious one that their satisfaction is also a social phenomenon. More precisely, we must identify, beyond the satisfaction of a need, the social confrontation which this apparently private fact implies. Just as a person, in order to think his ideas, must refer to the language he uses with the people with whom he is in a relation, so too, in order to value the utility of a good, a person must refer to standards of assessment recognized by those he lives among. Everyone agrees that the simple sensation of satisfaction cannot constitute a standard. We can take as witnesses to this the economists who, from Pareto to Allen and Hicks, and finally to Samuelson, have wanted to expel all psychological components from the concept of utility by transforming it, in turns, into the concepts of 'ophelimity', 'order of preferences', and 'revealed preferences'. They were able to do this because of the presence, in the definition of the object of their discipline, of quantitative criteria for the assessment of the effects of individual preferences. These preferences can be observed inasmuch as they act through the demand for goods and for labour. How they are formed on the basis of preferences over other systems is not explained. This is, however, the central object of explanation for a theory of social action, and raises the problem of the conversion of values relative to one system into values relative to other systems (for example, the conversion of wealth into prestige, political power, friendship, and so on).

To see things from the point of view of the nature of identification seems to make the problem more transparent. If we take the case of values in symbolic and monetary goods respectively, how can we establish a relation between them? The alternatives are: reward the valorous servicemen with money (pensions or other awards) or with medals; respond to the claims of an ethnic minority by investing in the region, or by recognizing its language officially; or give the working class higher wages or participation in power. The difference between the first and second solution of each of these alternatives cannot be based on a (purely nominal) distinction between material and symbolic goods. The distinction lies rather between the social systems within which those involved can evaluate the consequences of their choice. To distribute pensions, investment, or wage increases signifies a distribution of goods which the beneficiaries can use individually in the framework of a particular system, the market. The beneficiaries define and identify themselves as holders of monetary values, the market being the relational system in which this identity, and only this, will be recognized. The concept of individual freedom comes, at least in part, from the idea of a collectivity to which an individual can at any time claim to belong, and with the certainty of being recognized as belonging, on condition that he is the holder of exchangeable goods. If the distributed goods are, however, medals, linguistic rights, or positions of power, the individuals concerned must, in order to enjoy them, maintain a certain social identity which is defined by membership of the collectivity which alone allows them to profit from the distributed goods. The ex-serviceman must remain a member of the patriotic community and, more specifically, a member of the fraction of the patriotic community which still appreciates the value of medals; the member of a linguistic minority must continue to communicate within this minority; the worker must remain a member or a sympathizer of the workers' party which has conquered positions of power. It is not, therefore, a question of a difference between real and symbolic, between real and illusory satisfaction. It is a question of a difference of consequences for the social position of individuals, and therefore for their membership of another system, or 'circle' of recognition.

A parallel argument can be elaborated by analysing the conditions of possibility for a calculation of utilities. In order to decide one's interest, the subject must assume that his criteria for assessment (in economic language, his order of preferences) are identical when he calculates the cost and when he enjoys the benefits. If the two moments, the moment of expenditure and the moment of enjoyment, are not contemporary with one another, there must also be a convertible value which, like money in the economy, remains relatively constant, or whose fluctuations are foreseeable. In other words, the subject who calculates his interest must be able to count on the permanence of his identity as a calculator. This is not simply given, but depends, as we saw above, on the durability of the circle of those who recognize the same values which were taken into account in the initial choice. In order that he determine which are his interests, and calculate costs and benefits, the agent must be assured of his identity through membership of an identifying community. He will receive from it the criteria which will allow him to define his interests and to lend meaning to his action. An adequate theory of politics must therefore explain the constitution of identifying collectivities as products of an activity specific to politics. Its function of allocating utilities is not excluded, but this itself appears to be based on the existence of identifying collectivities and is brought into being through politics.[25]

One could then explain the participation of citizens in elections while avoiding the iron law of the free rider. If an action does not have as its aim the procurement of utilities which would flow from governmental measures, if it has rather as its aim a collective identification, it can be considered as an end in itself and cannot be considered as a cost. One would have no costs to avoid by remaining at home and not informing oneself. One would possibly have to choose between two types of identification (for example, identification with the family or identification with a party). Moreover, if action is considered as a way of identifying oneself, as an end and not a means, it is not possible that one will allow others to act in one's place. To the question 'why go and vote when you know that this vote will have no effect?', common sense replies: 'Well if everybody did that …'. This reply shows that the individual who accomplishes an act which is useless to himself perceives it, in fact, as a moment of collective identification. Such an act cannot be questioned on the basis that it would be an inadequate means, because it is not a means, in the same way as any ritual act is not a means. By going to vote, one is bearing witness to membership of a certain collectivity. Even the quantitative effect takes on its meaning: no one believes that one vote can decide an election, but if this vote can offer information on the relative strength of a party, of a collective position, the meaning of the individual act of voting changes.[26] The individual will add his vote in order to demonstrate the existence and the strength of his group. It is difficult to say if this voter is rational or irrational. What we can say is that he is not necessarily stupid. The notion of the utility he might draw from his act is simply alien to him. The partial influence on electoral participation of certain costs (dis-

---

[25] See A. Pizzorno, 'Introduzióne allo studio della partecipazióne politica', *Quaderni de sociologia*, 15/3–4 (1966), 235–86; 'Political Exchange and Collective Identity in Industrial Conflict', in C. Crouch and A. Pizzorno (eds.), *The Resurgence of Class Conflict in Western Europe since 1968* (London: Macmillan, 1978). For an original analysis of these positions *vis-à-vis* Habermas, see F. W. Reis, *Representation and the Autonomy of the Political*, report presented to the world congress of the International Political Science Association (Rio de Janeiro, 1982).

[26] I owe this metaphor to Guillermo O'Donnell.

tance from polling booth, bad weather, the abundance and confusion of information necessary to a decision) does not constitute an objection to this view. What is calculated, in terms of costs–benefits, is not the probability of obtaining future governmental measures, but the relation 'cost'–value of bearing witness. Electoral participation varies with the value given to this witness – in other terms, with the intensity of political commitment – and not according to the probability of benefits. Take the case of those who vote in spite of very high costs (for example, the case of being physically threatened if one goes to vote); or even the case of those who vote knowing that their candidate has no chance of being elected. These phenomena can be explained by a theory of identification, they cannot be by a utilitarian theory. All of this applies even more strongly to the phenomenon of political participation in its wider sense, for example, to activism, whose costs, if we accept the utilitarian point of view, are, clearly, too high for the utility of the favourable measures it can bring about. There is no need to dwell on this point.

We are now in a position to answer the question which we asked at the beginning of this section: the logic of individual political action should not be seen as instrumental, as a means–ends relation, but as a logic of identification: as the result of comparisons and conflicts between collective identities which tend to transform the aims of the participants. We need only remember Edelman's observation – and the daily experience of all political practitioners: if a group obtains satisfaction, far from feeling satisfied, it becomes more exacting, because the logic it follows is not a logic of satisfaction, but a specifically political logic of conquest.

The two political roles and the problem of representation

Let us now examine the traditional distinction between those who 'make politics', who produce policies, but produce also, as we have seen, a 'political discourse' – let us call them 'politicians' – and those affected by them – let us call them 'citizens'. Their relationship is constitutionally one of representation. Citizens choose from among politicians those who represent them or, more precisely, those who represent their interest. By expressing themselves in this way, one assumes that the citizens know what their interests are (that they are the best judges of their interests, as the utilitarian view would have it), and that they know also how to work out which politicians will represent them best. These two assumptions are, as we shall see, far from evident.

When the concept of interest and the concept of preference are conflated, tautology is inevitable: we can only infer preference from choices already made, any choice made is that which was preferred, and therefore all individuals always act in their own interests. To avoid this tautology, the utilitarians limit themselves to the following axiom: 'we have no means of determining if an individual clearly knows what his interest is, but it is certain at least that no one else can know it better than he does'. This seems to undermine ideologies, such as Marxism, which claim to know the 'real' interest of a social class, independently of whatever individuals belonging, by definition, to this class say or do. We know, however, that in certain conditions individuals cannot foresee the effects which might flow from the choices they face. They must, therefore, turn to specialists (the doctor, the psychologist, the financial adviser, etc.). These are situations where, not being well enough informed, we delegate to someone else the task of working out our interest.

Cases such as these are characterized by a scarcity of information on objective phenomena over which the individual does not have control (the condition of his own body, or of the financial market, etc.). The state of the political or politico-economic system belongs to this category of objective phenomena which the individual does not control, and about which he possesses only partial knowledge. One can therefore expect him to delegate to experts the task of determining the decisions to take in his interest.

But the individual must confront a more fundamental uncertainty, an uncertainty about his future identity. Will the present order of my preferences, from which I infer my interest, still be the same in the future? And because, for any calculation which is not a short-term one, costs and benefits must be assessed in different periods, am I properly able to assess the expenditure I make now in order to obtain benefits in the future? Losses or gains can only be calculated if I have reasons for thinking that my identity as an interested subject will remain identical. This identity, obviously, is not my physical identity — which also changes — but is based upon an inter-subjective recognition which is socially based in the collectivities to which I belong. And only such recognition allows me to assume that the objectives I attain, in terms of my social position, will satisfy my interest.

The interminable arguments on the concept of 'real interest', on the distinction between interest and need, interest and preference, or the possibility of false consciousness, can be resolved by distinguishing 'short-term' interest and 'long-term' interest.[27] This distinction appears here and there in the literature, but is never treated in a systematic manner. However, we all know—and we shall see that the constitutional practice of democracies implies this—that, if in the short term, when the moment of cost is not distanced from the moment of the enjoyment of benefits, the subject knows what he must do to obtain what he wants, in the long term, an individual's objectives, as well as the measures necessary to attain them, are uncertain, and one cannot calculate exactly where the road one is going to travel will lead. It is clear that the individual is not going to be the best judge of his interest in the long term. The definition of a long-term interest is the work of a process of social interaction in which the individual participates, more or less consciously, more or less actively, right through his lifetime from the moment of his early socialization, without ever being able to state that the horizon of aims is clearly defined. There is, therefore, no reason to refuse a priori the claims of infinite regression of psychoanalysis, or the infinite progression of the revolutionary interpretation (Marxist, or other) of an individual or a class in the reconstruction of true interests. It is always an open process which occurs, in particular, in that component of political activity which is constitutive of collective identities, and from which long-term interests derive.

The distinction between short-term and long-term interests can be deduced through common sense, as well as from psychoanalytic or ideological interpretations. However, although theoreticians of liberal democracies seem reluctant to admit it, it is also rooted in the constitutional practice of these regimes. Take, for example, the modern idea of political representation or 'independent representation', as opposed to the 'representation by imperative mandate' of medieval constitutions. In medieval constitutions, the representative had to obey the instructions

[27] This distinction does not appear in a work as exhaustive as H. F. Pitkin, *The Concept of Representation* (Berkeley, Los Angeles, Calif.: University of California Press, 1972); nor does it appear in the synthesis of theories of representative democracy by Pennock, *Democratic Political Theory*. It does not appear in Habermas's work, nor in the developments of Habermas's approach advocated by R. Geuss, *The Idea of a Critical Theory* (London: Cambridge University Press, 1981), in his chapter on the concept of interest. Only Schumpeter gives it importance, but he does not use it in a systematic way. A. Hirschman, *The Passions and the Interests* (Princeton, NJ: Princeton University Press, 1977) shows implicitly that the concept of interest, before taking on its economic character, was the opposite of the concept of 'passion', just as an enduring judgement opposes a momentary impulse.

of his electors; in modern constitutions, he is free to interpret the representatives' interests, and no one can force him to carry out a mandate. His task consists in interpreting the interests of his electors in the light of the general interest of the nation. But if the general interests are guaranteed by the application of the majority principle, why should the representative of particular interests have to interpret general interests and take them into account? This assumes that there is a common interest which is not determined by the application of the principle of the majority. All representative procedure therefore becomes contradictory. The representative would represent both a part and the whole at the same time. The only way of escaping from this paradox is to assert that the principle guiding the representative's interpretation of general interest comes from consideration of interests in the long term, whether of the overall or the partial collectivity represented, and that the two are supposed to coincide. The representative is qualified to determine which are the long-term interests of those he represents; that is why they elected him. This quality can be based on an ideological knowledge, on a general interpretation of the functioning of the system which allows him to foresee what is necessary to attain certain objectives, or on information that makes the development of a strategy possible. It can also be based upon a specialized knowledge of the functioning of economic, social, or international systems; or again upon a knowledge of the procedures of decision-taking acquired in the practice of negotiations, a knowledge which allows for the attainment of certain objectives by playing upon the relative strengths of antagonistic group interests. Whether it is in one or another of these areas, or in all of them, no one will deny that the modern political representative acts while assuming—an assumption which is constitutionally entailed by the absence of imperative mandate—that he knows more about things than do those he represents; that he knows better than they what might be their true interests.

The functioning of liberal democracies thus assumes that the best policy is that which, in the long term, will remove the conflict of contradictory interests. In other words, one assumes that there is a common interest which can be realized in the future, while the present remains dominated by the conflict of specific interests, a conflict which is taken as given in the practice of representative democracy. Naturally, what is taken to be the common interest can vary, but it is a question of a difference of view and not of interest, even if these ideological differences are rooted in social positions, and therefore in different sources of interest. We cannot, however, discuss this problem here.

If the distinction between short-term and long-term interest is so clearly implied in the constitutional practice of modern liberal democracies, we must conclude that the concept of a politics which is constitutive of identity (before being distributive of utilities) is more appropriate to these regimes than the theories of their doctrinaire apologists.

It is also the case that the function of constitutions in the modern state is to 'qualify' the majority principle. This is a function which is exercised—in the case of fundamental decisions—in the name of a more enduring collectivity, with an enduring identity and therefore common interests, and which is therefore more legitimate than the collectivity in existence on the national territory at any given time.

The distinction between short-term and long-term interests can be further elaborated if we re-examine the conditions of individual choice. We should remind ourselves that the distinction is based on the presence (for long-term interests) or the absence (for short-term interests) of uncertainty. The subject cannot be certain that the value of his acquisitions—satisfaction of need, or reward—will be recognized by others. Uncertainty essentially concerns, therefore, the stability of the collectivity which is taken as the reference group. In other words, if we fear that the value of our person (the significance of our identity) is not recognized, or if we are uncertain of the consequences of our choices, we will minimize uncertainty by identifying with a collectivity of reference in order to find a stable source of recognition which is itself indifferent to failures, setbacks, and individual defeats. The more an individual feels that the consequences of his actions are uncertain, the more he will adhere to a collectivity that will define his future aims. And he will work for the stability and permanence of that collectivity.

The orientation of individual action towards the satisfaction of the individual's interests—assuming that the concept of interest still has a meaning—is therefore a more complex phenomenon than it appears in neo-utilitarian theories. And the same complexities will be found in the process of representation which puts the citizens and politicians in a relation to one another. This relation cannot only be based on a calculation by the citizen of what utilities he can expect from the activity of the politician when the latter gains power. And the politician can no longer be defined as a representative of interests, or a producer of policies the efficiency of which can be evaluated in the light of interests represented. These definitions assume that politicians act in a society where interests are given, that is, structured independently of political activity itself. In reality, politics, understood as the production of collective identities, defines and redefines continuously the interest of the citizens.

In order properly to describe political activity, we will, therefore, distinguish between activity constitutive of identities and performing activity.[28] On the one hand, politicians take on the job of creating, preserving, or reinforcing the collective activities which appear on the political scene in multiple forms: groups, parties, movements, associations, states, etc. They produce symbols which allow the members of a collectivity to recognize themselves as such, to communicate their solidarity with each other, and to agree on proposed collective actions. In this way, ideologies and their various interpretations are produced more or less explicitly, and they define the long-term orientations of collective action. Thus, the signs which distinguish one collective identity from another are established. In this sense, politicians are the guardians of a language which is distinct from ordinary language, and into which information on social phenomena and the state of opinion must be translated in order that they acquire political significance. This language is what we called, using a common idea in a more defined sense, 'political discourse'. Political discourse is a mode of expression which is made up not only of words, verbal messages, information, rhetorical devices, and ideology, but also of gestures, relationships, exemplary actions, and suggested emotions. The voter will respond, therefore, not only to the politician's mastery of symbolic language, his propagandist and 'persuasive' abilities, but also to his ability to inspire confidence, to create ties of solidarity, and an intense and enduring loyalty, which is sheltered from the consequences of applied governmental decisions.

On the other hand, and this is the 'performing' aspect of political activity, politicians take decisions which have, as their direct aim, to ameliorate or preserve the relative positions of the collectivity they represent. They can do this when they are in power by using the state apparatus, or else through an alliance, conflict, or negotiating strategy which will allow a political subject to measure himself directly against

[28] This distinction is analogous to that between 'expert' and 'red' in communist analyses of the state.

others, and to win (or lose) battles. In this case it is expected of the politician that he use the state organization and the procedures of the system efficiently: knowledge of the bureaucracy, negotiating skills, legal expertise, etc. Obviously one must assume in this case that the ends are already defined and shared by the collectivity to which one belongs, and that the politician does not need to reformulate them, or create them.

The distinction between activity constitutive of identities and performing activity is simply an analytical one. These two types of activity can be simultaneous, and are complementary. Their relative importance varies and this variation allows for the classification of political activity. In spite of their complementarity, one can speak of the primacy of activity constitutive of identities over performing activity. A group whose identity is strong can maintain itself for a long time without gaining power, and even without winning significant victories over its adversaries (think of the socialist and communist parties through long periods of their history). One cannot, however, imagine the opposite situation: the conquest of power without the element of identification; by whom and for whom would power be gained? The case of a technocratic government is closest to this notion, but in reality this situation implies the identification of the whole national community with the state and its government.

This latter possibility reminds us that activity constitutive of identity and performing activity can be conceptualized either in relation to a part of the national community (group, party, movement), or in relation to the state. In the first case, activity constitutive of identity aims to strengthen the cohesion of a group, and performing activities help to defeat other groups, and eventually to gain power. In the second case, activity constitutive of identity and performing activity aim to strengthen a national state to the detriment of others. If we take the example of an economic policy dominated by the electoral cycle (the aim of which is to improve the economic indicators in a period preceding the elections, while neglecting the long-term effects of this), success will be measured in terms of a party's performance and not in terms of efficiency in governing the state.

The primacy of activity constitutive of identity enables us to determine the limits of the use of the concept of 'political exchange'. To say that a politician in power takes measures in order to obtain the votes of certain social categories is to express a realistic but incomplete view. It assumes that the processes by which the groups were formed and have become the partners of a possible exchange have already been described. And the processes themselves inform the possible modes of exchange. To assume that it is sufficient to promise favourable measures to senior citizens, or even to take effective measures, in order to obtain their vote is to forget that it is necessary to: (1) encourage them to inform themselves; (2) ensure that they compare political programmes; (3) ensure that they go and vote; and (4) gain their trust in the promises made, or their gratitude for the measures taken. Such trust and gratitude are not the components of 'normal' exchange. The process we have just described is a process of identification which transforms the social category of senior citizens; it modifies their number, because doubtless not all senior citizens will vote the same way; and it selects their interests, by taking certain measures and not others, in order to satisfy them. It is only after having reconstructed or understood this process that it becomes possible to speak of the exchange of 'political' resources between the actors in a system, and to understand how these resources can be evaluated.

Political action: choice or conflict?

Democratic regimes give citizens the possibility of choosing between two or more parties. To what end? Neo-utilitarian theories reply that the presence of different orientations allows citizens to choose the best 'policy', that is, the one most likely to procure utilities. At the dawn of the history of liberal regimes, when the electors were few and all were property owners who, as such, were concerned with, and able to understand, the consequences of economic and fiscal policy, this theory of choice might seem realistic. We have seen that this interpretation becomes unsustainable when the vote of a citizen disappears under the law of great numbers, abundance of information blurs distinctions, and the complexity and quantity of governmental interventions, in an uncontrollable international context, prohibits even experts—let alone legislators and bureaucrats—from assessing their consequences.

A theory of identification, on the other hand, suggests that competition between parties has as its aim, not the selection of the best political measures, but the strengthening of collective identities which have access to the political scene. We should speak of conflict which is, to a certain extent, analogous to conflict between national states, rather than of competition. Some questions, however, remain.

If the stuff of politics is to define the long-term interests of individuals, and thus constitute collective identities, why is this function not performed solely by the national community, that is to say, by the state? (This is sometimes the case in regimes other than liberal democracies.) The traditional reply is that in societies endowed with liberal regimes there were social forces, essentially those which were based either on private property or on a shared religious allegiance, which could not identify totally with the state. If this were the whole answer, one would have to conclude that political parties must present themselves as religious groups or interest groups. It is true we have to discount a partial correspondence between a community of interests or a religious community and a political party. But a political party, in its discourse and, above all, in the decisions it takes, does not confine itself to the defence of these interests. Collective political identity, as we have seen, does not simply bring together pre-existing social interests, but also sorts them, adds to them, invents them, and, if necessary, neglects or suffocates them.[29]

The presence of particular political identities which characterize liberal democracies should rather be explained in the following way. Given a society where divergent social forces exist which are, if so required, capable of opposing the politico-military power of the state—this is the case with forces based on private property, or religious allegiance—this society can only become a national political community if these forces are 'politicized', that is to say, if social conflict is transformed into political conflict. Political conflict can be subjected to procedures and, rather than remaining a simple means of satisfying interests, become a means of reinforcing collective identities. Whatever groups they represented, the first liberal politicians who used Parliament as an intellectual salon,[30] or the first democratic politicians who used it as a place of civic education, helped the state to restrain social, economic, and religious interests which might threaten it. Representative democracy seems essentially, therefore, to be a means of social discipline in a society where there are powers which are irreducible to the central territorial and military power. Representative democracy can fulfil this function, not only because it implies

---

[29] It is strange—and revealing of a compelling conformism *vis-à-vis* methodological individualism—that an observer as insightful as J. Elster, 'Sour Grapes: Utilitarianism and the Genesis of Wants', in A. K. Sen *et al.*, *Utilitarianism and Beyond* (London: Cambridge University Press, 1982), needs to use long and sophisticated utilitarian reasoning to arrive, and remain, at this conclusion.

[30] See L. Namier, *The Structure of Politics at the Accession of George III* (London: Macmillan, 1957).

that the same rules should be accepted by different parties, nor because it implies a familiarity between representatives, a shared language, or the possibility of translating one language into another, but also because the constitution of collective identities, when not destructive of individual interests, tends to impose limits on them. Identification with a political movement sometimes exacerbates conflict between economic, religious, or cultural interests, but more often it transforms it into a conflict between 'political positions', a conflict which submits implicitly to pacific procedural rules. This interpretation enables us to see that collective identifications with a strong ideological content are more functional to the life of the state than are weak identifications penetrated by pressure groups, which are not equipped to restrain interests.

The recognition of political plurality in democratic societies thus resolves a problem of social control which otherwise could only have been resolved militarily. Pluralist democracy was only able to resolve this problem because it presented itself as a procedure of democratic choice. In fact, it was a procedure which operated via political conflict as a way of strengthening identifications and predispositions towards negotiation. Furthermore, the potentially conflictual nature of political positions tends to widen political discourse into ideological discourse, a discourse which would have itself more global, more universal, than that of its adversary, and which refers, consequently, more to long-term than to short-term interests, more to hypothetical conquests than to immediate satisfaction. This form of political conflict in fact disciplines threatening social interests.

Democratic competition is not, therefore, a procedure which allows choice between policies, but is a controlled conflict between collective identities which in the ideological mirror (or in 'theatrical' representation) seem irreducibly opposed, but which in daily reality are constrained to negotiation and exchange.

Conclusion

According to one of their most important representatives, Anthony Downs, neo-utilitarian theories of rational choice claim to be able to elaborate a theory of politics which can adopt 'the traditional method of analysis and prediction'. This means that if a theoretical observer knows the aims of an actor, he can predict his actions by adopting the following approach: (1) He calculates the most rational course that the actor can adopt to arrive at his aims; (2) He assumes that the actor will in fact choose this course because he is rational.[31] In order to criticize these theories, it is not enough to point out that it is unrealistic to assume that an individual is isolated from society, or that one must take account of the social origins of his needs. All this the partisans of the theory know. It seemed to me that the best way to criticize a theory which not only dominates the specialized literature, but also corresponds to ways of thinking rooted in common sense, was to suspend judgement on its premisses and allow ourselves to be guided by our reason in order to reveal that there are decisive facts which the theory does not explain, and that it contains within it irreconcilable contradictions. In this way, I have been able to elicit the principles of a different theory which is not, however, the simple negation of neo-utilitarian theories. These principles can be summarized in the following way.

The concept of utility implies an inter-subjective recognition of the values which determine this utility. The processes of the satisfaction of needs vary, therefore, according to different collective identities. The calculation by an individual of the consequences of his actions is only possible when the moment of 'expenditure' and the moment of 'enjoyment' are relatively close to one another. When the calculation involves a long period, and therefore includes uncertainty as to the consequences of the action, it is not possible to show that the individual will remain the same, that the hierarchy of his preferences, and the criteria that he uses to calculate the value of costs and benefits, will remain unchanged. All experience, however superficial, teaches us how fragile is the identity of an individual. Security and stability are sought in collective identity: the individual can only, in fact, perceive himself as the same over time if other individuals perceive him thus. Uncertainty disappears when it is shared. It is therefore necessary to distinguish the calculation of interests in the short term from the calculation of interests in the long term.

In order to explain political activity we must substitute the notion of identification for that of utility. This cannot, however, be the basis of a theory diametrically opposed to neo-utilitarian theories, nor can such an approach give rise, of itself, to a new form of quantitative analysis.[32] What a theory based on identification can do is explain coherently

---

[31] See Downs, *An Economic Theory of Democracy*, p. 4.

[32] We should also note that when, in theories of utility, algebraic models are used, these only formalize the reasoning, and should not, as we have demonstrated, be confused with quantitative empirical models.

phenomena which neo-utilitarian theories cannot explain. It offers a description, from which we can generalize, of motivations shared by the citizen (or voter, or activist) and the politician: those who vote and those who fight for political power both seek, though in different ways, to secure the recognition of a collective identity. The observer must discover what this collective identity is, and describe it. It might be a group of friends, a party, a national community, or even a globally orientated collectivity which transcends the present and the national context. From this, one could work out a typology of forms of identification, and, ultimately, a historical description. In other words, it is a question of substituting a structural analysis for an equilibrium analysis, an analysis of identities for an analysis of interests.

Let us take the simple example of parties of different types in different national contexts. The difference between parties can be explained by the differences in structures of interests in the countries chosen, and the different policies can be explained by their possible utility for the voters. However, one could neither explain the existence of religious parties, nor account for the differences between parties which represent the interests of the same or similar social groups. Take for example the Democratic Party in the United States, the Labour Party in Great Britain, the Communist Party in Italy, the Social Democratic Party in Sweden, the Peronists in Argentina, and other parties which represent categories of workers in these countries. It is probable that, if they were in power, these parties would adopt similar economic policies. And we have an abundance of evidence which at least partially confirms this hypothesis. But as networks of political identities, which define the political commitment of their members and the relation between the political sphere and the private, the parties we mentioned belong to different types. If this is so, one can explain these differences by the different distribution of identities which characterize the societies in which the parties exist. This implies that analysis takes into account the factors defined by the relations of production, but also that it takes into account religious, ethnic, and other movements. Moreover, one must consider the collective identities which derive from political traditions themselves (political subcultures, etc.). In certain contexts these can explain to a great extent the differences between parties. A phenomenon as obvious as the stability of electoral geography in most European countries over the last sixty years—in some cases much longer than that—where the structure of the economy and institutions of these countries has been transformed during this same period, cannot be explained by the analysis of the structure of interests. One must refer to a theory of identification.[33] It is the same for the significance of hereditary electoral behaviour, whose influence has been demonstrated in those countries where this phenomenon has been studied.

Research on electoral behaviour takes these phenomena into account, and uses the concept of 'party identification' as the category which accounts for it as a residual phenomenon. If, for example, out of 100 voters who declare their disapproval of the policies of the party in power, or who believe themselves to have suffered because of them, 70 declare that they will vote against this party at the next elections and 30 declare that they will continue to vote for this party, the behaviour of the former is explained by the theory of the rationality of choice, that of the latter by 'party identification'. This is clearly an *ad hoc* explanation. In reality, the difference between these two categories of voters is a difference of identification. The latter 30 identify with the party and, even more probably, with its ruling group; as for the former 70, it could be a question either of voter-judges (in the sense that Fiorina uses the concept), that is to say, of voters who identify negatively, or voters who identify more strongly with the national community and who therefore assess policies in terms of their success in the defence of national interests.

At the beginning of this chapter, we asked if one could consider democracy as the most appropriate regime for the satisfaction of the different interests present in a society. We have shown that it is not possible to respond to this question without falling into tautology. Those who have tried have failed either because they simplified reality too much, or because they became entangled in the same inevitable

---

[33] See A. Przeworski and J. Sprague, 'Party Strategy, Class Ideology and Individual Voting: A Theory of Electoral Socialism' (unpublished, 1982), and *Paper Stones: A History of Electoral Socialism* (Chicago, Ill.: University of Chicago Press, 1986). Although they use an equilibrium theory, Przeworski and Sprague give an interesting demonstration of the reasons why identification with a party cannot be reduced to a choice between economic policies. I think I can sum up the results of their analyses of a hundred years of socialist voting in twelve countries with the following: the poorer a party is, the more it must appeal to commitment by its members (to ideology), and it cannot abandon its identification symbols and offer indeterminate 'policies'. We find in S. Verba, N. H. Nie, and J. Kim, *Participation and Political Equality* (London: Cambridge University Press, 1978) a demonstration of the process by which identifications can influence electoral participation.

contradictions. How then can we establish the reasons for democratic choice? Probably by beginning to revise our ideas on the relation between democracy and modern society. The theories based on a class analysis of society see the emergence and development of democracy in terms of the structural force — generally derived from the relations of production — of certain components of capitalist society (the bourgeoisie in a first phase, the working class subsequently). By refusing to accept the institutions of the absolute state, these social classes laid the foundations of the democratic state. Functionalist theories do not see the development of liberal and democratic institutions as the winning over of certain classes or social categories, but as the development of an ensemble of mechanisms (individual rights, the principle of representation) appropriate to the resolution of the problems of a complex society based upon private property and free labour.

In the view which has been sketched here, political democracy is seen rather as the emergent solution of a problem of social discipline in a society where certain essential resources (such as the ownership of labour and capital, and the ability to absorb religious and, later, ideological identification and devotion) remained in the hands of social agents who escaped obedience to administrative and military centres. Active social forces orientated towards the pursuit of particularistic aims operated on a terrain where no procedures, or rules for compromise or redistribution, were recognized. The terrain of political representation, with its institutions, its norms, and its constraints, offered itself as a site of agreements and possible compromises which were laid down and understood. Chaos was thus avoided and the mechanism for the material creation of a new regime was created. By thus politicizing collective identities of social, economic, and religious origin, that is to say, by transforming into politics what were originally social and economic objectives, the antagonistic drives which such collective identities express were checked, and eventually became the custodians of the efficient government of populations, and of the military defence of territorial integrity. In other words, by orientating the principal social groups towards gains made according to political rules, the potentially destructive drives of interests and religious devotion have been disciplined. It is in this sense that one can say that democratic representative institutions have acted as mechanisms of social discipline. Agreement on the rules of the game which have thus been established has also defined as enemies either those who live outside national frontiers, or those not considered as sufficiently responsible to be admitted into the system. The new boundaries of society were thus defined.

If democracy is nothing other than an ensemble of mechanisms of social control, why should it be accepted as anything other than an expedient? Our reply is that there is a value that only democracy can realize: not the freedom of political choice (we have shown that this is close to illusion), but the freedom to participate in processes of collective identification; and the fact that these processes cannot be destroyed or defined solely by the power of the national state. This freedom, in our hypothesis, was a response to the dissolution of traditional identities. For populations which were being driven to undergo or profit from the conditions of the most savage expression of individualism, and which were being placed under the control of a state administration that still did not have the means of remaking the social fabric, freedom of religious or ideological identification represented an attempt to reappropriate the conditions of an elementary social life and re-establish order through collective collaboration. But if this was the case, a new problem is raised today. The sources of social discipline function now across capillary instruments which make collective self-regulation via the mechanisms of political representation superfluous. These mechanisms now tend to be reduced to their surface theatricality. The traditional threats to democracy, some impending chaos, or the return to personal authority, seem no longer to apply. One threat, however, remains and grows, that of the loss of meaning. If, as we have seen, the rationality in democratic choice is not to be found in the guarantee of the effective satisfaction of the interests present in a society, it must be sought elsewhere. With which criteria? The view developed here can help us to see some aspects of reality. I see two which seem to offer a renewed meaning to the values of democracy. The first is the movement towards the recognition of new collective identities (ethnic, religious, sexual, cultural, etc.), towards the definition of their rights, their way of life, and their ability to generate devotion and commitment. The other is a movement which apparently carries an opposite significance, but which is just as profoundly rooted in the 'identificatory' terrain of democracy; it can be defined as the movement which claims the right to refuse imposed identities. This is also a form of identification, identification with the private. But this brings us to the threshold of another debate.

Index of names